Danny Boyle: Creating Wonder

Amy Raphael was born in London in 1967. She has worked on *The Face*, *NME*, *Elle* and *Esquire*, and now freelances for the *Guardian*, the *Observer* and *The Times*.

Her first book, *Never Mind the Bollocks: Women Rewrite Rock*, was published by Virago in 1995. She conducted the conversations for and edited *Mike Leigh on Mike Leigh*, which was published by Faber in 2008. She has also contributed to *The Rolling Stone Book of Women in Rock* and *Perfect Pitch*, a series of books about football. For more, visit www.amyraphael.com.

in the same series

WOODY ALLEN ON WOODY ALLEN edited by Stig Björkman

ALMODÓVAR ON ALMODÓVAR edited by Frédéric Strauss

ALTMAN ON ALTMAN edited by David Thompson

NICK BROOMFIELD by Jason Wood

BURTON ON BURTON edited by Mark Salisbury

CASSAVETES ON CASSAVETES edited by Ray Carney

ALAN CLARKE by Richard T. Kelly

CRONENBERG ON CRONENBERG edited by Chris Rodley

DE TOTH ON DE TOTH edited by Anthony Slide

FELLINI ON FELLINI edited by Costanzo Costantini

GILLIAM ON GILLIAM edited by Ian Christie

HERZOG ON HERZOG edited by Paul Cronin

HITCHCOCK ON HITCHCOCK edited by Sidney Gottlieb

KIEŚLOWSKI ON KIEŚLOWSKI edited by Danusia Stok

SPIKE LEE: THAT'S MY STORY AND I'M STICKING TO IT by Kaleem Aftab

MIKE LEIGH ON MIKE LEIGH edited by Amy Raphael

LEVINSON ON LEVINSON edited by David Thompson

LOACH ON LOACH edited by Graham Fuller

LYNCH ON LYNCH edited by Chris Rodley

MALLE ON MALLE edited by Philip French

MINGHELLA ON MINGHELLA edited by Timothy Bricknell

POTTER ON POTTER edited by Graham Fuller

SAYLES ON SAYLES edited by Gavin Smith

SCHRADER ON SCHRADER edited by Kevin Jackson

SCORSESE ON SCORSESE edited by David Thompson and Ian Christie

SIRK ON SIRK conversations with Jon Halliday

TRIER ON VON TRIER edited by Stig Björkman

Danny Boyle

Creating Wonder

In Conversation with
Amy Raphael

faber and faber

First published in 2010 as *Danny Boyle: In His Own Words*
This updated paperback edition first published in 2013
by Faber and Faber Ltd
Bloomsbury House
74–77 Great Russell Street
London WC1B 3DA

Typeset by Ian Bahrami
Printed in England by CPI Group (UK) Ltd, Croydon, CRO 4YY

A CIP record for this book
is available from the British Library

ISBN 978–0–571–30186–7

2 4 6 8 10 9 7 5 3 1

For Carol, my mother, and Bonnie, my daughter
(from AR)

Contents

Foreword ix
Foreword to the 2013 Edition xxiv
Introduction 1

Shallow Grave 46
Trainspotting 78
A Life Less Ordinary 109
The Beach 130
28 Days Later 164
Millions 196
Sunshine 218
Slumdog Millionaire 257
127 Hours 323
Frankenstein 360
The Opening Ceremony of the 2012 London Olympics 388
Trance 441

127 Hours Diary 456
Danny Boyle on Photo Albums 470
Acknowledgements 473
Filmography 475
Index 481

Foreword
by Amy Raphael

'Once I had it all. Now I just have everything.'
Jack McCann in
Nicolas Roeg's *Eureka*

The first time I meet Danny Boyle, he has a punky haircut that looks suspiciously like a Mohican. It's early 1996 and I am to interview him for the *NME* – after all, he is the director of the rock 'n' roll film of the decade. *Trainspotting* is just his second movie, but already Boyle – thirty-nine, northern, ambitious – is über-cool, his work defined by irreverence, reckless energy, dark humour and an outright rejection of social realism.

I interview him alongside producer Andrew Macdonald and writer John Hodge, the three doing press together as though part of an oddball pop band. While Boyle can barely sit still, Macdonald presents as laid-back and Hodge would clearly rather be elsewhere. Boyle's unrestrained enthusiasm is infectious. He raves about Irvine Welsh's novel, from which the film is adapted. He explains how they didn't want the film to be a period piece, and so they created a loose time span with the soundtrack: Iggy Pop, Lou Reed, Blur, Pulp, Sleeper and Leftfield. At which point Macdonald sighs and says: 'It was the biggest amount of work; more time-consuming and exhausting than the film itself.'

The timing of *Trainspotting*'s release was extraordinary. New Labour were in the wings, Britpop was mainstream and the newly coined term 'Cool Britannia' encapsulated a prosperous, optimistic country offering the best music, art and fashion in the world. After eighteen years of Conservative rule, things, they said, could only get better. And along came Danny Boyle with an aggressively honest film about heroin addicts in Edinburgh. Just as the Britpop bands sought mainstream success after too many years of indie bands pretending to be content with cult status and minimal sales, so Boyle and co. took the American approach to film-making and marketing: put in the simplest of terms, they wanted bums on seats.

It is no exaggeration to say that, with both *Trainspotting* and its predecessor, *Shallow Grave*, Boyle woke British film up from a kind of post-Thatcher stupor. Under Boyle's aegis, British film suddenly had – and still has – the possibility of being not only populist, but also anarchic, violent, disturbing. It doesn't have to be about gritty realism, although there are, of course, plenty of jobless underclass males in *Trainspotting*. It can – should – take risks, push boundaries, terrify or thrill. Above all, it should be a visceral pleasure, a physical experience.

Boyle is an unashamed visual stylist who cares about the plot, the narrative arc, the characters. He effortlessly finds humanity in the least sympathetic characters, most memorably in *Shallow Grave* with the three yuppie flatmates. Most directors fantasise about bigger budgets; Boyle is at his best when working under pressure, with money stretched to the max. He is not afraid to admit his mistakes and then learn from them: much of what went wrong on *The Beach*, filmed on a Thai island paradise with a largely British crew and lots of Hollywood dollars, was put right in *Slumdog Millionaire* with the help of a local crew and a relatively tight budget. Although it is the subplot of *A Life Less Ordinary* that lets the film down and not its rural setting, months filming in the vast expanses of Utah taught Boyle that he prefers an urban setting.

Perhaps unusually for a British director, Boyle is not scared of big ideas. After all, he made *Sunshine*, a sci-fi epic with Kubrick-sized ambition. He dips into genres, most notably with zombie flick *28 Days Later*. He can, when he chooses, allow a glimpse of his more sentimental side: *Millions* is an old-fashioned children's film about a young boy who believes in miracles; *Slumdog Millionaire* is a modern fairy tale, a Romeo and Juliet for our times.

On 22 February 2009, after winning the Best Director and Best Picture Oscars for *Slumdog Millionaire* – and after the film had picked up a further six statuettes – Boyle gave a suitably breathless interview backstage. First of all he quoted Plato – 'Be kind, for everyone you meet is fighting a hard battle' – and then Einstein: 'There are two ways to live your life. One is as though nothing is a miracle. The other is as though everything is a miracle.' His enthusiasm was such that nobody thought to ask which way he lives his life.

The second time I meet Danny Boyle, on 1 April 2009, I have fifteen minutes to persuade him to do this book. It is a wildly sunny day and, for some daft reason, I suggest we go outside. We sit – him with his chair tipped forward, elbows on the table – and squint and talk. He is fizzing with energy, intense, articulate. He doesn't know why anyone might be interested in a book about him. He is not, it seems, being disingenuous. I take a risk and tell him he's being ridiculous. There is no British film-maker alive so versatile, restless and resolutely populist. It would, I boldly suggest, be wrong not to document his experiences for present and future generations of film-makers.

When our time is up, Boyle doesn't say yes. But he doesn't say no either. So I wait. On 12 May, he sends a text message suggesting we start the book two days later. To help with research, he lends me the original photo albums he used as visual inspiration for his eight feature films to date: although the early ones are disintegrating, they illustrate perfectly why he has such visual flair. He searches out a DVD of *Alien Love Triangle*, a short film written by Hodge, produced by Macdonald and starring Kenneth Branagh, Courteney Cox and Heather Graham. Made in 1999 and running at just 26 minutes, it is unusually whimsical for Boyle. 'It was one third of a portfolio film – terrible idea, portfolio films – and never released, of course.'

He also entrusts me with his original, battered copy of Welsh's *Trainspotting*: in the back I find a postcard of Corrour Station (where Renton gives his impassioned 'It's shite being Scottish' speech) and an invite to the world charity premiere of the film at the Odeon on Renfield Street in Glasgow. On the inside back page are two columns of tiny writing in purple pen: Boyle's key moments from the book ('Sick Boy's black hole'; 'Begbie wants out briefly'; 'paranoia and fury').

Over the next seven months, Boyle and I meet eleven times, mostly in the Covent Garden office of Christian Colson, the producer of *Slumdog Millionaire* and *127 Hours*, which at the time is in pre-production. The office is spacious and simple: expensive scented candles, two huge *Slumdog Millionaire* posters, an Orla

Kiely sofa and a vast producer's desk dwarfing the silver Mac. As the seasons drift by – intense rain, stale heat, soft snow – a window nearly always remains ajar, revealing a cheap tin ashtray hidden on the window ledge.

We change location twice. Once, early on, we meet for lunch in Soho, where, as Boyle eats wild salmon and chips, I suffer a catastrophic technical failure and record nothing of our four hours together (informed of the recording blackout that evening, he sends a return text: 'Arrrrrrrgh. Understood.'). Another day, at the end of August, I find him at his modest Mile End home, sitting in the kitchen beneath a poster of *Sunshine*, writing a treatment for *127 Hours*. Inspired by the true story of Aron Ralston, a mountaineer who trapped his arm beneath a boulder in the Utah desert and, five days later, hacked it off with a blunt knife, it will be the first script for which he takes a co-writing credit – alongside Simon Beaufoy, who won an Oscar for his *Slumdog Millionaire* script.

Boyle pushes a hand through his hair until it stands on end, regrets his lack of typing skills, asks how to spell 'triptych'. He emails the treatment to Colson, shuts his laptop and offers fresh coffee with hot milk. I ask, a little embarrassed, to see his Oscar. He brings it down from his study, wrapped in a plain blue shoe bag, and hands it over. It's ludicrously shiny and incredibly heavy. As I stare at it, he busies himself in the kitchen; he is now embarrassed.

During all these sessions – which last three, four or even five hours – Boyle gives his undivided attention. But he rarely sits still. He straightens paper clips, peels labels off pens, spins paperweights. In Colson's office, he disappears regularly to make tea barely touched by milk. Sometimes, when he is explaining a particular scene in a film, he leaps off the sofa and acts it out in front of me; on one occasion, he mimes stuntmen pulling on the tightest of latex pants for the waterfall scene in *The Beach*, before collapsing with laughter at his apparent madness.

Although we start the book only a few months after *Slumdog Millionaire*'s Oscar haul, Boyle's life continues in fast forward – perhaps because he has so many stories to tell that there is barely time to pause, to reflect; perhaps because, devoted though he is to his kids, his life *is* his work. Between May and December, he travels to China to head the jury of the Shanghai Film Festival; twice visits the child actors of *Slumdog Millionaire* in Mumbai (to address the much-publicised, ongoing housing issues); flies to America half a dozen times in preparation for *127 Hours*; personally picks up the last award of the year for *Slumdog Millionaire* at the European Film Awards in Germany – reporting back with some excitement that he shook Ken Loach's hand for the first time.

One of those who appear to enjoy forty-eight-hour days, Boyle uses every minute to absorb popular culture: music, books, art, television documentaries, films. He talks about trips to the cinema, alone or with his son Gabriel (his two daughters, Caitlin and Grace, are living abroad; he separated amicably from the mother of his three children, Gail Stevens, in 2002. She lives just down the road and remains his casting director; Boyle describes himself as not lonely but 'solitary'.) Charlie Kaufman's directorial debut, *Synecdoche, New York*, troubles him: *Eternal Sunshine of the Spotless Mind*, which Kaufman wrote, is one of his favourite films of all time, but *Synecdoche* is 'not good'. J. J. Abrams's *Star Trek* impresses: 'I thought there was no way Chris Pine and Zachary Quinto would ever be able to step out of William Shatner and Leonard Nimoy's shadow, but they did it instantly. It reminds you that you have to believe in youth, always.'

He loves *Mesrine* and *Inglourious Basterds*, raves about *A Prophet*. We speak on the phone the morning after he has taken Gabriel to the premiere of James Cameron's *Avatar*. Boyle talks non-stop for ten minutes straight about its stunning visual effects, its incomparable gigantism, Cameron changing the way films are made. It may not be the kind of film he wants to make himself – the budget too colossal, the CG too central – and he doesn't say if he actually likes the film. But, for Boyle, *Avatar* succeeds where so many British films fail: it is all about the *experience* of watching it, the sheer physical thrill of being transported to Pandora.

For a director who has developed a personal style of directing that, at its best, is characterised by visual pyrotechnics, a beautiful chaos, the eclecticism of the Coen brothers and the intelligent energy of his favourite band, The Clash, Danny Boyle generated a surprisingly arty body of work prior to *Shallow Grave*. I watch a series of old VHS tapes lent to me by his twin sister Maria and am, perhaps naively, taken aback by how theatrical his early work is; after all, he went straight into theatre after graduating from Bangor

University, working for Joint Stock, the Royal Court Theatre Upstairs and the RSC.

The VHS tapes, over twenty years old, feel like relics. First up are two of the six television films Boyle directed and produced in Northern Ireland for the BBC, both of which were broadcast in 1987: *Scout*, written by Frank McGuinness and starring Ray McAnally and Stephen Rea; and *The Venus de Milo Instead*, written by Anne Devlin. Apart from one scene in which Rea violently pours vodka out of the car window as he's driving and playing The Undertones at full volume – which reminds me, very broadly, of what's to come in *Trainspotting* – *Scout* is a dialogue-heavy, slow-paced and gently entertaining story about a Manchester United talent scout looking for the next George Best.

The Venus de Milo Instead, which follows a school trip to Paris, is charming, lively and funny, but, even in retrospect, not a film that you could easily identify with Boyle. By 1993 – the year after directing the second of two episodes of *Inspector Morse* and just a year before *Shallow Grave* – Boyle is hinting at his ambition with *Mr Wroe's Virgins*. A three-part television drama starring Jonathan Pryce, Kathy Burke, Minnie Driver and Kerry Fox, and set in Lancashire in the early nineteenth century, it's the complex tale of a prophet of the apocalyptic Christian Israelite Church. Pryce – the prophet – is told by God to comfort himself with seven virgins, whom he systematically rapes and abuses.

Kerry Fox, who went on to work with Boyle again on *Shallow Grave*, remembers his 'incredible patience' on *Mr Wroe's Virgins*. 'He managed to get around twenty babies to sleep simultaneously. He wanted a shot of many, many babies asleep, and we just sat and waited as he set it up. He already knew by that stage where to spend his time.' She trusted him, without hesitation, from the outset. 'I never had *any* doubts about working with Danny. He's obviously incredibly manipulative, but I say that as a good thing; it's necessary for directors to understand what an actor has to offer and to encourage them to weave it into their character. He is completely engaged with what's going on with his actors. He's incredibly enthusiastic. All the time. I've never known him to be negative.'

While they were making *Mr Wroe's Virgins*, Fox and Boyle talked constantly about making a feature film together. Fox had already starred as Janet Frame in the Jane Campion film, *An Angel at My Table*; Boyle was, by now, bursting to get his work on the big screen. When *Shallow Grave* came along, Fox was the perfect foil to Ewan McGregor and Christopher Eccleston. They lived in a flat together for a week before filming, rehearsing, drinking whisky, watching films. When the three flatmates try to kill each other and run off with the money in one of the final scenes, the film stock had almost run out. 'We had no film and no time,' remembers Fox. 'After each take, Danny would ask how much stock he'd used. We did the conflict scene in a day; as far as I can see, it's a miraculous piece of film-making.'

Andrew Macdonald, who produced *Shallow Grave*, kept the film stock in his office, which was in a small Portakabin adjacent to the specially constructed set of the yuppies' vast flat. 'Danny had to come and ask me for more film as and when he needed it,' he recalls. 'It was the only way we could conserve it. There wasn't much leeway for mistakes and there's not much fat on the film. But when you're doing your first film, it's all about getting it made. It was incredibly exciting. I wanted to make a film like the Coen brothers; I believed, whether it's true or not, that they raised the money for *Blood Simple* through a group of dentists in Minneapolis. The reality was that we ran out of money to build or buy props and ended up borrowing furniture from my dad's house.'

Over time, I talk to various other cast and crew members who have worked with Boyle. I realise just how much Boyle thrives on having his back against the wall on set – as though he is endlessly trying to recreate the thrill of making *Shallow Grave*. Simon Beaufoy recalls feeling amused the first time he talked through the *Slumdog Millionaire* script with Boyle. 'Danny said, "This film is probably impossible to make." And that seemed to cheer him up no end. Then he added, "This film is impossible to cast." The more impossible he felt it was going to be, the more I could see him thinking, "Yeah, I'm going to do it!"'

Anthony Dod Mantle, the British cinematographer who has lived in Denmark most of his adult life, knows about Boyle's love of the impossible only too well. He first met Boyle in 2001. The director was bruised after his experience of shooting *The Beach*, on which he felt he'd lost control, and was about to make two back-to-basics films on digital video for the BBC. Dod Mantle got a message on his answer machine: Boyle talking about 'something he'd seen in the camera movement on *Festen*, which I'd shot a few years earlier'. The cinematographer's first instinct was to panic. 'What the fuck is Danny Boyle doing calling *me*? I didn't know him, but I had immense respect for his films. And he'd worked with amazing cinematographers: Brian Tufano on the first three films and Darius Khondji on *The Beach*. But we met and clicked immediately.'

Dod Mantle, who had been making 'mad hatter Dogme films' with Lars von Trier and Thomas Vinterberg, flew to Manchester and was thrown in at the deep end. Both *Strumpet* and *Vacuuming Completely Nude in Paradise* – written by Jim Cartwright and starring Christopher Eccleston and Timothy Spall respectively – had to be shot at breakneck speed. 'I worried about being good enough, but Danny made it very easy. He was bouncing around with the energy he still has today. He pushes you hard, but you know he respects you and it makes you keep going with him. We shot the BBC dramas back-to-back and then flew into *28 Days Later*. We got to know each other pretty damn quickly. His energy can be invigorating and exciting. I enjoy my sixteen-hour days with him as much as I enjoy my home life with my family and my dog. As long as Danny gets his tea and biscuits, he's got a sense of humour.'

After *Millions* – during which Dod Mantle looked on as Boyle 'became deeply engrossed on an emotional level: watching the boys in the film grieve for their mother, he regularly shed a tear for his own late ma' – they next worked together on *Slumdog Millionaire*. Dod Mantle says Boyle 'patiently held my hand' as he modified the SI-2K digital camera for use in the slums of Mumbai. 'I was taking Danny down the road of unexplored technology. We effectively found a visual language together and it's one of the reasons why the film communicated to so many people. It's also one of the things I love about him: he trusts me to take huge artistic risks.'

Yet, unsurprisingly given its location, Dod Mantle also hints that their experience together on *Slumdog Millionaire* wasn't without its problems. 'It was a big and ambitious film and we didn't have as much money as we needed. I certainly didn't sail through it. Danny had never seen me in such a state before; I was used to a calm set, and in Mumbai you had to almost execute half the people to get them out of the way. You'd look at the call sheet every day and think, "My God, there are two scenes too many." But you had to go for it. He sets his films up so they're tough. He's almost masochistic . . .'

If Dod Mantle was 'in a state' at times, Boyle – or 'Danny uncle', as the local Mumbai kids called him – found a way of keeping his cool. 'I've seen Danny with his back against the wall, which is when one assumes the less charming side of the ego might reveal itself,' says the cinematographer. 'But he just locks in, like Spiny Norman, the imaginary hedgehog from Monty Python. He won't retreat into a corner, he'll stay in the middle of the room, but his spines are out. He'll tuck his folder and notebook under his arm and you won't be able to read his face. His hair will be sticking up like Samuel Beckett's. You think he's going to say something to thin the air, but instead he says in that Mancunican accent, "Let's have a cup of tea, then."'

Danny Boyle's masochistic madness – if I may call it such a thing – is idiosyncratic, but not unique. It's what quite clearly propels certain directors to push themselves, their crew and their cast to the limit in the hope they will then do their very best work. Boyle is no Werner Herzog, no Francis Ford Coppola, but he readily admits film-making is a kind of madness. Yet he doesn't use this brief loss of sanity as an excuse for bad behaviour. He is dedicated to treating his crew and cast as equals. He properly respects his writers – Frank Cottrell Boyce, who wrote *Millions*, was astonished that Boyle would 'ring me up to change a line; he's got a knack of making everyone around him raise their game because he's the kind of person you want to please' – and refuses to assume the position of the autocratic, bullying, power-obsessed director.

He is not, of course, perfect. He has fucked up. Sometimes he will come clean; at other times he is less keen. When I discuss the shaky subplot of *A Life Less Ordinary*, he slightly petulantly says it's his favourite film. As we continue to talk about his other films, he insists on joking about my reservations with *A Life Less Ordinary* – even though I am hardly alone in my criticism of the subplot. He is being playful, but I am surprised at how defensive he is. When we move to *The Beach*, however, he has to stop himself from being too self-critical.

It's a particularly vulnerable film coming, as it does, after the commercial and critical disappointment of *A Life Less Ordinary*.

Boyle, Macdonald and Hodge had been the golden boys of British cinema thanks to *Shallow Grave* and *Trainspotting*; suddenly here they were, making two films in a row – *A Life Less Ordinary*, in 1997, and *The Beach*, in 2000 – that failed to live up to their promise and heralded the end of their three-way working relationship (although Macdonald, of course, went on to produce *28 Days Later* and *Sunshine*).

The Beach may have been a considerable commercial success – a fact often forgotten – but, in the end, its on-screen story was less interesting than its off-screen one.

Macdonald says he feels as though he 'forced John to write *The Beach*, and he probably should never have written it; he never really wanted to'. Hodge, in turn, says it's 'the least my script'. He doesn't think the film's failings – the lack of a three-dimensional central character in Leonardo DiCaprio's Richard; the film's strongest scene, between Richard and Robert Carlyle's Daffy, taking place inside twenty minutes – are anyone's fault. He puts it down to the experience of working in Hollywood: a big budget, a script that everyone tugs over and a Hollywood star fresh off *Titanic*, at that point the highest-grossing film ever made.

'DiCaprio wanted Danny to make him as cool as Renton in *Trainspotting*,' says Hodge. 'It's no criticism of DiCaprio, but he couldn't understand that it's not as easy as that. It put a great deal of pressure on Danny. The studio wanted *Titanic II* and DiCaprio wanted *Trainspotting II*. The film that Danny, Andrew and I wanted to make somehow never got discussed, not even among ourselves. We were so busy reacting to the pressures from outside. I didn't feel any ownership of the script in the end.'

And then there was Ewan McGregor. To use an emotive word, he was usurped by DiCaprio – or, rather, by the studio. Let's go back to the start of what might, from McGregor's perspective at least, be called a love story. Back in 1993, when he was just twenty-two, he had already appeared in two television mini-series, *Lipstick on Your Collar* and *The Scarlet and the Black*. He auditioned for *Shallow Grave* – Boyle, Macdonald and Hodge were, he remembers, 'self-assured and confident; it really was like meeting a rock band' – and was delighted to be given his first proper film role, as self-absorbed journalist Alex. 'There was a youthful arrogance in me, Kerry and Chris. The accepted rule is that you have to sympathise with the leading characters, but we wanted to break the rules. I think we proved that we could do it. It was great fun playing Alex as a bit of a wanker.'

McGregor – like other cast and crew I talk to – had an 'immediate connection' with Boyle. 'Being directed with such diligence and care was something new to me. When I was lying beneath the floorboards near the end of *Shallow Grave* – with a fake body lying above, attached by latex to my real neck – I had a claustrophobia attack. Danny very calmly talked about the size of the studio, the ceiling being far away. He talked me out of the attack. I've subsequently learned that it's rare for a director to be so dedicated to his actors.'

When McGregor was at Sundance with *Shallow Grave*, Boyle gave him the *Trainspotting* script. 'I have never felt more certain that I wanted to play a part. Danny, Andrew and John were worried because Renton had to be very skinny. I knew I had to lose weight to be in with a chance. By the time I met them about a month later, I'd lost a stone. We talked about Renton having a skinhead, so I went off during the meeting and had all my hair cut off. I would have done anything for Danny; it's why he managed to get the best work out of me. He really watches you on set, which is not as common as you might think. His direction leads you further down the path which you had already started travelling. He encourages you to explore the character and story based on what he sees you doing. He pushes actors to be brave, to take risks.'

McGregor dazzled as Renton. His on-screen chemistry with Cameron Diaz was then the best thing about *A Life Less Ordinary* – 'I'm not sure it works as completely as the first two films,' he says, 'but I'm very fond of it and I'll always watch it if I come across it on TV' – before his working relationship with Boyle came to an abrupt end. Put simply, McGregor thought he was to be Richard in *The Beach*, and it turned out that DiCaprio had got the part instead. 'I was very much under the impression that the part was mine. There had even been discussions about dates. I was doing a play and was told the dates of the film had moved to accommodate me. Then I started getting calls from my agents in both Britain and America saying that DiCaprio had the part. I kept dismissing it as a rumour, defending Danny, insisting he would have told me.'

In the end, Boyle asked McGregor to lunch. 'I thought we were going to discuss *The Beach* in more detail. We blathered for half an hour and then he told me . . . I understood that he was under pressure from the studio over casting and financing. But not being told earlier was very upsetting for me. I was going to turn down *Star Wars* to be in *The Beach* – being part of that film-making team with Danny, Andrew and John was part of my identity as an actor. Of course it couldn't go on for ever and I would never have wanted to have been cast for the sake of it . . . Anyway, it was a really sad time for me. The situation was handled badly and I felt betrayed. I don't think I've ever had such a great experience with a director. I loved being on set with Danny. It *was* very much like a love affair: I'd look across, see him and be very happy he was there.'

McGregor finally bumped into Boyle at the end of the Shanghai Film Festival in June 2009. 'I'd been waiting to see him for years. I'd have nightmares about bumping into him and wake up in a panic. When we were flying back from Shanghai, there were three of us in first class. My wife was asleep. My light was on, Danny's light was on. Here was an opportunity to talk about it, to sort it out, but for some reason we couldn't. So we sat in our respective seats for 12 hours and said nothing. When I saw him again in LA a few months later, to present him with an award, I was really, really happy. I've missed him so much.'

It is hardly unusual for actors to gush about directors. But there's something different about Boyle's relationship with his cast: not just the trust and respect, but a sense of utter control amidst the chaos. Timothy Spall, who turned up in Manchester to shoot *Vacuuming Completely Nude in Paradise* straight after filming *Vanilla Sky* with Tom Cruise, was 'nuts' with jet lag and flu. 'I instinctively knew that turning up half crazed would be required,' he remembers. 'I could see a glint in Danny's eye when he clocked I was in that state. He was enjoying the lunacy. Given that he's so urbane and equable, he loves a bit of torture. But the great thing about Danny is that he instils immense confidence: whatever happens, it's going to be all right. Given that his work is so visual and wild, he has a real calm sense of command over his domain.'

Robert Carlyle is not, of course, like the tough characters he often portrays on screen, but neither is he given to superlatives. Yet the ten days he spent rehearsing for *Trainspotting* remain 'the best time I've ever spent with a group of actors and a director'. Which is not to say that transforming himself into Begbie was easy. He had turned down the role of Alex in *Shallow Grave* because he saw him as a working- and not middle-class character ('How stupid was that?') and, already familiar with every paragraph of Welsh's novel, his initial response to playing Begbie was 'no way'. 'I saw Begbie as a monster, a huge guy who frightened everyone in sight. But Danny was his dogged self and insisted I'd be terrific as Begbie. We finally agreed that small psychos are the best!'

Carlyle wanted Begbie to look like a Hibs football casual from the 1980s, with Pringle jumpers, Lacoste T-shirts, Sta-Prest trousers, white socks and Bass Weejun shoes. 'Rachael [Fleming, costume designer] was brilliant; she understood exactly how I wanted Begbie to look. We had one fitting where she brought every colour combination of Pringle jumper imaginable. At that point I was struggling to accept how intimidating I was going to have to make myself. It was the first time I'd really played such a terrifying character. I decided everything about Begbie had to be a provocation. The way he sounded, acted, looked – everything. So I deliberately chose the pastel-coloured Pringle jumpers. They would make people turn around, and that would be enough for Begbie: "What are you fucking looking at?"'

Carlyle turned up on the first day of the shoot not only in a lemon Pringle jumper, but also showing off a moustache and an emerging mullet. 'No one had seen me until that point. Everyone's jaws just dropped. Danny was laughing so much that he had to cut several times. I know it's unusual for him to corpse; he usually is too possessed by his desire to tell a story to be distracted by how a character looks. But he gives you a platform to express yourself. You'd need to be an idiot to fuck it up with Danny Boyle.'

I remember watching *Trainspotting* for the first time at a press screening in Leicester Square towards the end of 1995 and being pinned back in my seat for the full ninety minutes. The story, the soundtrack, the cast, the set, the costume – they were all as irresistible as heroin was to Renton. If life can be measured by pop-cultural experiences, here was one of mine for the mid-1990s. Since then Danny Boyle – for all those *Slumdog Millionaire* Oscars – has remained a Hollywood outsider who is more excited by New York than Los Angeles, more interested in ideas than a career trajectory.

He doesn't want to live anywhere but London and isn't sufficiently interested in money to make films for the sake of it.

Christian Colson – who punched his fist in the air upon hearing that Boyle was interested in the *Slumdog Millionaire* script – says that Boyle couldn't currently be in a more perfect position. 'It doesn't get better than *Slumdog* and he hasn't fucked the next movie up! Right now – as we're just about to leave for Utah to start pre-production on *127 Hours* – is probably about as good as it gets.'

Boyle has, as might be expected, been made some absurd offers in the wake of *Slumdog Millionaire*. He was offered a $2-million fee to direct an indie film. And some £800,000 to direct an advert. But, even though he is in a position to write his own cheques, Boyle is no director for hire. His biggest ambition may be to direct a musical but, in the meantime, he will continue to make films that are all but impossible, building them from the outside in, using what he calls the 'architecture' of the script. Steven Spielberg once said that Stanley Kubrick 'reinvented himself with every motion picture', and it's similar shape-shifting that keeps Boyle's films appealing, engaging and impossible to ignore.

Andrew Macdonald says that, on some level, Boyle wants to be James Cameron, but I'm not so sure. Why would he direct *127 Hours* on a relatively small budget if he was chasing world domination? Having dismissed the notion, however, I remember that when Boyle was talking about *Avatar*, he mentioned in passing that he'd seen *Titanic* four times. He was surprised when I asked why. 'Because it was so good! Seriously! I went to see it twice with Gabriel, once with Caitlin, once with Grace. It's such a great movie. And it will live on way beyond us.'

By the end of our sessions, I have a sense of Danny Boyle as a director with an incredible life force, as an emotional person who can cry on the set of *Millions*, but who is ultimately contained. Who is, to use Anthony Dod Mantle's words, 'socially gracious', but who is happy to be on his own. It's not hard to pinpoint Boyle's strict Catholic upbringing as a – if not *the* – source of what Spall calls 'loving a bit of torture'. Dod Mantle says that if Boyle had, as his mother hoped, become a priest, 'it would have been a nightmare. He'd have led the second crusades! He'd have changed world history. Thank God Danny was allowed to make films instead.'

When I say, partly as a joke, that all he does is make films, Boyle's response is serious: 'That's fair comment, I'm afraid. I can't see that I contribute very much to society in other ways. So yes, as you have seen, my life is making films. What else would I be doing anyway?' I ask where his drive comes from, and he says it's about excitement, curiosity, being a child playing at make-believe. He finds it difficult to relax; every time he reads a book, for example, he can't help wondering if it might make a good film. He has a basic work ethic which he attributes to his background: his father was a physical labourer all his working life, and his own physical energy is channelled into film-making.

As cinematographer on *127 Hours*, Dod Mantle is embarking on his sixth project with Boyle and preparing to 'feel the fear' again – this time in the canyons of Utah. 'The first I heard from Danny on *127 Hours* was this: "It's a little thing shot from the hip – just a loose, simple thing to get away from *Slumdog* and move on." But that guy can't do anything loose and simple. He just can't! He's going to be on set every day, he'll never have a day off, he'll be a dead man walking by the end. He'll be like Rommel with his head sticking out of a tank, keeping morale up in yet another dust storm.'

Dod Mantle has met Boyle's father, Frank, and agrees that the source of Boyle's tremendous work ethic is probably hereditary. 'Danny is the brickie of the British film industry. He puts his script and all his notes in a bag, chucks it over his shoulder and goes out on set first thing, whistling away. He is always first to arrive, last to leave. He works damn hard. A great, creative, gifted director, but also a proper worker.'

Amy Raphael
Brighton
January 2010

Foreword to the 2013 Edition

'This is for everyone who has ever looked at the stars, or
gazed from atop a hill, or across the sea and wondered . . .'
Tim Perkins, *Worlds End: The
Riders on the Storm*

At just after 8 p.m. on Friday 27 July 2012, I sit in front of the television with my daughter. She is a few days shy of her eighth birthday. She is calm and composed. I am jittery, unsettled, consumed with childish anticipation. It is nearly two years since I teased Danny Boyle about rumours that he was going to direct the opening ceremony of the 2012 London Olympics. Boyle never had any doubt about accepting the job. I thought it was a bizarre, eccentric decision.

What was he thinking? Why would he want to deal with the International Olympic Committee (IOC), the sponsors and the inevitable politics of the opening ceremony when he could just make another film, safe in the knowledge that he always enjoys director's cut?

Slowly, however, his decision began to make sense. If he had turned it down, he would never know what he had missed out on. And why wouldn't the most successful British director of recent years take on one of the toughest and most exciting directing jobs on the planet? Boyle relishes a challenge. He thrives when working under stress, acknowledging that film-making is 'a kind of madness'. He can see the bigger picture and yet, even when proving himself human by teetering on the edge of exhaustion, doesn't let the smallest of details go.

In recent years, Boyle has decided not to make films for more than $20 million. He enjoys the pressure of producing spectacular movies out of relatively small budgets. He did it with *Trainspotting* in 1996 and again with *Slumdog Millionaire* in 2008, so there was no reason why he couldn't kick-start the Olympic Games with £27 million. It's said that the Beijing opening ceremony in 2008 cost at least ten times that amount, possibly even as much as $500 million. It was spectacular, but in attempting to flex its muscles in the new world order it gave a post-communist display that ultimately felt cold and clinical. The best decision Boyle made was not to 'better' Beijing, but to create something different altogether: a truly idiosyncratic ceremony.

On 12 June – an utterly miserable wet day – a press conference for the opening ceremony was held at 3 Mills Studios. Close to the Olympic Park, it was also where the control deck of *Icarus* had been built for *Sunshine*. In a cold, cavernous space, Boyle unveiled a model of the Olympic Stadium: fake grass, plastic toy animals, a village green, Glastonbury Tor, a mosh pit. Boyle, talking fast and fluent, discussed his vision of England's green and pleasant land. He had the air of someone in control. But only just.

At the end of the press conference, I spoke briefly with him. 'The whole thing is beyond pressure,' he said, with a huge grin. 'But we're having fun mostly because the volunteers are so amazing.'

I wanted to ask what the inevitable edge to the ceremony would be; I refused to believe that he would present a bucolic and anodyne vision of Britain to the world. I wanted to ask if the thousands of nurses invited to the stadium might provoke memories of Benny Hill rather than the intended celebration of the NHS. I wanted to ask how the alchemy of film-making, when the film somehow comes together in the edit, would work with the opening ceremony. Was he hoping that, almost by magic, it would all come together on the night? As Boyle was briskly whisked away by officials, my questions were left to hang in the air.

Despite my scepticism, I managed to write a positive preview piece for the *Radio Times* in which I surmised that '[Boyle's] ceremony will surely reflect the Britain we'd like to be: inclusive, caring, energetic, positive and quietly ambitious'. I concluded that he would either fail heroically or succeed spectacularly.

Back to the sofa. Back to the nerves. Back to the biggest night of Danny Boyle's working life. We watch Frank Turner sing 'I Believe' as men play cricket on the village green. We listen to the Four Nations Choirs sing 'Jerusalem', 'Flower of Scotland', the 'Londonderry Air' and 'Bread of Heaven'. I make a cup of tea and return to find the Industrial Revolution is taking shape on my screen. We sit, my child and I, transfixed. I give her a potted history of Britain. The dark satanic mills are erected. I get goosebumps.

And then the five steel rings, forged on the floor of the stadium by the workers, start to rise. Giving off dazzling yellow sparks, the Olympic rings light up the stadium. They light up Britain. For a moment, they even light up the world. I find myself in tears. Because this is my country and I have never felt proud of it before. And because Boyle, I realise, has cracked it.

When Danny Boyle agreed to direct *Frankenstein* at the National Theatre in the autumn of 2010, he had been away from the stage for fifteen years. He decided to use the Mary Shelley play as a dry run for the opening ceremony, as a way back into live entertainment. Designer Mark Tildesley and costume designer Suttirat Larlarb had experience of the theatre; composer Rick Smith had none.

Smith, who first met Boyle back in the mid-1990s when the director asked to use 'Born Slippy' in *Trainspotting*, was on tour with his band Underworld when Boyle sent him a cryptic text out of the blue. 'He said there were two things he wanted to discuss. One big and one not so big. We met a month or two later and discussed *Frankenstein*. I rather naively thought that the play was the big thing and that the little thing had gone away.'

Smith and his Underworld partner Karl Hyde wrote a soundscore for *Frankenstein* of violent industrial noises, soothing sea shanties, wedding toasts and gentle guitars. 'It was probably the most enjoyable experience of my working life,' says Smith. 'I loved everything about it, including being yelled at by Danny. Regularly. He's really demanding and vocal, but extraordinarily kind. He's always got guidelines and a brief. Yet you know there's so much space to bring in what you want. He desperately wants to be surprised. I love it when he comes to the studio in Essex; he's so passionate about music. It's very collaborative, very inspirational. I've been a man working in a techno shed most of my adult life, and I find working with Danny incredibly exciting.'

What Smith didn't know is that Boyle was effectively using *Frankenstein* to audition him for the opening ceremony. If he thought 'the little thing had gone away', Smith was wrong. When *Frankenstein* was in preview, Boyle invited him to come over to 3 Mills Studios and asked if he'd be music director of the opening ceremony. 'It sounded as though it was a really difficult project in terms of bureaucracy and organisation,' recalls Smith. 'It took me less than a minute to say yes. I was delighted. Let me at it!'

Larlarb had just finished work on *127 Hours* when she got the call. She was back in New York, taking some time out, and her boyfriend asked her what she was going to do during her break. 'I said, without really thinking, "Read, see movies, catch up with friends. Unless, of course, someone asks me to do the Olympics." I had no idea Danny was involved. It was an "if I won the lottery" comment.' Two weeks later, Boyle called her up to say he was being courted by the head of ceremonies for the 2012 Olympics and was she in?

Frank Cottrell Boyce, writer of the opening ceremony, says that Boyle knew he was going into battle and 'wanted to have people around him who genuinely liked and cared about him and whom he could trust'. In the small room in Soho he set up two years ahead of the ceremony, Boyle, Cottrell Boyce and designers Larlarb and Tildesley – the 'gang of four' – talked and talked about British popular culture until the evening began to take shape.

Like the opening ceremony itself – and this is absolutely not a criticism – the meetings were more punk than polished, more DIY than formal. 'What was brilliant and troubling about working on the opening ceremony was that I never quite knew what my role was,' says Cottrell Boyce, laughing. 'And I never quite knew whether I was doing it right. I felt slightly out of my depth, which was good. Danny, for example, never told me that I was officially the writer. He just mentioned it in passing in an interview.'

Cottrell Boyce, who thought that Boyle was talking about some kind of sports movie when he first asked him if he'd like to be involved in the Olympic Games, says modestly that he was 'quite good at putting together the others' brilliant ideas and giving them emotional logic'. When pushed, he admits that with his vast knowledge of poetry, literature, television and music, he would be a natural king of the pop quiz.

He also, vitally, gave Boyle a copy of an out-of-print book called *Pandaemonium* as the director was preparing to direct *Frankenstein*. Inside the Humphrey Jennings tome, which explores the development of the machine age in Britain, Cottrell Boyce wrote a note: 'You'd better read this. It cost me £42.50.'

Boyle is a bibliophile who often makes films out of books: Irvine Welsh's *Trainspotting*, Alex Garland's *The Beach*, Cottrell Boyce's *Millions* (which, strictly speaking, only turned into a book as the film was being shot), Vikas Swarup's *Q&A* (the foundation of *Slumdog Millionaire*), Aron Ralston's *Between a Rock and a Hard Place*. While *Pandaemonium* was never going to be turned into a screenplay, it ended up being worth more than £42.50. It gave Boyle a starting point for *Frankenstein*, which is set in the early nineteenth century as scientists are desperately trying to harness electricity, and for the Industrial Revolution sequence of the opening ceremony.

When the book was reprinted recently, Boyle wrote a quote for the cover: '*Pandaemonium* was the biggest single inspiration for the Olympics opening ceremony . . . the book is the equivalent of Pepys giving you a guided tour of the birth of electricity and the mechanical age – it's brilliant, exciting and essential.'

Without *Pandaemonium* there might have been no Industrial Revolution sequence in the opening ceremony, or at least not one that worked so brilliantly. It was an organic source of inspiration upon which everyone agreed. But, of course, the gang of four spent just as much time throwing ideas out because they wouldn't travel around the world: no to the 1970s children's TV show *The Clangers* (much to Cottrell Boyce's disappointment); no to *Dr Who*.

Boyle and his team decided very early on that the protocol which is written into the opening-ceremony format – the Olympic rings going up in the first fifteen minutes so that the image can be beamed around the world; the arrival of the head of state; the doves of peace – should be treated as part of the show rather than as an irritant. Hence the blazing rings rising above the satanic mills and James Bond escorting the Queen to the Olympic Stadium. And Larlarb's graceful, magical dove bikes.

'The doves are meant to illustrate the Olympic idea of promoting peace in the world,' she explains. 'In the 1988 Seoul Olympics, the doves flew straight into the cauldron and were burned. From that time forward real doves have been replaced by an expression of doves. At one point we had an extensive sequence about bikes, and the dove bikes were an extension of that. I looked at the work of Eadweard Muybridge, who created world-famous photos of animals and humans in motion to isolate how doves move as they fly.'

The dove bikes were approved immediately, which gave Larlarb and her team time to attend to them properly. Not everything, however, proved so straightforward. The Olympics organisers had, for example, clear ideas about the cauldron. It was to sit on the roof of the Olympic Stadium, which had been strengthened specially. There was talk of bringing in the cauldron from the 1948 London Olympics (a plain-looking slab of stone reminiscent of a giant holy water font) on the night. There were to be no moving parts after an issue with those in the cauldron for the Vancouver 2010 Winter Olympics.

Boyle tore up the rule book. He asked British designer Thomas Heatherwick to design the cauldron. It would sit on the floor of the stadium. There would be no old cauldron turning up. And, as far as he was concerned, Heatherwick's idea of having 204 petals to symbolise each country taking part in the Olympics was nothing short of genius. 'I felt enormously guilty about the cauldron being made up of a thousand moving parts,' says Heatherwick. 'But I went to see Danny at his house the day after Boxing Day [in 2011], and he immediately got it.'

Heatherwick had never met a film director before, never mind collaborated with one. He was impressed. 'If you locked Danny in a room by himself, he'd be phenomenally creative. He is self-confident and therefore doesn't need to impress you. There's no posturing at all. I often had the chance to watch him with the volunteers because we had to wait for them to leave before we could rehearse the cauldron. Danny managed to make everyone feel they were doing this not for the IOC, not for the Queen, not for David Cameron, but for him. Everyone there felt they had an intimate tie with him, and he was the creative glue holding it all together.'

Boyle certainly possesses outstanding leadership qualities. Larlarb offers the perfect analogy. 'When I was living in London and working on *Frankenstein* and the opening ceremony, I felt homesick. I'd unwind at the end of the day by watching all 156 episodes of *The West Wing*. I really appreciated it being about this group of people against the world. There's the President – whom I shall equate to Danny – surrounded by these very opinionated advisors. Disagreements and conflicts of personality happen when you put a group of people in a room who are solving really hard problems with not enough time, money or sleep.'

In the opening-ceremony chapter, Boyle talks extensively about the importance of belief. He always makes the people who work with him raise their game, but this time he also gave complete or relative strangers the belief that they could bring something to the opening ceremony. It was for him that the volunteers turned up in the freezing rain to rehearse week after week. Rick Smith's sixteen-year-old daughter Esme had the courage to sing 'Caliban's Dream' as the cauldron was lit. Emeli Sandé, who astonished with her rendition of 'Abide with Me' in a perfectly silent stadium, says that 'Danny made everyone feel as though they were important.'

Frank Cottrell Boyce watched the ceremony with his wife and two of their kids. 'We sat with Rick and his family. So we were watching Esme sing her dad's composition while sitting with her mum. It was just like a nativity play. My daughter, who was just back from Zambia, said this really amazing thing: "I feel as though my dad chose all my favourite things and put them all in a big show for the world."'

The opening ceremony was a spectacular international success. The *New York Times* called it 'noisy, busy, witty, dizzying'. The Chinese official Wang Nang, director of the Beijing Olympics' opening and closing ceremonies, gave Britain ninety marks out of a hundred. Ghana's biggest news website concluded it was 'bloody brilliant'. Even Rupert Murdoch, who could not quite bring himself to embrace the opening ceremony fully, tweeted that it was 'surprisingly great, even if a little too politically correct. Danny Boyle is a creative genius.'

Maybe. But what everyone appeared to immediately forget is that few people truly believed in him in the lead-up to the opening ceremony. Cottrell Boyce was lined up to appear on Radio 4's *Today* programme the next morning to defend it. Larlarb's friends couldn't imagine how they would 'best Beijing'. Everyone thought Boyle was on a suicide mission. As Cottrell Boyce points out, the director took a massive risk: 'Danny bet his whole reputation on the Olympics. Had he screwed up, he'd have gone all the way back down the line to square one. It was genuinely courageous of him to take the opening ceremony on.'

In my *Radio Times* preview I concluded that Boyle would either fail heroically or succeed spectacularly. He not only did the latter, but he also allowed us all to feel a new kind of patriotism. In a diary piece for the *London Review of Books*, Alan Bennett's entry for 22 August 2012 read thus: 'There are different ways of being English, one of which is not to want to be English at all.'

Before 27 July 2012, I would have agreed with the playwright. Now, I'm not so sure. Maybe there are different ways of being British, and this was one of them. The opening ceremony wasn't a flag-waving exercise, but a celebration of the complexity of identity. It was about the rings moving us to tears as we remembered our industrial heritage rather than our colonial shame. It was about the volunteers turning up come rain or shine. It wasn't, in the end, a Danny Boyle production. It was a ceremony by the people for the people.

Amy Raphael
Brighton
January 2013

Introduction

AMY RAPHAEL: *You were born in Radcliffe, Lancashire, in 1956 to a strict Catholic family. What do you remember about your childhood?*

DANNY BOYLE: I was very aware of my Catholic, Anglo-Irish roots. My mum came over from Ireland in the 1950s when there was a huge influx of post-war labour to the north-west of England. She was a hairdresser. We had one of those stand-up driers in the house; she'd sit underneath it to curl her hair. She met my dad at a dance in Bury in 1952 and they married in 1954. He was brought up beside a tiny farm where his dad worked, all this in Radcliffe, six miles north-west of Manchester. He left school at fourteen to be a labourer but he educated himself, which he's very proud of.

When he had kids, he was determined to pass on that gene. In fact, both my mum and dad were desperate for me, my twin sister Maria and my younger sister Bernadette to get into good schools. They got us through the eleven-plus and into single-sex grammar schools that were also really good Catholic schools. They were quite tough schools in certain senses, but they were good schools. Having a decent education changed our lives.

When I was eleven, we moved house. Until that point we had lived in a tiny house with two bedrooms, and I had shared a room with my sisters. But once I was eleven, we were no longer allowed to share. So we were allocated a three-bedroom house on a decent council estate in another part of Radcliffe, and I had my own bedroom for the first time. Moving house was another life-changing moment: we were just far enough from the original house to lose touch with the friends we'd been at junior school with. The new friends I eventually made were what I'd now call middle-class kids, but back then, of course, we didn't give them that label – they were just mates.

My sisters went to a convent in Bury, while I used to travel five or six miles every day to my grammar school in Bolton. I have a very clear memory of simultaneously moving house and starting secondary school. For a while I didn't have any mates in my neighbourhood because my old friends lived down in the town and my schoolfriends lived in different towns and villages around Bolton.

Was it a difficult time?

It wasn't difficult but I do remember it. Then I got absorbed in school. I didn't rebel against school because we had been brought up to value education.

You didn't at any point rebel against your parents' educational directive?

No, no. I never thought about it like that. Part of me hated school, but I worked hard to get O-levels and A-levels. I pushed myself really hard. Because Maria and I were twins, my dad was very comparative. When we were at the same primary school, he used to do this terrible thing of putting our school reports down side-by-side on the table. The competitive relationship forged by my dad benefited me most, despite the fact I always felt my sisters were much brighter than me.

Maybe your father thought you and Maria would thrive on the competition?

I'm sure he did. It's also important to remember that punishment is the key to Catholicism. When I was growing up, there was certainly very little of the modern ethos we embrace about encouragement. If we fell below a certain level of achievement or behaviour, we had to be punished! We had to feel guilty! I had to try and jettison that with my own three kids.

Lose the guilt or the strictness?

Both. But it's too easy for me to go round the whole time feeling guilty about everything. I can't shake it off.

Are you and Maria non-identical twins?

Yes. And I was born a few minutes earlier. We get on really well now, but we didn't for a long time. You can't really when your dad is constantly comparing you. There was also that male working-class notion that the son is allowed to do whatever he wants – it's even okay if he wants to go off and do drama – whereas my sisters became teachers. They've both given it up now: Bernadette stopped to have a family, while Maria, being too conscientious, just got burned out. She's now an administrator for special-needs provision in Rochdale. Going back to the guilt: I have always felt guilty about my sisters doing more important jobs than me and getting paid fuck-all comparatively.

How relevant was – or is – it that you were the older twin?

We used to refer to it a lot when we were younger. I was the slightly heavier one.

Were you close to your parents? How strict were they?

It was quite a strict household. My dad has always been a hardcore socialist, a big Tony Benn supporter, and I was brought up to think like that. My mum's Catholicism defined everything for her, but she loyally voted Labour as my dad did. When I was growing up, I hated my dad, like you do; my son Gabriel, who is twenty, is going through exactly the same thing with me now. I was very, very close to my mum until she died in 1988. I learned things from my mum that I really value and I inherited things from my dad that you can't really do anything about: aggression, stubbornness, doggedness. All of which are of great value to me as a director – it means I just keep going and going.

How does aggression help as a director?

I mean in the sense of pushing. Having to be on the front foot. If you want something, you'll push for it. You've also got to be willing to push people around sometimes to get things done.

What did you learn from your mother?

Tolerance and respect. She instinctively had both. She came from the same background as Noel and Liam Gallagher's mum. Both our mums were uneducated Irish women who came over to the north-west of England. Both were dinner ladies. My mum started working at the primary school I went to, St Mary's, in 1963 or '64. There's a generation of people who came from Ireland to Manchester and got similar jobs. Our family stayed together because they had this ambition for us to be really educated.

Where did that ambition come from?

It was common sense. My dad looked at me and thought, 'He's not going to be working where I'm working. He's going to get a better job.'

What were you like as a kid, before you sat the eleven-plus and moved house?

(*laughs*) Just a normal kid! My uncle Tom, who sadly died in spring 2009, was mad about football. He used to run the football teams at St Mary's. When I went home after the Oscars, he brought a framed photo along of me and my mates as ten-year-olds about to win a tournament. Oh my God, this photo!

Is it like a scene out of Kes?

It's totally like *Kes*! None of us look as though we'd ever been fed – what were we eating? And of course you realise how conscious we've since become of nutrition and diet. But then, for fuck's sake, we all looked like Billy Casper. Grey, sallow, but beautiful as well. It's a really beautiful picture. Anyway, I was mad about football. Really mad about both playing and watching. My dad used to take me to see Bury, the team I've supported all my life. He was a big Manchester United supporter as well. In the back of our family album there's a beautiful grey and red photo of the Busby Babes lined up just before eight young players were killed in the 1958 Munich air crash.

4

St Mary's primary school football team, 1967: (back row, left to right) John Bailey, Tony Dallas, John Fletcher, Kevin Holt, Terry Dolan; (front row, left to right) Danny Boyle, Malcolm Lee, Leonard Toye, Mick Collins, Steven Worthington, Paul Greenhalgh

I saw Georgie Best play a number of times at Old Trafford; he was *such* a fantastic player. When I was working as a director for the BBC in Northern Ireland in the late 1980s, I made a film called *Scout* which was written by Frank McGuinness and inspired by Best. The guy who discovered Best in Northern Ireland was called Bob Bishop; he was Matt Busby's scout. Bishop used to find these young lads, take them away to a cottage in the countryside and test their character to see if they could cope with a big club. Although I'm not sure the test of character really worked; look at what happened to Bestie.

So you'd go to games on a Saturday afternoon and in between play reasonably well at school?

I wasn't very good. My dad was naturally ambidextrous but, as was customary at the time, he was brutalised out of writing with his left hand at school. I'm right-handed but I could play with both feet. I wasn't good enough to be on the right side, so I was on the left, where there was less competition for places.

Were you more academic than sporty? Were you bright and focused even at primary school?

Bright enough to pass the eleven-plus. I didn't have any training other than what I got at school. I knew the paper was important. It wasn't particularly hard. I remember some of it very clearly: there was a word with letters missing; you had to work out that 'ach' was 'yacht'.

And, after passing the eleven-plus, you got into the Salesian College in Bolton, which is run by priests.

Yes, it was a very Christian, heavily Catholic education. It wasn't quite *Angela's Ashes*, but it was hard. The teachers were tough. Still, it was a good education. I was lucky; I had an English teacher who changed my life. Mr Unsworth, whose nickname was Ticker, refused to compromise just because we were teenage lads. So we did *Northanger Abbey*! How the fuck did he sit there and think, 'I'm now going to teach you fifteen-year-old boys *Northanger Abbey*. All thirty of you are going to read it out loud, and I'm going to tell you why I think it's a work of genius and why Jane Austen is one of the greatest writers'? He persuaded me! He was a brilliant, secular teacher. He was clearly unattached, except to his mother, and he told us that he took a Jane Austen novel on holiday with him each year to re-read. You can imagine what a bunch of young lads thought of that. He also taught us Shakespeare – *Richard II*, *Antony and Cleopatra* – and directed us in stage plays. He was a pivotal figure in teasing out what you had an inclination for.

Had you always been a big reader as a kid?

Always. I read every single one of Franklin W. Dixon's Hardy Boys mysteries. I made a natural progression to the Bond books, which I read multiple times. They were *so* cool. Ian Fleming was an amazing writer. Bond lived in a godless world and the books dissolved everything I was meant to respect – it was just sex, pleasure and guns. Then came Graham Greene; my favourite was always *Heart of the Matter*. Although he converted eventually, Greene was the great doubter; I was drawn to his doubt as much as anything.

You say 'Ticker', the English teacher, directed you and your class-mates in stage plays. What other drama projects were you involved with at this point?

I had a really loud voice, which basically makes you a good actor at school, so I got all the lead parts in the plays because they could hear me at the back. Later, I put on plays in school assemblies which were entertaining and a bit outrageous.

The first directing I ever did was in the sixth form. One play was about a Polish cardinal who had been appointed to a very high office. He was called Cardinal Vincenti, but I renamed him as Cardinal Sinplenty. Everybody who came on stage had to kiss his ring, which was a deliberate double entendre. There were, of course, whispers about the abuse of some of the pupils. It didn't happen to me, but other boys said they had their trousers taken down.

Didn't that make it a terrifying environment?

I don't know . . . the majority of boys just dealt with it, which is why so many priests got away with it. We traumatise it so much in our minds now, but back then we did just get on with it. It used to happen to the pretty boys, but I wasn't a pretty boy – I had National Health specs.

Being a skinny lad with glasses, were you bullied?

No, never. There was a bully in our class, but he never took me on. One of my best friends, Dilip, took a bit of racist stick on occasion. There was an effeminate guy who was bullied in an invisible way. He was constantly finding pictures of penises in his desk.

What happened when you put on the Cardinal Sinplenty play?

I was told by the priests not to do it again. I remember getting thrashed a few times. On my backside and hand. It really hurt. This was the 1970s, and thrashing really belonged to the 1950s, but they still used it for major offences.

What did you do to get thrashed, other than subvert and challenge Catholicism with a play?

Bunked off. Lied. Covered various things up. Went into the country with this guy who had an air rifle and shot birds: terrible cruelty. We were young men obviously testing boundaries. And I very quickly rebelled against the school's heavy Christianity. That was how my rebellion manifested itself; it wasn't against education as such, it was against Christianity. So I'd try to skip Mass constantly.

You rebelled against the school's religious indoctrination, but you were then coerced into attending church with your parents on Sundays.

I went to church until I was thirteen, fourteen, and then stopped. I put my foot down and said I wasn't going. I was an altar boy for many years, so I used to go to church every day before school. On Saturday you'd serve and on Sunday you'd go to church with the family in the morning and then back in the afternoon for Benediction. It's such an Irish tradition; your whole day off is devoted to worship. So, until I hit my teens, I'd go to church eight times a week. I still know the Mass in Latin backwards because I served for so many years!

The pressure to go to church came from my mum. My dad would thrash me if I was out of order about something major but, basically, he didn't really believe in God either. Not in the same way as my mum, anyway; she was devout.

What happened when you stopped going?

It was a big act of rebellion. A key moment. But it was also a gradual process. I started by not going to Benediction on a Sunday afternoon. At a certain point I said, 'No, I'm not doing that. I'm not going on a Sunday afternoon.' I used the excuse of having too much homework. So they'd traipse off to church and, when they came back, my mum always put her hand on the back of the telly to see if it was warm. To check if I'd been watching telly. She did it every week. Surely she'd worked out that *I'd* worked out to turn it off fifteen minutes before they got back (*laughs*)? Then I dropped out of being an altar boy; again I said I was at big school and had no time. I gradually established my own independence and, eventually, I stopped going to church altogether.

If you turned your back on the church at thirteen, fourteen, at what point were you considering becoming a priest?

I was around twelve. I was designated a place at the seminary in Upholland in Wigan. I was due to go when Father Conway, whom I didn't get on with particularly well, stopped me. I remember him saying, 'I don't think you should do this, you're not cut out for it. I think you should continue your education here.' He must have passed his thoughts on to my mum because the whole notion just vanished.

Until Father Conway had other ideas, did you really think you were going to go off and be a priest?

I didn't think about it that much. I wasn't even into pop music at that stage; I was thinking about football all the time. I went every week to watch Bury and in between played for the school team. Everything else passed me by. I was only interested in getting to school so I could play football before the day began. Every break I was out playing football. Or cricket. It's only in retrospect that I look back and think, 'Bloody hell, that could have been it!'

If Father Conway hadn't advised against it, would you have entered the priesthood?

Yes, because it was my mum's dream. It's not like wanting your child to be a journalist or a bank manager; it was a calling, a vocation.

You would actually have given your life up for the church?

I can't tell you that. I just don't know. I didn't wonder if I'd made the right decision, I just played more football. And then I started to be interested in music and girls and smoking. Everything else just drifts away. I suppose my mother just watched it happen. It must have been heartbreaking for her. Now that I have three kids of my own, I see it in a completely different way – now in their late teens and early twenties, they want to establish their absolute independence. It's as it should be, but there's always at least a small element of heartbreak involved.

When you stopped going to church was it more than teen rebellion?
Did you also question the existence of God?

I didn't want to be told what to do any more. My mates at school couldn't believe I was still going to church. I certainly didn't want to turn up to church with my sisters and stand next to them. To begin with, I started standing in a different row from them. Then I stood at the back. I wish I could remember the day I said I'm not going. I do remember my mum being very upset and anxious.

What did your mother feel when, in your late teens, you decided to become a director?

She didn't really understand the world I was going into. Religion and devotion have connections with showmanship, but she wasn't bothered about any kind of performance. I know she would have liked *Millions*. It's about her really. It's weird because it's Frank Cottrell Boyce's story, but as soon as I read it I felt so close to it. She'd have found the saints very funny. She died on 15 February 1988, so never got a chance to see *Millions* or any other film I made. It's tough when your mum goes. I was working in the BBC office in Northern Ireland when she died. I got a phone call from my sister. It was the saddest day of my life so far. I flew from Belfast to Manchester. The flight was unbearable. I got there and saw her dead body. They close dead people's mouths and seal them up, which is the weirdest thing. It makes you realise how people's mouths are so rarely properly closed. She was so cold. Her skin was like icy marble. For lads, losing your mum is such a major thing . . .

Let's go back to your gradual rejection of the church. When did you begin to question the existence of God?

The more I started to read, the more I became aware of secular writing, of music and popular culture. The *New Musical Express* was one of the big things in my life; I defied religion by getting into it. It was about desecrating everything to do with Him. There was outrageous writing by journalists such as Charles Shaar Murray, Nick Kent and, later, Julie Burchill – what they were writing was unbelievable! I'd look over my shoulder as I was reading in case my mum caught me. It was profane; it was wonderful. The *NME* was so important for lonely suburban kids. It was a lifeline.

What sort of music were you into?

Music has always been a huge part of my life. I've been lucky in that I've been the right age to experience pivotal movements: at grammar school it was glam rock, at university it was punk and, when I was about to hit thirty, house music started. In the mid-1990s, when I directed *Trainspotting*, it was Britpop. So, as a teenager, I was a big fan of Led Zeppelin, David Bowie, Roxy Music. We used to dress up in what would now be regarded as incredibly effeminate glam-rock gear. We used to buy clothes from women's shops because they were the only place to find the right T-shirts. And we'd somehow get into these glam-rock clubs in Manchester.

Bowie remains everything for me. He's the ultimate superstar in my mind. So much so that I don't ever want to meet him, just in case he proves to be a disappointment. I always found it hard to make my dad interested in the music or films I loved, but when Bowie sang with Bing Crosby it was extraordinary. Both my parents were

Danny Boyle at seventeen.

huge Bing Crosby fans, and there was Bowie singing with him! It was great for me.

Alice Cooper was a big part of my life too. We used to write out the lyrics to songs like 'Dead Babies'. The more profane, the better. The more we tempted God to damn our souls, the better!

Were you ever in a band?

No, I was hopeless! I was in the school brass band, but I was even kicked out of that for being flat.

You were never even in a crap punk band?

Not even that, despite the fact that punk started when I went to university! I have this theory that, sadly, I think is true: in America lower-middle-class parents would give their kids Super-8 cameras and, years later, a Spielberg would turn up; in Britain we just don't have that tradition of talented or expressive people going into film. You join a band instead. I guess my circle of friends just weren't interested in forming bands; we loved music and we went to concerts.

What was the first gig you went to?

Led Zeppelin at Belle Vue in Manchester when I was fourteen or fifteen. I remember seeing Jimmy Page with his double-neck guitar; I was mesmerised. I didn't have the look, I never had long hair. It wasn't allowed at school. To my horror I never saw Bowie in concert. But then punk happened and took over everything.

At which point you fell head over heels in love with The Clash.

They were the business. I never met them. Joe Strummer was clearly accessible to everybody, which I always respected, but I never sought to meet him. I wish I had. When he died, I couldn't believe it. It was like one of my immediate family had died. Really bizarre.

What exactly were you responding to in The Clash?

In retrospect, it's their eclecticism that is so extraordinary. There were dozens of other interesting punk bands around – X-Ray Spex,

Siouxsie and the Banshees, Joy Division, The Jam, The Specials – all of whom we went to see. But The Clash were the ones willing to dip into different genres, from reggae to Americana. Listen to *London Calling* or *Sandinista!* now and it's clear they were experimenting constantly. I loved that about them. They were bold. And, politically, they were my cup of tea. They were very clear about their left-wing allegiances, whereas a band like The Jam weren't – not initially at least. The Clash are the perfect pop heroes.

Music was a central part of your teenage years. Had you also been to the cinema regularly as a boy?

The first film I went to see was *Battle of the Bulge* with my dad; it was a big WWII tank movie, directed by Ken Annakin. Years later, George Lucas got the name for *Star Wars*'s Annakin Skywalker from him. It must have been my ninth birthday and therefore Maria's too; I think my mum took her to see *The Sound of Music*. The gender stereotyping started early! But we didn't often go to the cinema as a family – it was a special treat.

You often talk of your admiration for Nic Roeg. Do you remember the first film of his you saw and where?

I think it was *Walkabout*. I can't remember how old I was or where I saw it, but I got hooked on his films. I probably saw it on my own. Between the age of fifteen and eighteen, I used to go to the Aaben, an art cinema in Hulme, Manchester. Back then, Hulme was a wasteland, a really tough area. The Aaben, which has since been knocked down, wasn't famous, but I'll bet Morrissey used to go too because it showed everything that wasn't mainstream Hollywood. It was hard for me to get there – I had to take two or three buses – which shows how interested I was. I'd wander off there alone and watch two or three films in a row.

There were also two cinemas in Bolton: one which showed mainstream films and a boutique cinema next to it which showed non-stop porn. My mate Declan and I used to go for the sex scenes – being at a boys' school was frustrating. I was fifteen and, looking quite old for my age, could just about get away with buying us tickets for an 18. The sex was blinding: *Decameron*; *Nada*, the 1974 Claude Chabrol film; *Blow-Up*; *La Grande Bouffe*; Alejandro

Jodorowsky's *El topo*. I remember those specifically. There was so much sex on screen it was fantastic. Some of those films I've seen subsequently and they're terrible. Awful.

You say attending a Catholic boys' school was 'frustrating': did you date any girls?

Not enough! On the other side of Bolton was a girls' convent, Mount St Joseph. We used to do that embarrassing thing of meeting for dances. That was about it. There was a lot of talk, most of which was hot air.

Were you allowed to take girls home?

I had a couple of girlfriends while I was at school, but I didn't introduce them to my parents. In fact, I had a girlfriend named Elaine, whom I met in the Turf in Radcliffe, the pub I worked evenings in, and my dad made me finish with her as I was coming up to my A-levels. My parents were fanatical about me and my sisters getting into university and learning to drive. They obviously made a lot of sacrifices to make those things happen. Actually, I went down to Asda in Radcliffe recently and saw Janice, my first-ever girlfriend, who works there. She said, 'Ah, they mentioned you were in!'

How old were you when you started dating Janice?

I was about sixteen. I used to work every summer, and that year I was working in a paper-bag factory in Radcliffe. We made trillions of brown paper bags for Woolworths! Janice worked in the office and she was gorgeous. Then I worked at Warburtons cake factory making cakes for two or three summers. Bad hours but really good money for a student. While everyone went on holiday, they covered their staff with students and gave them the full rate. It was serious money. Fantastic.

What did you spend the money on?

Records, clothes, the cinema. Declan and I saw *Clockwork Orange* in the boutique porn cinema in Bolton just before Stanley Kubrick himself banned it in 1973. We wanted to go because of the controversy around it. I didn't really know anything about Kubrick and I don't think I'd seen *2001: A Space Odyssey* at that point. *Clockwork Orange* blew me away; the risk-taking was phenomenal. It was really refreshing. *Trainspotting* was certainly inspired, in part, by *Clockwork Orange*. With *Clockwork Orange* and, to a lesser degree, *Trainspotting*, people objected to the notoriety that comes with taking risks. But I would argue that it's partly why people go to the cinema.

Clockwork Orange *must have been the most violent film you'd seen at that stage?*

I remember the violence very clearly and, of course, the speeded-up sex when Alex takes the girls back from the record shop. I remember the record shop itself and the weird way they played records, which was Kubrick's vision of the future, of what would eventually become CDs. Now I know about him, you think of all the research Kubrick must have done trying to find out how we were going to listen to music in twenty years' time. I also remember the extraordinary scene at the end in the fake snow as Alex had sex with a girl wearing long black gloves . . . These things get burned in your mind. More than the rape at beginning with Adrienne Corri, which is partly why the film became notorious.

Watching *Clockwork Orange* was – and is – an overwhelming experience. It stimulates your senses so much. I think it's one of the points of cinema – to be visceral rather than intellectual or reflective. The reflection can come later. It should be the sensation of experiencing ninety or a hundred minutes of live imagery. It should be unstoppable. You shouldn't be able to walk away. You should feel trapped in a dark room. That's what really turns me on about cinema.

Did seeing Clockwork Orange *make you want to direct films?*

Anybody who sees *Clockwork Orange* wants to make a film because it's so exciting to watch. But, coming from my background, I never thought being a director was a possibility. Pop stars often came from backgrounds that weren't particularly privileged, but not film-makers. Around that time I got a job as an usher at Bolton Octagon. It was amazing; I was seventeen and I'd never seen a play before. It was a theatre in the round, so it was astonishing just to stand in the aisle as an usher and watch these actors.

Did you get the job to see plays or was it just a way of earning money?

Both. I was really interested in drama; I'd been inspired by my excellent English teacher at school. But I needed the money too.

When you went to study English and Drama at Bangor University, how did your interest in the theatre develop?

First of all, I'd never lived away from home before but, by 1975, I was desperate to leave. It was very lonely to begin with because I was in my David Bowie/Roxy Music period and I turned up at Bangor University in all this glam-rock gear . . . I was defiant for a while but finally realised that what I needed more than anything was a duffel coat. And then I started doing drama and it was fantastic. I picked the right combination of subjects: the English course was hard work, while the drama course was more practical.

I directed my first play at Bangor and decided I enjoyed it much more than acting, which I then gave up. I directed a Howard Brenton play called *Christie in Love*, the weird one about the life of the 1950s serial killer John Christie. It's a fantastic student-union play. There's a plastic doll in it, so I had to go home to Manchester to buy a blow-up sex doll in this sex shop – there weren't any in Bangor. Before I even asked for the doll, I started clumsily explaining that it was for a play. They must get that kind of excuse all the time. Years later, when I was working at the Royal Court Theatre in London, I ended up directing two of Brenton's original plays – *The Genius* and *Berlin Bertie* – and, of course, met him. He was one of my heroes. And, as it turned out, a lovely, lovely man.

Did directing simply make sense to you as soon as you started working on Christie in Love?

I just knew. Straight away. Why be an actor when you can do this? I can control it all! Directing is really just about control. All directors are control freaks.

However, I don't remember working out how I could actually be a *proper* director one day. I just loved the experience. Everything changed when I heard on the grapevine about Joint Stock visiting a new theatre in Mold, Gwynedd. Joint Stock was a fairly radical theatre company founded in London in 1974 by David Hare, Max Stafford-Clark, David Aukin and William Gaskill, and co-operatively owned by its members. A few of us from Bangor went to Mold to see *Fanshen*, Hare's play about the Chinese revolution, and *A Mad World, My Masters*, Barrie Keeffe's modern version of Thomas Middleton's Jacobean play. It was total theatre. I felt completely liberated watching the plays.

I wrote to Joint Stock straight away to ask for a job and got an interview. I made one of my first-ever trips to London, met Alison Ritchie, the stage and company manager, and was offered a job as assistant stage manager. It basically meant I had to drive the truck and make the tea but, because it was a collective, I was paid the same as everyone else. It was a fortune: everyone was on £80, £85 a week. My mates at home were on £35, £40. And also you had a voice in the company because, theoretically at least, everyone was equal.

There were all these meetings that went on for ever about what the company should put on. But the work itself was fantastic. The first professional work I was involved in was *The Ragged Trousered Philanthropists*, an extraordinary production of the Robert Tressell novel directed by William Gaskill. Bill was one of the great directors of the time – he did all the early Edward Bond plays. It was just dazzling to watch. I was hanging around hoping some of it would rub off on me.

When you got the job at Joint Stock, were you pushy or ambitious?

Well, I remember having incredible enthusiasm, and the people in the company responded to that. I think they were surprised at *just* how much enthusiasm I had. It was inexhaustible because I loved what I was doing. I don't ever think of myself as being pushy. Now I always tell people to show enthusiasm when they feel it. If I interview someone for a job and they enthuse about my work and their own work, I'll always be inclined to give them a chance. It's not a guarantee they will be better at their job, but there's a good chance they will be.

Other than the sheer, inexhaustible enthusiasm which still defines your approach to work now, what were your strengths around this time?

Total immersion. No distance on anything. No peripheral vision. Complete focus. As you say, I always had all this energy. I can't do it any differently. Which is why I'm not a very good producer. I can't stop myself taking over, trying to take control.

What were your specific responsibilities when you were ASM with Joint Stock?

When they were touring the UK, I got the gear in and out, got the set in and out, got three nights sleep a week touring from Scotland to Plymouth. I loved it. And of course when people now ask for advice on how to get on, that's *exactly* how you get on: young people have this phenomenal energy. That's your initial calling card, not talent. You find out later if you've got talent or not. Don't be afraid to flatter because it works amazingly well. Alison Ritchie at Joint Stock was this nice, rather proper woman from Highgate, and I was all over her, telling her what I thought of the company's work. It was disarming. I got the job. You can only hope people give you a chance. Although I remember a few bollockings when my enthusiasm went too far.

I was talking to Ken Loach recently about the advice he would give to young film-makers and, without hesitation, he suggested starting in the theatre.

I think he's right. I remember writing to film people when I was at Bangor and getting no replies. I loved cinema more than anything, but theatre seemed more accessible. So I very loosely decided that directing theatre and then television might lead, one day, to directing feature films. If you are insanely devoted to theatre, then you're almost automatically promoted. It's not a meritocracy as such because it's as much to do with devotion as ability – you have to be mad enough to work long, long hours and, most of the time, be poorly paid for doing so.

It's weird how many British film directors come from a theatrical background. It's one of the things that really differentiates us from the Americans. It's rare to find an American film director who has worked in theatre. Apart from David Mamet, obviously. You'd never imagine the Coen brothers started off by working in the theatre. Whereas here you've got Anthony Minghella,

Stephen Daldry, Sam Mendes, Roger Michell, Antonia Bird, Mike Leigh . . .

Which isn't to say that the transition from theatre to film is necessarily an easy one. When I was a theatre director, I was endlessly told that I couldn't then become a film director. I was told my films would look really flat, like a tableau. Like a Peter Greenaway film. In fact, theatre teaches you a wonderful visual sense – especially more modern theatre, which is a bit more stripped back and isn't so much about lavish recreations of realism as imagistic impressions. I think it freed up directors like me.

The most important experience theatre gives you is working with actors. Because it is an actors' medium. Theatre has been with us for thousands of years and yet the director has only been with us for a hundred years; he was a stage manager before that. As a theatre director, you get all this time with actors. You learn to empathise with them, to get the best out of them within the given time frame. And to glimpse what they can give a story.

It's very different in America, and not just because they don't have the same tradition of directors and actors learning their craft in the theatre and then moving into film. Over there it's much more about the actors just getting on with it. I remember Jonathan Pryce talking about working with Martin Scorsese on *The Age of Innocence*. I was very excited to know what Scorsese was like as a director. But Pryce revealed that Scorsese never said anything other than, 'Can we do it again?' An American director such as Scorsese will cast the right actor and let them get on with it. You rarely watch a Scorsese film and think an actor has been miscast.

And Woody Allen directs even less than Scorsese.

I remember Ken Branagh talking about working with Woody Allen on *Celebrity*: all he said was, 'It wasn't very funny.' Or, 'It needs to be funnier.' It's weird, the way it works. There's no one way.

Let's go back to your time at Joint Stock and the Royal Court. Who were the most influential people you met around this time?

There were three guys. Bill Gaskill, who was a genius and whose work was very much to my taste, and Max Stafford-Clark, who was brilliant but very precise in a way that I'm not. The third was

Richard Wilson, whom I worked with at the Royal Court. Richard was delightful. His work as a director is completely different to his work as an actor – he's obviously most famous for his larger-than-life role in *One Foot in the Grave*. But, as a director, he'd strip people down and tell them to stop acting. He used to bellow, 'Stop acting!' Richard was the first guy to let me be an assistant director; Max then developed me over a number of years.

What were the specific skills you picked up from these three?

On a broad level, I learned that theatre is an actors' medium. For three or four weeks you are important as director and then the actors push you away. It's really shocking when it first happens, but then you learn. When I started directing at the Royal Court, I was still giving the actors notes once the play was in production, and they would say, 'With respect, Danny . . .' I might as well just shut up. They've got the live performance, which is all that matters. They know how to direct it themselves then. It's weird. Of course, in film you don't get that, which is one of the attractions. If anything, you push the actor away; they do their job, you tell them when to go and then you manipulate what you've got.

On a more detailed level, I watched them work. Learned tricks. Max did one of the best tricks I ever saw in the theatre. The actors would each pick a card from a pack. The card would indicate their status; ace was high, two was low. They then had to improvise a scene and somehow play the comparative status of whatever card they'd got. It was really interesting. A two and an ace were easy but how do you play a seven? When the exercise was over, everybody had to work out which number everyone else was playing.

Richard had this exercise in which eight actors lined up at an imaginary bus stop. It's real time, so they'd wait. Everyone who was looking at their watch in an exaggerated manner would be told to stop. They'd stand there and Richard would jump time forward – twenty, forty, sixty minutes. He was trying to ferret out overacting. When you're a theatre director you need all these exercises because you have so much time with the actors. Obviously you have no such luxury on a film.

Although I watched Max and Richard carefully, I was inspired more directly by Bill. He didn't adopt the exercise or improvisational approach. He was right on the script straight away; he sought out the truth in the text. I felt more at home with Bill's style, which was less about precision and more to do with sweep.

I was never very good at improvising, either in the theatre or on film. It amazes me how a director like Mike Leigh works. It can produce extraordinary work; look at David Thewlis in *Naked*. Something emerged in that film which could never have been written. It's so out there. But I've never been into that. I like to bounce off the writing.

You worked with Joint Stock and, after graduating from Bangor at twenty-one, moved to London. How did you end up at the Royal Court, where you became director of the Theatre Upstairs and stayed until 1987?

Max took over the Royal Court, and I went with him in 1982. He took me as a young assistant to learn the ropes. I started going to as many plays as I could. I saw Jonathan Pryce's *Hamlet* at the Court and it was extraordinary; I later got to work with him on *Mr Wroe's Virgins*. There are certain actors with whom you work – Pryce, Gary Oldman, Kerry Fox – who are really different. They have this frightening energy. It's like they are doing everything in second gear until they can find a way to release themselves. Thoroughbreds, I call them.

Was your life at that point dominated by the theatre?

I didn't do anything else. Apart from music and concerts. One of the joys of my life is that all my relaxation is a form of research in one way or another.

Did you go to the cinema too?

Of course! One of my first memories of London was seeing a poster of *Apocalypse Now* in 1979. A black poster as big as a building on the Fulham Road. It just said, 'Apocalypse Now'. That is mass marketing! It's a film that deserved the ultimate mass marketing. I went to see it and was blown away. I had no idea why I was going to see it, I don't even think I connected it with *The Godfather*. I still think *Apocalypse Now* is the ultimate action movie. That term has come to define anything with Bruce Willis in it, but *Apocalypse Now* is a true action movie: it's all movement. And whenever the movement stops, you get this extraordinary crisis.

Does it elicit a similar response of awe when you watch it now?

I agreed to write a piece about *Alien* for the twenty-fifth-anniversary DVD and made the point that it's a timeless film. It's the same with *Apocalypse Now*; even now it doesn't look dated. It's my complete, absolute favourite film of all time. Ever (*laughs*). It's mad. It's flawed. It's total film-making on a gargantuan scale. It never even crosses your mind to say that it has stood up well to the passage of time. Nobody would be allowed to make a film like that any more. The last guy who was allowed to do it was Michael Cimino with *Heaven's Gate*, and it went wrong. It wasn't remotely mesmerising. Whereas you can't rip your eyes away from *Apocalypse Now*.

Which other films did you see around that time?

This is God's honest truth: I never ever saw *Star Wars* when it came out in 1977. I find the industry's obsession with the franchise baffling. Not because I don't admire them – I have since seen them – but I find people's breathlessness in their presence odd. I didn't want to be watching kids' films at that time; I was into Siouxsie and the Banshees. However, as we now know, *Apocalypse Now* is the end of that era of film-making, and, in the end, George Lucas won.

I would have loved to have seen *Apocalypse* when it was shown at the Cannes Film Festival. Can you imagine just turning up to watch it? Didn't it share the prize?

It did. The audience were shown a three-hour work-in-progress, and it went on to share the prize with Volker Schlöndorff's The Tin Drum.

That's right because, at that point, Francis Ford Coppola still didn't know quite how to cut *Apocalypse*. It was really fresh and wet. It must have been extraordinary. I remember taking my dad to see it at the Prince Charles in Leicester Square, back when it sometimes showed feature films and sometimes showed porno. And – can you imagine? – it was preceded by trailers for porno films (*laughs*). I wanted my dad to see *Apocalypse so* much. But he wasn't very impressed. I don't know why. A few years earlier I took him to see *The Man Who Fell to Earth*. And even, at one point, tried to get him to listen to Led Zeppelin. But it's pointless trying to convert people – you've got to let them discover things for themselves . . .

Despite your father not sharing your good taste, you had a great time in London, moving up from assistant director to artistic director at the Royal Court Theatre Upstairs. Then, in 1987, you moved to the BBC.

I stayed at the Court for what seemed like quite a long time. The first play I directed there was an allegorical Polish drama called *Cinders*, written by Janusz Głowacki. It was literally translated by a friend of Janusz's and then adapted by Hanif Kureishi. To get a feel for the country, Hanif and I flew to Warsaw – it was the first time I'd ever been in a plane – and stayed in the translator's flat. It was winter and so cold that Hanif barely left the flat, choosing instead to stay in bed. He was already establishing himself as a bit of a writer and I was slightly intimidated by him.

While Hanif was in bed, I took a bus out to a workers' estate, which was impressively vast. I don't know if I was followed; I suppose I might have been. Hanif and I then went to midnight Mass at a church in Gdansk, where they sang the Polish national anthem. It was a memorable experience; we were crammed into this big church like commuters on the Tube at rush hour. Two weeks after we left, General Jaruzelski clamped down on Solidarność, Lech Wałęsa's trade-union movement. Janusz wasn't in Poland at the time, but his wife was trapped inside the country and he couldn't get back in.

The other key plays I directed at the Theatre Upstairs were *Salonika* by Louise Page, *Victory* by Howard Barker, *The Grace of Mary Traverse* by Timberlake Wertenbaker and *Saved* by Edward Bond.

By the time I left the Royal Court, I was institutionalised. I had no idea what freelancing was: I'd gone straight from university to Joint Stock and then on to the Court. In 1987, I saw an advert for a two-year contract as a BBC Northern Ireland TV producer. I knew a couple of people at the BBC through the Court, so I asked them what the job entailed. I basically found out that the BBC didn't appoint directors – they were signed up for one-off films – but that if I got this producing job I might be able to direct as well.

At that point I'd already been to Northern Ireland a number of times: I'd done a play about Derry and one of my close friends from university was from Ballymoney. I applied for the job and got it. David Hare wrote me a reference because he'd seen some of the work I'd done at the Court. The guy in Northern Ireland who was making the appointments was really impressed by his letter. I said to them that I'd direct the films as well, but wouldn't charge for doing so. For one fee I'd do both jobs.

Between 1987 and 1989, I directed and produced seven one-hour drama films in Northern Ireland. I loved being there. From the outside it looked tough politically, but once you lived there it was just wonderful. You'd hear a bomb going off every now and again, but the compensation was the friendliness of the people. I'd recommend Northern Ireland to anyone.

On two of the drama films I worked with writers I'd met at the Royal Court: Frank McGuinness wrote *Scout* and *The Hen House*, while Anne Devlin wrote *The Venus de Milo Instead*. The latter's a beautiful little drama about a Protestant girl going on a school trip to Paris. I had Anne on the set the whole time, and the Northern Ireland drama crew were clearly affronted: what was the writer doing on set? Was she going to come with us everywhere? I could never get over how little writers were paid. Anne was on about £3,500 for a drama. And all these other people I was in charge of were comparatively paid staggering amounts of money.

This was your first time working with a camera. Did you learn on the hoof?

You learn from the cameraman; he tells you everything you need to know. Orson Welles said you can learn everything you need to know about a camera in an afternoon, and it's true. The one thing you have to get your head round is left to right, right to left. I wanted the camera to be in a certain place, but it would look like the two actors were looking the same way rather than at each other. Phil Dawson, the BBC cameraman, patiently explained the process and finally, over time, it clicked.

I was lucky that on the first television film I directed, *Scout*, I worked with a wonderful Irish actor, Ray McAnally. He'd been in *The Mission* the previous year. He was an old, experienced actor who was happy to help me work my way around making a film. He knew I didn't know what I was doing. Well, on the one hand, I thought I knew what I was doing; on the other, I had so much to learn. He'd deliver his lines on one side of the camera and then offer to deliver them on the other side too. He knew that I'd have a cutting problem, that I didn't fully understand left to right and right to left yet, and that I'd need him to be looking in a different direction for some of the scenes. He was really lovely. A really sweet guy.

He was working alongside all these young lads who were playing aspiring footballers, and I remember him opening his shirt to show them the scar from his heart bypass surgery. He was this great big barrel-chested Irish actor and he had train tracks all over his chest. It was like Frankenstein. He loved showing it to the boys. Sadly, he died in 1989.

Despite various teething problems, did the transition from stage to television drama feel relatively natural?

Yes, because both are writer-based. I was commissioning TV plays in the same way I had done at the Royal Court. I liked working with the writers and I treated them with respect, which was unusual – most TV writers, apart from the Potters and the Bleasdales, are treated appallingly. But I kept the writers involved at all stages. Until recently, I haven't been in a position where I've had to push the writer away. Certainly, with all the early stuff, I would never have done so. Although I might have disagreed with them and, at times, had to overrule them. The rule at the Court was that if there was a disagreement, the writer wins. If Caryl Churchill said to Max Stafford-Clark, 'No, I want it that way,' it would be that way. Whereas in film it's the opposite. So my experience at the Court helped me to build proper relationships with writers, and they were happy to trust me too.

It took time to adjust to working with the actors in a different way. I'd run the scenes all the time and I could see them looking at me, thinking I didn't need to do the whole scene, I just needed to pick up that one line saying, 'I'm going!' But I'd run the whole five-minute scene that led up to that character saying, 'I'm going!' because that was what you did in the theatre.

Did you enjoy learning on your feet?

God, yes. While I was in Northern Ireland, I directed three or four films and produced twice. I produced *The Rockingham Shoot* for a very nice director called Kieran Hickey, who's dead now. It was a lovely script by this wonderful writer John McGahern, but I wouldn't leave them alone. I just knew how it should be done; I couldn't stand back and watch from a distance. I learned that producing wasn't really my thing (*laughs*). Kieran was so patient with me, even though I wasn't supporting him properly.

The second film you produced, in 1989, was the late Alan Clarke's Elephant.

We have only ever had a few genuine mavericks like Alan Clarke. I meet directors all the time who still talk about him; I get invitations from all over the world to go and talk about working with him on *Elephant*. His work has that resonance. As a teenager, I used to watch the Play for Today at home; there was always a good chance there'd be sex in it, but I could pretend I was watching a serious piece of drama. So, in 1974, I watched a play called *Penda's Fen*, which was written by David Rudkin. I only found out years later that Alan had directed it. It had a big effect on me: it was visually different – surreal. In 1977 and 1982, I was blown away by *Scum* and *Made in Britain* respectively.

When I first thought about leaving the Court, I wrote to Alan Clarke and asked if I could watch him film. He agreed; he was incredibly generous because he didn't know who I was, although we had worked in the same office at the Royal Court earlier, when Lindsay Anderson was around. Alan was pretty dismissive of the Court and, with his macho northern sarcasm, talked of 'a lot of gay people mincing around in the corridors'. Anyway, I went to see him make a not-very-good film called *Christine*, which he shot with a Steadicam around the streets of Ealing. It was incredible to watch him work. It was total film-making: he works in a much lighter way than I do, but he had everybody marching everywhere. He used his Scouse charm to get everyone going the way he wanted them going (*laughs*).

When you say he had a lighter touch, what exactly do you mean?

He was less serious than me. Although he was *very* serious about what he was doing. His commitment to violence was certainly serious! He worked in a slightly more playful way than I do. There would be slightly more humour around on set. I keep things affable but focused. Even though we have a different approach to directing, Clarkey's manner to the crew and the actors was genuinely inspiring. He wasn't autocratic; he was a leader but he was also genuinely a team player. He didn't indulge in any of the status stuff, didn't shout at people. He said the director should have control but not abuse it. As director you are probably being paid more than anybody, so why would you be shouting at people? If it's not going well, it's your fault, you're to blame. It's brilliant advice.

He was affable and also supremely talented. He was innovative, dangerous, experimental. Sometimes it didn't work and sometimes it was breathtaking. He was always provocative; he used to say, 'Don't read the *Guardian*, lad, everything you need to know is in the *Sun*.' He told me to read *Hitchcock* by François Truffaut, citing it as the only decent book written about film-making.

Did you go straight out and buy it?

Yes. It's outdated now because times have changed so much. Hitchcock said, for example, that you could never put a camera inside a fridge because the camera could actually never be there and it would look too artificial. And, of course, now cameras are everywhere. Hitchcock was talking about those huge old cameras that he somehow managed to move around.

Clarke was, as you say, experimental, which also meant that he was regarded as left-field. He used Steadicam for the first time in 1983 on Made in Britain, *and then, on* Elephant, *he uses it to startling effect.*

Traditionalists distrusted Steadicam because anyone can use it. It means that, on one level, it takes away all the skill. But if you used it as effectively as Alan used it, it actually required more skill than a classicist approach to film-making. He was such an experimentalist in the way he made films, but his mantra nonetheless was, 'Get lots of coverage. Get as many shots as you can. It's the only thing you need to remember.' Which is, of course, what classicists do: they over-cover everything. But Clarkey said at some point you will need that cover. He knew you could do all these big, spectacular tracking shots, but actually if they don't work, what you need is coverage.

He taught me that films are made in the editing room. And it's true. Cameramen might *think* they make films, but more than 50 per cent of a film is made in the edit. Sometimes it's as much as 75 per cent. And yet cameramen are often disdainful of editors; they think they ruin their work.

It must have been a real coup when Clarke agreed to direct Elephant.

It certainly felt like it. He came over to Northern Ireland, and, because I was producing, I always wanted to take him out. But he wasn't interested. All he wanted to do was sit and watch the rushes the whole time. Back then, you'd get the rushes two or three days after you'd shot them. I understand that now; I just want to see what I'm getting and see if I can improve it. If I can somehow not make the film fail (*laughs*).

Sadly, he died the year after making Elephant.

He eventually got a big movie in America – a political movie about Central America – and he was setting it up when he collapsed. He had cancer. They flew him home. He was in the Cromwell Hospital in London and then in a hospice. I went to see him there in July 1990. There was football on the telly – and he was a mad Everton fan – but all he was interested in was the birds on the balcony. It just shows you that it all gets stripped away; the swallows and swifts were more important even than football. He had so many visitors. Women who were devoted to him, who slept on the floor to keep him company. It was incredibly sad. He was a Joe Strummer-type guy for me. Another one of those . . . He was very special.

After an incredibly productive time in Northern Ireland, you moved back to London.

I came back and did a couple of one-off dramas for the BBC that were effectively Play for Todays, including *For the Greater Good* and *Not Even God Is Wise Enough*. In 1990 and 1992, I directed two *Inspector Morse*s. It was an important job in the development of a young director because you work with a proper film crew. The crew would do something like a Spielberg film – *Raiders*, or whatever he was filming in the UK – and the other six months they'd do *Inspector Morse*. It was high-end television with lots of equipment and a proper budget. John Thaw pulled in an audience of 18 million every week back then.

Did you get along with him?

He was a proper lead actor. It was the equivalent of working with Tom Cruise. You have an actor who is the kingpin, who is paid more than everyone else and around whom everything revolves. John was really interesting because, as soon as I walked on set, he put me in my place. I remember talking about continuity in the first or second set-up, and he insisted he didn't pick up the cup on line five but on line ten. We disagreed. I was just about to ask the continuity woman to check, but I could tell it was the point at which I had to say he was right.

And was he right?

No! I think I was right. Directors always do. But you have to give in and allow it. Actually, we got on well and I grew to really like him. Despite it being within the usual confines of television, you worked with considerable scale on *Morse*. They were also prepared to listen to ambition. The openings were famous because it was where you set out your stall, and you were encouraged to be ambitious in setting up the murder.

Did you work with interesting writers?

The first one had a very good, classic *Morse* script by this guy Julian Mitchell, who had written *Another Country*. And then I met a friend of his, Amy Jenkins, the daughter of the late Peter Jenkins and who, of course, went on to write *This Life*. We became good friends and she introduced me to rave culture. She invited me to an early rave; it was extraordinary. Once you got into the music, it was fantastic. We used to make each other tapes and then drive around playing them, and the odd car would be playing the same music. You'd look at each other at traffic lights and just know. The spirit of it was incredible. It was clearly an antidote to Thatcherism. It was blindingly obvious: people were determined to share their experiences, find an alternative to right-wing individualism and competitiveness.

Amy and I wanted to make a film about Ecstasy and we tried to sell it, but nobody would touch it. The timing wasn't great; it was when tabloid headlines were screaming 'Save our children!' Endless images of children in fields, off their heads. Amy wrote these really good scripts with superb dialogue; a young, middle-class playground of London and Brighton. You could see she harnessed that skill to great effect in *This Life*. Anyway, we ended up putting the rave-culture storyline in *Morse*. Amy reworked the dialogue of the young characters in Julian's script. Meanwhile, Julian dealt with Morse's bafflement at this new world perfectly. It was the first appearance on British mainstream television of rave culture.

ITV must have been thrilled.

They were horrified! Nobody really understood. I remember setting up this rave in a country house and getting a party crowd in who were all off their faces. These ITV producers came along and were totally bemused. John Thaw himself was very amused.

Still, you were offered a three-part BBC series called Mr Wroe's Virgins, *which was critically acclaimed upon its broadcast in spring 1993.*

Mr Wroe's Virgins was very special to me. I worked with terrific actors – Jonathan Pryce, Kathy Burke and Kerry Fox, among others. I met John Chapman, an excellent producer, who set it all up. He introduced me to properly creative producers who think about a script. They are not stealing your ground, but they think about the shape of the drama in a way that's complementary to your vision. John wasn't telling me how to do it, which I used to do when I produced; he just made gentle formative suggestions.

John introduced me to Brian Tufano, who had been one of the great BBC cameramen and had worked with Ken Loach and Stephen Frears. Then he went off to America and came back with his tail between his legs. However, he was brilliant for me: my first proper movie cameraman. I'd express an idea, and he just got it. He introduced me to these lenses I'd never come across before. He introduced me to one in particular, the Zeiss 10mm wide lens, which makes everything bigger. Television people are terrified about everything looking too big; it's got to look like it's set in a living room. But the Zeiss made everything look as though it was in the Wild West. It made it difficult because there was nowhere for the crew to hide, given that you could see everything in the room.

Which I presume is why, just the following year, you wanted the flat in Shallow Grave *to look so vast?*

Absolutely. People kept saying the rooms were too big, but it's a film! They have to be as big as you can make them! So, back on *Mr Wroe's Virgins*, John introduced me to Brian Tufano and then to Masahiro Hirakubo, an editor who had a growing reputation within the BBC. They were wonderful collaborators. I'm very proud of the work I did on *Mr Wroe's Virgins*. It was a big stepping stone for me. In fact, it got me *Shallow Grave*: I was recommended to producer Andrew Macdonald on the back of it.

As you detail in the chapter on Shallow Grave, *your relationship with Andrew Macdonald and scriptwriter John Hodge was based on your own idealism, namely your wish to share the profits from the films you worked on. After* Shallow Grave, Trainspotting *and* A Life Less Ordinary, *however, your relationship floundered. You may have been disabused of your anarchistic idealism by the time you had finished shooting* The Beach, *but did your approach to film-making remain essentially the same?*

It's got to be total film-making. Absolutely total film-making. I encourage the crew to get on with it themselves, to be mini-directors. I started to work with production designer Mark Tildesley on 28

Days Later, and he was perfect for me. He's the designer, he works closely with a small team and that's that. There's no chain of command. I like to feel as though I'm working with a gang of thieves as opposed to an anonymous group of experts who are handing out a series of delegations to other experts.

Once the gang is up and running I expect commitment. As director I'm always first on set and last away. I'm on a mad mission. I live and breathe the film. Your insanity has to persuade other people to give everything too, to share the madness. Every single person who works on the film has to be completely dedicated to it. They are not allowed to outsource to anyone else during that period, which involves pre-production, the shoot, post-production. It may sound autocratic, but it's the only way to make it work as a team, to ensure that everybody is on the field at the same time.

When did you learn to work this way?

I've always been like that. But I only became self-conscious about it when I was making feature films. I've never understood why people I work with aren't 100 per cent committed. It doesn't make any sense to me. There can, of course, be an unreasonable side to it: if I see a cameraman on the phone about another job and I get pissed off with him . . . (*laughs*) In one sense it *is* unreasonable because we're all freelancers, but I want his mind to be on the job in hand.

And converting your cast and crew is down to sheer enthusiasm?

Yes.

And absolutely knowing what you want, even though you have the right to change your mind?

Yes. You *have* to know what you want – almost instinctively – because you spend all day answering questions. Somebody said it's like being a primary-school teacher. Films basically get made; as director you're just there to answer the 600 questions that get asked along the way. Which are as meaningful as, 'Can I go to the toilet?' (*laughs*). Simon Beaufoy tried directing and hated it because he couldn't answer questions that quickly. He really likes to stop and think about questions, but you just can't on set.

Questions are designed to slow everything down. That's the other thing: pace. For some reason, film-making has inertia built into it. It's all designed to not quite happen. You have to defy it. That's one of the jobs you do as director.

Are you good at being patient?

I'm very patient with people – I don't want or need to be rude – and very impatient with the process. If you can combine those two things, you can defy the inertia. And yet still let people think they like you. Think you're all right.

Do you want and need to be liked?

I just know how much it helps on set. You feel like you've suc-ceeded in converting the cast and crew if they like you. You could say it's being cunning, because you are obviously after extra effort for free. You're after the overrun (*laughs*). Because if you're a nice guy and you go to them at the end of a hard day, they'll give you more. If you're a fucker and you behave like a fucker all the time, at some point they're going to say what they think of you. And not hang around for that extra shot you desperately need.

Do you ever lose your temper on set?

No, you can't. I very rarely do. People expect you to – you can see it written across their faces. They're expecting you to yell, 'You fuck-ing idiot! Don't you know which hemisphere we're in?' It sounds a bit heroic, but you've got to remember how privileged you are. My sisters were teachers – think of what they had to deal with in an average day – so what have I got to complain about? If you are shouting at anyone, it should be the producer, because you're equal. Otherwise, it's just bullying. You've got to keep thinking about teachers, nurses: we get paid huge amounts of money to do what many consider a dream job. There is no excuse to behave badly.

You said earlier that you learned tolerance and respect from your mother. Do you consciously apply these values to film-making?

Yes. I've always had a strong belief in those values. I think a lot of northerners have a chip on their shoulders about southerners, about people who've been to Oxford and Cambridge or the perceived bias in the media towards southerners. However, once you get over that chip, the field is then clear to apply more important and positive values. The tolerance and respect I try to maintain on a daily basis definitely come from my mum. She wasn't interested in drama – although, of course, religion is drama in a way. She was very devout and not at all oppositional. And yet her values keep me in a really good place. I fail her sometimes, but it's what I aim for. I remember her really clearly. When I'm tempted to lose my temper, which is rare, I think of her.

As you say, your mother was devout. What effect has the legacy of a Catholic upbringing had on your films, either directly or indirectly?

It's hard to judge it myself. One of the key aspects of Catholicism is the extreme guilt one carries in relation to enjoyment, pleasure and success. It's easier to discuss in direct relation to my mum: she was incredibly optimistic, and I've always believed in trying to find an optimism in the work, even in the most difficult circumstances.

Have you found a way of dealing with the guilt by now?

(*laughs*) I've tried to. I can't completely, of course, because it follows me around.

I suppose what I'm asking is: can you enjoy your success?

No. Only in a very private way. I always doubt my success, which is a good thing. I see other people enjoying success in a more emphatic way, and I think, 'Fair enough,' but I could never naturally do it. I can pretend to do it.

How do you pretend to do it?

You watch how it's done and think: I can do that! But I never genuinely feel it. Definitely not. Part of me always thinks I'm a charlatan, which is as important as doubting one's success. Alongside every other creative person, I'm always waiting to be found out. It's a cliché, but film-making isn't about any single person. Directors shouldn't consider themselves special. Films are dependent on so many different people; so much of the work is not creative; it's not about having 'a gift' but how well you carry out man management. I always find it really odd when film-makers are referred to as artists. I think artists are people like Picasso.

Would you ever refer to yourself as an auteur?

No, I don't think so.

But it just means that your films reflect your creative vision and have a distinct quality.

I'd be happy to accept that word if it didn't have such indulgent associations! That one word shuffles everybody else's contribution sideways, and it's obviously unfair.

Other than total film-making, extreme guilt and being a nice guy, what else defines you as a film-maker?

Outrageousness! In the sense that, in cinema, you have to be bold and push things beyond the limit. I remember feeling it the first time I saw *Shallow Grave* in the cinema. Films are there to make the audience go, 'Fuck!' Or, quite literally, to be on the floor laughing. I remember going to see *Dumb & Dumber* in Glasgow when we were making *Shallow Grave*. At one point Jim Carrey gets his tongue stuck, and I was on my hands and knees in the cinema aisle laughing. I was in pain from laughing.

Have you always set out to achieve cinematic outrageousness?

Not at all. My early television films are very Tarkovskyesque (*laughs*) – more about the dangers of '-esque' later. Back then, I was going through a high-art stage. It's embarrassing. Actually, the early films are not *that* bad because most of the scripts were by very good Irish writers. They have a kind of earthiness . . . I was wearing my influences on my sleeve at that point. I've always enjoyed bold films. Nic Roeg is my favourite film-maker, and his films are like that. In one sense they are high art, but in another they are deeply provocative. Roeg is provocative by nature. He's pushing to see how he can cut you. I always loved his films instinctively without really understanding everything about them.

Do you believe in living dangerously when making films?

If you can make it up on the day, it's always much better. Films are set up to discourage you from making it on the day, but, instead of relying on a large crew who know exactly what is going to happen in advance, I'd rather use a small, intimate crew who are up for inventing something on the day. And if that means botching together pieces of equipment over lunchtime, then that's part of the spirit of it. You can quickly identify who is up for working like that, and it's very exciting. You achieve little things that feel like big triumphs. That spirit is partially passed across to the audience and infects the film in the end. You get the idea that the film was made live.

Do you think rigid storyboarding – apart from on a sci-fi film like
Sunshine *where it's unavoidable – encourages the possibility of making a dead, mechanical film?*

I would be instinctively inclined to think that, but there are plenty of films that are storyboarded and are very exciting to watch. Spielberg's early work was storyboarded frame by frame. John Ford worked like that in his mind: he shot exactly what he needed so no one else could recut it in a different way. Of course, there are certain sequences that have to be storyboarded for technical reasons. I always try to contradict them if I can and find another way.

Not all directors are storytellers. But, given that you work so closely with writers, do you feel as though you serve the script or do you bring it to life?

I'm absolutely script-dependent. I'm not a great improviser; I don't like improvising as a technique. I don't really know how to manipulate it. I can't see the point of it. I'm not a big fan of improvised films. I see writers as architects and I like that sense of being manipulated. So I think I serve the script, but some writers, such as John Hodge, hardly describe anything. They use the bare minimum. It's just dialogue and the hidden structure, which I call the architecture. In which case I get plenty of room to inhabit the script. I'd like to think I serve the script, but I've no idea if I do; in a way, it's an impossible question to answer. You'd have to get inside the writer's head and see the film they thought would be made, and then you'd have to get inside my head and think . . . oh my God! Most writers think their vision and mine do coincide, but Simon Beaufoy didn't. *Slumdog* wasn't what he was imagining at all. Luckily, it was much better! Or maybe it wasn't. Luckily for me, you'll never find out.

Are you concerned with plausibility or just good storytelling?

Plausibility is always there, but then you overcome it. You judge everything in terms of moment-to-moment plausibility: could this happen? Is this real? Even within a fantasy sequence you want things to be authentic enough to be reasonably realistic. So I have an eye on plausibility but, at the same time, good storytelling lets you get away with anything. The British are not naturally outlandish storytellers. We don't embrace sweeps away from realism and plausibility. We have a less flamboyant, more down-to-earth manner of doing things.

How far you can push the plausibility threshold is a big part of the job of being a director. Especially if you are going to do anything more than realism: if you can push a film into a joy or an outrage or a horror, you automatically go beyond the plausibility threshold. If it works, you make a pact with the audience; they know it wouldn't happen but they watch and think, 'Wow! That's great that it did.'

What comes first, storytelling or entertaining?

Hmmm . . . You've got to be committed to storytelling. I don't know exactly what you mean but I take it as: entertainment is *Dumb & Dumber*, where the story doesn't really matter as much as the exhilaration of just watching people larking around. Some good gags. For me, storytelling is more important. Partly because my focus is on the script.

Do you generally like the characters you bring to life on the screen?

I do actually, yes. A lot. They are writers' characters really, and then the ownership is shared with the actor and director. Having said that, Alex Garland tends to make his central character separate from the others: he did it with Richard in *The Beach* and Capa in *Sunshine*. I'm not so sure I like those guys as much as, say, Jamal in *Slumdog* or Robert in *A Life Less Ordinary*. Richard and Capa are much colder, somehow removed from the other characters. I love the characters John creates, but he thinks he's a cold writer.

That's interesting. He's not at all.

Not *at all*! It's that weird fucked-up thing he has as a former doctor: 'I've seen everything, nothing moves me.' In fact, of course, it does. He writes in this amazing way where the actors go 'Wow!' and chew the lines up. Alex's writing is much more about refusing to join in, to engage. Characters who try to remain at the periphery until they are dragged to the centre – that's really what the drama is.

Of all the scripts you've worked with, which was the most complete?

God. I don't know. I've got no idea. The problem with *Trainspotting* is that we didn't really have a story. There was no compelling forward narrative. It's just 'and then Tommy died and we went to the funeral'. *Shallow Grave* is a much more complete, controlled, architectural script. The same with *Slumdog*. I can't answer that question. I wouldn't feel qualified to choose.

Is directing ever satisfying?

If it is, it's very temporary. Alan Clarke used to say get plenty of coverage: he knew that directors would sometimes show off and say they're going to cover everything in one shot. It may be four pages of dialogue from the script but, hey, let's do it in one shot! So you rehearse it and the actors are happy and you feel exhilarated at having done it so quickly. Fuck! I can fucking show those people how to direct! I can direct four pages in fifteen minutes! And – this has happened to me a few times – you get back to the cutting room months later and the film is turgid. That feeling of elation you have on the day doesn't necessarily translate in the rushes.

So if it is satisfying on the day, then it's often an illusion. Make sure you get the coverage! Oliver Stone was right when he said film-making is done 'inch by motherfucking inch'. And there's not much satisfaction involved in that.

Do you get frustrated?

No. It's part of the process. I think actors do. If they are honest, they admit it's laborious.

You once said, 'Filming itself is a bit of a madness, a tunnel: the less detours you make, the better.'

That's definitely true. You get in there and think some detour is fascinating. You get back in the cutting room and wonder what you could have been thinking. I think it's especially true in narrative films, where you've got to be very careful. You get a script ready and shoot it. If you want to change it, do it afterwards in reshoots or pick-ups. But stick to the script when you're shooting. There have been so many times when I've thought we should drop a scene, but I've made myself shoot it.

Various crew members such as assistant directors and line producers are always asking if scenes can be dropped to help with the schedule or budget. I insist on shooting all the scenes, even if one or two are below standard. You can get lost in a film trying to work out what is important. In a weird kind of way, you're the worst judge there is of what is and isn't important. It's a bizarre thing to say but it's true. Then you get a coolness in editing and the scales fall away from your eyes about what you've done or not done.

What happens when you don't want to hang around on a film – I'm thinking, of course, of The Beach?

I couldn't wait to leave Thailand, which is a very bad sign. I had quite the opposite feeling on *Trainspotting*: I was really angry with the crew because they didn't want to keep going. And on *Slumdog* I wanted to keep going; producer Christian Colson literally closed the bank accounts and left. You have to be on a journey where nobody can keep up with you. They all tire and you just keep going. It doesn't necessarily mean you're making a good film . . . but I just wanted to get away from *The Beach*.

What happens when you get back from somewhere like India? What do you do with yourself to prevent post-production comedown?

(*laughs*) I have a couple of weeks off. I usually walk around

London. I have weird dreams where I wake up and everybody is looking at me, waiting. It's a variation on the dream actors have in which they wake up live on stage in front of 400 people. They've no idea where they are, which play they're doing; all they know is that it's their cue.

I let the editor assemble. Some directors dominate the editor throughout the assembling, but I never do that. When they ask, I try not to answer. Editors are extraordinary; instinctively, they never come to the set because they'd rather not fret about what the director might have left out. The editing process is amazing. Extraordinary. Because you go from 100 to 250 people asking what they should do to just you, an editor and one or two assistants just sitting there for months.

One thing you have to learn is to show the film to people and not be frightened. You do get precious, but one of the great things you learn is how much value there is in watching it with other people. Partly because of what they then say to you about the film, but also how *you* feel as they are watching it. It's weird. You suddenly see things and think, 'Oh God, I shouldn't have done that.' They haven't twitched in their seat or anything, but you sense so many things just because people are in the room with you.

You've had to learn to love focus groups.

They are torture but they are also wonderful. It's a big job for producers to get directors, especially those starting out, over the hurdle of not resenting or fearing those kinds of screenings. In fact, you're going to learn about your film more than you ever thought possible. You think you're coming to the end because you've done your eight weeks of editing, but it's just the beginning!

It must be good for you as a director, because you can't be touchy or sensitive about your work.

You've got to learn not to be touchy or sensitive very quickly. It can be painful. You learn to understand the testing process as well. The biggest score there has ever been for a film in a test – almost 100 per cent and therefore judged as being perfect by the test audience – was *City Slickers II*. The problem is that everyone then hides behind it, saying that *City Slickers II* tested so well, yet did nothing at the box office. It allows everyone to dismiss test screenings, if they so choose. It becomes every director's refuge. It's also true that, in the end, you can't be swayed by test screenings. You've got to stay focused on what *you* want to do. You can only learn from them.

Which weaknesses would you admit to as a director?

I learned quite a lot in India about using the persona of a star like Anil Kapoor. I hadn't done that before. It wasn't so much because I was fearing it, but I certainly tried to avoid it. I think it's a weakness in a director not to use big, iconic actors such as Brad Pitt, Angelina Jolie, Leo DiCaprio. They are a crucial part of film-making. Really great directors like Hitchcock and Roeg are not frightened to take on big stars. I always worry that big stars distort a film because you're watching the star rather than the character. Of course you are, but if you do it well enough, audiences are capable of adjusting the algebra in their head. Although I worked with Leo on *The Beach*, avoiding stars is a genuine shortcoming in my films.

I will also admit to relief that part of the reason *Slumdog* worked is because it's a love story. And I always used to think I couldn't do a love story. I thought my cynical side wouldn't let it work. If you're going to do a love story, you must not apologise. No one's interested in half-hearted love.

A Life Less Ordinary *is a love story.*

It is, but it flopped. It made me insecure. I thought I was better at the more cynical side of it, where deals are made, as they are in *Shallow Grave* and *Trainspotting*. Both those films are cool rather than exposing; nobody's heart is exposed or trampled on.

That's typically male storytelling.

It is, and I've always felt better at it. Finally – I'm still on my weaknesses – I've never made a film with a woman at its heart, properly leading it. It's a terrible shortcoming. Women make up more than half the world, and there's a long list of extraordinary women who helped make these films happen for me.

Why do you think you haven't made a film with a woman at its heart? Do you plan to make amends?

I'm not sure. This isn't an excuse, but it's partly about engaging with the more commercial side of cinema. You know a film such as *28 Days Later* will appeal to a male audience. You put a woman in it and she's a wonderful character, but she's not the absolute driving force. Sadly, and to its shame, the film industry is a more male business. Particularly if you want to attract a mainstream audience.

I loved directing *The Venus de Milo Instead* and *Mr Wroe's Virgins*. There are so many stories with women at their centre, but I still haven't managed to direct just such a feature film.

Because of the scripts you are sent or what you naturally gravitate towards?

Both. You have to blame yourself for everything in the end. As you become more well known, there is less and less excuse for circumstance to explain something you've identified as a failing. I'd love to make amends but perhaps I'm not a light enough director, given that women's scripts often have a lighter touch. I'm in no way denigrating the material, rather commenting on my own directing style.

Some people believe that female directors should tell women's stories, but I think women should tell men's stories too. Kathryn Bigelow made *The Hurt Locker* and then refused to discuss being a female director and making a film about war. And she's right: the film shouldn't be about her gender; it should be about her instincts as a human being.

The Hurt Locker *is a great film. What makes a great film as opposed to a good one?*

Personally, it goes back to the madness in the film. Either in an actor or in a vision. Or even in an attempt of some kind, because great films aren't necessarily successful. *Apocalypse Now* is the most perfect example of it. There is an attempt in there that is mad, which elevates it. A madness where things have been forgotten, like technique . . . All the slightly colder things about marketing and target demographics get thoroughly trampled on. You can see it even in the Pixar films. They are a hugely successful franchise now, but when you look at the early films, they're mad! They thought people were really going to watch this stuff? It's so plastic looking! But we all sat there and watched *Toy Story* in awe.

It's the same with Nick Park. He has an insane vision of spending nine months moving plasticine figures of Wallace and Gromit around. The railway chase at the end of *Wrong Trousers* is one of the greatest pieces of action directing ever done. That really *is* doing it inch by inch.

Does your love of animation go back to being a kid?

It goes back to my kids. I watched *everything* with them. I'm sad now because I don't see everything as devotedly as I did before they grew up. It was great to experience movies through their eyes.

We've talked about what makes a great film. How many great films have you made?

(*laughs*) Twenty-seven! Actually, I'm very proud of *Millions*. It was outside the comfort zone I had established. *Slumdog* was outside the comfort zone too. A film like *28 Days Later* was terrific, but it was inside my comfort zone. It was in a world I kind of knew. It's not about making great films so much as working outside your comfort zone if you can. It's scary.

What do you want people to feel or think after watching one of your films? In fact, do you want them to be feeling or thinking?

Feeling. Initially. It can be reflective afterwards. I want them to be caught in its spell as they are watching it. You have no option to look away. It's compulsive, urgent, insistent, visceral.

So the feeling is more important than the thinking?

For me, sitting in there watching it, yes. It's not an intellectual pursuit, it's . . .

. . . an experience?

That's a good way of putting it. It's one of the things that makes films unique; I don't think the other art forms are like that. They are much more selective.

How do you think your films will be enjoyed in the future?

I was asked to do a drawing for an exhibition at the BFI; they asked people what cinema would be like in the future. I did this drawing of a two-sided cinema screen as big as a football pitch. I'd been to one of the screenings at the O2 where 10,000 people watch this huge screen. It is going to go like that relatively soon: movies will be beamed in, as will Ultimate Fighting, tennis from Australia, Latter-day Saints Masses from Utah. And we will all go there for the collective experience of watching it together. There will be boutique events as well, but I think these enormous gatherings will become the norm.

Like some kind of pleasure dome?

Yes. They've already started building huge franchise stadia in America.

Without wishing to consign you to history, you've made eight feature films to date. How many do you have left in you?

It always used to be said that writers and directors have a ten-year golden period. Nic Roeg is the great example of that. For ten years – to my mind – he just blew the world away with *Performance*, *Walkabout*, *Don't Look Now* and *The Man Who Fell to Earth*. Having said that, he made *Eureka* in 1983, outside the ten-year golden period. So perhaps there's hope for us all . . . But you basically have ten good years during which you have a real thirst and energy for film-making. You get truly exceptional artists for whom that rule doesn't apply, but for most of us it's confined to a decade. After which you keep working for your own dignity, finance or whatever personal reasons.

So how do you explain your own career trajectory? Slumdog came out fourteen years after Shallow Grave.

It's only a theory. I'm well outside the time frame. I deserved those Oscars years ago!

Roeg is perhaps the exception to the rule in that he made four brilliant films in succession in a decade. Very few film-makers achieve that.

I agree. It comes and goes. It's very hard to sustain good work. Again, you think you can control the idea but you can't. Sometimes ideas you're working on will go out of focus, out of orbit. Maybe you, as director, lose sight of them. Films take a minimum of two years to make and it's hard to maintain absolute control from beginning to end. It's difficult to stay within people's orbit through that time. Especially over a number of films. You're always going to make a film you were, with hindsight, deluded about.

But which, presumably, you learn from?

You should learn all the time. Doubt is really crucial to film-making. It drives you mad and you long to lose it, but you can't do without it. You need it all the time. You constantly think your work isn't good enough. And some days you'd be right – your self-doubt is eventually proved correct. That's when some kind of film-tsar figure should step in and say, 'Enough! We're going to retire you now!'

Shallow Grave (1994)

Juliet Miller (Kerry Fox), David Stephens (Christopher Eccleston) and Alex Law (Ewan McGregor) live on the third floor of a large Edinburgh tenement. Sitting in a row on a sofa, they interview Cameron (Colin McCredie) as a prospective fourth flatmate. They are superior, smug, sardonic; he is nervous, uncomfortable, daunted. Several other contenders turn up, are interrogated and dismissed. Finally, Hugo (Keith Allen) rings the doorbell and tells Juliet that he has been away travelling and is now trying to write a novel. When the phone rings, she instructs him to pick it up and say she's not in.

Juliet, David, Alex and Hugo sit around the dining table, eating the last of the food, drinking wine and whisky. They decide Hugo can have the room and ask if he can afford the rent. He immediately pulls a wad of notes from his pocket. When David asks Hugo if he has ever killed a man, Hugo says no. All three flatmates appear satisfied with him.

The action moves to a high street: Andy (Peter Mullan) assaults and robs a man withdrawing cash from a machine.

Hugo arrives at the flat with two suitcases and shuts himself in his new room. As the flatmates come and go to work – Juliet is a nurse, David a chartered accountant and Alex a journalist – they wonder where Hugo is. Alex knocks on the door but there is no answer. David flings himself against the door and it opens. Hugo lies naked and dead on the bed. Juliet partially covers his corpse with a sheet. Alex starts to rifle through the drawers and cupboards; he finds needles, syringes and a bag of white powder in the bedside cabinet. He pulls an empty case from under the bed.

Juliet dials 999 and waits in vain for a response. Alex discovers *a large bag stuffed with money and takes it into the hall to show Juliet. Just as the operator answers, Juliet puts the phone down.*

Juliet, David and Alex sit around the table, the bag in front of them. They are clearly stunned but also excited. Alex is tempted to keep the money, while Juliet and David accuse him of being immoral. He sarcastically suggests they phone the police, but they just sit there in silence. The next day, Hugo's corpse is still lying on the bed, the money still sitting on the table. We see Juliet, David and Alex in their respective places of work.

The three flatmates have a short, final conversation about Hugo. It seems none of them will call the police. In a voice-over, David simply says: 'OK. Let's do it.' They go to a DIY warehouse to shop for appropriate dismembering and burial tools. Alex tackles the task of disposing of Hugo's body with relish and suggests they bury him in the forest. David says he could never cut the body up. Alex is disappointed, irritated. He says Hugo has to go; he is starting to smell.

They hire a van to transport the body to the forest. Juliet also has misgivings about chopping up the body.

Meanwhile, Tim (Leonard O'Malley) is seen plunging a man's head into a bath full of water as Andy looks on. The man says he knows nothing. Tim gets carried away and the man's body becomes limp.

Juliet, David and Alex wrap Hugo up in plastic. They wear face masks. Even Alex is nervous and agitated as they carry the corpse to the van. Once in the forest, they draw straws to decide who will cut the body up. David draws the short straw, says he can't do it, although he has no choice. Alex digs a shallow grave, and David saws through Hugo's limbs. Alex hands him a hammer to knock out the teeth, to make identification harder. Juliet looks on, clearly disturbed but also detached.

Back in the flat, David lies on his bed, staring into space. Alex drinks beer and watches Chris Tarrant present Lose a Million *on television. He appears unaffected by the burial. David climbs into the loft to hide the bag of money. Hugo's room is now clean.*

Juliet casually dumps Hugo's limbs in the incinerator at the hospital where she works.

Juliet, David and Alex attend a charity ball. David wants to talk, but Juliet is busy fending off an admirer and Alex is interested only in drinking himself into oblivion.

The next day, Juliet and Alex spend some of Hugo's money. David returns from work and is furious. He has changed; he is angry, impatient, troubled. He spends an increasing amount of time in the loft with the money. Juliet and Alex worry about him – and the money.

The doorbell rings one evening: it's Tim and Andy. They kick the door down, tie Juliet and Alex up, whack Alex across the shins with a crowbar and force him to reveal the location of the money. Tim and then Andy climb into the loft; David kills them both.

The three flatmates return to the forest and David dismembers Tim and Andy. He is stoical; Juliet and Alex think he's gone too far.

Juliet secretly books a flight to Rio de Janeiro. Alex watches The Wicker Man on television. David drills holes in the loft floor and suddenly the gloomy room is pierced with light.

Detective Inspector McCall (Ken Stott) and DC Mitchell (John Hodge) turn up at the flat to ask about a burglary in a neighbouring flat and briefly question David.

Alex takes a torch into the loft. Juliet waits below. David, downstairs all along, clamps his hand across Juliet's mouth. Alex finds the money in the water tank, brings it down and is confronted by David holding a drill to his face. After teasing Alex, he decides not to use it. Later, David returns to the loft and spies on Alex and Juliet through the holes.

Juliet takes David to bed in an attempt to both pacify and manipulate him. At work, Alex is asked to cover a breaking story of three decomposed and mutilated bodies found in the forest. He returns to the burial site, listens to the police brief, has a panic attack.

McCall and Mitchell interview Juliet at the flat. They show her and then Alex photos of Hugo, Tim and Andy. Both flatmates claim never to have seen these men before.

David is about to leave the flat – with the money and his passport – when Juliet appears and asks why he's going without her. Alex comes into the hallway. David, having found Juliet's ticket to Rio, accuses her of going it alone. David attempts to leave with the money, Juliet tries to stop him; he punches her in the face. Alex and David fight. David puts a knife through Alex's body, pinning him to a floorboard. Juliet stabs David through the neck. She calmly removes a shoe and hammers the knife in Alex's body firmly to the floor. She leaves.

Alex, still lying prostrate, is surrounded by police. Beneath the *floorboards lies Hugo's cash. Juliet has taken a bag full of ripped-up newspaper to the airport. David lies in the mortuary and his voice-over laments the loss of trust amongst friends.*

* * *

AMY RAPHAEL: *Did you realise you were about to rejuvenate British cinema with your feature-film debut?*

DANNY BOYLE: *(laughs)* Those are not my words! You've got to deflect such sweeping statements because the responsibility is unbearable. We were ingénues making it up as we went along, trying to get away with it. All we were trying to do was make a highly entertaining, decent first film. It's interesting because, although it's completely sealed as a film – it's about three people in a flat – it's really about British society at the time. It's not a directly political film, yet it's deeply embedded in post-Thatcherite decay in Britain. Greed, aggrandisement, pleasure, selfishness, individualism. And nothing is worth worshipping other than money.

We'll talk about money and morality later. By the time you came to make Shallow Grave, *you had worked at the Royal Court and the BBC, and presumably you felt ready for the challenge of making your first feature film.*

Danny Boyle on the set of *Shallow Grave*.

49

I was nervous, yet desperate to do it. I had no idea how it was going to turn out. I lost sight of the bigger picture immediately; the experts on the film are often those who are not actually inside it. As director, you work on tiny, disparate parts and therefore have little idea of what the final product might look like. It's not like in the theatre when you do runs of the whole play, get a feel for it and see how you might improve it. On a film you become the expert of nothing. You're in charge of all the minutiae and you simply have to trust that the bigger picture, such as the arc of the story, will work.

John Hodge started writing Shallow Grave – *his debut script – in the spring of 1991 and met with first-time producer Andrew Macdonald. They spent a few years developing the script with Channel 4. At what point did they come to you?*

Channel 4 suggested they interview some directors. I don't know who else they saw; they never told me. I do know they weren't impressed by the directors who clearly exhibited the 'I'm-going-to-rewrite-the-script' syndrome. I was very honest with John and Andrew: the script was way better than anything I'd read. I was astonished at how good it was. I did, however, say that the ending needed a further twist in which Alex gets the money. You've got to keep twisting with these thrillers right until the very, very last moment. Take your foot off the pedal and you quickly lose momentum. I think they instinctively agreed. I also said a lot of *Shallow Grave* was stolen from the Coen brothers, to which they could say very little. It was a case of honour among thieves.

I assume that Hodge and Macdonald were aware of your work with the BBC?

Allan Scott, who executive-produced *Shallow Grave* and who was Nic Roeg's producer and writer – he adapted Daphne du Maurier's *Don't Look Now* – recommended me to Andrew Macdonald on the basis of *Mr Wroe's Virgins*. I remember John talking about Alan Clarke's last film, *Elephant* – he knew I produced it and obviously loved it – but the truth is that Andrew wasn't sure about working with me because he thought my work was a bit arty. Which is ironic, because I later saw his attempt at making a short which was *so* arty . . . God!

So you met Shallow Grave *producer Macdonald and writer John Hodge as the arty outsider.*

(*laughs*) There's probably some truth in that! But, at this stage, any creative differences were eclipsed by the sheer joy of getting the chance to make a film. Although a million quid is the minimum budget with which you could make a film like *Shallow Grave*, it was still an extraordinary opportunity for three young guys to be entrusted with this money by a television channel – and for us to actually be sent off to Scotland to do as we pleased for five weeks. It's unbelievable really. We were well paid, well looked after and working with great actors.

What did you learn from working as a trio?

There's something wonderful about working so closely with two other people. Andrew, John and I were very different people. And it's rare to find three very different people who agree to join together and make a film. You could argue that it was amazing we were able to deflect the inevitable ego issues for so long; we worked incredibly well together until we made *The Beach*. I had always benefited from the people I'd worked with, but never as intensely and informatively as I did in the beginning with Andrew and John. Each of our jobs encompasses a hugely creative vision, though more obviously with the writer and director than with the producer. But Andrew's vision was equally important. He always put maximum emphasis on storytelling. He didn't think it mattered so much where the film was set or who was in it; it was all about the story. Of course, I cared as much about the set and the cast, so there was a wonderful creative tension between us. And then John would come in with cruel and heartless dialogue that seemed so effortless to him.

What else did you learn from Macdonald, who was just twenty-eight at the time?

To start with, he's a brilliant producer – and there aren't enough in the British film industry. There are very few world-class producers in this country who can hold their own with Scott Rudin and those other big guys in Hollywood. Andrew has this completely un-PC approach to everything he does. He's driven by popular

Top: Andrew Macdonald. Bottom: John
Hodge (right) as DC Mitchell with Ken
Stott as Inspector McCall.

entertainment, but with a twist: he wants to make it as fascinating and yet as accessible as possible. It was a source of tension
sometimes because of my background at the Royal Court and the
Tarkovskyesque films I had directed at the BBC. Andrew was right
to be wary: there was a danger I'd turn *Shallow Grave* into an arty
indie film. I benefited enormously from Andrew's commercial sensibility; it helped shape my taste in the way Max Stafford-Clark had

at the Court. So Andrew's approach, combined with the vivacity and energy of John's scripts, made the perfect combination for me.

Did Andrew Macdonald talk about being the grandson of Emeric Pressburger? Working collectively as the Archers, Pressburger and Michael Powell gave themselves the unique joint credit 'Written, Produced and Directed by'. Did this offer a loose blueprint for the three of you working on Shallow Grave *half a century later?*

Given that my first job was with Joint Stock, a co-operative theatre company, it was how I wanted to work anyway. I suggested to John and Andrew that we share fees and divide the profit. As *Shallow Grave* was our first film, the profit didn't amount to much, but I was very keen to start that way. I learned over time that Pressburger's shadow does indeed have a hold over Andrew. He has a suspicion of directors taking hold over everything: despite Powell and Pressburger sharing the credit for their films, Powell assumed the role of the big director. In the end, it did come between us.

I remember you, Macdonald and Hodge doing press together to promote the film, which was highly unusual.

I always tried to share the publicity duties, but basically no one wants to interview three people. And John hasn't ever been particularly interested in talking to journalists. So I became the focal point, and then the dreaded 'auteur' word became attached to me.

Yet you were still doing interviews as a trio when promoting Trainspotting.

We always used to do as much as possible together. Of course, the grander you become as a director, the less anyone wants to talk to the producer or scriptwriter. I did a six-month press tour of America for *Slumdog Millionaire* – because producer Christian Colson would rather have died than done press, and the same goes for Simon Beaufoy as writer. So in the end I probably get more publicity than I deserve. It's just the way the film industry has focused in recent years.

You made Slumdog Millionaire *as an established director and* Shallow Grave *largely as an unknown. Right from the start, press attention was particularly focused on you: not only because it was such an assured, confident and impressive debut, but also because you were working with largely unknown actors who didn't automatically generate their own publicity.*

It shifted when we did *A Life Less Ordinary*. Unfortunately, ego hovers over everything, waiting to destroy everyone. I always used to say I preferred the rock-band role model, in which a group of individuals collaborate on a record, as opposed to the traditional film-industry model, in which the focus is very much on the individual director or star. It's very easy to get an inflated sense of your own importance.

In the introduction to the Trainspotting *and* Shallow Grave *scripts, John Hodge describes you thus: 'In conversation he came across as a man of sensitivity and endless patience, but with a thuggish streak and a certain low, animal cunning: in short, a man who could work with actors.' There's an element of tongue firmly in cheek, but is it an accurate assessment?*

Ha! Andrew and John always used to pretend that they could direct, if only they could be bothered with the actors. That was their excuse. What he says is true: there is a cunning at work. Directors have different approaches to getting what they want on the day. You have got to know what you want and then you've got to make everybody who's there work towards that goal. Afterwards, everyone decides if it was worth it or not.

You gave Hodge a small role in Shallow Grave, *as DC Mitchell.*

I like to keep the writer involved in the film by casting them – which I did with John in *Shallow Grave* and Irvine Welsh in *Trainspotting*. I later cast Frank Cottrell Boyce in *Millions*. John is a weird actor but excellent. Irvine was an interesting presence. Frank is just really rather good. I could never persuade Alex Garland, he was too shy. I haven't tried with Simon yet.

Was Hodge offended when you suggested adding a further twist to the final scene in that initial meeting?

Not at all. Luckily, I've always loved writers, for which I have the

Royal Court to thank. So I always preface suggestions by saying it's okay for them to be ignored. What normally happens with good writers is this: they hear you, go away and return with something far better. It was the main change we made. Otherwise, it was a tight script. We worked really hard on the script and then agreed that whatever happened, we'd shoot the script.

Hodge's background was in medicine. What did that bring to the script?

I loved it when I found out he was a hospital doctor! He was still practising when we were making *Shallow Grave*. He had to keep his hand in once every twelve to eighteen months, so he used to dabble as a locum somewhere for a few weeks. Some of the medics who helped us film the injections on *Trainspotting* were friends of his. John is really fascinating, very bright, very smart, with a really good, awkward take on films.

John always used to say that doctors could have two basic responses to the situations in which they found themselves: dark and depressive or cold and funny. Doctors often go cold and funny, which is what makes them great observers of human life and, in turn, great writers. They look at someone on an operating table and either pass out or compare it to something completely inappropriate and make everybody laugh. I always remember John telling me about the secret acronyms hospital staff used to communicate without the patient overhearing. T.F.BUNDY was the best: 'totally fucked but not dead yet'. If you're doing a tough Q&A and everyone's sitting there looking bored, I always tell that story. It puts everyone in the right frame of mind.

Despite your arty background, were you, Hodge and Macdonald all opposed to the notion of making art-house films?

Yes. And it united us. I love an art movie – I'm a big fan of Tarkovsky, Krzysztof Kieślowski, Michael Haneke, Jacques Audiard – but I didn't want to make those kinds of feature films. I'd made a few arty films for the BBC, including *Hen House*, which was sub-sub-sub-Tarkovksy. And I knew I didn't want to do any more. So when I read John's script, I was just elated.

Did you have a specific audience in mind – perhaps popular-culture fans under the age of thirty?

I don't know if anyone ever thinks so crudely in terms of an audience. I've never really thought much about it. You trust your instinct: 'Fuck, I love this story!' And in some insane, egotistical way you think other people will too. Especially if you can make the film as you have visualised it while reading the script. You can't think about an audience or else you'd be trying to second-guess them and engineering the film accordingly.

Of course, you do start to meet the audience when you do test screenings. And it's always interesting coming face to face with them. You realise there are some things you can change about the film and others you can't. I suppose if you're making a huge movie, you have to consider the potential audience because you are being reminded every day that you have to recoup the money. Which is, of course, the benefit of working with small budgets; you just don't have to think like that.

Yet some reviews around the time of release accused you, John Hodge and Andrew Macdonald of being ruthless in your branding and of being opportunist.

(*laughs*) I was asked to do an interview with my favourite periodical, *Sight and Sound*, just before *Shallow Grave* came out. Basically, the journalist thought all the things we wanted the film to be were awful. He dismissed the film as commercial, infantile, irresponsible. I was absolutely charming with him as he laid into my work. We had a big row about *The Simpsons*, which had just started and which I thought was the best thing to happen to British television for a long, long time. He didn't like the show at all. So I felt fine about the interview.

It's fair enough for anyone to dislike *Shallow Grave*. Or any of my films for that matter. However, there was a buzz around *Shallow Grave* before it even came out. Others seemed to understand that it's not a classical film nor is it serious. It hasn't got an easily identifiable moral. You don't quite know where you are as the flatmates start cutting someone up because you're enjoying yourself too much.

The Sight and Sound *journalist wrote of 'the freezing and cruel emptiness at the film's heart. The absence of any character to sympathise or engage with made it hard to find an emotional response as the unpleasant, greedy trio destroyed themselves and each other.' Do you think he was perhaps hoping for more depth?*

Yes, of course. And like its title, it was shallow. I remember asking John to change the title on the premise that no one would go and watch a film called *Shallow Grave*! At one point we were going to call it *Cruel*, which is very moralistic. Thankfully, we stuck with *Shallow Grave*.

I have to agree with part of Sight and Sound's *exposition: none of the characters in* Shallow Grave *is appealing. Yet I'd argue that the film has a moral centre.*

It's one of those occasions where the moral centre works despite the characters. *Shallow Grave* has got elements of film noir, in which you get a sense that what the characters are doing is wrong and they will ultimately destroy themselves. Stick a moral, appealing character in there and you kill it dead.

It's also interesting that, as with most of your films, Shallow Grave *has heart despite, and not because of, its characters.*

It had more heart than it should have done, in a way. It was written as having not a chink of light in terms of empathy or sympathy. I think I encouraged it to have heart. John is less inclined to do so – he won't give any of his characters an inch. He's happy to let them suffer! It helped to have Ewan McGregor playing the part of Alex because he has a twinkle in his eye that makes you think he can't be so bad. It makes you think you could get hold of him and turn him into a nice guy.

I was also sympathetic to Eccleston's character's predicament. I could understand the load David was carrying. I felt less for Juliet than any of them. Kerry Fox's whole job was to be unreadable. When she goes into David's accountancy office, her face is like a mask of make-up; she looks like Elizabeth I with this strip of red lips and white skin. It's fantastic for the moral tone of where they're going: nobody is going to be able to read anything about the flatmates from that point onwards. They are not going to tell the police about the money; they are going to cut Hugo up and keep it.

Did your Catholic background – and the religious backgrounds of both Hodge and Macdonald – have a bearing on the film?

They're not left-footers, not Catholics. We used to joke about it because, astonishingly, they support Celtic. I support Celtic because I'm Catholic, but I couldn't understand why those two, as Protestants, didn't support Rangers.

Anyway, there's also a work ethic in what we do that comes out of those slightly different religious backgrounds. It's guilt or something: you just feel the need to work. And if you're in trouble, you work harder. You don't give up. Whereas the characters in *Shallow Grave* are the opposite of that – they'll always find the easiest route to something.

Both Shallow Grave *and* Trainspotting *have been called the cinematic equivalent of a three-minute pop song. Is that a compliment?*

I love that idea because I'm such a big music fan. I was watching a music show on TV last night and wondering what it is about a microphone that is so sexy, so magical. We all want to stand on stage in front of a microphone and sing in front of an audience. Yet most of us can't. I think the best work in this country over the last forty years has come from pop music. It's unquestionable. Occasionally, we throw up a decent film-maker, but it's a pretty poor average. There just aren't that many people who feel entitled to be film-makers. It's so restricted. It definitely holds back our contribution to world cinema. Whereas there is no inhibition when it comes to music. If you can persuade a couple of your mates to form a band, you just get on with it and do it. There's always been a flood of exhilarating music in this country. No other art form here compares to it.

Do you think the Gallagher brothers, from a working-class estate in Manchester, could have become film-makers? I don't think so. Thank God, whether you like Oasis's music or not, they became pop stars. They wrote some fantastic songs. Blur, like John Lennon, went to art school. So there's no inhibition – anyone can do it.

Think of Manchester, my home town, and the music that's come out of the city: Joy Division, New Order, The Smiths.

Going back to your question: comparing our films to three-minute pop songs is meant as a deep insult by classical film-makers, but I've always been delighted about it. MTV was starting in Europe around that time, and we were partly responding to that. I saw MTV not as something to worry about, but as an opportunity for enjoyment, pleasure and expression.

I always very deliberately say that I find the whole David Lean way of doing things with such perfection a dead end. It elevates film-making into such an art form that it almost becomes a quest to turn it into opera. Yet the roots of film-making are in popular culture: Victorian audiences screaming in cinemas as trains came hurtling towards them on the big screen. The danger with art films is that they forget those roots.

And become elitist?

Of course there is a place for elitist and specialised films, but the popular art form shouldn't be sneered at. It's useful to think of the way stand-up comedians work: can you sell your goods to the ordinary people? We used the three-minute pop song as part of that technique, alongside humour, fresh casting, a slightly flippant eye on the form and a conviction about the narrative.

We were lucky because PolyGram, who distributed *Shallow Grave*, were developing a business plan that reflected our ethos: British films can be sold like American films. It hadn't really happened before. *Shallow Grave* came out at the same time as another PolyGram film, *Four Weddings and a Funeral*, and they managed to market both films, diverse as they are, incredibly effectively.

Is that partly why Shallow Grave *became an immediate hit – the luck always associated with the timing of a film's release and the sympathetic backing of PolyGram?*

It's certainly good fortune when these things work out in your favour. British film magazines like *Empire* were growing too and were enthusiastic for decent British films. Constellations align and the film doesn't vanish, which it could so easily do. Having said that, *Shallow Grave* did vanish in America. I don't like it when film-makers blame a film's lack of success on the way it's sold, but I did see it vanish in America, where it was sold as a Hitchcock film. In fact, the only quote on the poster was about Hitchcock. It was totally the wrong reference: although there were moments of tension in *Shallow Grave* that you could relate back to Hitchcock, it was essentially a pop-culture film and not a classic thriller.

Let's talk about the cast: how did you choose the flatmates?

Chris Eccleston I knew as a brilliant actor from around Manchester. Ewan McGregor, who by this time had been in *Lipstick on Your Collar*, was a rising TV star. He was obviously the business, but we didn't know if he was a movie star, so we had to audition him. In fact, David Aukin, as commissioning editor for films for Channel 4, said that both Ewan and Chris had to be screen-tested. Kerry Fox didn't need a test because she'd done the Jane Campion film, *Angel at My Table*. She was already a bit of a pull on the arts circuit. She was the star.

You offered the role of Alex to Robert Carlyle, but he was apparently concerned the film wasn't going to be Scottish enough and the role not working-class enough.

I think Bobby wondered who this English git was, coming up to Scotland and working with John and Andrew, two middle-class Scottish intellectuals. How on earth are they going to portray Scotland? So yes, he turned it down. Thankfully, by the time it came to *Trainspotting*, he had seen *Shallow Grave* and liked it.

Did he regret turning down Shallow Grave?

No! He was busy doing other projects. And thank God he did turn it down, because Ewan was great as Alex. He had that duality, which is a bit female, a bit male, a bit truthful, a bit deceitful. You didn't quite know which way he was going to go.

Yet Ewan looked so innocent with his long, fluffy hair and puppy fat, on the edge of manhood . . .

And completely on the edge of what is acceptable to say to people. He was brilliant in the charity-ball scene. He spots Cameron, the

The flatmates: Chris Eccleston, Kerry Fox and Ewan McGregor.

red-haired guy they interviewed as a prospective flatmate at the start of the film, and humiliates him by calling him over and then sending him away again. He was horrible but nice as well. He had that lovely quality about him. And Chris was extraordinary as David: tight, controlled, responsible and yet out of his depth. Terrifying.

Which was vital because, as we discussed earlier, the characters are largely unpleasant.

It's also easier to be sympathetic towards David because he's taking the situation so seriously and the other two run rings around him.

You enjoy using unexpected actors in the cast, so Keith Allen turns up as the flatmate who soon becomes a naked corpse.

I've always thought that casting should be mixed up. I worked with Keith's brother Kevin on stage, which was a big risk because he was just a comedian. I gave him a big role in a Howard Brenton play at the Royal Court called *Berlin Bertie*. He was superb in it, really funny. So we cast Keith in *Shallow Grave* and he was excellent. He loved being naked in front of the whole crew. Most actors want as few crew around as possible and to take their clothes off at the last possible second. Keith was naked in the breaks, sitting around smoking. He adored it.

I didn't quite know where he was coming from or what sort of part he might play. I like being in that uncertain position. We then used both Keith and Kevin in small cameo roles towards the end of *Trainspotting*. The wonderful thing about film is that you can take

The flatmates discover the naked corpse (Keith Allen).

those kinds of risks because sometimes you're casting personality. It's a flavour, a colour that comes with a certain kind of personality. They often develop into proper actors: Keith Allen is now a skilled actor. But in the mid-1990s he was a personality, a slightly surprising flavour wandering through the flat.

Peter Mullan was a great discovery too.

I don't know where we got him from, but the gods were looking after us on that day. He was probably around on the Scottish circuit. And I'd seen Ken Stott in the theatre in London. He was one of those amazing actors. He's still very underrated. The scenes in which Ken and John Hodge play the coppers who sit side by side on the sofa in the flat is wonderful. We tried to shoot those scenes chronologically. I remember it was Guy Fawkes night – you can hear the fireworks on the soundtrack – and we were trying to shoot all these scenes in one day. It was impossible.

Everyone thinks the sofa scenes are very stylish, but they were done in one shot with one camera. These days you'd have three cameras. We didn't have much film stock left and we'd already sold some of the furniture in the flat to buy more. We didn't have any time left to do close-ups, so we had to just shoot quickly, and both Ken and John were brilliant. If a great actor like Stott knows you're really in trouble, he'll get you out of a corner. And John loved it because he knew he had a proper actor beside him and it made him feel like a proper actor too. And of course a great script to work with! You can see their confidence as they intimidate the flat-dwellers.

So you were taking risks with the cast – McGregor as a relative unknown, Allen as an untried actor – but also relying on Kerry Fox to lead the ensemble?

I'd worked with Kerry before on *Mr Wroe's Virgins* and knew she was a thoroughbred – you just unleash her on an idea. It was great to have her because she was leading the others both as an actor and in character. When she takes her clothes off, it's clear that Alex and David don't know how to deal with it. It's the power a woman has in that situation.

I remember doing this scene where she's at the end of her sleep cycle because she's going back into hospital on the night shift. It's very simple but it's also the kind of scene you could never do on TV. She wakes up and the camera tracks over the bedclothes and she opens her legs under the sheets. It's an invitation into the story. Me, Kerry and Brian Tufano, the director of photography, had a conversation about the scene, and she knew exactly what she had to do. We did it in one take. It's about sex and power and control. That's what you get with a great actor.

Before you started filming, you lived with the three main actors in a real flat in Glasgow. How did that work out?

We lived in the location manager's four-bedroom house and took a bedroom each. We'd rehearse during the day and play out the scenes. We advertised for flatmates and got real punters in to interview them for a place in the flat. The actors would try to run the prospective-flatmate scene as it was written, even though they were interacting with real people. Of course, it fell apart straight away because the punters didn't follow the script!

Did Fox, Eccleston and McGregor carry out research for their respective jobs?

Yes: Ewan went and worked on a newspaper, Chris spent time at an accountancy firm, Kerry did a night shift at a hospital. I like to burst the actor's bubble, move them away from their previous piece of work and get them into the new role. There's something about the three characters that makes them hate the outside world and, on some level or other, hate their work. They just want to be in the flat. They were leading an indulgent, cosmopolitan, professional, middle-class life that hadn't really been celebrated in Britain at that point.

Given their collective desire to hide away from the world in the flat, you had to get the look of it just right. Did you spend most of the £1-million budget on building the set of the flat?

I think we did in the end, yes. This sounds very pretentious, but it was expressed in the film: I wanted the landscape to be interiors, whereas the norm is for it to be exteriors. Kave Quinn, the bold and dazzling production designer, didn't try to break up the set by making the walls smaller, but instead went for these washes of primary colour. We had a mixture of references, including Edward Hopper and Caravaggio. There were so many potential set-ups in the flat. It wasn't perfect; there was no running hot water. When Chris is naked under the shower, he's being drenched in cold water! And this was October in Glasgow, so it was pretty cold anyway.

How did you divide the thirty-day shoot between interior and exterior shots?

We spent ten days doing exteriors. Normally, when your location shoot overruns, your studio shoot gets compressed. But we made a blood pact that once we'd done the exteriors, we wouldn't go back. We had a date to move into the studio and we stuck to it. Anything we hadn't managed to get during the location shoots, we'd have to live without.

So we shot the exteriors upfront and out-of-sequence before moving into an old factory. We used to play football if we had any spare time. Chris is a really good footballer. I can reveal that Ewan isn't. After *Trainspotting* we did a charity game and Robbie Williams was there – he's a good left-footer – but Ewan was the star. The photographers were there waiting for him to score the photo-opportunity winner, but he couldn't.

Anyway, the set of the flat was being built in the old factory while we were doing the exterior shots. We'd go back every day and it was frightening because the flat was just so big, especially without furniture. I'd look at the set and think, 'What have we done? It's too big!' But the first time you go to one of those Edinburgh flats it's phenomenal, like walking into a Tardis.

Filming in a real flat would have been very slow because the crew have nowhere to go and, consequently, you get them traipsing over one another. But on this vast set the rooms were like football pitches and there was room for everyone. And room, vitally, for camera movement. Your audience want to feel like they're inside the space, so your movement is three-dimensional.

Did you end up using the first or second take due to time pressures?

Most of the time, yes. With three really good actors, you just don't need to keep reshooting. Provided nobody's fucking around, fluffing their lines and insisting on going again – if everyone's on the same side – you can get it pretty quickly. Especially if the set-up is right, the actors are firing and the writing is strong.

You said earlier that John Hodge's script was 'way better than anything I'd read'. What did you particularly respond to?

I loved the fact that Hugo isn't murdered; the flatmates cut him up when he's already dead. So we didn't need guns. In *Shallow Grave* they wander round a hardware store choosing a shovel, a saw and a hammer; in America the characters would be choosing pump-action shotguns. One of the constant dangers of film-making here is the temptation to imitate America. Especially with anything noir-ish.

Shallow Grave *has simple American noir values, but at the same time it's firmly rooted in British culture.*

And it knows British culture. The first time I read it, I thought how clever that was. Because it stops you pandering to the Americans. You often wonder why so many British films go wrong, and it's often because they pander to America and bring in the guns. Whereas the truth is that you can live most of your life in Britain and never see one. There are sub-machine guns at airports but that's about it – especially if you think back to the mid-1990s.

You're very good at violence – which suggests you enjoy directing it.

Yes! I love shooting it – thank God, because it's absent from my own life. Violence is very visceral, physical and full of momentum. I'd always rather do it with actors and not with stuntmen, even if it means working out the mechanics so they can do it safely. It's triply effective if you use the actors. When you're watching a film, you may not be registering the fact that the actor has been swapped for a stuntman, but subconsciously you know it's a stuntman being dragged along under the car. It's one of the problems with CGI at the moment: the brain subconsciously knows it's not real.

We were lucky that David Aukin chose to come up to Edinburgh and see us on the day when the thugs come to the flat and tie up Kerry Fox, put a plastic bag on Ewan McGregor's head and smash his knees and shins. Normally, set visits are so boring, but this particular one was exciting because there was so much shouting and screaming and cameras crashing in and out of the action.

Weren't McGregor's battered shins in that scene inspired by an injury footballer Nick Barmby sustained when he was at Tottenham?

They were indeed. Barmby was just eighteen when he had this horrific shin-splints injury and was sidelined for six months. So we decided that Ewan would be whacked on the knees with a rubber crowbar – it could be smashed across the knees without it hurting at all. And, of course, he wore shin pads under his trousers as extra protection. With sound over it – which is 70 per cent of the effect – it looked agonising. It led to a great follow-up gag: when he drives to the woods in a later scene, Ewan asked if the car door could fall on his shins so the audience could be reminded how sore his shins are. Good decisions lead to other good decisions. Boy, can Ewan do pain. No idea why. It's not easy to do, but he's brilliant at it. It's extreme and delicious to watch.

How did you ensure the plastic bag on Ewan's head didn't nearly suffocate him?

Oh, we just put it on . . . I asked if he'd do it, and he was up for it. It's a gift for an actor because as soon as he breathes in, it sucks up to his face. You can't recommend people to do it at home, of course, but it was perfectly safe on set. And if he had fainted, someone would have pulled the bag off him. It was great fun.

I had a very clear idea about how the film would look, from Ewan sucking the bag onto his face to the high-heeled shoe Juliet uses right near the end to hammer the knife into Alex's body. I love the moment where she tests whether the knife is touching any vital organs before hammering it further in to keep him there. Alive, but out of her way. The last thing you're expecting a doctor to do is look at somebody who is gravely hurt and hammer them with a shoe. I had, as usual, collected various images as visual inspiration for the film and, for this particular scene, I showed everyone Cartier-Bresson photographs of shoes.

Just before Juliet drives the knife into Alex's body, a knife goes straight through David's throat and ends up poking out at the front of his neck.

That was a shocking moment at the time. I remember sitting in cinemas and being palpably aware that the audience were shocked. They couldn't work out how we'd done it. There was no CG involved – if only because CG was barely out of its trap in the mid-1990s. Instead of using special effects, we got these two guys from Glasgow, Grant and Tony, who create prosthetic bodies. As they talk you can feel them looking at your skin texture. Their workshop is full of skin, hair and body parts. But they're lovely guys! So they built a body for the stabbing of Alex at the end and they also built a neck to sit in front of Chris Eccleston's own neck. Inside it was one of those spare blades you get in a Stanley knife; they cut it out and put it on a spring mechanism so it could pop out of his neck.

We shot right until the knife-in-the-neck scene and then Chris went away for five hours to have the prosthetic neck fitted. When you saw it happen live, with Kerry timing the attack, it was very cool. Fantastic. Meanwhile, Ewan's real body is under the floorboards as his prosthetic body lies on top – we had to do the stabbing of Alex for real. Chris was in method mode, wielding this knife, and Ewan was under the floorboards thinking, 'It isn't my body lying up there but it feels like it!' And, of course, it was his real head, pushed up through the floorboards, inches from flashing steel.

And you shot this complex scene with just one camera?

On the prosthetic day we might actually have got a second one in. But, for the most part, we just had one camera, and it had no monitors. I watched from behind Brian Tufano most of the time. He's a fantastic cameraman. Although we'd worked together on television, he was already an experienced cameraman from the Loach generation at the BBC. He shot *Quadrophenia* before going to America and, he told me, making a couple of terrible decisions, such as turning down the first *Terminator* film. Bad, bad idea! When he came back from America, we worked together on *Shallow Grave*, *Trainspotting* and *A Life Less Ordinary*.

Brian Tufano taking a rare look at
the monitor.

He is brilliant with first-time directors. He really helped me, and
then he went on to shoot *Billy Elliot*, *East Is East*, *Adulthood*. He's
so experienced and yet gracious about passing on his skills and
letting you benefit.

Tufano introduced you to the Zeiss 10mm camera.

He sensed on *Shallow Grave* that I'd like the lens because, after
years working in the theatre, I was always trying to shoot wide. We
used the Zeiss 10mm to an almost annoying degree on *Trainspotting*
because I was so fond of it by then. It gives you this huge, wide perspective, which is the other difference between television and film:
you should really shoot everything wide on film because you're
shooting a universe. This lens doesn't distort till you get right up to
it. It doesn't look like a goldfish bowl. It looks real but big – I love
the fact that it makes Britain look bigger than it really is.

Thanks in part to its visual ambition, Shallow Grave *has several
iconic moments: the static shots of the sofas; Eccleston hanging his*

head out of the trapdoor to the loft; the shards of light in the loft itself.

I used to love sofas because they're perfect for the cinema screen – they offer a beautiful framing device. At the start of the film, the flatmates are interviewing prospective lodgers, and towards the end they are interviewed by the police. You subsequently saw a lot of sofas in TV adverts. The shards of light in the loft are, of course, stolen from *Blood Simple*. It was very difficult to get them to register on film because we didn't have the big powerful lamps we needed. Brian had to slow the speed of the camera down, which is just one example of his technical expertise. There's a similar shot in *Trainspotting*, where Ewan's in the social club with his family and he's like a ghost – everyone around him is speeded up. Brian worked out how to capture that shot without the budget you'd usually need.

Chris Eccleston surrounded by shards of light.

The relatively small budget forced you to be inventive: David Lean always talked of the director declaring his or her ambition in the first five minutes, which is exactly what you did with the opening shot of Eccleston laid out on a trolley.

I had this idea – and it's probably stolen from somewhere; *Sunset Boulevard* is certainly where the original story comes from – that as you hear Eccleston's voice-over, you also see his face. You assume he's alive at the beginning, which is why we completed the image by returning to it at the end of the film; it is suddenly obvious he's in a mortuary. We went to the mortuary on the fourth day of filming; it was a location shot and so had to be done within the first ten days.

The film nearly fell apart at that point because the first AD phoned up David Aukin and told him we were pissing about in a mortuary and had shot nothing all morning. I had to speak to Aukin on the phone myself and, to his credit, he just asked if the scene was important. I said it was the last shot of the film. He told us to resume filming, and we replaced the first AD later that week.

So Chris was laid out naked on a trolley in a working mortuary. There were real cadavers in the drawers which were being kept chilled just below zero. When the camera finally pulls out into a wide shot, the guy shuts the door of the mortuary and walks out. There's a forty-five-second hold in which Chris is in this mortuary, in the pitch black, with all these dead bodies. The first time he did it, he said it was really freaky, so we put a props guy in there with him, in the next drawer. We could hear them whispering to each other in the dark as we were recording forty-five seconds of black to put the titles over. Very touching, actually, them whispering away.

Were you able to be as experimental as you hoped on Shallow Grave?

I certainly felt very excited about what we were doing. I didn't get to shoot everything, but I certainly felt we shot the film we wanted to shoot. As I said earlier, Andrew was always worried about me being too arty to direct a film-noirish piece. At one point, he sent me a note and we had a row about it. The three of us never discussed things openly. Typical boy stuff. I was annoyed that he hadn't confronted me face to face.

Andrew wanted *Shallow Grave* to be more brutal, whereas I wanted it to be seductive as well as brutal. I thought part of the equation of the film was that they seduced you with their world. I wanted people to watch the film and wish they lived in such a vast, colourful flat. Whereas Andrew didn't think it mattered where the action took place; it was the story that mattered.

I think you are seduced into their world if only because you find yourself wondering what you'd do with a dead body and a Gladstone bag bursting with cash.

So there's the scene where they sit round the table, with the open bag full of money. It's a great example of where everything comes together. John has written a brilliant scene which culminates with Alex saying to David and Juliet: 'Telephone the police . . . Go ahead. Tell them there's a suitcase full of money and you don't want it.' So I put the three round the table and talked about how to play the scene. They were convinced they wouldn't be able to move, and they were right. Other actors may have wanted to pace about, but they didn't. Brian frames every shot with the money, which you shouldn't do because the money is just going to jump around all the time in the edit.

I then did a good bit of directing, which I remember because it's

'Everything comes together.'

rare to do actual proper directing as opposed to just organising things: I told them they should feel like they wanted to go for a piss. They all started laughing, then they played the scene.

After living in the flat with Fox, Eccleston and McGregor before the shoot even started, you must have felt closely bonded and able to tackle anything.

One of the wonderful things about having very little money is this: if you all work together there's almost a siege mentality. We did it our way and we'd stand or fall by it. By the end we felt we'd shot the film we wanted and we were quite pleased with it. Later, we had a screening in the cutting room with David Aukin. Andrew said he looked at Aukin's face when it was finished and Aukin was absolutely thrilled; he knew the film worked. Which must have been a relief, as he had spent a twelfth of his budget on these unknowns.

Were you reluctant to let the film go?

We only edited for six weeks because we had no money. I'd only ever worked on television before, which is very strict in terms of deadlines. You hear about a film being edited for eighteen months; as a proportion of its total cost editing is nothing and it can always improve the film. Whereas a film like *Shallow Grave* has to be finished quickly. It's a very good discipline and one I embraced again on *Slumdog*. I could have spent longer editing it but, after a year in the edit with *Sunshine* – partly due to waiting for the CG – I deliberately turned down more time. There is an energy that you dissipate dangerously by relaxing and taking your time. We started editing *Slumdog* properly in April and it was in the Telluride Film Festival at the start of September. That's pretty quick.

Once you'd finished the shoot, you turned your attention to the music. I believe Hodge and Macdonald thought you were a mad raver and that the soundtrack was going to reflect your love of electronic dance music?

Oh yes! I *was* a bit of a raver at the time. In the end we used a more eclectic selection: Nina Simone's 'My Baby Just Cares for Me' and Andy Williams's 'Happy Heart', alongside two Leftfield songs – 'Release the Dub' and an original track, 'Shallow Grave', which we commissioned them to write. There's a good story about the Andy Williams song. When I was a kid, my dad used to play his records all the time, as well as other crooners like Frank Sinatra and Perry Como. I can sing virtually all of Andy Williams's songs by heart. When we were filming *Shallow Grave*, we'd buzz around Glasgow in taxis because they're so cheap. I was climbing into one when I heard 'Happy Heart' on the radio. I turned to Andrew and said, 'We'll use that at the end of the film.' And it works perfectly; it gives the audience such a lift.

My dad, by the way, has been to see every single one of my films and always has the same thing to say afterwards: it was good, but not as good as *Shallow Grave*. And not just because of Andy Williams – I genuinely think he likes the film.

You have already talked about PolyGram being in sync with your way of thinking. They also went to great lengths to generate interest in Shallow Grave *and elevate it from being a low-budget Scottish thriller.*

Channel 4 had a screening for a few movers and shakers in London. In that audience was this guy Robert Jones, who had a deal with PolyGram to tip them off about strong films. He left the screening before the credits came up and rang Stewart Till, chairman of PolyGram. He told him he had to buy it. Till wanted to see it, but Jones was insistent he must buy it straight away. Which, luckily for us, he did.

PolyGram had an idea that what we needed in this country was to sell films for people to watch on a Friday night. After a tough week at work, the films they could either unwind with or get fired up by didn't necessarily have to feature Tom Cruise or Harrison Ford – they could actually be British films. So they unapologetically sold *Shallow Grave* like that. It wasn't a case of 'people will find the film', that passive acceptance of waiting in line behind the big US movies; they would *find* the people to watch the film. I was very proud of the campaign because ordinary punters would stop me in the street to say they liked the film. I remember this young guy who worked at HMV in Glasgow running out to talk to me about the film – it really meant something to him.

PolyGram were brave enough to put the spade on the poster rather than a boy's face next to a girl's.

Andrew is a genius at this side of the business. He wanted *Shallow Grave* to be marketed mercilessly. Great producers have a sense of showmanship about them. He was one of the first guys in this country, I think, to say we're not going to worry about taste, we're going to sell it. People can make their own minds up when they've noticed the film – because, at that time, British films would just disappear, vanish. Andrew was a bull at that gate, ensuring poor marketing wasn't going to stand in the way of the film. Stewart Till was equally prepared to be bold about the marketing. Spades were sent out to journalists. The poster was a calculated risk. There was an insolence about the advertising which I loved.

Was it a thrill seeing your first feature film playing at cinemas?

I very clearly remember seeing the letters up in the sky at the Haymarket cinema advertising three films, and one of them was *Shallow Grave*. *Sense and Sensibility* and *The Specialist* – a terrible Sylvester Stallone and Sharon Stone movie – were out at the same time. It was weird seeing *Shallow Grave* up there too. On the opening night we introduced it at the Gate cinema in Notting Hill and were then driven around town in a limo.

You don't appear to be particularly interested in the world of flash cars, but did you, even for a fleeting moment, think to yourself, 'I've arrived'?

No! But I remember going into the Haymarket cinema towards the end of the evening, and the manager said it was playing really well. It was a buzz, though, I'll admit that.

What happened with Cannes? Wasn't Shallow Grave *supposed to be shown there?*

We'd tried to get it into Cannes. They did this terrible thing of putting us on a shortlist and then keeping us waiting for weeks. We kept thinking, 'We're going to be in Cannes!' It was unbelievable for first-time film-makers. And then, of course, we got dropped at the last minute. I've never forgiven them for that! In the end PolyGram organised a midnight screening, and it was better because you could feel people really discovering the film themselves. When we were leaving, a producer gave me the script of *Se7en*. I remember walking down the road with her. I saw the film when it came out and thought, 'That guy David Fincher's a good director.' He'd done a brilliant job with that script.

As well as being immediately offered high-profile Hollywood films, you were also being sold, by critics, as the British Tarantino.

I remember seeing *Pulp Fiction* at a film festival in Spain with Kerry Fox. She urged me to see it. I hadn't seen *Reservoir Dogs* at that point, but *Pulp Fiction* was amazing. Still Tarantino's best film. Brilliant writing, of course – not just the dialogue, but the structure. It's proper architect writing.

So you didn't mind briefly being the British Tarantino?

It's just embarrassing really. And I think we're very different; even back then he was making films about American pop culture which were very different to the films I was making about British pop culture. When I think of British pop culture I think of music – although, having said that, I admire Tarantino's love of music. You can taste it in his films. I think we both choose music we love for our films, music that is part of the fabric of our lives – not music to attract a certain demographic.

Is Shallow Grave *your best film? I was thinking of that Milos Forman quote: 'You can only lose your virginity once.'*

I got a beautiful card from him about *Slumdog*. I was thrilled. It was an 'oh-my-God' moment. The only *Slumdog* award I felt really nervous about was the DGA, because you're in the same room as great directors like Milos Forman. But to answer your question: I do have this provocative theory that your first film is always your best. Exactly for the reason Forman gives: there's something you can never get to again. It's a simplicity. A lack of technical cunning.

As soon as you've made a feature film, you've got access to the technical-cunning manual. You learn how to make people cry, how to frighten them.

When you're making a film for the first time, you don't *really* know what you're doing, and so to an extent have to make it up as you go along. I love that feeling. It's unrivalled. I'm sure that technically *Shallow Grave* is not as good as my other films but . . . I'd quote *Blood Simple* as a good example: did the Coen brothers ever make a film as good? And in early Scorsese films you can see him working out how to do it on screen. That virginity is really precious and valuable. You never quite get the same feeling again.

Trainspotting (1996)

Mark Renton (Ewan McGregor) and Spud (Ewen Bremner) are running hell for leather down a shopping street in Edinburgh. Shoplifted items spill from their pockets. They are pursued by two store detectives. Renton bounces over the bonnet of a car as it screeches to a halt in front of him.

Renton's voice-over urges us to: 'Choose life. Choose a job. Choose a career. Choose a family. Choose a fucking big television, choose washing machines, cars, compact-disc players and electrical tin-openers.'

On a floodlit five-a-side pitch, Renton, Spud, Begbie (Robert Carlyle), Sick Boy (Jonny Lee Miller) and Tommy (Kevin McKidd) are playing football. Renton's voice-over continues: 'Choose leisurewear and matching luggage. Choose a three-piece suite on hire purchase in a range of fucking fabrics . . .'

In Swanney's (Peter Mullan) flat, Allison (Susan Vidler), Sick Boy and Spud are injecting heroin. Renton is lying on the floor, already high. His voice-over eulogises heroin – 'Take the best orgasm you ever had, multiply it by a thousand and you're still nowhere near it' – but Swanney's dilapidated flat and Allison's ignored baby suggest the reality is more complicated.

In a pub, Begbie is smoking and drinking. He doesn't like all the 'fucking chemicals' in heroin. Tommy also denounces the drug.

Renton declares he is going to get clean. In his sparse bedsit, he lines up his cold-turkey kit, which ranges from ten tins of tomato soup to pornography and paracetamol. He needs one final hit to ease the pain. He visits Mikey Forrester (Irvine Welsh), picks up two opium suppositories and shoves his hands down the back of his pants. On his way home, he suddenly, desperately needs a toilet. At the back of a betting shop, he finds a door displaying the legend 'The worst toilet in Scotland'.

The toilet is flooded with shit. Even Renton grimaces. Desperate, he sits down. Realising the suppositories have, of course, fallen into the bowl, he pushes his arm deeper and deeper into the pan. Slowly, his whole body twists down into the toilet. He reappears, swimming in an expanse of clear water. He retrieves the suppositories and climbs back out of the toilet.

Back in his bedsit, Renton is ready to go cold turkey.

Renton and Sick Boy are in the park with binoculars, an air rifle and beer. Both have, for now, given up heroin. They chat about the relative merits of various pop stars and actors. Imitating Sean Connery, the friends spot a thuggish man and his dog. They shoot at the dog, who immediately bites his owner.

Renton and Spud, dressed for job interviews, share a milkshake in a cafe and discuss the art of staying on state benefits long-term. Spud's interview is a masterclass in avoiding employment.

In a large pub, Renton, Spud, Sick Boy, Tommy, Lizzy (Pauline Lynch) and Gail (Shirley Henderson) watch as Begbie throws an empty pint glass over his head and high in the air. He doesn't seem to care where it may fall. In voice-over, Begbie and Tommy offer alternate versions of a game of pool they recently had with each other; in Begbie's mind he was distracted by a 'hard cunt', whereas Tommy says Begbie picked on a 'speccy wee gadge at the bar'. Tommy concludes that Begbie is 'fucking psycho, but he's a mate, you know, so what can you do?'

In a nightclub, Tommy and Spud discuss Spud's girlfriend Gail withholding sex and Tommy's girlfriend Lizzy still being angry that he forgot her birthday. Renton, his libido returned now that he's off the heroin, gazes at the girls on the dance floor. He spots Diane (Kelly Macdonald), likes her style, follows her out of the club and into a taxi. Meanwhile, we see Tommy and Lizzy kissing in their flat, then searching frantically for a sex video that's gone missing. In Gail's flat, Spud has passed out on her bed.

Diane sits astride Renton and they orgasm together. Renton's voice-over conveys his euphoria: 'Christ, I haven't felt that good since Archie Gemmill scored against Holland in 1978.' Diane sends him to sleep on the sofa. In a dark corridor, we see Renton alone, *pulling the condom off. The next morning, Diane appears dressed in her school uniform. She is fifteen.*

Meanwhile, Spud wakes up in Gail's bedroom to find the sheets covered in vomit and excrement. He removes the sheets and, while arguing with Gail's mother about who is to wash them, accidentally lets the contents fly all over the dining room.

Renton walks Diane to school and, pointing out that underage sex is illegal, says he can't see her again.

Renton, Spud, Tommy and Sick Boy take a train into the wilds of the Scottish countryside. Tommy enthuses about 'the great outdoors' and asks his whining mates if it makes them proud to be Scottish. Renton shouts: 'It's shite being Scottish. We're the lowest of the low, the scum of the fucking earth . . .' As they head back towards the platform, Renton's voice-over adds: 'At or around this time, we made a healthy, informed, democratic decision to get back on drugs as soon as possible.'

Back in Swanney's flat, Renton shoots up again. Renton and Spud, needing money for drugs, steal a television from an old people's home. Tommy, ditched by Lizzy after the disappearance of their sex tape, tries heroin for the first time.

Renton's voice-over details the number of prescription drugs he has tried, from temazepam to pentazocine. Begbie mugs an American tourist and shares the cash with Sick Boy, Tommy, Spud and Renton. Renton returns to Swanney's flat. Allison starts to howl; baby Dawn lies dead in her filthy cot. It's clear from his response that Sick Boy was the father.

We return to the opening sequence, in which Renton and Spud are running away from the store detectives. This time, we see what happens next: Renton and Spud are caught, apprehended and appear in court the following day. Spud is sentenced to six months in prison; Renton, already signed up to rehab, is given a suspended sentence. In the pub, Renton's parents (James Cosmo and Eileen Nicholas) are relieved. Begbie tells him to 'Cut that shite out for ever.'

Renton leaves the pub and heads for Swanney's flat. He shoots up and seems to sink through the floor and into a coffin-shaped space. He is having a bad trip. Swanney drags Renton, who has passed out, into a taxi; the taxi drops him off at A&E. Later, Renton's parents take him home, vow to get him clean and lock him in his bedroom. He sweats, shakes, hallucinates. He finds Begbie in his bed, admonishing him for his continued reliance on heroin. He watches baby Dawn crawl across the ceiling. Diane sits at the end of his bed, singing New Order's 'Temptation'. The hallucinations continue.

Back in the real world, Renton is clean. He is surprised to have tested HIV negative. He visits Tommy in his flat. Tommy is not so lucky: he has tested positive. His flat is a mess; his once-beloved Iggy Pop poster is falling off the wall. He asks Renton for money for heroin. As Renton hands over the cash, their eyes meet. There is a sense of friendship but also of the random nature of life: Renton is a survivor, but Tommy is not so blessed.

Diane turns up at Renton's bedsit. They lie on the bed, smoking a spliff. She tells him he has to find something new in his life.

A montage of tourist London – from Pearly Kings and Queens to the Routemaster bus – is followed by an unexpected image: Renton in a suit and tie, working in an estate agents in the capital. Diane writes to him, tells him she's not pregnant. Begbie, on the run after an armed robbery, turns up at Renton's bedsit. He sits around in the flat, smoking and betting on horses. After a win, they go clubbing. Begbie picks up a transsexual without realising and is horrified. Sick Boy turns up, and Renton now has to share his single bed with two old friends. Later, they sit and eat fish and chips staring at the space left by the television, which Sick Boy sold earlier.

Renton, Spud, Begbie and Sick Boy return to Scotland for Tommy's funeral. Sick Boy tries to tempt Renton into a heroin deal. He is reluctant but finally agrees. He even tests the drug. Renton, Begbie, Sick Boy and Spud get the bus down to London and check into a cheap hotel. They sell the heroin to a drug dealer (Keith Allen) for £16,000.

In a busy London pub Renton, Spud, Begbie and Sick Boy sit drinking, the bag of money on the table in front of them. Begbie goes to the bar and, on his way back, a man accidentally spills one of Begbie's pints. Begbie immediately sees red and thrusts a glass into the stranger's face with terrifying brute force.

Spud, Begbie and Sick Boy are asleep in a hotel room. Renton carefully prises the bag of money away from Begbie's clutch. Spud is watching and crying but won't go with him. Renton strides out of the hotel. He leaves money for Spud in a locker. Renton's voice-

over explains why he ripped off his friends: 'Begbie, I couldn't give a shit about him, and Sick Boy, well, he'd have done the same to me if only he'd thought of it first, and Spud, well, OK, I felt sorry for Spud . . .'

As Renton walks across London with a smile on his face, his final voice-over takes us right back to the start. He is cleaning up, moving on, choosing life. 'I'm going to be just like you: the job, the family, the fucking big television . . .'

* * *

AMY RAPHAEL: *Did you set out to make a British version of* GoodFellas, *or was it* A Hard Day's Night *on heroin?*

DANNY BOYLE: *(laughs) Trainspotting* is often compared to *A Hard Day's Night* – more than anything, I think, because both have scenes in which the central characters run away from the police. *GoodFellas* inspired both *Shallow Grave* and *Trainspotting*. We certainly learned how to do the voice-overs in *Trainspotting* by studying *GoodFellas*. There's this idea that voice-over can solve problems, but in *GoodFellas* it actually created problems: Scorsese had to shoot ten times more material than usual. He tried to tell

Danny Boyle with Brian Tufano and Robert Carlyle shooting *Trainspotting.*

more story than was being relayed to us via the voice-over – by not just illustrating the voice-over but also counterpointing it and throwing in some apparently unconnected visuals – and it's one of the reasons *GoodFellas* hurtles you forwards.

The voice-over in *Trainspotting* allowed us to relish John Hodge's wonderful script, from Renton's 'choose life' speech which opens the film to the list of drugs he rattles off. John's wife Lucy is a pharmacist and the list is pretty comprehensive; I remember Ewan McGregor trying to pronounce some of the harder ones, such as dextromoramide chlormethiazole.

On *Shallow Grave* we had the discipline of ten days on location and twenty on set; on *Trainspotting* we were going to have to shoot ten films at once simply because of the voice-overs. We were always going to end up with a vast excess of material, some of which was going to be very bitty. The actors had to carry their characters through this blizzard of scenes, which I'm sure is one of the reasons the characters are so bold: they're being carried through so many fragments of little scenarios and scenes. And yet the fragmented scenes are linked together by the characters and the voice-over.

You even held a screening of GoodFellas *at Channel 4.*

David Aukin, who was still commissioning editor for films at Channel 4, screened it for John, Andrew Macdonald and me before we started work on *Trainspotting*. I remember talking specifically about needing more material than it would ever be possible to shoot. We needed an inexhaustible amount of material, which influenced everything. At the time John had written just eighteen pages of the script, which I remember reading on the Tube going home and just roaring with laughter. The problem with *Trainspotting* the novel is that Irvine Welsh didn't write a story in the narrative sense; it's rather a series of vignettes in which the characters go on and off drugs in various ways. Yet the spirit of the book is irresistible. I think it's a modern *Ulysses*. It's full of truth and insight and much of it is unacceptable. It cuts through that anaesthetising effect of modern life.

We tried to capture that same spirit in the film via music, voice-over, costume and boldness. Babies on the ceiling. Scenes in toilets. Writing a sign declaring: 'You're now in the worst toilet in

Scotland'. The film was like a Jackson Pollock; you could throw all these things at it. We had the cocky confidence from having had a hit film with *Shallow Grave*. And then we found these actors who were clearly on top of their game for different reasons. It was a heady concoction, to say the least.

Let's go back to the very beginning: when did you first read Irvine Welsh's novel?

A friend of Andrew Macdonald's gave him a copy. Only 2,000 copies had been printed and it was a cult book in Scotland. Andrew read it and gave a copy to me and John; I've still got my copy. We all thought it was extraordinary. I clearly remember the first sentence: 'The sweat wis lashing oafay Sick Boy; he wis trembling.' By the end of the first page – and it wasn't even a full page – I swear to God that I just knew we'd make a film about it. I knew after ten to fifteen pages of Simon Beaufoy's *Slumdog Millionaire* script too. Sometimes you just know. It may seem ridiculous because anything could happen in the subsequent pages.

Wasn't John Hodge reluctant to adapt the novel?

Yes, but John's reluctance wasn't related to the novel's excellence; it was the lack of narrative. But he decided to have a go anyway and wrote those eighteen pages I read for the first time on the Tube. They were nothing like the book, except the characters had the same names, and yet it felt faithful as well. Andrew had bought the rights by this point, but there wasn't any competition; being in the vernacular it was difficult to read and nobody wanted it. In fact, it's like any vernacular – if you stick with it for ten pages, it unlocks.

We then had a meeting with Ewan. He had read the book and was determined to play Renton. We all thought, 'No way.' Renton is a skinny, shaven-headed ginger in the book. Ewan is a sexy young leading man. He insisted we give him six weeks to show us how serious he was. During that period, John was writing, while Andrew and I were prepping for the film. So, six weeks later Ewan reappeared. He'd shaved his hair off, much to the horror of his agent, and lost all this weight – by cutting out alcohol and milk. It was a key moment for us. The actor was declaring the part as his.

How could you not respond to such dedication and determination?

It was dazzling! However, we also had a problem. At the time, Ewen Bremner was playing Renton on the stage, and he was excellent. But we had to persuade him that we wanted a very different Renton in the film. Ewen had great grace giving up the part. In the DVD interviews for *Trainspotting*, he's told that I think he is graceful, and he retorts: 'He hasn't hired me since, the cunt!' But Ewen was Spud. I can't explain it. It was just a feeling. Thankfully, he was up for it. Susan Vidler was in the same stage play as Allison, the junkie mother of the baby who dies – and we cast her in the same role in the film.

Bobby Carlyle agreed to play Begbie. He's a big, physically

Top: Ewen Bremner as Spud (with Ewan McGregor). Bottom: Robert Carlyle as Begbie – 'an actor on a ride'.

intimidating guy in the book, but Bobby knew guys like Begbie; he said they are often in fact small and have something to prove. He developed it further by the whole Pringle, lambswool sweater thing – in pastel colours, no less! He was an actor on a ride, with a vision. Duncan Heath and Sue Rogers, my agents in London, introduced us to Kevin McKidd, who at the time looked like a Beach Boy. So beautiful.

What role did Gail Stevens, who casts your films, play in Trainspotting?

Casting directors are among the first interpreters of the film. Gail reads the script and then immediately begins to influence the film by the kind of actors she introduces you to. To my mind she's one of the first mini-directors that influence the film beyond the triumvirate of producer, director and writer. In this instance, she introduced us to Jonny Lee Miller. He's from Surrey, not Scotland, and I initially thought it had to be an all-Scottish cast. But he was Sick Boy, he was this sliding presence.

Was he dating Angelina Jolie at the time?

Yes, he was. She came up and stayed in the hotel with Jonny near the end of the shoot. I didn't meet her because it was mad hectic. I didn't have time to meet anyone, although I spotted Ken Loach in the lobby of the hotel one day. I didn't talk to him because I thought he probably hated *Shallow Grave*. I always used to say that Loach could have made another film out of *Trainspotting*.

So Loach would have done the naturalistic, gritty, political version of Trainspotting, *as opposed to your pop-culture version?*

Yes, but the fact that we took a popular approach wasn't an attempt to do a commercialised version of the book; it was to inhabit the pop-culture spirit of the book. The film is profane. And being profane meant not doing it in the way drug movies had been done up till that point: in a depressing way. It was profane and much riskier to do it in a different way.

Avoiding the style of Christiane F.?

Yes. The real risk wasn't to make a film nobody would see but to make one that was different. The most important thing to remember is that Ecstasy was everywhere in the mid-1990s, and so it was the prism through which people saw drugs at the time. Which is a different prism to heroin in the 1970s. In a funny way *Trainspotting* has a euphoria you associate more with Ecstasy than a drug like heroin, which just leaves you in a corner for fourteen hours till you're ready to search out your next fix. Heroin is all about passivity. It's a bliss of nothingness, in a way. No pain, no highs, no lows. With heroin it's all about the quality of the supply; the big problem in Scotland is the shit that's in it. It causes clogging. Irvine knows all about it – he's riveting on the subject.

There's a Blur tune which plays over the end titles, and Damon Albarn couldn't think of a title for it. I suggested 'Closet Romantic', which he used, because it's a phrase Irvine has in the book: the people who are most susceptible to heroin are closet romantics. There are people who can take it, have a great time and yet never want to touch it again. Then there are people who will never be without it again. It will follow them around their whole lives.

Did anyone take heroin in an outlandish attempt to research their roles?

No, not so far as I know. Instead, we did most of our research through this drug-recovery group, Calton Athletic, run by Davey Bryce and populated by a wonderful bunch of people – Eamon, Little Davey, etc. – forcing their lives back into coherence after smack. They told us all we needed to know. They also proved that although Irvine's book seems very extreme, it's not in fact an exaggeration. What happens in the film and the book doesn't exceed what happens in real life. Calton were inspirational to us all. Their spirit affected the film because they had come through the other side and had replaced heroin and methadone with sport. Marathons and five-a-side football filled the vacuum in their lives. The film reflects their upward spirit; the effect they had on all of us is there in the unquenchable life spirit of the film.

By avoiding Loach-style gritty realism it sounds as though you set out to inject Trainspotting *with the black comedy at the heart of*

Welsh's novel, with life as well as death. Did you discuss this specific approach with Hodge and Macdonald?

We just knew it was the approach we were going to take because we talked about how funny, but also how shocking, the novel was. You expect to read this terrible story of amputation and abuse, and instead it's hilarious. The characters are unbelievably lifelike. Their obsessions, for example, are totally regular: they are jealous of each other, they worry about getting a girl, about ever getting a shag again. The fact that everyday neurosis is juxtaposed with this terrible struggle with a drug that pervades life in that social class simply makes the story more acute and doubly funny.

And there is Ewan McGregor again, adding charm to his role, making Renton more engaging than he perhaps should be.

Why shouldn't he be engaging? We wanted his peer group to watch, not just cultural commentators. However, when we were about halfway through the shoot, Ewan said he was worried about not doing enough. It's rare for an actor to say that; he probably only said it because we'd already worked on *Shallow Grave*. He thought he was going to be eviscerated within the film. He thought he was

Ewan McGregor as Renton: 'The centre through which you look.'

going to look boring and dull. It was because he was in these scenes with actors like Bobby and Ewen, who were just blazing. They gave quite extreme performances. Of course, John had written Ewan more as an observer. He was watching and then taking advantage of things when he needed to. Sick Boy was a watcher too, but he was also an arch manipulator of circumstances.

I instinctively said to Ewan that it wouldn't work if he didn't hold the centre of the film. And it was true in the end. He is the centre through which you look. You can't look through Begbie or Spud's eyes because they are too far out on the extremes. It's weirdly effective, of course, because Renton is very compromised as a character. So if he is your supposed hero, what do you think of him taking the money at the end? He cheats his supposed friends out of their money. He redeems himself only by leaving a bit of money for Spud. John hated that idea, of course, but I was determined he leave it.

Ewan McGregor may have expressed concern about 'not doing enough', but in the DVD interviews for Trainspotting *he talks frankly of his relationship with you and says: 'I loved him . . . I'd have done anything for him.' How do you develop such a relationship with your actors?*

Well . . . I don't know. Maybe he's being a bit romantic. There are certain people you get on with really well. Listen, the ones you get on with very well are those you don't direct very much. I didn't really direct those *Trainspotting* guys. You set the framework and they're intelligent people, so they see what's going on. My job is then to say: 'You can come down a bit there or you can push that a bit more.'

It comes down to similar tastes. When they start dressing up, I suggest one outfit works but not the other, and they obviously agree. Which in itself builds trust. I wouldn't have been able to suggest that Bobby Carlyle wore pink Pringle jumpers or even that it was a good idea *(laughs)*. But Rachael Fleming, the costume designer, worked with Bobby on Begbie's outfits and I thought it was best to run with it; they were on a roll together. I thought it would bear fruit later, which it did. If only because it's so unexpected.

I think it's also to do with John's writing. John, like Ewan, comes from that Scottish sensibility which is not working class but is an observer of it. As soon as I started to work in Scotland, I found its culture irresistible. It grips you. You can't just walk by; it's mesmeric. And both John and the largely Scottish cast are experts on that culture. In terms of a writer writing for an actor, it's a perfect match.

The male members of the cast had all acted before, but you ended up casting a novice as Diane. What did you see in Kelly Macdonald, who was nineteen at the time and working in a restaurant?

The audition was held in a big hall at the University of Strathclyde. Hundreds of young women were waiting to be seen. We took pictures of them, got some basic details; we were flushing out the ones who weren't right. There was a basic problem: in the club scene where she first meets Renton, Diane had to look like a sophisticated young woman in her early twenties, and the next morning she had to be a plausible fifteen-year-old schoolgirl. As soon as Kelly walked in, I caught her eye and I thought: 'That's her.' I've had that sensation twice since: once with Alex Etel, the little lad from *Millions*, and again with Freida Pinto on *Slumdog*. You restrain yourself and put them through the whole audition process, but you always know it'll be them.

It's a casting process in which you throw something in that's risky in one sense, but also exciting. The audience don't recognise Kelly Macdonald, and yet she appears to have all this confidence. As well as being surrounded by conventional actors and it being her first time acting, there was the explicit sex scene. We were very clear in casting that Diane would appear full-frontal naked and that there would be simulated sex. You have to be absolutely brutally, rudely frank about what you're going to see. And Kelly was brilliant.

How did you rehearse the sex scene with Diane and Renton?

Kelly and Ewan rehearsed it fully clothed in a room with ten or fifteen people. You put a blanket over a table, the actors go under it and they have to convince people they are having sex. The conceit is they *could* be having sex. It's great for the actors because it puts them on their own, looking in each other's eyes as they gasp and pant – it turns it into a joke. It's a great way of ensuring they feel in control. When we came to shoot the scene, we reduced it to a minimum crew. Kelly just took off her clothes and threw a condom on the bed. Ewan said it would be fine, but that if he started to get a hard-on – she was a very attractive girl – I had to stop. About halfway through he started yelling: 'Woah! It's happening! Stop!' Everybody went running out of the room and left him on his own for a minute.

I noticed when I watched Trainspotting *again that Renton stands in the dusky corridor after he's had sex with Diane and pulls the used condom off.*

Details like that are fantastic. Condoms are part of modern life but usually you are unable to film them, other than show the awful shot of the used condom on the floor as a cutaway. Which no one wants to see. But putting Ewan in silhouette and showing him pulling the condom off his cock was great. He's got quite a big cock and he's not shy in that regard.

Just before Diane kicks Renton out of her bedroom, he says: 'Christ, I haven't felt that good since Archie Gemmill scored against Holland in 1978.'

It's a very, very funny piece of writing. It's John writing about what it's like to be a Scotsman.

A little later, when Renton has been locked in his bedroom by his parents and is mid-way cold turkey, Diane turns up and sings a line from New Order's 'Temptation'. But you originally wanted her to sing David Bowie's 'Golden Years'.

Diane turns up and sits on the edge of his bed in her school uniform. We decided she'd sing 'Golden Years'; the scene isn't in the book but the song is. Then we discovered that Kelly had never even heard it. I played it to her, sang it to her but it didn't register. It was a frightening moment in which I realised how old I was! Pop culture ages very quickly. We had to come up with a song that had similar significance, so we came up with the New Order song. She knew the song and sang it beautifully.

You were determined to assemble a strong soundtrack, using both tracks referenced by Irvine Welsh in the novel and a selection of Britpop and rave songs.

I was very keen that the music should be a journey from Iggy Pop and Lou Reed, the godfathers of punk, to songs that were around in the mid-1990s. I had a very clear idea of that specific musical arc. We were fortunate that David Bowie unlocked the Iggy Pop/Lou Reed songs. *Trainspotting* was a low-budget film made by a nobody film-maker, but Bowie, who is obviously a big factor in both Iggy Pop's and Lou Reed's lives, had apparently seen *Shallow Grave*. So he unlocked the permissions for 'Lust for Life', 'Nightclubbing' and 'Perfect Day' for us. For which I shall be for ever grateful.

I'd played Underworld's *Dubnobasswithmyheadman* album to John and Andrew and said I wanted it to be the pulse of the film. They thought the film would be unbearable if the whole soundtrack sounded like *Dubnobass*, but I only wanted it to be the heartbeat of the film. There are some songs on the album that feel deeply druggy, but we ended up using just 'Dark and Long (Dark Train Mix)'. I went to HMV one day while we were in the edit and came across an Underworld single called 'Born Slippy', which had been a big flop and wasn't on the album. I took it home, listened to it and thought, 'This has to be the finale of the film.' It was one of those moments where a door opens effortlessly, like getting into the black cab in Glasgow and hearing 'Happy Heart' playing when we were shooting *Shallow Grave*. I took it into Masa – Masahiro Hirakubo, who edited *Trainspotting* – and he laid it up. It became a great roll call for the film and helped Underworld too.

Why did you use Sleeper's 'Atomic' and not Blondie's original?

I liked Sleeper a lot. Louise Wener is very smart. Masa and I wanted to use 'Atomic', and he played and played with it in the cut. Either the original cost too much or I wanted a Britpop interpretation of it. I can't remember. Anyway, Sleeper re-recorded it for us.

There are also some classical-music tracks, notably 'Habanera' from Bizet's Carmen, *which reminds me of the way Kubrick used classical music.*

That was Masa. He's music-mad too. But he loves traditional film scores.

Although the Trainspotting *soundtrack remains the most cele-brated, you have always given music high priority in your films. You are also a visually motivated director. Were you worried about style taking preference over substance in* Trainspotting?

That concern – or accusation – is partly a result of using so much music. And we shot very boldly. Some people thought *Trainspotting* was like MTV; a selection of pop videos strung together. It's a fair accusation. But it was an intentional approach; it was something I was proud of. It seems easy to say it now, but back then it was quite difficult to admit to having a pop-culture sensibility. It wasn't established that this was the way cinema was going to go. I think it's fair to say that music was hidden in films until Scorsese and David Lynch started to use it very deliberately. They also used music you were familiar with; pop songs instead of a score. The soundtrack became part of film language.

If some were unsure about the way Trainspotting *embraced pop culture, others were horrified by the explicit drug use. You must have been wary of the inevitable storm that would be whipped up by the anti-drugs right-wing press?*

We bumped into that hysterical anti-drugs reaction all the time. The hysteria even spread to classical exponents of cinema: Barry Norman saw a clip and condemned it in his show. He thought it was outrageous that such a film was coming out. The *Daily Mail* was equally appalled. Then Muriel Gray wrote an article in the *Evening Standard* saying why she thought it was actually an impor-tant film. It was a tipping point. Until then I was thinking, 'We are going to get fucking killed here.' I had a brief panic: you cannot show drugs like this because everyone is going to blame you for a whole nation becoming addicted to heroin.

It sounds ridiculous saying it like that now, but it's how it felt at the time – until Gray wrote the article. It created a sensibility in which people then sucked up the film. They went mad for it. It attracted an audience who felt uncatered for, who wanted to see British culture in a film in a pop-culture way. And, of course, the

Britpop scene was simultaneously exploding.

It's all about the timing. You need a key, cool figure like Gray who has read and enjoyed *Trainspotting* the novel to speak up and be on your side. We were also – and inevitably – attacked for not doing an exact adaptation of the book, but Gray identified the fact that the spirit of the book was also the spirit of the film. Another important figure at that time was Jarvis Cocker: a couple of people who came to previews of *Trainspotting* thought it might be a pro-drugs movie, and Jarvis said they'd got it all wrong: it was a kosher film.

Newsweek *called it 'the most secular of drug movies. There's no spiritual quest; the highs are purely visceral, the lows even more so.'*

It's interesting that it's not spiritual in that sense. It *is* a visceral film. It is so physical. It's what I loved about Steve McQueen's *Hunger*. I'd worked for the BBC in Northern Ireland, and to see a guy make a film about the hunger strike without it being really political was very impressive because it's a minefield. McQueen did it by focusing on the body and the body's endurance. It was phenomenal. There's a similar obsession – though obviously in a very different context – in *Trainspotting*. About what we can do with our bodies, what we can put in them and how far we can take it. It's in the book and also the film.

Trainspotting – *the book and the film – is seen as an exhilarating black comedy about Edinburgh's heroin culture of the 1980s. Your initial reading of the book, however, was that it was about the relationships between a group of young men.*

I always read it as being archetypal, partly because I'm like those young men. Which is to say that men basically jettison all their friends from school and college, while women seem more adept at maintaining friendships over time. Men tend to be terrible at friendship and so what Irvine wrote about in *Trainspotting* felt incredibly real. We had these big discussions in which we asked what the narrative of the book was. When you make a film you should be able to describe it in a couple of lines. Of course, you could say *Trainspotting* is about a guy giving up drugs, which would not only sound grim but also would fail to hint at the depth of Irvine's book.

So I always thought the story was about Renton jettisoning each of his friends. They were all stained with drugs and drug culture. And trapped by the small-town culture of Leith, the Edinburgh suburb they come from. Renton's decision to leave his drug friends behind doesn't necessarily make him a better person, but it does give the possibility of a future. Yet nobody reviewed *Trainspotting* from this angle because nobody could see beyond the drugs and the pop-culture world. I could truly address the issue of friendship in a sequel.

There has been much talk of a sequel over the years – an adaptation of Irvine Welsh's novel Porno, *in which we meet the characters again a decade later – but the pressure to make it as good as* Trainspotting *would be immense.*

Yeah, it would be rubbish!

It would be different!

It would have to be different. The actors would have to look as though they had aged a decade, which might be a challenge given how carefully they look after themselves these days. The scenario is similar to *The Likely Lads* and *Whatever Happened to the Likely Lads?*, between which there was a ten-year gap. Another idea behind doing the sequel would be that the characters would no longer be able to abuse their bodies. They'd no longer be indestructible. Part of the journey of life is that you risk destroying your body by doing various things to it. Most of us get away with it, if only because we reach the point where you have to stop. The invincibility of youth is no longer there.

Going back to Trainspotting, *what was the hardest scene to shoot?*

I never got over the fact that we didn't shoot the vampire scene. There's a sequence in the book where the lads walk through Edinburgh at night, imagining themselves as vampires. It was always crucial in my mind that we filmed that scene. We were going to put Iggy Pop's 'Nightclubbing' over the top of it. There's always a scene that is impossible and you think you'll never get because of money, time, etc. But you refuse to take it off your wish list.

Top: Renton running. Bottom: Princes Street – John Hodge on the right.

Secretly you feel you'll have proved yourself if you do it. Of course, in this case, we never did.

One of the weirdest scenes was in the pub towards the end where Renton is thinking of running away with the bag of money and Begbie glasses the guy at the bar. It's an incredible moment but I remember working on it and thinking, 'What the fuck is it about?' It wasn't very dynamic. I think the actors sensed this vacuum and produced a brilliant scene with what we'd given them. The guy who took the glass in the face was a stuntman, Terry Forrester, who has died since. Stuntmen are mad. It was sugar glass but it still cut him. I remember watching Bobby in that scene and thinking, 'Wow . . .'

A tough scene was the opening shot of Renton and Spud running through the streets. We had permission to film on Princes Street, but no one knew we were going to bring a quad bike, which is illegal to use on the street. We justified it to each other by saying it would be on the pavement and not on the street! We had no control of Princes Street, so you can see people looking at Renton and Spud. I was on the quad bike with cinematographer Brian Tufano, and at one point Ewen fell and we went over him on the bike. Oh fuck! We went back and he was a bit shaken but okay. He came straight out of character. He doesn't stay in character all the time, but he does keep the character's spirit going. You could see him thinking, 'You fucking ran me over, what's going on? I thought we were making a film!'

We got just about enough footage for the opening sequence. You'd never get permission to film there now. It's like the *28 Days Later* scene when we closed down London and even filmed in Whitehall. You'd never be allowed anywhere near any of those places now. They've got CCTV cameras and alert squads ready to jump on you. But back then we were able to spend all day shooting on Princes Street, and Edinburgh shoppers assumed we had permission to use the quad bike because why else would we be on it?

Working with a limited budget obviously forced you to take such risks – and it's what gives the film its energy.

Well, we had £1 million for *Shallow Grave* and just over £2 million for *Trainspotting*. The money was more evenly distributed on *Trainspotting* than on *Shallow Grave*, where we spent most of the budget on the set of the flat. There was a larger cast and bigger players on *Trainspotting*. John, Andrew and I got double the money. We each got £25,000 for *Shallow Grave* and £50,000 for *Trainspotting*. Grant and Tony, who helped us out with our prosthetics for nothing on *Shallow Grave*, now got properly paid. And we filmed for thirty-five, thirty-six days.

The flats – or squats – were filmed in the Wills cigarette factory in

Glasgow, which has now been converted into luxury flats.

It's one of the ironies about any kind of renaissance in the British film industry: you usually find it shooting in closed-down factories before they are turned into flats. We had a great time in there. People used to rollerblade on the upper floors. In fact, Jonny Lee Miller and Angelina Jolie used to rollerblade upstairs, and I had to ask someone to stop them because we were filming downstairs.

The *Trainspotting* set didn't have the simplicity of *Shallow Grave*'s because it had to be multifunctional. A lot of flats in Glasgow and Edinburgh had been closed down and sealed by the respective councils. People had taken them over and created rat runs. We tried to recreate that and then did it up in an arty way. It wasn't like standard British realism, in which flats are always painted in dowdy colours; we put drawings on the walls as though the characters actually lived there. Kave Quinn, who designed the first three films, again found this balance elevated realism beautifully. She then went off to raise a family, and I missed her badly on *The Beach*.

The costume not only looks great but also stands the test of time; it stops Trainspotting *from looking like a period piece.*

We found this costume designer, Rachael Fleming, who was in a

The Wills cigarette factory: Ewan McGregor, Kevin McKidd, Jonny Lee Miller, Ewen Bremner, Robert Carlyle.

league of her own in terms of modern-costume design. Oscars and BAFTAs are always given to period-costume design, which is so unjust. Period-costume design is done by academics, by reference, by stores who keep the costumes, by cutters who've done it before. Great. But the really original spontaneous thinking and creativity is often done by modern costume design. *Trainspotting*'s costume design is timeless, as you say, which is a brilliant achievement. Rachael deserved an Oscar for that.

You may have had twice the budget of Shallow Grave, *but you were still restricted in what you could do: you couldn't spend much money, for example, on the baby which crawls along the ceiling of Renton's bedroom.*

You have to improvise those things. The baby definitely had a home-made quality. Usually you'd shoot the baby on the floor: create a false ceiling, shoot it and then flip it. But I loved the idea of it really being on the ceiling and Ewan being in the shot too. It goes back to my love of wide shots. I always thought it was much more disturbing than a cutaway of a baby on the ceiling.

It's weirdly disturbing given that it doesn't look real; it's like something out of a budget horror film. Did you use the same baby as the dead one we see in its cot earlier?

They come from the same cast. It was a four-month-old baby. We had to meet the parents and be honest with them. They couldn't just turn up on set and discover their baby was going to die on screen. Grant and Tony had to take a cast which was then used as a dead baby. It was hugely unsettling. It's hard to make an accurate cast of a young baby and so it always looked a bit weird. But it suited us that it looked weird. Susan Vidler plays the scene when she finds the dead baby brilliantly. It's Sick Boy's child. No one says anything. You just know. You just look at Jonny and you know. They don't know what else to do but cook up more heroin.

Just before we see baby Dawn crawling along the ceiling, Renton has another hallucination about Begbie being in bed with him.

We did that with the old sheet trick. A great actor like Bobby knows when the camera can see him. If he can't see it, it can't see him. So he knew when to fall off the bed. It's a stupid magic trick. When Renton's in that state, he also dreams about the HIV game show. I asked Richard Wilson to do it first – he's from Greenock and I knew him from my Royal Court days. He couldn't do it; it must have been a very odd scene to read. So we got this guy Dale Winton, who was just starting off. He was delightful. He turned up and he was quite orange. He had a lovely day. He entertained everyone. It was nice having his presence on set.

Irvine had a great day when he came. All the crew, who were Scottish, brought their copies of *Trainspotting* and he ended up signing books all day. Everybody who visits for the day loves the catering, loves the fact that lunch is laid on.

When a non-actor comes on set like that for what is effectively a cameo, are you gentle with them?

You have to be. You have to frame everything carefully to benefit them. The actors then cover for him and support him.

The bedroom scenes – with the baby, Begbie and Dale Winton – are comical and dark in equal measure. As is the now famous

Danny Boyle with Irvine Welsh.

toilet scene in which Ewan McGregor dives into the worst toilet in Scotland. Although I know you used chocolate mousse in the scene, I still can't stop myself from flinching as soon as Renton goes into the men's . . .

It's just chocolate! It's all sterile. We had a bunch of Scottish prop guys who had worked with Bill Forsythe and who were brilliant. They just knew how to squeeze it out of a tube and onto the surface. In the toilet scene in *Slumdog* we used crunchy peanut butter and chocolate. The *Trainspotting* toilet was the simplest thing in the world: it's just a cutaway toilet like you'd use in the theatre with a shoot down the side like a baby's slide. Tufano suggested twisting Ewan's legs at the end to make it look like he's going down the U-bend. And then the props guys start chucking water up in response.

We filmed the underwater shots in a swimming pool. Ewan's a fantastic swimmer. I hadn't asked him; you ask actors about any skill like swimming, horse riding or driving, and they always say they're brilliant at it. 'Of course I can speak French, fence and drive off-road vehicles!' There I was looking at him at the edge of the

The worst toilet in Scotland.

pool and I suddenly thought, 'Fuck, what if he can't swim?' But he dived in fully clothed and it was clear he was a great swimmer. The multitalented Mr McGregor.

It's also hard to watch the close-ups of heroin being injected into the vein.

The injections were cut when the film first came out on video, as you weren't allowed to show skin penetration with a needle. You can show it now. Anyway, we shot it for the theatrical release by injecting saline solution into both a prosthetic and a real arm. The injections were set up by medical practitioners John knew from his days as a doctor.

You talked earlier about the importance of being willing to improvise on the day. What did you do when Ewan McGregor and Jonny Lee Miller turned up one morning still drunk from the night before?

There has to be a plan A and a plan B. You are supposed to have a very clear plan where everybody knows how things are going to go. But it's really dull because actors – and even me as director – are a different person each morning. You might have met the love of your life the night before. Or you might have lost a relative. Or not slept, as in this case. So I always used to have a bit of a plan, but basically make it up on the day.

Quite close to the end of the shoot, we had to do the dog-in-the-park scene. There were only three days left to film, so Ewan was able to drink alcohol again without it noticeably adding weight to him. Boy, did he make up for lost time. All of them had been out all night, I think, but Ewan and Jonny were the only ones who were called. We were there in the park in our shirt sleeves because it was a lovely day, and I got word from the AD: Ewan and Jonny were absolutely wrecked. But if you use it rather than fight it, you can get away with it. So we shot it static because they literally couldn't walk. All they could do was lie down. They had sunglasses on that they lifted up to look down the gun. It was particularly entertaining because Jonny does a wicked Sean Connery. Although the wildest impression of Connery I've ever heard was Chris Eccleston's. He's a brilliant mimic.

The dog-in-the-park scene – 'Ewan and Jonny were absolutely wrecked. All they could do was lie down.'

How did you excite the bulldog without letting it get out of control?

It was just playing, and we added the growls afterwards. It's all suggested. You can't get a dog like that angry because it would bite someone and never let go.

Although they are shooting at a dog, the scene between Renton and Sick Boy shows an unusual degree of intimacy and lends the film some heart and emotional warmth.

There are other moments of heart in the film too. There's a wonderful moment where Renton goes to see Tommy and he's really in a bad way. Tommy asks for some cash. In the book it says something passes between them, and the two actors play it perfectly. Renton knows he's not going to see Tommy again. He's on his way out. The book has moments of heart too: the little girl goes to her dad's funeral and dreams about him going to heaven, and how it'll be better than Wester Hailes. I was desperate to try and get that in, but just couldn't work it out.

Renton, Sick Boy, Tommy and Spud bond in their Scottishness in an earlier scene, when they catch the train up to Corrour Station on Rannoch Moor. The station is at the summit of the West Highland line. It's incredibly beautiful – and remote. Tommy says: 'Doesn't it make you proud to be Scottish?' and Renton offers his 'I hate being Scottish' rant. They don't know what to do in a rural setting, but at least they're all in it together.

We shot that scene in a day because there's only one train up to Corrour Station and one back each day. We shot a scene on the

Top: Spud, Tommy, Renton and Sick Boy bond in their Scottishness at Corrour Station. Bottom: Andrew Macdonald, John Hodge and Danny Boyle at Corrour Station.

train on the way there, but it was cut in the end. We then filmed the four young men standing around amongst the heather and also filmed the teaser trailer. There was a six-hour gap between the trains, so we ended up waiting around for hours. The great speech, which was taken from Irvine's book, was nailed by Ewan on every take. It's a Scottish actor's dream. It addresses the chip on the shoulder front on.

It's also an indirect comment on the lasting effect of the Thatcher years.

When you and I were talking about *Shallow Grave* being very British and not involving guns, it was really about money. It was about football managers taking back-handers in motorway serv-ice stations. About the Hamiltons taking cash for questions. It addressed those incidents through the three characters in *Shallow Grave. Trainspotting* is, in part, about a Scottish city that declined to die despite Tory attempts to bring it to its knees. The people of Glasgow and Edinburgh said 'Fuck you' to Thatcher. They didn't want her 'help'. You look at those northern cities now and they are relatively reborn.

The characters in Trainspotting *are so congenitally Scottish that they look rather odd when they migrate, however briefly, down to London. There's even a change of pace when the action moves down to the capital.*

It's a nice, natural change of rhythm. They walk round London as though they're in a slightly alien world, which is why, at one point, they cross the road in a line, emulating The Beatles' *Abbey Road* cover. It's a world of estate agents and the NatWest Tower. A strange world of Pearly Kings and Queens. It's literally a chance for them to catch breath before they are inevitably drawn back to Scotland. And, in the first instance, to Tommy's funeral.

Is it true that the film was subtitled in America because the Scottish was thought to be impenetrable?

There was a great story that the Weinsteins, who were distribut-ing the film in North America, decided to have the film revoiced.

They didn't do it in New York and LA because they knew we'd be there on the press tour. But everywhere else it was dubbed into American. At least those were the rumours – Jonny Lee Miller even met the American actor who claimed to have dubbed his voice. But we never found any real evidence.

Did the Americans also cut the sex scene between Renton and Diane?

They may have made some changes to the sex scene, but I never noticed them; in fact, I didn't watch the film all the way through in America. I think they cut the physical injections because it would have meant an NC17 and then all your advertising changes, magazines won't carry the advert for the film and so on. Contractually, you're not allowed to get an NC17, so scenes can be cut to make it an R.

The film was strongly marketed by PolyGram. Lorenzo Agius's black-and-white photos of the lead actors were particularly memorable.

As he had done on *Shallow Grave*, Andrew effortlessly organised and orchestrated the whole campaign. Brilliant producing. PolyGram then had the machinery to push the film. Chairman Stewart Till was determined to sell this British film starring British actors to a British public. He would use any and all means necessary to do it. There were *Trainspotting* mugs, posters, T-shirts, the lot. The photos still look great today. Kevin McKidd didn't appear in them because he was on holiday when Lorenzo did the shoot. The photos had a very bold dynamic, with the characters set against a white background so that they were unreal; they weren't realistic people in a realistic place. It wasn't about pretty boy, pretty girl mugshots. It was defiant: quite literally a fuck-you attitude. The orange and white screamed at you.

Both Trainspotting *and* Four Weddings *were marketed in a bold way by PolyGram. Given the success of both campaigns, how did they influence marketing strategies in subsequent British films?*

Success always gives a confidence about marketing films. The truth is that to do a marketing campaign like that, considerable sums of money need to be spent upfront. PolyGram certainly spent a lot more marketing the film than we spent making it, which is always a leap of faith by a distributor. It simply points to the importance of someone like Stewart Till: he is willing to put his neck on the line; he has vision that allows him to sense the mood of the country and how it relates back to the film. You don't get many guys around like that. It's about the courage of an individual who is willing to take risks: 'Dare I spend £2 million putting up bus-shelter posters advertising a film about heroin?'

With the marketing campaign up and running, you started the round of international festivals, including a frustrating trip to Cannes, where Trainspotting *was shown out of competition.*

I've still no idea why it was out of competition. They said it was because it had already been released in the UK, but I think it was because they didn't really know if it was a good film or a bad film. They couldn't quite work it out. The zeitgeist was clearly hovering around it somewhere, so they wanted to be associated with it in some way. They had a huge screening and a big party afterwards. They brought all these people to the party, like Elton John and Mick Jagger. And then, I remember, they wouldn't let the Calton Athletic guys into the party, which I thought was pathetic and terrible. Leftfield were playing and it was just too loud. Everyone raves about that party but it's what the film world does, of course – it distorts events like that terribly.

I remember the screening very clearly: I turned round at the end, as is tradition, to receive the cheers or boos. My memory of it is completely different to Andrew's: he says it was a rousing reception, while I looked at these bourgeois French faces and thought they had not a clue about what they'd just watched and whether they should approve or not.

At least John Hodge was nominated for an Oscar for Best Screenplay Adaptation.

Which was extraordinary! We went and sat at the back. It's not like it is on television, because you can't see anything. Madonna was singing, and you couldn't hear her. All I remember were these professional clappers positioned every twenty seats to make you clap. It was my first experience of professional sitters: a lookalike would come and sit in someone's chair to give the illusion they'd been sitting there the whole night, whereas everyone was out on the balcony smoking.

John was robbed; he clearly should have got it because as a work of adaptation it's beyond adaptation. It doesn't bother with the original. He just genuflects to it, then makes something else up equally as good but bearing its name and reflecting its spirit. I remember coming out saying he was robbed. Then when we got home he won a BAFTA. Home advantage paid off there.

The biggest buzz of the Oscars was being crushed up against Muhammad Ali on the way out. He was surrounded by all these minders. And Joe Frazier was there. They won an Oscar for *When We Were Kings*.

Trainspotting *has enjoyed an amazing international afterlife on DVD. Do you often come across people in unexpected places who have seen it?*

It doesn't apply to any of my other films, but the number of people around the world who have seen *Trainspotting* is just amazing. People of all different ages. People who clearly had no access to it in theatres. I was in Uzbekistan, in this terrible town called Munyak on the edges of what was once the Aral Sea, now drained dry. I was in this place that you could barely call a shop, and there, sitting on a shelf, was a pirated copy of *Trainspotting*. I swear to God they didn't know I was coming. My translator said who I was, and the shopkeeper didn't even blink – he said, 'Sign it!' And, to my shame, I did.

A Life Less Ordinary (1997)

In a series of completely white-washed rooms that suggest a police headquarters based in Heaven, Gabriel (Dan Hedaya) leads Jackson (Delroy Lindo) and O'Reilly (Holly Hunter) into his minimalist office. All three are dressed in white. Gabriel is furious: he flicks through a series of files, commenting on each as he does so: 'Divorced. Divorced. Wedding cancelled. Separated with divorce pending . . .'

He says he's been getting 'pressure, from above' for more couples on earth to get together and stay together. He sets Jackson and O'Reilly, whom he refers to as his chief operatives, a tough task: if they don't do some good work, they'll be consigned to life on earth with no special powers. Neither Jackson nor O'Reilly are thrilled with this new deal.

On a gloriously sunny day in a lavish villa, Celine (Cameron Diaz) is teasing Elliot (Stanley Tucci), an orthodontist and slimy suitor who wants to marry her. She asks him to place an apple on his head so that she may shoot it. He does so but, as she takes aim, he loses his nerve and lunges towards her. He lies next to the glistening swimming pool in a puddle of blood. Celine casually asks Mayhew (Ian McNeice), her butler, to ring for a doctor.

Robert (Ewan McGregor) is a young janitor employed by Celine's father's company. He learns that he is about to be replaced by a robot and is fired. He goes to a bar to drown his sorrows. The barmaid, who turns out to be his girlfriend, announces that she is leaving him for another man. Robert is woken up the next day by Jackson and O'Reilly knocking on his door: dressed in regular clothes and posing as collection agents, they evict him for non-

payment of rent, taking his possessions in lieu of money. He is left alone on the pavement.

Robert sneaks into his old workplace. Picking up a cleaning robot on his way, he heads straight for the boss's office. Here he finds a petulant Celine being berated by her father, Mr Naville (Ian Holm), for shooting Elliot. Robert throws the robot at a reinforced window and is apprehended by security. He grabs a gun from one of the guards and drops it. Celine kicks it back across the floor to him. Robert demands his old job back and then, encouraged by Celine, shoots Naville in the thigh.

Robert abducts Celine and forces her to drive off in her father's car. When it becomes clear he has no plan, she mocks him, sarcastically calling him 'a real evil genius'. They arrive, finally, at a small, simple cabin in the middle of nowhere and break in. Celine reveals that she has been kidnapped before; Robert asks how he's doing. She wonders if he's going to try and have sex with her. He says no but clearly feels awkward and nervous around her. He ties her up and throws a patchwork quilt over her.

The next day, Robert returns from the shops laden with food and discovers Celine reading. She has untied herself.

Sitting around in a cheap urban apartment, grumpy Cupid's angels Jackson and O'Reilly wonder if 'they' – presumably Robert and Celine – have fallen in love yet.

In the cabin, Celine teaches Robert the rules of kidnapping. They bicker like an old married couple, but she has no intention of walking out on him. They squeeze together in a phone box as Robert rings Naville. Robert introduces himself as 'me', fails to assert himself and is cut off by Celine until he finally gets the tone right. This time, however, he dials the wrong number.

Jackson and O'Reilly are in Naville's office, posing as bounty hunters. They offer to find Celine for a large fee.

Tod (Maury Chaykin), an eccentric neighbour, knocks on the cabin door. He wants to know what Robert and Celine are doing there. Celine claims they are newlyweds, introducing herself as Lucille and Robert as Ritchie Vanderlow, a hugely successful pop star.

Robert has written a ransom note. Celine says it's an opportunity for them both to make millions of dollars.

Robert leaves Celine in the cabin and drives till he reaches an empty stretch of road. Here he finds an empty car containing a package and a fake bomb. He is suddenly and violently shot at before driving off. He stops for a hiker, who steals the car.

Later, Robert and Celine go to a karaoke bar. Tod introduces Robert as his good friend Ritchie Vanderlow; Robert takes to the stage and sings 'Beyond the Sea'. Surprisingly, he is a consummate performer, a great showman. Celine does a duet with him. They appear to be the perfect couple.

Naville receives a ransom letter written in Celine's blood.

Robert and Celine hijack a car. He ties her up again to show the bounty hunters what an effective kidnapper he is. They meet Jackson, and Robert hands over Celine in exchange for a bag of money. Robert drives off alone and, a little later, sees O'Reilly lying in the road. She points a gun at him, and he stops the car. Jackson and Celine turn up; O'Reilly stays with Celine, while Jackson makes Robert dig his own shallow grave in the depths of a forest. Celine hits O'Reilly and runs through the trees to find Robert, fearing the worst. Jackson is pointing his gun at Robert; Robert is cowering in his grave. Celine knocks Jackson out with the spade; she rescues her kidnapper.

Robert and Celine drive off. O'Reilly appears at the back of the truck; Robert flings her off by braking suddenly. She reappears at the front; they jump out and watch the truck, O'Reilly and the ransom money disappear over a precipice.

Robert and Celine have no cash, so they rob a bank. They have their first kiss in the car park afterwards. Security appears. Robert takes a bullet for Celine. In another stolen car, she drives him to see Elliot, who admires Robert's teeth as he passes out in pain. Later, Robert awakes to find himself in Elliot's house, his leg wrapped in bandages. Elliot and Celine are drunk, high and half undressed. Robert is jealous; he and Elliot fight.

Robert and Celine leave Elliot's house together, but it's not long before they start to argue. He gets out and walks away.

Jackson has written a love poem. He and O'Reilly survey Al's diner, where Robert now works. Celine turns up, clutching the poem she thinks Robert wrote for her. She reads it out to him; he says he has never written a poem in his life. Humiliated, she storms out.

Celine's car won't start. Jackson sprays her face with mace and *puts her in the back of the car. Robert, emerging from the diner, fails to stop Jackson and O'Reilly driving off with Celine. In their cheap apartment O'Reilly makes a ransom call to Naville. Robert turns up, knocks O'Reilly out, threatens Jackson with a gun, sets Celine free and declares his love for her.*

Mayhew and then Naville appear and take everyone back to the cabin. Jackson and O'Reilly appear to be dead. Celine is in the trunk of the car. Gabriel, meanwhile, is on the phone to God. Celine appears with a gun and shoots Mayhew, who drops his own gun.

Jackson and O'Reilly climb out of their body bags and head back to Heaven. Robert – in kilt – and Celine are married.

* * *

AMY RAPHAEL: *How would you introduce* A Life Less Ordinary *at a film festival or retrospective?*

DANNY BOYLE: With astonishment that it was included! I don't know . . . I'd talk about how the original script was set in France

Andrew Macdonald, Danny Boyle and John Hodge on the set of *A Life Less Ordinary*.

and Scotland and was much more graphically violent. And that, initially, the Holly Hunter and Delroy Lindo characters were not angels but human bounty hunters or detectives. Moving the location to America, toning down the violence and introducing the angels made it into a completely different film. We made changes to it that were, in retrospect, a mistake.

Let's talk about the genesis of the film first. You were originally going to direct Alien: Resurrection *around this time.*

I was a massive *Alien* fan, always at the first screenings in London's West End, so I was shocked to be sent the script for the fourth one. And it was a really interesting story about cloning; at the time, the technology to clone was becoming available. The script was by Joss Whedon, who had written the *Buffy the Vampire Slayer* film and co-written *Toy Story*. You could tell he loved *Alien* like I did. So I agreed to direct and got into pre-production. I met the transcendent Sigourney Weaver and Winona Ryder. Then two things happened: I realised I'd be hopeless at directing *Alien 4* because I had no knowledge of puppeteering. CG was just being introduced, and you had to have a knowledge of it. At that point I had no experience in – or real interest in – working with CG. So I very quickly understood I just wouldn't be able to do it properly.

Simultaneously, John and Andrew gave me a script called *A Life Less Ordinary*. So I backed out of *Alien 4* and started work on *A Life Less Ordinary*, which was much more my cup of tea. I knew John had been working on it because we'd talked about it a bit. But he's not very talkative, John, he just does it.

The original script was, as you say, set in France and Scotland.

And we moved it to America, home of road movies. We probably should have stuck with France and Scotland. But we'd done two films set in Scotland and we wanted to branch out, to try our hand at what we imagined was the bigger stuff. The other interesting aspect of the script was its extreme violence. Severed heads and all sorts. We took all of that out deliberately. Although I'm very proud of Ewan McGregor's and Cameron Diaz's work in *A Life Less Ordinary*, it is bedevilled by the Coen brothers. The shadow they cast is so colossal . . . They mix violence and comedy in a way that is almost unpalatable, yet somehow they engineer it so that it's really effective. We cut the violence because we thought we couldn't make it play with the comedy.

How did John Hodge feel about the change of location and the toning down of the violence?

We worked on it together, so it was fine. And we were very pleased with the film in the end. Yet when I look back at it now I can see where we made mistakes. John is a very good writer and it was always unlikely we'd improve his script by challenging his initial instincts about the location or the level of violence. When I worked with Bill Gaskill at the Royal Court, he was adamant that, as a director, he could always spot rewrites. The fluidity of the writer's voice is interrupted by the addition of something clever that doesn't quite fit. Whether the writing is perfect or not is immaterial; it's about the fluidity. Objectively, it might be an improvement, but you can tell the flow has been interrupted.

Once the action had been moved to America, why did you shoot the film in Utah?

Utah is interesting; it's a Mormon state. And we had to work in a non-union state so that we could bring crew over from the UK. And Ewan. We didn't know whether to make him American; in the end, we decided there are so many different nationalities wandering around the country that it was okay for him to be Scottish. We wanted to use a mix of British and American actors. When we were in Cannes with *Trainspotting*, we'd met the Coen brothers at a dinner, which was quite intimidating. We inherited Holly Hunter from them – she'd been in *Raising Arizona* in 1987. And I was a big fan of Delroy Lindo from Spike Lee's work.

Ian Holm came over from Britain. He's a god in my eyes. One of the best things about directing *A Life Less Ordinary* was seeing how he works. He's just fantastic. I couldn't stop laughing at his scenes, which is probably a very bad thing; if the director is amused on set, it tends to mean that the audience won't find those scenes funny. But I was happy to be in the presence of an acting genius and a lovely man. Ian told these great anecdotes about Stanley Kubrick and *Napoleon*. He was deeply involved with the film for a long

Top: Heavenly creatures: Delroy Lindo and Holly Hunter.
Bottom: Ian Holm.

time. And suddenly, pffft! Nothing. He never heard from Kubrick again. Kubrick dropped him, dropped the whole project.

A Life Less Ordinary was packed with American actors. Gail Stevens normally casts all my films but, because it was set in America, Gail cast some of the parts and then Donna Isaacson, a fantastic casting director who works at Fox, introduced me to a lot of American actors – Stanley Tucci, Tony Shalhoub, Dan Hedaya.

At this point, after the critical success of Shallow Grave *and* Trainspotting *and as the cool British director* du jour, *I assume you could pretty much take your pick of actors both in the UK and the US?*

Within reason. There are two things worth pointing out about the movie business in America: they love success, and everyone wants to attach themselves to it. If you have made films that work, then you have a lot of leverage. But they also do give people a chance. They love the idea of taking a risk. Directors ask me about where they should work, and I say if you want to get a break, you might as well go to America, because you'll probably get a break quicker there. There are American actors who are also willing to take a risk.

Did you always have Cameron Diaz in mind?

Yes. At the time she was just beginning to arrive as a hot girl. The first thing you notice about working in America is the extent to which actors prepare. In Britain at the time you could barely persuade an actor to read a script in front of you. An American actor has not only learned and rehearsed the script, but has also probably put him or herself on tape as well. So Cameron flew on the red eye from Chicago, where she'd been working, came in to meet us and already knew the part.

She was a delight. The loveliest woman you could ever meet. Smart, down to earth. Cuban background. Family is absolutely everything to her. As a director you're watching actors all the time, for weeks on end. And I don't think I saw her look in a mirror once. I couldn't believe it. I thought it was a front. I thought I'd discover that her motorhome was secretly covered in mirrors. It wasn't.

So we all got on well, had a good time. It was a lovely family atmosphere. But I think, in the end, as I said, everything is dominated by the Coen brothers. And although you may love them, you've got to find your own way of doing things. If you're just imitating them, you'll just come a cropper.

Cameron Diaz – 'The loveliest woman you could ever meet.'

You sound pretty disaffected with A Life Less Ordinary, *as though it's a weak imitation of* Raising Arizona.

No. I like the film and I'm very affectionate about it, if only because it's the film that nobody likes and everyone has forgotten. There are elements in it about falling in love that are really good. It has that slightly dizzy feeling you get when you fall in love. You don't follow rational thought; it doesn't apply any more. That's what I love about the film.

I like it with reservation. The relationship between McGregor and Diaz works well and there's clearly chemistry between them. I like the fact that she's the tough guy and he's the wuss. There are some strong scenes, such as his comical ransom call from the phone box.

If you want to be reminded of how gifted an actor Ewan is, watch that scene. Technically very difficult, carried off as simple as fresh air on the mountain top.

Screen chemistry – Cameron Diaz and Ewan McGregor.

McGregor is a joy to watch, but the subplot with the angels doesn't work. Were you trying to introduce a Capraesque subplot into the middle of a fairly traditional road movie?

It hurts when people don't like the film. When you make a film like *Trainspotting*, you don't realise that you are always going to make one, two or even three films that will suffer. You may be lucky and delay it by one, but it's coming. As Irvine Welsh says, it's in the post. A negative verdict on your work will be delivered at some point.

At which point I suppose you have to learn to fail better, as Beckett would have it. Anyway, I'm not saying it's a bad film. It just doesn't hang together as a whole.

I spent so long watching American movies and suddenly, oh boy, there we were making an American film. Or at least making a film in America. It was a bit of a thrill. It's probably why we got carried away with being Coen brothersesque, Frank Capraesque.

Yes, but you always steal from other directors in your films. Why does it work on some occasions and not on others?

I'm happy to admit to it. You steal better. Nothing is any good when it's '-esque'; it has to be its own thing. I certainly learned that along the way.

You mentioned the thrill of shooting in America. Did it feel like a very different form of film-making?

The landscape is the first thing. We went from inner-city Glasgow to the Utah desert. And, despite the fact that we were a small movie with a budget of $20 million, there were still so many film trucks. Dozens of them! It felt like film-making on a different scale.

Did you feel out of your comfort zone?

Yes and no. I was very well provided for. I had everything I wanted. But you learn what you're better at. There is a natural instinct in the industry – especially after a success – to expand from film to film on every conceivable level, whether it be budget or status or expectation. Everything inflates. You have to do one of two things: learn how to resist it or inflate it even further. If you're going for inflation, you'll probably be thinking: 'At last! Here's my chance to make a film about the Holy Roman Empire! I'm going to fill it with every actor I can think of, who will of course join me because of the success I've had previously . . . '

Over the course of *A Life Less Ordinary* and *The Beach* I learned about myself. I learned what I'm better at. It doesn't matter what you like going to see at the cinema; it's about what you're best equipped to do as a director. What, if you have one, is your craft or skill?

And you learned that dozens of trucks in the middle of nowhere or a huge film crew in Thailand don't result in your best work. You'd rather work on lo-fi indie projects in an urban rather than rural setting?

Yes. But it has little to do with working in America. Everyone thinks *A Life Less Ordinary* and *The Beach* are American films, but they're not. For a start, one was shot in Thailand. Both were made here: British writing, British editing, everything. As you say, the central factor is that neither film was made in a city. When I was making *The Beach*, I couldn't believe I was on this paradise island with all these hippies. I hate hippies. I don't like paradise islands. I'd rather be in Shanghai or Mumbai.

Are you always drawn to the energy of cities?

Absolutely. It's also about appetite. Although I don't know the private library of films in your mind, I guarantee most of them will be set in a city. Although we have this ridiculous idea that film is all about escapism, the truth is that it's only escapism to other cities. A huge percentage of the people who watch movies live in cities. They go and watch films about people who live in other cities. All the stories are in the city. It's where the humanity is. It's where the crazy people go. So it's not about escapism at all. There are much fewer good rural films. Period films are, of course, an exception.

Did you have the same uncomfortable, isolated feeling you had in Thailand when you were shooting in Utah?

It was emerging. There were no cities to shoot in. We had a couple of city scenes in the big but bland Salt Lake City, such as the tower-block scene in the boss's HQ. There was nothing to shoot really. Salt Lake has very little texture or character – unless you want to investigate the Mormon control of the city, which wasn't our concern.

Or make a film about The Osmonds.

We saw them at a concert in Salt Lake. Donnie and Marie flew in on a helicopter. It was the full Mormon experience. I also remember that Ewan couldn't get served alcohol because you had to show ID to prove you're at least twenty-five. He ended up sending assistants out to get cigarettes or alcohol. If we were having dinner in a restaurant and ordered wine, they wouldn't leave the bottle at the table; we had to ask for the glasses to be replenished. And they wouldn't serve doubles in a bar. I think it's changed a lot since the Winter Olympics in 2002.

Before your feelings of discomfort and isolation began to emerge, how did you envisage A Life Less Ordinary *on a fundamental level? Did you, Hodge and Andrew Macdonald want it to be slick, stylish, fast?*

We wanted it to be about the irrational side of love. What happens when you fall deeply in love with someone. Some people who have seen the film – and mostly it's women who trust that side of themselves more than blokes – really like that element of it. I like talking to those people because they get the film. Of course, it clashes with its predecessor: *Trainspotting* was poppy, urban, black, undermining.

Whereas A Life Less Ordinary *is unashamedly romantic and warm?*

Yes. I like that. But I tend to think all the films have a romantic side to them.

Yet you've often said in the past that you're not romantic.

Well . . . I'm not in my real life, but I am in my imagination. I think I am anyway. Without that sense of romance, I might make cold films. There are elements of the films that are superficially modern and pitiless. The films may have that veneer, but they are not cold. That sense of romance is what, of course, allowed me to make *Slumdog*.

I think you direct romance almost as well as you direct violence: some of the scenes between Robert and Celine are drenched in passion. I'm thinking particularly of the string of saliva that hangs between them after they kiss.

That just happened as you see it. I didn't ask them to create the saliva! It was good, that.

Did McGregor and Diaz have a strong affinity?

They became very close friends. But there was no romance involved. Ewan's wife Eve was there. There was a genuine family atmosphere on set.

The karaoke scene works well: it's the first time you see McGregor not with the chubby cheeks of Shallow Grave *or the wasted elegance of* Trainspotting, *but dressed up in a suit, looking like a proper movie star.*

You don't really think of actors like that, though. He just needed to dress up for that scene. I love anything to do with music and dance. It was great fun rehearsing the dancing. Just fantastic. We had a great song to work with. I think John originally wanted an Elvis Presley song, but we went with 'Somewhere Beyond the Sea'. It was probably cheaper.

You rarely focus on just two people in a film. There's usually a group dynamic to be explored.

The group dynamic has always interested me. *Shallow Grave* is not the classic two people; there are three people who are murderous equals. I like that kind of structure. Both *Trainspotting* and *The Beach* are about gangs of people. *28 Days Later* is about a pack of people in a taxi who drive out of London; a different film-maker would have put the focus on Cillian Murphy and Naomie Harris. It would be a love story about those two.

The karaoke scene: 'I love anything that has to do with music and dance.'

Are you saying that A Life Less Ordinary *is not so strong because the focus is on McGregor and Diaz, or that it fails because it's not on them enough?*

Both. It would have been more successful had the focus been exclusively on the two of them. I did try to put the focus on them, but you end up adding Holly Hunter and Delroy Lindo. And Dan Hedaya from *Blood Simple.*

How easy is it to ensure all these disparate actors work together?

Very experienced actors work in a bubble; one of your skills as a director is to make sure all the bubbles coincide. Actors who play character parts often join you for a few days for a pay cheque. The studio is happy because they're surrounding young actors with quality actors. But you don't get such an effective sense of a group working together. I thrive on the group dynamic. But it's more difficult in America and India to get everybody working together at the same time.

The film subverts audience expectation with the behaviour of the angels and McGregor's inept kidnapping. Did you really respond to those elements of the script?

I loved all that. The inept kidnapper is great fun. Ewan's very funny doing that. Cameron asks if he was going to try and have sex with her, and he gets very nervous. Even when we rehearsed those scenes they were natural together. They were also very skilled at the comedy element of the film. Maury Chaykin plays Tod, the mountain guy who comes to their cabin door. He's a big Canadian guy and, shit, he was funny. Ewan and Cameron found it very hard to play those scenes because Maury was genuinely funny in a really odd way. We built the exterior of that cabin in the middle of a field and a moose visited the set one day. We had to clear everyone and hide in our trucks. The moose was fucking terrifying; it was huge. It sauntered through the set to see what we were doing on its land. You're not allowed to scare them off, so it mooched around for an hour or so.

Where did you shoot the interior of the cabin?

In a studio in Salt Lake City. Heaven was created in a building in downtown; we just sprayed it white.

It must have been a challenge to shoot white on white, given that the costumes as well as the set were white.

Brian Tufano is a very good cameraman!

Did he enjoy working in America again?

It was interesting for him. He could talk to us about all things American. We'd only been there on promo trips for *Shallow Grave* or *Trainspotting*, whereas he'd worked and lived there for ten years. He relished telling us all about it. It was definitely useful having him around as a negotiator, as the UK and US systems work slightly differently, especially for camera and lighting.

Although, as you said earlier, you didn't have the technical skills to direct Alien 4, *you actually ended up shooting your first CGI scene at the start of* A Life Less Ordinary.

We shot the opening scene with Cameron Diaz and Stanley Tucci, who played her suitor, in Los Angeles. John's script describes Celine firing a gun at an apple balanced on Elliot's head. This is what I'm like: I wanted to do it for real. Couldn't we get a camera that can record the bullet travelling towards Mayhew's head? I had got hold of all this footage from National Geographic about slow-motion cameras. We investigated them; they are extraordinary. They will record what the eye can't see – such as a bullet firing in slow motion – but they only run for about fifteen seconds. The film is running through the camera so fast that it takes two or three minutes to get up to speed. Then it shoots for fifteen seconds before taking another two or three minutes to slow down, otherwise it breaks. So each time you shot you had to strip the whole camera down and oil it all before putting it back together again. It took hours. Just to record a bullet.

Someone suggested we do the scene in CG as it would not only be far simpler, but also much safer. So we did. Those were the really early days of CG.

Celine firing the gun.

Did you enjoy working with CG, if only out of technical curiosity?

Not really my forte. I've never been very good at CG, even though I directed *Sunshine*, which is essentially a CG movie. I don't think technically enough about it. You have to break everything down into little elements for CG and, maybe because of my theatre background, I don't tend to think of things in units. My brain just doesn't think like that. I run a whole scene, even though it's wasting film. I learned how to do CG by basically working with good people who can explain it and cover for my inadequacy.

I assume you felt more comfortable shooting the action sequences, notably the one in which Holly Hunter flies over the top of Robert and Celine's truck?

I love doing them! Holly and her stunt double were very brave.

McGregor is almost run over in a back street in Edinburgh at the start of Trainspotting, *and here he is in the middle of Utah, trying to kill Holly Hunter.*

Renton is nearly run over in *Trainspotting*; Ewan did a pretty good stunt. That's a young man with no fear. I'm a big believer of momentum in film. I've got a theory that will, of course, change because digital film-making is different: film as a mechanical process is about momentum. The film moves through the camera and then through the projector, and it's moving at staggering speeds: twenty-four frames per second is quick! Film's origins were about motion and the capturing of motion. And astonishing people by motion.

I love action movies more than any other genre. No matter what a film may be about, I love making it look and feel like an action movie. If you can make it interesting as well, as opposed to a series of mechanics leading you from one sequence to another, then you are doing pretty well. I find stillness on film very difficult.

Which is strange, given your theatrical background.

You would think. I remember a critic recommending a Turkish film which was so slow that I vowed to die rather than sit through it again.

The action in A Life Less Ordinary *is carried along in part by the soundtrack. There are great tracks by Sneaker Pimps and The Cardigans, yet I wouldn't have recognised the list of songs as belonging to a Danny Boyle film.*

It's interesting because it's more influenced by other people. It was compiled considering an American business model, so that it would appeal to an American audience as well. It's not something I would normally have worried about; Americans like good music, regardless of where it comes from. They wanted me to use a Beck track, and I can see he's very good, but he's not really my cup of tea. Still, it's important to have one's horizons challenged.

At least Ash wrote the title track.

Yes. I liked their singer Tim Wheeler big time. Really lovely guy. And a great track.

You are clearly dissatisfied with several elements of A Life Less

Ordinary. *What sort of responses did you encounter while doing press for it around the world?*

You learn quite quickly that everybody wants to talk about *Trainspotting*! I remember touring *Millions* and everyone wanted to talk about *28 Days Later*. You have to be okay with it; it would be rude not to be. I'm not trying to make a case for *A Life Less Ordinary*, but very few people ask me about it. Which is why it has a special place in my heart.

Do you feel the need to defend it?

Not defend it, but certainly to speak up for it. I always get asked to choose my favourite film, and of course I can't. But if I had to, I'd choose the one that nobody likes.

So you'd seriously say A Life Less Ordinary *is your favourite film? Above, say,* Trainspotting *and* Slumdog?

In many ways, yes. Why not? One of the problems with *Trainspotting*, *28 Days Later* and *Slumdog* is that people know so much about them that they don't feel like yours any more.

So the ownership has shifted from you to them?

Very much so. There are people who know more about those three films than I do. So you tend to relish the ones that nobody remembers any more.

I read that you thought A Life Less Ordinary *was doomed . . .*

(*Laughs.*)

. . . when you read Richard Curtis's script for Notting Hill.

I remember! I read it just after we'd finished cutting *A Life Less Ordinary*. I remember thinking that *Notting Hill* had real warmth. It was beautifully written. I was trying to work out why I had reservations about our romantic comedy. Then it came to me: our film obviously wasn't a true romantic comedy. *Notting Hill* was the real deal.

I can't imagine you directing Notting Hill.

I certainly wouldn't have done as good a job as Roger Michell. Definitely not. I just don't have that sensibility. I constantly want to contradict things. I want to experiment. Richard Curtis's work is brilliant because it's full of mainstream warmth. It's often despised by critics, but it is, in fact, very, very difficult to pull off.

Did you like Michell's film?

I did. I love the line where Julia Roberts stands in front of Hugh Grant and says: 'I'm just a girl, standing in front of a boy, asking him to love her.' Whoa! You could search through billions of feet of celluloid before finding a moment like that. It's a delightful film and very funny. Hugh Grant is a brilliant actor. The casting of Julia Roberts is brilliant, when it could have been disastrous. So yes, I knew we were doomed if we were hoping to be anywhere near as successful as *Notting Hill*. Cutting the violence and turning the detectives into angels in an attempt to find mainstream appeal after the cultiness of *Trainspotting* didn't work.

A fucked-up rom-com.

I'd argue that A Life Less Ordinary *still works as a fucked-up rom-com.*

Which is what it is. It's the fucked-up bit you can't forget because it powers everything you do. That's what you learn. At least I learned I'm better at doing that kind of stuff in a city with less money than I ideally need. It's oxygen to the fucked-up bit. Whereas a proper romantic comedy can happen anywhere because you're involved in characters' hearts.

I like the stop-motion animation sequence of Robert and Celine at the end of the film. I assume that was inspired by your love of Nick Park?

I'm a big Nick Park fan. My son, Gabriel, has always made me appreciate the world of animation. And we have perhaps the world's greatest. After *Trainspotting* came out, there was a style-magazine piece featuring the best directors in Britain. They asked to take a photo of me, and I wanted to know if Nick Park would be there because I'd love to meet him. They asked who he was. I told them he was the best director in Britain! So they got him along.

After the critical success of Shallow Grave *and* Trainspotting, *were you disappointed about the lukewarm response to* A Life Less Ordinary?

Well, it was a big hit in Belgium. There's this theory that if you have a big hit, there's always one country where it doesn't work and, conversely, if you have a big flop, there's always one country where the film confounds all expectation. *A Life Less Ordinary* was number one in Belgium for three weeks!

The Beach (2000)

Richard (Leonardo DiCaprio) is a young American backpacking through Asia, looking for an unusual adventure. He introduces himself thus: 'My name is Richard, what else do you need to know?' He is happy to explore the city alone. As he wanders down the Khao San Road, a Thai street salesman disdainfully passes comment: 'Like every tourist, you want it all . . . to be safe, just like America.' As if to prove the salesman wrong, Richard finds himself in a dark, oppressive den knocking back a shot of snake blood.

Back in his cheap hostel, which shows Apocalypse Now *and* The Simpsons *on a large screen in the communal area, Richard meets his neighbour Daffy (Robert Carlyle). Richard doesn't quite know what to make of the rough, boisterous Daffy. They share a spliff, and Richard ventures: 'No offence and all, but you're fucked in the head, right?' Daffy just laughs. He tells Richard about his time on an island paradise in Thailand not to be found on any regular map.*

Later, Richard discovers a map pinned to the door of his hostel room and then, next door, Daffy's blood-splattered corpse. He testifies to the police but his mind is elsewhere: he is already planning his trip to the island paradise. Unwilling to go alone, he rehearses asking the beautiful French girl Françoise (Virginie Ledoyen), who is staying down the corridor – only to find out that she is with her boyfriend, Étienne (Guillaume Canet).

Françoise and Étienne are unable to refuse the offer of a trip to this exotic Utopia, so the trio set off on their adventure. On the way, Richard gets drunk and stoned with a couple of American surfer guys staying in an adjoining beach hut. They mention the myth of the paradise island. Thinking to himself that he's 'shit scared of the great unknown', Richard slips a copy of Daffy's map under their door before he leaves.

Richard, Françoise and Étienne have to swim across a daunting stretch of water to reach the island. At one point, Françoise disappears underwater, and Richard panics. When she pops up again, she laughs with Étienne at Richard's obvious anxiety. They arrive at the island exhilarated, but their journey is far from over. First, they have to escape the enormous marijuana fields protected by armed guards and a fierce monkey. Next they jump from a high waterfall: Françoise takes the first leap as the two boys waste time arguing.

As they edge ever closer to paradise, Richard has a fleeting but prescient thought: 'I suddenly became aware that we weren't even invited.'

Keaty (Paterson Joseph), a member of the paradise community, spots Richard, Françoise and Étienne and takes them to meet Sal (Tilda Swinton), the stern, vigorous leader. She interrogates them – How did they find the island? Who gave them a map? Did they give a copy of the map to anyone else? – before finally accepting them into the community.

Richard, discussing the island in voice-over, is in heaven: 'I settled in. I found my vocation: pursuit of pleasure.' He is quick to set himself apart from other backpackers following well-trodden routes: 'It was just a beach resort – for people who don't like beach resorts.'

Françoise takes photos of the night sky. Richard and Françoise walk alone on the beach one night, kiss under water lit by iridescent plankton and vow to keep their affair a secret. It isn't long, however, before Étienne discovers and reluctantly accepts their liaison. Cuckolded and disappointed, he sits on the beach in the rain alone.

Later, Richard goes diving for fish and is attacked by a small shark. When he stabs it to death with his harpoon, he gains hero status in the community. Richard's voice-over suggests that the elation will be temporary: 'For a while, we were untouchable in our happiness.'

When the rice, which forms the staple part of the community's diet, is found to be contaminated, Sal organises a trip to the mainland with Richard in tow. Her partner Bugs (Lars Arentz-Hansen) clearly feels usurped. Sal and Richard take supply requests from everyone and end up with a huge shopping list of home comforts, ranging from chocolate to painkillers.

In Ko Phangan, which is pumping with house music, Richard bumps into the American surfer guys and is unable to stop them from discussing the island. Sal overhears and is furious. To compensate for his indiscretion, Richard must have sex with Sal.

Richard and Sal return to the island and, for a short time, everyone has their commodities and is jubilant. Then the Swedes go fishing: Sten (Magnus Lindgren) is killed by a shark and Christo (Staffan Kihlbom) is seriously injured. The perfect golden sand is stained with their blood.

Christo is slowly dying and, when the others can no longer stand his feverish raging, they banish him to a small tent in the jungle behind the beach. Richard is complicit with the decision: 'Out of sight really was out of mind.' Only Étienne is able to maintain any humanity and it is he alone who sits with Christo.

Richard has vivid nightmares about Daffy's death. The two American surfers are spotted on an adjoining island with two friends, and Sal banishes Richard to a remote part of the paradise island to keep an eye on them and somehow retrieve the map: she has made a deal with the local farmers that no more people will join the camp. Meanwhile, Françoise discovers that Richard had sex with Sal on the mainland and, heartbroken, confronts him in his new jungle retreat.

Although he calmly watches the sunset at one point, Richard's exile quickly sends him over the edge. King of the jungle, he hallucinates, talking to Daffy and imagining himself as a character in a video war game. Alone again, just as he was at the outset of the story, he concludes: 'The longer I stayed away from the community, the less I missed them.'

The Americans arrive on the paradise island, discover the marijuana field and are immediately shot by the armed guards. Richard, attempting to save his compatriots, gets blood on his face but escapes.

Richard returns to the community and tells Françoise and Étienne they must leave the island. He has lost sight of himself: 'I tried to remember the person I used to be, but I just couldn't do it.' Étienne initially refuses to leave Christo, who is dying an appallingly painful death, but eventually agrees to a mercy killing and lets Richard smother the Swede.

A Thai farmer turns up at the camp and says there are too many of them. They must now go home and forget about Thailand. Sal refuses to leave. She reveals to everyone that Richard gave the Americans a copy of the map. The farmer hands her a gun housing a single bullet. If she wants to stay, she must point it at Richard and play Russian roulette. She points and shoots a blank. Richard simply says: 'Game over.'

Sal is the only member of the community to stay behind on the 'paradise' island.

Sometime later, Richard is in an internet cafe. He opens an email from Françoise showing the community jumping up in the air in unison on the beach. She has written across the photo: 'Parallel universe. Love Françoise x.'

* * *

AMY RAPHAEL: *Do you have a very clear memory of reading Alex Garland's novel* The Beach?

DANNY BOYLE: A friend of mine – Chris Fulford, who was the bad guy in *Millions* – recommended it. It was like reading *Trainspotting*

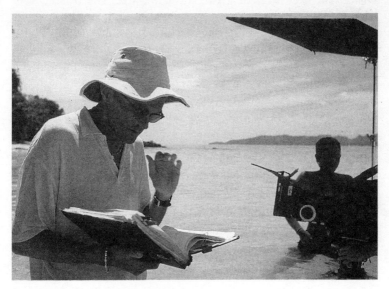

Danny Boyle on location in Thailand for *The Beach*.

133

in the sense that it wasn't, at that point, very well known, but it already had a cultish following. I had such pleasure in reading it and sensed it would make a fantastic film. So Andrew Macdonald and I got in touch with Alex, met him and said we'd like to make a film. He was thrilled. He said he'd help us as much as he could. He'd just finished his second novel, *The Tesseract*, which was also excellent. In many ways it's a better book than *The Beach*.

Garland heard the rumour about a secret island while travelling in the Far East.

Alex's book was based on the idea that there was a community like this somewhere. Alex has travelled all over the Philippines, and the rumour was that a community existed. But he never found it, so it has remained speculation. We never found it either! Andrew, John Hodge and I went to Thailand and followed the route of the backpackers. We did the whole journey as backpackers. I remember having this weird experience when we were waiting for this ferry to Ko Phangan. We were surrounded by backpackers whose mobile phones started ringing simultaneously. It was news that Princess Diana had been hurt in a car crash in Paris. The frisson went round. And then news came that she was dead. It was bizarre. We were so far away and yet news came so quickly. All the phone calls were from America, where they'd already had the news; I found out before my family, who were at home in London and who didn't hear the news till they got up.

Did you enjoy backpacking, given that you never had a gap year?

It wasn't quite the same as being a student taking a year out, although we did try to spend as little money as possible and stayed in crappy places. But we were always looking for the film. We had some surreal experiences. When we wandered along the Khao San Road we saw *Trainspotting* being shown in some of the bars. And not, as it happens, *A Life Less Ordinary*!

We then made a subsequent trip which proved to be one of the most extraordinary things I've ever done: we went on a little tour looking for the most beautiful beaches in the world. It coincided with the opening of *A Life Less Ordinary* in countries like Australia. I went to this incredible place called Whitehaven Sands on the Gold Coast. We couldn't set the film there because it's a completely open beach that's protected by a barrier reef so ships can't get in. They don't allow anyone to live on the island. But it was just the most beautiful place I'd ever seen. We ended up travelling around Australia, Malaysia and Thailand looking at all these beaches – until we found the island cluster of Ko Phi Phi a two-hour boat ride from Phuket. What a job!

So even though you're resolutely urban you could still appreciate these natural wonders?

They were just so visually striking. And the challenge of *The Beach* was initially appealing: it was essentially about exploring a community of modern, urban hippies who wanted to abandon their Western lifestyle. However, while making the film I realised that I didn't really like any of the characters. I found it was impossible, in the end, to have sympathy with what they'd done, the world they'd created.

You didn't have much sympathy with how the characters in Shallow Grave *behaved, yet you felt the film had a moral centre which worked despite its characters. The sole character with rectitude in* The Beach *is Étienne; he is the only person in the entire camp who cares about Christo, the slowly expiring Swede, ravaged by a shark and raging with fever.*

It's also a shame that so many of Étienne's scenes were cut. We shot, for example, several scenes in which he speaks French. It is obvious that he would have returned to his mother tongue to both denounce Richard taking his girlfriend and to articulate his discomfort at the moral vacuum being created when Christo is mistreated. Perhaps we should have given Étienne's moral core to Richard . . . Anyway, the fact is that Étienne's scenes were cut because he is not the central character. Only a film-maker like Altman or a playwright like Chekov can keep lots of deeply rooted and rich characters in the air. Even Shakespeare only has two or three main characters.

Shallow Grave *is perhaps saved by its consistently dark humour. Maybe the lack of humour in* The Beach *doesn't help its cause . . .*

It's an accusation you could fairly make of it. The humour is certainly more intermittent than in *Shallow Grave*.

Was the inherent lack of humanity a problem in The Beach? *To what extent do you need to be able to identify or empathise with characters in order to direct them well?*

I think it helps in a very odd way if the lead character is some kind of version of you. And in a way you try to make them like you. Not because you want to be in every film, but because you can then say, 'Surely *he'd* do this, because I know *I'd* do it.'

How did you try to address these core issues?

We tried to shift the perspective in *The Beach* late on so that we could see the hippy community more from the Thai point of view, so there's the Thai farmer at the end who hates them because they just keep turning up and taking more and more. The modern hippies in *The Beach* go to Thailand and show absolutely no interest in the country whatsoever – other than what it can provide them with in terms of this glorious beach and this secret community.

Did you think it was a continuation of post-colonial arrogance?

Yes, and the film should have been more about that. The problem is that when you make a film for $55 million, it can't really be about that. In the end it's going to be about a movie star, Leo DiCaprio, and there has to be romance and adventure.

So I learned not only about my dislike of shooting away from cities – *The Beach* cemented what I started to realise on *A Life Less Ordinary*: I infinitely prefer the energy of cities – but also about compromise and money. I think we also felt a heavy responsibility to earn Fox their money back. A rather principled attitude which comes from Andrew, John and I having a strong work ethic.

What we should have done, although we didn't realise how to go about it at the time, was turn down huge amounts of money upfront in favour of taking some back end; in other words, taking a percentage profit from the film's box office after it breaks even. Everyone's paid pretty well in the film industry, but the real benefit comes afterwards. Back-end deals also make everyone invest more energy in the film. So in each subsequent film I've worked with a relatively modest budget and have taken a back end.

Hugh Grant accepted a decent fee for Four Weddings *and no back end, while Andie McDowell took a back end and, given the film's subsequent success, did extremely well.*

The famous case, of course, is Alec Guinness in *Star Wars*. He said, 'Oh no, dear boy, I don't want anything to appear in the film but I'll just take a point afterwards.' Everyone was wondering what on earth this film was, and he recognised its huge global potential. But it's not just about the money. Even if the film doesn't have a huge amount of commercial success, it allows you ownership of it.

Before we go any further, I'd like to get the Ewan McGregor story absolutely straight – it's been reported in so many different ways for so long. Did you or did you not offer the role of Richard to him and, when the role went to DiCaprio, did McGregor fall out with you?

We gave Ewan a copy of Alex's book. Which obviously indicates a clear intention. What then happened in my recollection is this: Andrew realised we couldn't raise enough money to make the film in the way we wanted to. At this point we'd been to Thailand and we'd begun to cost it. We were taking a lot of people – cast and crew – to Thailand. We had this idea that we would behave well. We would treat people well. We'd hire local crew to shadow our crew, but it would nonetheless principally be our crew, so that we weren't outside our comfort zone. I subsequently learned that this approach is not helpful, and as a direct result I made *Slumdog* differently – of which more later.

Given that we couldn't raise enough money, we were told we'd need a big movie star to pay for the kind of budget we thought we needed, which must have been about $30 million. Ewan was obviously an arriving actor because of *Trainspotting*, but he still hadn't done *Star Wars*, so he wasn't yet a movie star.

This is the problem with big-budget films: it's all about the business. John and I were very reluctant to lose Ewan. John was persuaded next and I last. I then went to tell Ewan on my own – I don't quite know why I had to go alone. I probably volunteered. It wasn't a very nice thing to have to do. I've said a number of times that I don't think we behaved very well. Ewan was entitled to be treated so much better. But you learn. Some actors might disagree with this, but I think I've only behaved really badly twice: I double cast an actor once at the Royal Court and ended up with two actors for one role. Fuck knows how that happened. I never thought I'd do it again. And in effect it was what I did with Ewan and Leo.

Was Ewan pissed off when you gave him the bad news?

No, he was very gracious. He dealt with it in a very dignified way to my face. I don't blame him for feeling mistreated. The group loyalty that John, Andrew and I had to each other included Ewan because we'd done the first three films together. It's a difficult dynamic to keep going with actors. Some directors manage it. I didn't.

The biggest problem, in fact, was not who we cast as Richard – Ewan and Leo are both fantastic actors – but the part itself. What we didn't do in the end was create a really decent part. I couldn't locate Richard's disinterest in both the West and his loss of faith in what they were doing in the community. Because the hippies are mostly European, Richard is basically an American in a completely European world.

Would it have been any easier if Richard had been English, as he was in Garland's book?

I'm not sure. I just couldn't find him. I couldn't see what drove him. Partly it's the writing of modern characters who lack orientation or a moral compass that always proves to be very tricky to translate onto the screen. It's partly what the film's about: you experience it right at the start when Richard is fascinated with seeing Daffy's dead body. It's barely a real experience for Richard; it's more like watching a movie.

I know you dislike characters with obvious back stories, but might Richard have been an exception?

Yes, I guess so. But as you say, I can never think in terms of back story. I like the scene where he rings home from the telephone booth because he's got nothing to say to them.

And, right at the end of the film, when he's in the internet cafe, Richard chooses not to open a 'Where are you?' email from his parents in favour of one from Françoise. Do you feel that the audience don't need to know any more about him, they are just watching him respond to the here and now?

Yes, I think that's okay. The overwhelming problem was losing contact with everyone on set. Making such a big film is a huge, industrial exercise. A staggering amount of money is spent each day. It becomes a chain of command, and so I had hardly any contact with Andrew while I was shooting the film. He and Sarah Clark, our brilliant press person, were driven to despair trying to get our story across. Andrew was off handling the row over the removal of the island's palm trees, and I was left to make the film with people who had just been hired and with whom I wasn't particularly familiar. I'm just not interested in working that way. It works for other directors, but not for me.

Were you all staying in the same place at least?

We were all at the Cape Panwa Hotel at the bottom tip of Phuket so we could go back and forth to the island. Staying there also allowed us easy access to the studio, which was an abandoned shoe factory in inland Phuket.

Despite the idyllic surroundings, was it not a remotely enjoyable experience for you?

It was my least enjoyable personal experience on a film. It's not to do with the actors, but rather, as I've said, the lack of empathy I felt with the characters and the situation they had created for themselves. I should have twisted the film to be much more about Thailand. We also went about the working method in the wrong way. We were an invading army. There's no way around it. Although they weren't reported as such, our intentions and behaviour were completely honourable. But that didn't matter. Local people can only relate to you as a cash cow; you turn up in their country with a staggering amount of money compared to their own standard of living. So what is going to happen? It's going to go wrong . . .

When it came to *Slumdog*, I told producer Christian Colson that we would only take ten crew with us. We took hundreds on *The Beach*. It was insane. In a post-colonial world it's not the way to make movies.

We'll discuss the negative reports around the shoot later. If you hadn't made The Beach *and learned from your numerous mistakes,* Slumdog *would not be the film it is.*

We would definitely have feared going to India. As it was, I knew the risk of going to India was much more interesting than any fear you might have about being outside your comfort zone.

Did you feel pressure from the studio for the first time while working on The Beach?

There was absolutely no pressure from the studio whatsoever.

I read they wanted you to create a romance between Richard and Françoise that wasn't in the novel.

It's one of the misconceptions about *The Beach*. I've never had any real pressure from a studio. Apart from when Warners decided not to release *Slumdog*! In fact, when you hire a star like Leo and get on very well with him – which we did – then the studio are incredibly cautious about staying on the right side of him. It's absolutely in their interest to keep him happy. So any problems were just deflected. He used to say that he would inform the studio if we wanted to reshoot any scenes. He has the power to do that. He kept saying, 'Do you want more time, Danny? I'll get it for you.' I think he probably sensed I wasn't firing on all cylinders.

Leo seems to use his power well: for a start, he's given Scorsese a third or fourth wind with films like *The Departed*. Given that he has this image as an all-American beach boy, his sensibility is completely European, in part because of his ancestry: his mother is German. His whole interest is in working alongside directors and not in being a movie star as such. He's not like he's reported at all.

He's one of those actors who, like Cameron Diaz, seems to be almost luminous on camera. Was he worth his alleged fee of $20 million?

Danny Boyle with Leonardo DiCaprio – 'He's a dazzling actor.'

He's a dazzling actor. People's reactions to him are as intense as his talent. One of the weird things about doing *The Beach* was shooting street scenes with Leo which also involved the general public. I've never seen anybody being looked at so intensely. It was terrifying. It was like being with Jesus Christ. *Titanic* was just coming to the end of its complete global domination and here we were in the middle of Thailand, in the middle of Phuket with this guy who was a megastar.

How did DiCaprio respond?

I can't imagine how he remains sane. It's extraordinary. Every girl he came across was trying to get off with him, but he didn't seem to be interested. He just stayed up late at night playing video games with a couple of mates who came along. His mother and grandmother turned up too. They are in one of the scenes in the beginning at the hostel, sitting at a table and watching *The Simpsons* on the big screen. His grandma, who only spoke German, sadly died in 2008. He was very close to her. So he dealt with the attention brilliantly as far as I could see: he just wanted to do good work. He'll do anything you ask of him.

Including the three-day shoot in a jellyfish infested sea when Richard, Françoise and Étienne were swimming to the island.

Oh God, that was because I wanted to film it for real between two small islands. The sensible thing would have been to shoot it offshore somewhere, but it wouldn't have looked the same. Thankfully all three were really good swimmers. These huge jellyfish get cut up by outboard motors and all the strands remain live. So you get stung by these shredded jellyfish bits. Although I was watching the actors swimming from the safety of a boat.

Were the underwater shots done separately?

We built this huge pool at the old shoe factory for the underwater sequences and used it for the shark scene too. We had two or three big accidents during the making of the film where people very nearly lost their lives. We were filming the love scene with Leo and Virginie Ledoyen in the pool at night using a light fixed onto a big crane way up in the sky. I was on the monitor, but both the actors

The three friends about to swim to the island.

and Darius Khondji, the cameraman, were in the water. This huge light started falling and it took for ever to hit the water. Everybody could see it coming and they were all shouting, but they couldn't get out of the water. The English gaffer – the guy who organises the electrics – had brought the circuit breaker and plugged it in before we started shooting. If he hadn't plugged it in, everyone in the tank would have died: Darius, Leo and Virginie. The gaffer's sleeve was torn off by the crane but that was all.

That sounds like an unbelievably close call.

It wasn't the only near miss. There was a second accident when we were on a small rowing boat with Tilda Swinton and Leo. We didn't know that when the tide changes a washing-machine effect is created. So the tide changed and we got caught in this incredibly choppy and unstable sea above a barrier reef. It was pretty scary. The crew boat sank and everyone had to get into the water. All the equipment was in the water. It was like being in a theme-park wave machine, only we couldn't get out. All these steel boxes of make-up equipment suddenly became lethal missiles hurling around.

We were all in a panic and instinct made us want to swim towards the shore. The diver who was with us was screaming at everybody to swim out to sea. People drown by trying to get to dry land because they can't swim against the tide. So we swam out to sea and boats came to pick us up – they couldn't reach us while we were in the swell.

The third accident we had was during a recce scout up a mountain. The Thai location guys and I climbed it too late in the day, and by the time we got to the top it was dark and we couldn't get down. All we had for light was a mobile phone. We rang the police and they basically told us to fuck off. We had to feel our way down the mountain using our hands and we were all terrified of snakes. We managed to get down eventually but it took hours. It was pretty scary.

Even though we'd taken this enormous crew of hundreds of people – justified, I suppose, by the gaffer plugging in the circuit breaker – you can't be sure of safety standards. There was little health-and-safety tradition in Thailand then.

You took a largely British crew, an American megastar, a few British and European actors and then cast a handful of Thai actors. What were the Thai actors like to work with?

They were fantastic in the audition process but as soon as they got in the room with Leo they turned into gibbering wrecks. They forgot all their lines. Their English, which they had perfected for the audition, suddenly went to pieces. They were shaking. They kept calling him 'Leo' instead of 'Richard' on camera. I've never seen anything like it in my whole career. You forget the whole star thing is so powerful sometimes; people are completely intimidated and decentred. I don't know what goes on in people's minds.

In Asia movie stars are afforded a completely different status: for anyone from Europe or North America it's probably comparable to the hysteria around Charlie Chaplin in the early days. It's like the gods had come down to earth.

It must have been disconcerting.

I had to work out what to do very quickly. The only solution was to take Leo out of the room. If you watch the relevant scenes, there's a shot of Leo followed by a separate shot of the Thai actor's reaction to him. Very bizarre.

When Richard is peacefully watching the sunset alone as he contemplates being in exile from the community, weren't there 20,000 people off camera also enjoying the view?

We couldn't film the sunset on the actual island, so that scene was on Phuket. We had to ask the 20,000 to be quiet. There's a deleted scene where Leo climbs down one of the cliffs. He was pretty brave. It was a little hair-raising.

It sounds as though you were taking considerable risks with Fox's star asset.

Leo takes risks. He's completely in love with the craft of acting. Once he gets on camera it's like he's being mainlined oxygen. But we also had all sorts of problems related to Leo's star status. The bodyguards who protect him had to be armed, and Thailand won't allow foreign arms into the country. So this huge rigmarole developed. It's all to do with scale in the end. Some directors relish such setbacks and still make a great movie. As far as Ridley Scott is concerned, the more hassle the better. Whereas I like the hassle of not quite having enough money and not knowing what to do next. 'Okay, let's empty London for *28 Days Later* by using small cameras.'

So you're constantly forced to be inventive?

Yes. It's really good for me. I thrive on it.

Did you consider contrasting DiCaprio's Hollywood cachet by casting real backpackers who were already hanging out in Thailand?

That's what we should have done. I think it would have been a richer film. Holiday film-making – which is what it turned out to be, and which is entirely my fault – doesn't suit my puritanical instincts. The cast had a great time. Can you imagine? What a job! They were paid nice per diems, lounged by the pool when they weren't needed. And they got Leo's autograph when they could work out a cool way of asking for it. They were a lovely bunch, actually.

You can always rely on Tilda Swinton to give a powerful performance; she was pretty convincing as the controlling, uptight and essentially cold Sal.

I loved casting Tilda in this because she was a complete outsider to this whole world. We flew up to Scotland to meet her and flogged her the project. It's not a great role – it needed to be developed more – but she's fantastic. You talked earlier about Cameron Diaz and Leo DiCaprio being loved by the camera. Well, Tilda has got it too, and it's frightening. It's probably to do with her upbringing – her father, Major-General Sir John Swinton, is the former head of the Queen's household division and lord lieutenant of Berwickshire – and the way in which she has intersected that upbringing with a total immersion in art. She's a hybrid creature who regards her body as an exhibit. I think we introduced her to Hollywood, where she's done very well. She's carved a nice niche for herself.

When you say you 'flogged her the project', are you just being

Tilda Swinton – 'A hybrid creature who regards her body as an exhibit.'

colloquial or did you have to really sell it to her?

No, she was up for it. She constantly challenges herself. *The Beach* looked like a mainstream Hollywood film, which for someone like her was a challenge in itself at the time.

There are lots of gorgeous people in The Beach, *not least the French actors Virginie Ledoyen and Guillaume Canet.*

Before I knew Virginie's work I saw a picture of her in a magazine. I didn't even know she was an actress, never mind a very good one. So we met and cast her. Guillaume, who's gone on to be a film director as well, had some terrific scenes cut, and they didn't even make it to the deleted-scenes section of the DVD.

As DiCaprio's Richard becomes increasingly feral, prowling around the island in exile, Canet's character Étienne – as we touched on earlier – shows himself to be about the only empathetic character in the entire film.

He has a genuine decency that doesn't seep away on the island. He objects to the community exiling this suppurating Swede into

Guillaume Canet and Virginie Ledoyen.

a tent. There are definitely some fantastic ideas in *The Beach*: the shark story, the shark attack, the Swede suffering. I do like elements of the film: one of my favourite scenes is when Richard goes to Koh Phangan and tourist backpackers are having their photos taken pretending to be astronauts on the moon.

Why did you decide to recreate the Khao San Road, instead of actually filming there?

The Khao San Road, where the backpackers congregate, is mad. It's got everything you could ever ask for: Asia delivers the West its dream with cheap everything. As you say, what we should have done is filmed on that fucking street. Because it was a big movie and because no one wants to film in Bangkok, I let myself be persuaded that we should recreate the Khao San Road somewhere else. So we recreated it pathetically on a quiet street. The scene where Leo is invited into an illegal den to drink snake blood is bearable, but the street itself isn't credible. My fault.

Leonardo DiCaprio sits in front of the polystyrene Buddha.

When it came to making *Slumdog*, I had exactly the same problem: no one wanted to film in the slums, so they suggested recreating them on a set. I was told the set would be clean and calm and would look just like the slums. But because of the Khao San Road experience on *The Beach*, I knew it wouldn't work. I said that if we couldn't film in the slums, I'd go home. The film would be over. So we filmed in the slums. And we gained everything.

As a result you can almost smell those scenes in Slumdog.

I think you really can. So you learn how to do things.

I like the opening scene of The Beach, *where Richard could be in any city in the world and suddenly he slides across the screen, stands next to the Sleeping Buddha and locates himself in Bangkok.*

Our Buddha was built to real size out of polystyrene by these incredibly gifted Thai craftsmen. The journey to the island, the

Leonardo DiCaprio (right) with Robert Carlyle.

swim, the false shark attack, the real shark attack: it's all good fun.

It's a shame Robert Carlyle had to be killed off so early in the film. When he meets the fresh-faced DiCaprio over the mosquito net in the Bangkok hotel, there's a moment of real edginess and darkness. Was there a strong rapport between the two actors?

Bobby was fantastic. He has no respect for the star system. He's also so intimidating, if only for the roles he's played: Leo was quite scared of him after seeing him as Begbie in *Trainspotting*. Bobby is the sweetest guy, but he can just turn it on. They were both on their toes – literally – that day. *The Beach is* a good adventure yarn at the beginning. The film should then have gone one of two ways. It should either have remained more of an adventure yarn and turned into a mainstream, Sunday-afternoon adventure about escaping the island; or it should have become more of an analysis of the interaction with native Thai culture, or lack thereof. It's not quite either.

I think my argument about why it went wrong is right. We had all this money. Stacks of money. And yet when, for example, I wanted there to be a fucking huge tropical storm at the end of the movie which kills lots of people, we didn't have enough money. I'd no idea where the money was going. If I'd have done the movie for $20 million all in, I'd have had my tropical storm. That's my argument anyway!

Apart from the absence of a huge tropical storm, where do you think the film loses its way?

The film's okay . . . There was a lot of disappointment around it. Maybe if expectations could be lowered then people could just enjoy it on a simple level. Sometimes people say to me, 'It's not that bad, you know.' I just feel that with the resources I had – good story, Leo, Bobby, Tilda, Virginie, Guillaume – I should have made a better film.

So it's less about the film losing its way in, say, the third act and more about it not being quite right throughout?

The whole approach was wrong. Praise for good work is great, but equally you've got to hold your hand up when you haven't done a good enough job. I'd certainly make a better job of it now. I'd know to film on the real Khao San Road. I'd talk to the producer every day; it's one of the ways to keep yourself disciplined because, as a director, you're the gateway for everyone, and as such you're indulged. The producer is the only one who can ensure that doesn't happen.

In terms of the casting, everyone wants to talk about Leo v. Ewan. That's beside the point! Richard the character is the real issue. I don't think either of them would have had sufficient material to play with in the end. Richard was a bit of a blank, and yet we didn't go the whole way and make him a modern blank character. He wasn't cold and empty, which would have been more interesting. Nor was he a fascinating character with lots of back story. He ended up being a vacuum. Leo was desperately trying to fill the role with all his ability and stardom.

Yet there are interesting ideas in the film, not least Richard living his life via a succession of cinema, computer and video-game screens.

Sure there were good ideas. But I didn't make them compelling in the way they should have been. You always want your films to be traps that you can't take your eyes off, and you can with *The Beach*. The rhythm of it wasn't right. And with everyone's commitment to it . . . it should have been more insane.

Apocalypse Now, your favourite film ever, is shown in the hotel cinema at the start of film and it clearly influences the Richard-in-exile scenes. It's interesting that both you and Alex Garland take your references from the same film.

The film hovers over Alex's book *and* it hovers over me and my whole career! As we made the mistake of allowing the Coen brothers to influence us too much in *A Life Less Ordinary*, so we allowed *The Beach* to be too Coppolaesque. Much as you might want it to be, it's no flattery to him. You've got to keep it as your dream film – and, as you say, it's my favourite film of all time, ever – but you can't copy it. *Apocalypse Now* is as close as you'll get to a cinematic experience of Vietnam. Perhaps it's not so appropriate to use it on a fantasy island full of annoying hippies.

You also pay homage to The Deer Hunter *in the Russian roulette scene.*

Yeah . . . As all the films I've done have some reference to other films. They all loop round. It's how successfully you do it.

The Russian roulette scene is pretty gripping.

That's because Leo and Tilda are brilliant. Thoroughbreds, waiting for decent scenes. We reshot that scene; Andrew insisted – probably because someone told him to. So we did it again but no one offered any reason for reshooting it. I kept asking him, half-embarrassed, half-needy, and he just looked blank. In the end there was no difference; Leo and Tilda were brilliant in both versions. Insane. I guess it was a sign to me that things weren't great. Although that's one of the best scenes in the film.

And it gets interesting, of course, because the Thai farmer has turned up and he's pissed off.

That's what I liked. In the modern world the Thai farmers should have had a much more significant presence in the film. As I keep

Playing Russian roulette.

reminding myself, the idea of a group who have sealed themselves off is ultimately reductive.

The film still has something to say about our search for paradise, which is, perhaps, a search for something that doesn't exist.

Yeah. All that is there. The buzz, the thrill. All the ways you go to seek thrills.

Despite your misgivings, The Beach *did very well commercially, although it was endlessly described by the press as a flop.*

Before *Slumdog* it was my most successful film by a long way. Even in an unpopular movie Leo's stardom took it to $150 million around the world. It's a lot of money. I managed to pay off my mortgage. *28 Days Later* made $80 million. *Trainspotting* made $75 million – in other words, half of what *The Beach* made. And it's why the studio is prepared to pay those vast sums of money upfront.

Did you call your house The Beach?

Ah, humour! That's very funny. No, I'm going to call it *A Life Less Ordinary*!

Do you feel that neither A Life Less Ordinary *nor* The Beach *follow your notion of total film-making?*

Yes. I can only make films well if I'm completely immersed in them. When I'm not fully immersed, for whatever reason, it doesn't work as well.

You mentioned the near-death experiences during the shoot. When people began to protest about your treatment of the island, did you feel the film was cursed?

Fuck, those accidents weren't funny. When we worked on *Slumdog* in India we did some really tough stuff and we never had any encounters even close to those on *The Beach*. It's weird the way films seem blessed or cursed. You shouldn't believe all that stuff, but looking back on *The Beach* it's hard not to. Once people start talking about the palm trees there's nothing you can do to turn that kind of publicity around.

You filmed around Maya Bay on Ko Phi Phi Le, one of the smaller islands in the Ko Phi Phi cluster of islands. Environmentalists accused you of damaging the island's ecosystem; stories appeared in the media at the time suggesting you and your crew left the island in a state of disrepair. What's your side of the story?

We put trees back on the beach because every few years these huge storms flatten the beach and everything on it. So there's not enough time for palm trees to establish themselves. We left the money to repair the beach, but it made no difference; in two years' time it would be ripped apart by a storm. It's the natural cycle of the beach.

Tragically, the Indian Ocean tsunami happened on Boxing Day in 2004 and wreaked havoc on the Ko Phi Phi islands. I am familiar enough with Phi Phi Le to know which channel the tsunami would have pushed itself through. It would have been terrible. There was an opening on the beach which we blocked off using CGI, to make it look as though the beach was in a perfect cove. The tsunami wouldn't have come in that way, it would have come in the back way, through this 300–400ft-high corridor. Horrific.

You are pointing out that the island is vulnerable anyway, no matter what a film crew might do to it. Yet the criticism about the environmental damage caused by The Beach *is ongoing.*

I don't think it matters any more. We left a lot of money to care for the island for five years after we left. We went about it the right way.

You were criticised again on Slumdog, *the objections mostly relating to a Westerner's portrayal of Indian slums and the slum kids.*

But people wanted to see the film, so it had very little effect. It's strange how these things work. The opposite happened on *The Beach*: it got bogged down in the criticism.

The Thai environmentalists even brought a law suit against Fox. But was it really a way of protesting against the Thai agricultural ministry and its attitude to island tourism on a world stage?

The truth as far as I understand it is that the protesters were mobilising Leo's power and the profile of the film as vehicles to protest against the government. There are so many examples of real encroachment on protected land throughout Thailand, and the environmentalists used our film to draw attention to that. Which I can completely understand.

Have you been back to Maya Bay since making the film?

I went back a couple of times after we finished to check on the way the land had been replanted. It had all been done properly, but since then everything will have been ripped out by the tsunami. I haven't been back since the tsunami. I imagine the beach will have slowly rebuilt itself over time.

You had to make Ko Phi Phi Le look incredibly seductive. How do you then square the inevitable knock-on effect of the film encouraging mass tourism?

That whole nightmare . . . How do you get round all that? Tours of the slums in Mumbai are already being organised. There's so much business enterprise in Asia. They even used to do *Trainspotting* tours in Edinburgh . . . However, I'm not sure I can be responsible for mass tourism in Thailand.

Okay, let's move on. How hard was it to shoot DiCaprio, Ledoyen and Canet jumping off the waterfall when they first arrive on the island?

We took a couple of stunt guys with us to check out the waterfall. We stood at the top; it's as you see it in the film. They said the problem with such waterfalls is not the jump, which is okay for stuntmen, it's the rocks underneath the water. Without a full inspection you've no way of knowing what the rock formation is like. We were busy discussing this when a Thai stunt guy just leapt into the water. He had no idea about the rocks. He was fine. He took off a bit like Françoise does while Richard and Étienne are squabbling.

They then carried out a detailed inspection of the rocks in the water and built an extension on the top of the waterfall so that they were guaranteed not to be anywhere near the hidden rocks. In order to match up the skin colour with the three actors we used British stunt guys. When they jump from such a high waterfall they

Leonardo DiCaprio, Virginie Ledoyen and Guillaume Canet about to jump off the waterfall.

have to wear these special thick rubber underpants. The problem is enemas. When you're hitting the water at that velocity . . .

They also use a special pump in the water to disturb the surface, which causes less damage than sheet water if you hit it wrong. The three stunt people – two guys and a girl – jumped twice and one of them hit the water wrong once. You could hear the slap of the rubber pants through their clothes. It was painful just to hear.

Why, after three films, did you stop working with Brian Tufano as DOP and move on to Darius Khondji?

You sometimes come to a natural point with your collaborators when you've done enough together and you both need a break from each other. Also I had no idea what Thailand was going to be like, but I knew it would be a tough, gruelling shoot. Brian was doing something else at the same time, and I also felt it was the right moment to have a change. What is extraordinary about Darius – apart from his work, which includes *Delicatessen*, *The City of Lost Children* and *Se7en* – is his absolute loyalty to the director. He's half Iranian and half French, and he has that French thing of being devoted to what he sees as the auteur. If I'd asked him to shut his eyes and shoot a scene, he would have done so. Yet he wouldn't listen to anyone else! Only the director. It's one of the reasons he's a great cinematographer; he inhabits your vision as director so intimately. He's a really wonderful man.

How did you shoot DiCaprio and Ledoyen – or rather, Richard and Françoise – getting intimate in the sea late one night?

We shot day for night as we couldn't afford to light the island at night. We did a lot of day-for-night shoots. You shoot in daylight but expose it differently and then grade it so it looks like night and slightly magical. And the phosphorescence in the sea was added with CG. The sex scene was basically Leo and Virginie just swimming around. Kissing underwater isn't a good idea, but it looks good.

Richard and Sal later have sex on the mainland.

No problem for Tilda doing that. She's so brave. They were both just at it straight away. Faking it masterfully, both of them.

Was it a challenge to work in such intense heat?

We were careful to go at the most pleasant time. Early on I talked to John Boorman, who'd made *Beyond Rangoon* in 1995. He'd filmed at the wrong time, in the pre-monsoon heat, and couldn't film for full days.

Did the actors have to get fit and buff for The Beach?

They trained for a few weeks and went on diets because the characters were living off rice and fish. Aesthetically, they needed to look like a bunch of yoga teachers.

Why did you decide not to show the female characters topless, as they probably would have been?

There is some topless stuff. I'm sure we had a discussion about the women being topless all the time, but I can't remember. It's probably because of the certificate in America. When you get $55 million of a studio's money, they give you a maximum running length and it also can't exceed a certain film certificate. These are contractual obligations, and the budget won't be released unless you agree to them. There was a lovely scene where Richard sees the women bathing in a waterfall. Deleted eventually. But there you go.

You said earlier that the studio put no creative pressure on you, but didn't they have an issue with the fact that Richard often resorted to lying?

If morality mattered to Fox, then Leo protected us from all that. Studios are happy to take risks with huge film stars. And Fox would do nothing to upset Leo.

Despite working with a big studio and a fat budget, you still tried to do things for real as opposed to relying on CGI. Didn't you actually grow an entire field of dope?

The dope field was so complicated. There are a lot of real dope fields in Thailand, but the government burns them within twenty-four

The marijuana field.

hours of discovery – or at least they say they do. They offered to let us shoot in a real dope field but couldn't guarantee that the field would actually be there for long enough. We therefore decided to create our own field. Obviously we couldn't grow marijuana, so we grew hemp, which looks very similar. So yes, we grew an entire field. By mistake southern hemisphere seeds were ordered and Thailand is in the northern hemisphere. The daylight requirement for the seeds was wrong – it was two hours short. A series of fluorescent lights had to be built above this field which came on when it suddenly went dark each night at 6 p.m. It was an extraordinary image.

When the hemp was fully grown and we were ready to film, local people started stealing it, thinking it was dope. You'd have to smoke 20kg of hemp to get any kind of hit!

It sounds like an adventure.

Can you imagine someone coming up in the middle of a tropical paradise and saying, 'It's the hemp seeds, there's not enough day-light to grow them'? And you go, 'What???'

You also wanted Françoise to be taking real photos of the night sky.

I love all that, it's very romantic. I talked to night-sky photographers, who explained that they virtually always shoot in the desert where there's no humidity at all. You can shoot time lapse all night and you only need one drop of humidity to ruin it all. Imagine doing it in a humid climate . . . In the end I gave in and we did it all CG at the Framestore CFC studios in London. They did a lovely job enclosing the island too.

And the Swedes mauled by sharks – their wounds look appallingly real.

The prosthetics guys were amazing. It was pretty horrible to look at. Why would you want to surf after seeing that? The Swedes are very funny: those scenes are typical of John's mordant wit.

Were you thinking about the music while you were in Thailand?

It was on my mind, yes, but of course we didn't put the soundtrack on until we got back to London. I'd got a bit out of touch with music, so I started to catch up. I had great fun doing it. It's

Taking photos of the night sky.

a really good soundtrack. The Underworld track '8 Ball', which they wrote for the film, is maybe their best song. It's wonderful. All Saints wrote 'Pure Shores'. Then I found *Play*, a Moby album that nobody had picked up on yet. We put 'Porcelain' on the soundtrack and people started picking up on it. Then almost every song on *Play* was used for an advert. I was already a Moby fan so I was very pleased to find it.

I told the Radio 1 DJ Pete Tong about Moby, and he started playing the album on his show; later he told me about Godspeed You! Black Emperor and we used 'East Hastings' at the start of *28 Days Later*.

It was also the first time you used a score.

I was a huge fan of Angelo Badalamenti because of his work on David Lynch movies. But in the end there isn't enough Angelo on the soundtrack because my instinct is always to use pop music. I'm sure if you asked Angelo he'd tell you that he wrote me a beautiful theme and I hardly used it!

Were you happy to be back in London once filming was over?

I was so relieved! I wanted to come home. We were in Thailand for eight months, including the prep.

Were you depressed when you arrived home?

I don't really get depressed. I'm admitting to you that I couldn't wait to come home because that's how I felt. Which is unusual for me. Just because of the stress levels that were involved, I suppose. I began to enjoy *The Beach* again when I started editing. And then you go and do tests in America! You get all this incredible stuff where the audience fill in cards and hand them back in. They wrote things like, 'Oh, you have betrayed us!' – mostly prompted by their loyalty to *Trainspotting*.

Were you happy with the ending of The Beach *when you were in the edit?*

It's very depressing when Sal kills herself and they all leave the island. And, on top of that, there's Richard Ashcroft singing on the

UNKLE track. The internet cafe scene was a pick-up. We'd already shot the scene in which they all jump in the air on the beach for the group photo. It's based on that famous photo of the Duke of Windsor and his wife jumping for the camera. We wanted to give a sense of . . . not hope but . . . something living on after the experience – their deeply flawed sense of community.

So Françoise sending Richard the photo is all about nostalgia rather than a suggestion their relationship might be resurrected?

I think so. It was a moment in time. It often is when you're that age.

DiCaprio looks like James Dean in the internet cafe.

He does! We shot that up at Leavesden, where they were just getting ready to shoot the first Harry Potter film.

It's hard to feel sorry for DiCaprio, but when he was nominated for a worst actor Razzie for The Beach, *I thought it was a bit mean.*

I didn't know that. That *is* a bit mean. I think that's less to do with acting ability and more to do with his status amongst young men in America who are a bit threatened by him.

Have you contemplated revisiting The Beach?

It's interesting. I've always been tempted to have another go at it. To re-edit it. I don't know if there's enough there to make it worth while or if I could make enough difference. But I'd certainly do without the voice-over, which was a cardinal error. It was never conceived with a voice-over; I didn't shoot it with one in mind. There's a voice-over in *Shallow Grave* but it's very different; it's just used at the beginning and end of the film, *Sunset Boulevard*-style. In *Trainspotting* we decided to really go for the voice-over and use it like Scorsese used it in *GoodFellas*. The one in *Trainspotting* is a litany and you're challenging the audience to keep up. Either you really go for it or you don't do one at all. In between is lazy. It's an easy way to try and get the audience to sympathise with the main character.

Of course your experience on The Beach *radically changed your attitude to film-making.*

And that's no exaggeration. I decided as a direct result of my experience in Thailand to make a series of digital films. It was an incredibly refreshing experience.

And you were back in control again. I presume you'd admit to a loss of control on The Beach?

A bit. But not in a whingey way. Those big films don't suit me. I certainly learned that.

Was it almost as though you were running away from that other world of big budgets and Hollywood stars?

And those experiences fed 28 *Days Later*. One of the great things about that film was that it gave me control again. Because it's not monolithic, you can do it in your back garden – and we did, in fact, shoot a bit of it in my back garden. You can take the cameras home with you or head off somewhere with Cillian Murphy and shoot something. It totally freed me up. The alternative would have been to continue making big films like *The Beach*, which just wasn't an option for me.

Did The Beach *feel claustrophobic and the lo-fi digital projects liberating?*

Weirdly for me, yes. I quite literally found my feet again by working on digital projects for TV. It wasn't anything against film per se – *Millions* is shot on film because it suited the story more – it's more to do with the approach, the set-up of the crew and the sense of collaboration. It's that whole idea of wanting the people I work with to behave like mini-directors. They feel such responsibility themselves that you get the best work out of them.

So you want your crew to have the same level of absolute dedication you have?

Oh God, yeah. And working in what I call the Pinewood way doesn't suit me because I'm not that organised. You'd think that all the money in the world would allow you to make the kind of impromptu decisions I like to make, but it doesn't. People used to say a big-budget film is like an oil tanker: weighed down with wealth and riches and yet if you want to turn it around, it takes half a day. If you've got a small crew, you'll just react. The difference between the two schools of film-making are going to become more pronounced. There's very little in between the vast films being made on an industrial scale by directors like James Cameron and small films. I really hope the small films will survive and prosper.

So you left the oil tanker behind and, with digital film-making, took control of a sprightly speedboat. You also struck out on your own: The Beach *was the fourth and final film you made with both Andrew Macdonald and John Hodge – though you went on to work with Macdonald on* 28 Days Later *and* Sunshine. *All good things come to an end, but, after the brilliance of the first two films you made together, it's a shame you didn't part ways on a high. Your initial idea was to work loosely as a co-operative: in hindsight, do you think you were perhaps naive?*

Well, I still believe in it as a dream. I was determined to share the back end of each film's profit three ways, which is unheard of really. But when a film is working really well and it's truly a collaboration, why should the director take more money? As well as the idealistic side of it, there is also a very important practical result, which is that you sustain people's involvement in a project by treating them as an equal. It's particularly relevant to writers, who are usually working on four or five different scripts because they know, sadly, that if they're lucky only one of them will get made.

But yes, maybe I was naive thinking the partnership between Andrew, John and I could be equal. Maybe it was a ludicrous idea.

Did things fall apart? Did you fall out with each other?

We were never close friends. We never hung out together. But, for a while, we had an excellent working relationship. Andrew and John were certainly disillusioned with me after *The Beach*. They went off to make *The Final Curtain* together, while I did what I had to after such a negative experience: I got back to basics.

28 Days Later (2002)

A bank of television screens shows a series of catastrophic news events that suggest a world out of control: lynchings, wild fires, police v. the public. In the Cambridge Primate Research Centre, animal-rights militants in balaclavas liberate rage-infected monkeys from their glass boxes. A scientist begs them not to: 'They're highly contagious . . .' Seconds later, a monkey kills a militant. Her eyes turn red; she is now infected.

Four weeks later, Jim (Cillian Murphy), a former bike messenger, awakes, naked and Christ-like, in a hospital bed. Drips feed into both arms. He peers through the shutters and shouts, loudly and hopefully, a simple 'Hello?' What he sees is an empty corridor littered with the contents of an overturned trolley; what he hears is his own voice echoing out into the heavy silence.

Dressed in hospital scrubs and white pumps, he wanders through the hospital. The pay phones are disconnected and no one responds to his periodic cries of 'Hello?' He empties a vending machine of fizzy drinks and puts them in a white carrier bag. Outside, ambulances sit abandoned. A shot down the Thames towards St Paul's shows an eerily empty, post-apocalyptic capital.

Jim walks over Westminster Bridge, stepping over the souvenir replicas of Big Ben and miniature Union Jacks scattered on the pavement. He shouts a more frustrated 'Hello?' A double-decker bus lies on its side. He finds hundreds of pound notes on the steps which lead up from the Mall towards Pall Mall; he stuffs as much money as he can in the carrier bag. He peers into a silver car and the alarm goes off: this is the first noise he's heard since waking up, and he leaps away, momentarily terrified.

A newspaper headline screams 'EVACUATION'. Its subheading explains further: 'Mass exodus of British people causes global chaos . . . Blair declares a state of emergency.' In Piccadilly Circus, the statue of Eros is surrounded by scaffolding and boards; these in turn are covered in desperate notices and pleas from those searching for lost loved ones. Jim is starting to realise the gravity of what has happened while he's been in a coma. He may be the only survivor.

In a dark, silent church, Jim finds himself in a congregation full of dead people slumped on top of each other. Looking down on them, he is visibly shocked. A priest appears, staggering and lashing out. Jim, still trusting, says 'Father' softly. As the priest comes straight for him, Jim says: 'Father, are you okay?' At the last minute, Jim smashes him over the head with the carrier bag and runs from the church. He is followed by a stream of 'infecteds' who can move with surprising speed and agility.

Jim is grabbed by a non-infected stranger, who leads him down into an Underground station. Here, behind the metal shutters of a small shop, Selena (Naomie Harris) and Mark (Noah Huntley) introduce themselves. They confirm the bad news: an infection spread so fast that there was no time to evacuate cities. Reports of the virus spreading to Paris and New York were followed by radio silence. No television, no government, police or army.

Jim, Selena and Mark walk along a railway track. They arrive at Jim's parents' house. Upstairs, his mum and dad are in bed, dead from an overdose. His mum clutches a photo of her son. On the back a message says: 'Jim – with endless love, we left you sleeping. Now we're sleeping with you. Don't wake up x.' Finally, Jim cries.

While Selena and Mark sleep, Jim watches an old family video by candlelight. An infected, drawn to the light, breaks into the house. Mark kills him with a huge kitchen knife, while Jim exclaims: 'It's Mr Bridges!' Mark is cut and therefore infected; Selena hacks him to death without hesitation.

Jim and Selena walk down yet another disturbingly deserted London street. She tells him the rule: 'If someone gets infected, you've got between ten and twenty seconds to kill them.' She is tough, unsentimental: 'Have you got any plans, Jim? Do you want us to find a cure and save the world or just fall in love and fuck? Plans are pointless: staying alive is as good as it gets.'

They spot fairy lights flashing in a tall block of flats. They clamber over the shopping trolleys blockading the hall and climb the stairs. Frank (Brendan Gleeson) welcomes them into his flat. His teenage daughter Hannah (Megan Burns) is initially terrified. Frank is thrilled to meet two more non-infected adults and celebrates by drinking crème de menthe. Jim cuts his hair and shaves without water. In their tank, goldfish hang in barely an inch of water.

Frank shows his new guests the roof, which is covered with thousands of multicoloured plastic buckets. It hasn't rained for ten days, but he remains hopeful.

They pick up a transmission on the radio from soldiers based north-east of Manchester and all four set off on a long road trip in Frank's hearse-like black taxi hoping to find a cure for the virus, for salvation. They get a puncture in a tunnel overrun with rats and the infected. They go on a shopping spree in Budgens. They stop for petrol and Jim is jumped on by an infected lad whom, following Selena's advice, he kills with a baseball bat.

They sleep in a ruin and, the next morning, watch horses running free in an adjacent field.

As they head up the M6, they see Manchester on fire on the horizon. They arrive at a blockade of parked trucks, and Frank, thinking they have been misled by the radio transmission, is disappointed. He wanders off, hears a crow squawking, looks up to see it pecking at a cadaver. A single drop of blood falls in his eye. He tells Hannah he loves her but she must stay away. Jim sets off to kill him as Selena restrains Hannah, but an officer shoots Frank first. The three survivors are driven in the taxi to base camp, which is set up in a grand stately home.

Major Henry West (Christopher Eccleston) – cold, remote, autocratic – shows Jim around, pointing out trip wires, landmines, an infected straining on a chain in a courtyard: 'Eventually, he'll tell me how long the infected take to starve to death.'

After an oddly formal dinner, infected invade the lawn, are exposed by industrial lights and are shot as if in a video game. Soldiers try to chat up Selena and are stopped by Major West, who later tells Jim that 'women mean the future'. When Jim tries to escape with Selena and Hannah, he is captured and chained to a radiator. Later, Jim is taken to the woods to be executed. He escapes, spotting a vapour trail in the sky as he heads back to the house.

Meanwhile, the soldiers are forcing Selena and Hannah to dress up; it is clear they intend to rape them.

Jim, now semi-feral, unchains Mailer (Marvin Campbell), the infected soldier in the courtyard. Mailer starts to kill and infect his colleagues. Jim finds Corporal Mitchell (Ricci Harnett) holding Selena hostage and ready to rape her. He violently kills him, smashing his head against a wall before gouging his eyes out.

Selena and Jim kiss. He tells her they will be okay. Hannah appears and whacks Jim round the head: 'I thought he was biting you!'

Major West shoots Jim in the stomach and is then bitten by an infected. Hannah drives Jim and Selena out of the house in her father's taxi. The gates are locked. The taxi lurches forward in slow motion. The action cuts to black.

Selena, in love and petrified, injects Jim. A flash of green with 'HELL' written in capitals.

Another twenty-eight days later, Jim awakes to find himself in a remote cottage. Selena sits at a sewing machine, Hannah is busy with a huge white sheet. They rush outside and unfurl the gigantic banner, which now reads 'HELLO'. A jet flies overhead as the infected lie dying on the roads. Selena, smiling, asks: 'Do you think he saw us this time?'

* * *

Danny Boyle in the stately home in *28 Days Later*.

AMY RAPHAEL: *After* The Beach, *in which a $55-million budget felt stifling rather than liberating, you craved low-budget projects that were resolutely low-key and urban.*

DANNY BOYLE: It was back to the BBC and back to Manchester. I got cinematographer Anthony Dod Mantle on board and we shot two television films on small digital video cameras. We had very little money and *then* I said we'd do two films for the price of one. So we filmed these completely mad, crazy Jim Cartwright scripts, *Strumpet* and *Vacuuming Completely Nude in Paradise*, back to back in Manchester. I very quickly got back that feeling – which characterises indie film-making – where you feel you can shoot anything if you believe in it. Just do it.

You must have had tremendous fun shooting Vacuuming Completely Nude, *in which Timothy Spall plays a coarse door-to-door salesman who drives around like a maniac.*

Oh, we had a great time with a young, energetic, can-do producer, Martin Carr. We put cameras in all sorts of odd places in the car. Spall is just . . . outrageous fun. And yet humane and epic too. I remember wondering how he was going to learn all the lines – there were so many! Jim's writing is vaudeville, it's performance. It's up and at 'em. You can't teach an actor how to take on a larger-than-life role. It's all about innate bravura. There are a handful of actors who could carry it off: Roy Chubby Brown was a left-field idea until Spall signed up. Jim Broadbent could have done it. Or, if he were older, David Thewlis. But Spall is one of the greatest at it.

Strumpet was fantastic too. One of the highlights of my career is Chris Eccleston chanting a John Cooper Clarke poem in front of a bunch of blokes in Collyhurst – a really tough area of Manchester – who didn't know what the fuck was going on. They didn't know who John Cooper Clarke or Chris Eccleston were, and then they heard 'Chickentown', realised it was about their lives and thought it was just fantastic. They loved it.

We also crammed twenty dogs into a white stretch limo for *Strumpet* and, unsurprisingly, there was shit everywhere. We went into the *Top of the Pops* studio for a couple of hours after they'd finished recording and let loose these dogs. They were shitting all over the stage. It was absolutely insane but good fun.

After the despair you felt making The Beach – *assuming you'd go so far as to say it was despair – did your love of directing return?*

I realised I'd moved into a slightly different type of film-making. One of the problems with success is that you get everything you want first time of asking, and it's not good. You should have to work hard for what you want. You should have to sell it to people. Persuade them.

Working under pressure, on your toes, against the odds?

Yes. You fight for an idea or vision that's a bit different.

Which is when the good ideas turn up . . .

For me. They certainly don't come out of a large number of technicians telling you this is how they did it on the Spielberg.

Your best films certainly have adrenalin flooding through them.

And you need that adrenalin. You want to see something on the screen that you haven't seen before. I always say to people that if you get the chance to make a film, be bold. We go to the cinema for a reason. We want to have an experience. Not just sit thinking about other things as we might when watching television. In all my time watching films, it's almost always the case. When people really take risks, it pays off. It doesn't even particularly matter if the film is not very good.

Films don't have to be flawless if, at the end, you take something away with you. It's what you say about not being able to take your eyes off the screen, as with Clockwork Orange *or even* Trainspotting.

It's interesting, because Kubrick made his films through a studio system but he worked with very few people. He had a tiny crew. Which is why Warner Brothers allowed him to shoot for so long: day by day it didn't cost very much. So he kept going. It's the key to it, I think. You reduce costs and give yourself the chance of being evangelical. You can persuade everybody that this is a mission you're all on together. Richard Stiles, who was the first AD on 28 *Days Later*, has a real eye and he'd go off and shoot things without even being asked. The crew aren't just clocking off at 5 p.m., they've invested their hearts in it.

Kubrick didn't trust people outside his close circle. It's as though you had to relearn to be intimate with your crew after not having daily contact with producer Andrew Macdonald on The Beach.

I certainly learned a tough lesson. Everything was spread out too much on *The Beach*.

Did earning money on The Beach *make a difference? Your head doesn't appear to be turned by money and success, but they must have some effect.*

Yes, of course. It's nice to earn money but it marks you, definitely. And if you chase it, then it gets worse.

After Strumpet *and* Vacuuming Nude, *you confounded all expectation and directed* 28 Days Later. *Why choose an apocalyptic horror flick, a zom-com?*

I love doing scary. It's a delight. I think it's why so many people make horror movies. It's that Hitchcock thing: it's so delicious working out how to frighten people. There are a series of rules you have to obey and exploit. And then try to create them afresh so people feel really scared! And anyone can get killed at any time.

Were you a zombie fan?

No, I don't like zombie movies very much. I find them implausible. Why do zombies just lurch around instead of running after their victims? When you suggest this to aficionados, it makes them furious because the not-running-away is the whole point. Alex Garland, who wrote the script, knows everything about zombie movies and, to be honest, I know next to nothing about them. So we had this good tension. Normally, I would watch everything and immerse myself totally in a genre. But on this occasion I tried to maintain my ignorance. Some of the scenarios in 28 *Days Later* are borrowed from other zombie movies, but I didn't realise at the

'I immediately said the zombies had to run.'

time. I think that's fine; it was an innocence I was after rather than being too knowing.

I immediately said to Alex that if I was going to make the film, the zombies had to run. There is a George A. Romero running-zombie movie that I didn't watch – and still haven't seen – called *The Crazies*. Making the zombies run immediately presented us with a problem: actors running is not unlike them riding horses; they tend not to be that good at it and you end up having to cut round the action.

So, instead of actors playing the infected, I wanted to use athletes. The only time I'd ever been in the room with an athlete, I had an immediate sense of their physical power. They are different to me and you. Gail Stevens, the casting director, discovered this agency in Leytonstone, east London, where former athletes sign on at the end of their careers. The agency sends them to places like Dubai to turn somersaults, cut a ribbon and open a supermarket. I did a physical workshop with them in which I acted out bits of the scenes. It was amazing. Really scary. They can bounce on you without hurting you. So all the zombies are athletes. There's a genuine tension, a muscular power in them. It was a great discovery.

It's a brilliant idea; instead of staggering around, the zombies leap unexpectedly out of dark corners. They seem more human than the usual celluloid zombies, which makes them quite terrifying. When 28 Days Later isn't making you jump out of your seat, it's satisfyingly chilling, disturbing and eerie. Even the stillness and silence of a deserted London near the start of the film is scary. And you don't even usually like stillness.

The idea of Jim waking up in hospital was borrowed from *The Day of the Triffids* with a tip of our hats. It's a bold, wonderful and very classic idea: the protagonist wakes up to discover that London appears to have been abandoned. There were just a few lines in the script about Jim walking around London on his own. The silence is fantastic. You know the rules of the genre dictate that the silence will be followed by a very loud, sudden noise and movement. A zombie will be right behind you.

We shot the deserted London scenes in summer. We shot on seven consecutive mornings from 4 a.m.; for two or three hours there was enough light but few people around. It only rained on one of the days. Anthony and I had developed a way to use numerous cameras

Jim wanders through deserted London.

on the two television films. It took Jim about two minutes to walk across Westminster Bridge. There were ten hidden cameras that could be left running without an operator. They record on mini-DV tapes and cost £1,500 each. We picked out the footage showing Jim walking past on each of the ten cameras, junked the rest of the tape and then cut it all together. It makes it look as though he's taking a long time to walk around a deserted London, yet all you've got to do is stop the traffic or the people for a few minutes each time.

We discovered a very funny thing: on a film of this scale, you're not allowed to stop the traffic. It's only a film like *101 Dalmatians* that's allowed to shut part of London on a Sunday morning, presumably because such big films are in a position to pay staggering amounts of money. So, for us, the police wouldn't officially stop the traffic. We appointed our own marshals in jackets to ask drivers to stop; if there was a dispute, the police stepped in.

The traffic marshals who came on the first day were students whom we paid a few quid. My daughter Grace, who was eighteen at the time, turned up with a few mates. They were all attractive girls. There was a heatwave, they weren't wearing many clothes, and of course the drivers around at that time of the day were mostly men. If I asked them to stop, they'd tell me to fuck off; a beautiful girl leaning into the car did the trick. The next day we hired more girls, until we had a rather beautiful gang of traffic marshals. And the traffic stopped.

So you actually relished the tranquillity of the city at rest?

Sounds a bit prissy but shooting that scene was so evocative of the William Wordsworth poem 'Upon Westminster Bridge'. The only thing moving was the river . . . It was really weird but a joy to shoot. We cut it together and put the Godspeed You! Black Emperor track 'East Hastings' on it. Other than Cillian Murphy as Jim, we hadn't even cast the film at that point. We just knew, from very early on, that the film would work. You don't often get that feeling, but we did then.

London is a perfect setting for post-apocalyptic films because of its postcard iconography.

I suppose so, although every time I visit a city like Shanghai for the first time, I think you could make *28 Days Later* work there. Cities without people are extraordinary. The whole point of them is people. They're weird without people.

At the start of 28 Days Later *you can't help but think an empty London would be amazing, but within minutes you change your mind as it's so eerie and unnatural.*

It's so scary! When I go to the countryside sometimes I'm frightened and spooked. It's so lonely. We were transferring that empty-country feeling onto the streets of London.

The eye almost can't deal with images of an empty London: it moves constantly around, searching for people.

You need to see movement, so your eye can't keep still.

I like the way editor Chris Gill edits and compresses time. It's very effective.

Up until *28 Days Later* I'd worked with Masahiro Hirakubo, who's a very good classical editor. However, Masa didn't want to come and work on the TV films we made in Manchester; he wanted to stay in London and in films. I didn't care where I worked, I just wanted to get back in control again. I met this guy Chris Gill, who was from Manchester. I loved the way he compressed time. You can compress time without people noticing it – which is what all editors do because to watch real life in real time would be painfully slow – but Chris also compresses so that you can actually see it happening. It adds tension and aggression and adrenalin. I like that a lot.

Did you use any CGI in those scenes of empty London?

No. All we took out were the traffic lights changing from red to green. You're not allowed to black out traffic lights, so we only did it occasionally when no one was looking.

Shortly after you started shooting the rest of the film, 9/11 happened. How did it change the mood of the film?

We started shooting on 1 September 2001. It was strange because, before 9/11, my vision of *28 Days Later* was of a film about social rage. It had something to say about how we've lost all patience with each other. There was the famous case of Kenneth Noye, who was involved in the Brinks Mat robbery in the early 1980s. They couldn't find the bullion despite digging up his houses in Surrey and Spain. He served eight years for handling gold and had been free for two years when a student in a Mini cut him up on a round-about. He got out of his Range Rover, stabbed the student and killed him. I remember thinking *28 Days Later* was about just that: why would a guy who has so much to lose get out of his car and do something like that? They nailed him and he's in jail now.

But then 9/11 happened and it changed the whole film. Not least because, post-9/11, we'd never, ever have been given permission to film scenes like we did in London. In the week before 9/11, we were pushing our luck a little: we'd be filming somewhere, someone would eventually spot us on CCTV, come and find us and ask what we were doing. Did we have permission? We'd say 'sort of'. But it was 7 a.m. and nowhere was open to check and so we were just left alone. We even got permission to upturn a red double-decker bus in Whitehall, yards from Downing Street. It was so innocent . . .

So the film changed. It became about how we all felt vulnerable to something happening, whether it be an epidemic, a pandemic, an attack of some kind. It became about how vulnerable cities are. Because usually cities feel impregnable: we're so confident, we just keep building them. In fact, as we've discovered, they are intensely vulnerable. It's bizarre the way films can go out of your control. We set out to make a film about social rage, and instead it became a more complex response to 9/11. I think it's one of the reasons it became a big hit. It was the first film off the block that was about the vulnerability we felt post-9/11.

When Jim finds the boards around Eros *covered in missing-people notices, it echoes those desperately posted up around Ground Zero.*

We wanted to film a sequence in Piccadilly Circus towards the end of Jim's short journey across London. We went to have a look at *Eros*; it was being repaired and was covered in scaffolding. We put boards up around the scaffolding and covered them in photographs of missing people. I got the idea from a Chinese earthquake

Jim in front of the noticeboard – 'It's what people do in a crisis, when all communication breaks down.'

or flood where survivors desperately put up photos of their loved ones. Angela Day, bless her, worked on those boards for months in 3 Mills Studios. All she did all day was make up these notices and stick them on the board.

And then, as you say, after 9/11 similar notices went up all around Ground Zero. It's what people do in a crisis, when all communication breaks down. They leave a note for someone saying, 'Look for me here . . . look for me at a fixed point.' It's really moving. But we only put the boards up as a result of the scaffolding around *Eros*.

Cillian Murphy has a dreamy quality which is perfect for Jim, especially as he makes his way across a London which is both familiar and alien. Were you already a fan?

Gail Stevens, the casting director, suggested we see Cillian Murphy; she'd seen him on the stage in *Disco Pigs*. We saw a lot of guys before finding Cillian. I have to be honest here: I didn't know how Cillian looked naked; I never auditioned his body. It's like Iggy Pop's. He's the sweetest, gentlest guy who doesn't exercise and who's got a body like iron. As soon as I saw his naked body in the hospital sequence at the beginning, I thought we had to get his shirt off whenever possible. He became a big gay icon when the film came out.

Cillian Murphy – 'A dreamy, slightly
de-energised, floating quality.'

His journey is, of course, towards this terrible violence – which
gives the film a great arc. Cillian has this dreamy, slightly de-
energised, floating quality that is fantastic for the film.

*Murphy is shy and therefore inclined to look slightly away from
the camera . . .*

He's just not aware of how beautiful he is. When he told me he was
from Cork, I thought of all the fighting men who come from there.
I was intrigued. We knew he could do the beginning and float and
just not know what's going on. His challenge was whether he could
do the ferocity of the ending. He did it beautifully.

*By the end, when he's trying to escape from Christopher Eccleston's
soldiers, he's feral in an utterly convincing way.*

Yeah, he actually takes the army guy's eyes out! Naomie Harris
makes the opposite journey. It's very simple and very brilliant. She
moves from this implacable violence, this defensiveness she has at

Naomie Harris as Selena.

the beginning, to an openness at the end. So they cross in a way. I've never done anything as simple as that in terms of character arcs. But it's really interesting to have a trajectory like that which is so clear from the outset. It gives you something to map and follow.

Naomie was really interesting. When I first met her, she talked like Princess Anne and had a similar hairdo. She seemed posh. I'm not sure why: she's from a London housing estate and her mum was a scriptwriter on *EastEnders*. She was interested in the role of Selena but, like many of the actors we approached, thought it was a bit trashy doing a horror movie.

Even after reading the script and despite your reputation?

Serious actors aren't really interested in horror movies. And I wanted to cut Naomie's hair, toughen her up. She's a brilliant actor and very much underused. She can do anything. As can Cillian. But both were quite young and inexperienced, and it made sense to use an established actor to work alongside them. I knew Brendan Gleeson's work and thought he could centre the film. It's the way the Americans work: when they use young actors they always try to surround them with established character actors to protect the film. He's the kind of wonderful guy you feel okay around – until he gets killed.

I presume he didn't procrastinate after reading the script?

He didn't hesitate at all; he thought it was a great script.

Brendan Gleeson – 'I thought he could centre the film.'

When you were discussing the film with Alex Garland, did you talk at length about the film appealing to both zombie and non-zombie fans?

Because I'm not a big zombie fan, I wouldn't have been able to make it for hardcore fans anyway. I don't really understand the genre. As I said, the tension between Alex and I – him loving the genre, me not – is a very good tension. Whereas on *Sunshine* we both loved sci-fi so much that it wasn't as helpful to us.

On Sunshine *you couldn't avoid the ghost of Kubrick. Did the spirit of Romero haunt you on 28* Days Later?

It didn't haunt me because I avoided zombie films or almost saw them by accident. After *28 Days Later* had been quite a success, someone came up to ask about the scene in the house where one of the soldiers is chained up in a backyard. It was apparently like a scene in another zombie film, but I had no idea.

Do you remember watching Threads, *the 1984 BBC play about the UK in the aftermath of a nuclear war, and the original* Survivors, *the mid-1980s BBC series in which a group of people survive a global plague?*

I saw *Threads* but not *Survivors* because I was at college by then and had stopped watching telly. But Alex was into it and it was definitely an influence on him.

Did you read around the subject of a global plague?

We all read *The Hot Zone*, Richard Preston's fantastic true story about the origins of the Ebola virus. This guy gets on a plane in Africa and discovers he's been infected with Ebola. He fills these sick bags as he flies back to America. He gets off the plane still able to walk and disappears into Washington. It was the ultimate nightmare. What stops Ebola killing us all is the fact that it breaks out in remote in villages in Africa, where it's so intense that it burns itself out very quickly. The villages can be isolated immediately. It's an amazing book, a key reference point.

With the blood being infected it's hard not to think of Aids as well as Ebola.

It's all about people's fear of infected blood. A drop in Frank's eye kills him within minutes. I remember reading how the blink instinct works so fast in order to avoid infection. If danger is sensed, nothing moves in the body as quickly as our eyes.

Frank's death is surprisingly moving. After Richard's coldness in The Beach, *did you want the audience to empathise with the central characters in* 28 Days Later?

Big time!

The audience is, in fact, curious about Jim from the moment he is seen lying, Christ-like, on his hospital bed.

I think it's to do with affection for the inner city. Part of the story is obviously the four characters escaping the city, but in a way they remain inside the city in the taxi. *28 Days Later* is different from *The Beach* because it has all the human touches that are missing with people you don't relate to – such as the modern hippies on their secret island. Jim does exactly what you'd do if you woke up in an empty hospital: he gets drinks out of the vending machine because he's thirsty; he tries the phones.

And there's the heartbreaking scene on the steps adjacent to the ICA on Pall Mall where he's stuffing the money into his carrier bag.

That image is taken from Pol Pot's rule: when the National Bank of Cambodia was blown up by the Khmer Rouge as they retreated before the Vietnamese army, money was left lying in the streets. Like Jim, I'd have picked the money up from the steps – you'd think to yourself that you might need it. It might be useful.

Did you and Garland plan such scenes together?

Alex is a very interesting guy to work with. Like all good writers, you give him your notes and he comes back with material that's better. He senses what you want and filters it through what he thinks you need. Because *28 Days Later* is a road movie, it allowed us a certain amount of freedom. We could show Jim, Selena, Frank and his daughter Hannah on the M1, but where would they be going? Okay, let's send them to Manchester because I'd quite like to show my home town burning down in the distance (*laughs*). We wanted Manchester to burn like Dresden, but this was now post-9/11 so we had to resort to CG. We discussed the action ending up at the Lake District. Alex had this big thing about the third act. I can never tell which is the first, second or third act.

Not even after all those years at the Royal Court?

No, because you have five acts in Shakespeare or two acts in a modern play. This idea of a three-act structure comes from Robert McKee – the idea that a film begins with an inciting incident, proceeds with progressive complications and ends with a crisis, climax and resolution. Executives in Hollywood are forever saying, 'I love the script but the third act doesn't work.' Having said that, *28 Days Later* has a slightly clearer notion of a third act in my mind because it begins when Jim and co. find Chris Eccleston and his soldiers.

Did you have several endings in mind?

We had an alternative ending where they found a scientist in a bunker who possibly had an antidote to the virus. We developed the idea so much that Alex and I did voice-overs for a series of storyboards for the DVD. The conceit was that the infected had to have blood transfusions to become human again. Inspired by Kathryn

Bigelow's *Near Dark* – one of my favourite films – in the end it was too obvious a steal. Instead, we stayed with the soldiers and the Garden of Eden idea of starting again. It's a wonderful idea. Alex has those really bold, anthropological ideas. Eccleston sees Naomie and Megan as an opportunity to get society going again.

There was a second alternative ending in which Jim dies in hospital, but it tested badly.

That was an incredibly bleak finale which was shot in a 1970s hospital in Greenwich which has since closed down. Alwin Kuchler and I shot it during editing because Anthony wasn't available. Naomie was awesome when he dies. Then we had this third ending in the Lake District where the fighter plane comes over and they do the big 'HELLO' letters – which is what Cillian was shouting at the start of the film in an empty London. I loved the idea that it was the only word that mattered.

Basically, we couldn't make our minds up about the endings. I couldn't see that much difference in the audience response when we were testing the film. It was put out in America with both endings: people went to see the film with the 'HELLO' rescue coda and then went back a while later when it was advertised as having an alternative ending in which Jim dies. It was astonishing, but it's partly why it made so much money there. American studios can be very inventive when there's money to be made.

The 'HELLO' ending is shot on 35mm as opposed to DV.

We were defeated by the weather! The idea was that after looking at this grainy film which is relentlessly tough to look at, the screen would just explode with life. The day we got up there to rehearse was glorious. Heaven on earth! We turned up the next day and there was the white cloud that covers Britain all the time. So it doesn't look as significantly different as it should. It's testament to Anthony's skill on DV that he made the film work so well visually.

I read an interview with Dod Mantle in which he talked about his frustration at having to shoot those beautiful London skylines on DV: had he been able to shoot on 35mm it would have looked even more incredible.

The great thing about DV is that if you're missing a shot, you can just go out and grab it. So some of the scenes when the infected break into Jim's parents' house I shot in my back garden, with my kids helping. The biggest problem when using DV is this: if Cillian is very small in the wide shot, in reality he's a couple of pixels because the image has been blown up so much. Your eye microscopes in on him and it's unsatisfying. He hasn't got a face, he's two blobs of green. So we had to cut quite quickly. However, most people don't care about all the technical stuff; it's wonderful to have great cinematography, but it's the story and the actors that count. It's a very hard point to make to cinematographers sometimes.

I think Dod Mantle was just being a perfectionist.

Anthony is fantastic. I love him. I'm not that bothered about the cinematography in the end. What I love is the operating. For me it's everything. On big movies they don't want the cinematographer to shoot the film. He's just lighting it while the operator shoots it. I can't deal with that. I insisted with both Anthony and Alwin that they had to do the operating themselves if they were working with me. I had it with Darius [Khondji] on *The Beach* too. He didn't operate at first, and I couldn't bear it after a few days: he actually had to be the eyes of the film.

Danny Boyle with Anthony Dod Mantle.

Does it feel too removed?

Too many people, too many opinions.

And then you lose focus?

Well, then they get another guy in to operate the wheels for the remote crane. And someone else to shoot the underwater scenes. And Steadicam, of course, requires another specialist. A cameraman is a cameraman; he carries the camera and that's the direct link with the audience. His eye is capturing what the audience is going to eventually see on screen. Anyway, Anthony, Alwin and Darius are *brilliant* operators. It's insane not to have them as close to you and the actors as possible.

Let's talk about Mark Tildesley, the production designer you worked with for the first time on 28 Days Later *and who then collaborated on* Millions *and* Sunshine. *He did an amazing job of creating a post-apocalyptic world in* 28 Days Later.

Mark is a genius. He's one of those mini-directors I'm always talking about. He has a kind of vision which may or may not reflect my own; when it does, we don't even need to talk to one another. The wonderful thing about Mark is that he has huge technical ability but he's also very hands-on. He can do all these expert 3D drawings if you need them, but he's also on set creating his vision. One of his protégés, Marco [Mark Digby] – who was production designer on *Slumdog* – is the same. That's what you need: a breed of highly creative, hands-on designers, like Picassos working at the coalface.

There are some terrifying scenes at the start of the film, the first being when Jim wanders into a church and comes face to face with an infected priest.

That was in a church in Limehouse. The infected priest that comes at him is Toby Sedgwick; I told Gail that I wanted an actor for this particular zombie instead of an athlete. As well as being an actor, Toby teaches stage actors about physicality. Gail got him along to do some physical workshops with the core cast. That's an example of a mini-director like Gail contributing more than her job description.

Did you shoot the bodies in the church as they appear on screen, lying on top of each other?

Some of the visuals for the film were sourced from the incredibly disturbing images which came out of Serbia and Rwanda: from the massacres and the dumping grounds for the dead bodies; from the churches in Rwanda that were burned down with bodies inside them. There were stories of people who escaped those massacres by playing dead, which inspired the scene towards the end of the film in which Jim escapes from the soldiers and plays dead amongst a pile of inert bodies.

The imagery was built out of extensive research, and initially, as I've said, the idea that social intolerance eventually leads to a kind of genocide. I talked about social rage when the film came out, but no one really picked up on it.

Films are taken out of your control as soon as they are released. It happened on *Slumdog* too. I'm not the kind of director to give up explaining a film, but I can see why others do: there's something to be said for sitting back and thinking, 'The audience are either going to pick things up or they're not.' As director you have a bizarrely meaningless position in that scenario. But you still do six months touring *Slumdog* around America talking to anyone who appears to be listening.

All you can do is be in control of the film as you're making it and then let it go. At least 28 Days Later worked as a real collaboration and what you describe as your 'madness' on set inspired the crew. I heard that Tildesley even painted the stairwell of the abandoned tower block.

Mark would do anything. He's mad – and I mean that in the politest possible way. Other designers might think painting the stairwell doesn't matter as you won't see it. Not Mark. He'll do it anyway, just in case you get a glimpse of it.

Was the tower block actually abandoned?

It was. We found one not far from Waterloo that was about to be knocked down. We were filming in it and there was something slightly odd about the access we were granted; no one was allowed on the third floor. There were these Nigerian security guards looking after it till it was pulled down. Red rag to a bull of course, and we eventually discovered that the third floor was covered with hundreds of sleeping bags. People were renting it for £2 or £3 a night from these security guards. There was still running water in the toilets. The sleepers weren't allowed to be there in the day as they would be in danger of being discovered, so they'd just return at night. It made me think of the Stephen Frears film, *Dirty Pretty Things*, the hidden world of the megalopolis.

I love the aerial shots of the tower-block roof when it's covered with hundreds of multicoloured buckets to collect the non-existent rainwater. It's like a Damien Hirst picture.

That's Tildesley again. I told him I wanted to cover the roof in buckets. I figured that if you couldn't get out of the tower block, that's what you'd do. It's obvious how short they are of water; at one point you see the fish tank in the flat with barely enough water to keep the fish alive. I turned up one day to find hundreds of black and grey buckets sitting on the roof and they were lost against the tarmac. I don't know how he did it, but Mark – who was as disappointed as I was – went and found thousands of colourful buckets in an hour. Literally thousands. It looked beautiful in the end. And

The buckets on the roof.

the Bengali shopkeeper has shifted three years' supply in an hour.

Mark knew exactly what I needed at the end of the film too. I said the letters for 'HELLO' on the parachute silk had to be vast. Sometimes when you say that to designers, you turn up and the letters aren't really that vast. But with Mark you just know they'll be beyond vast. It was a nightmare trying to get the parachute silk outside: the wind kept trying to carry whoever was holding it away.

Was it also Tildesley's idea to make the soldiers' stately home Gothic?

The stately home was a disaster. We started out at Luton Hoo and were chucked out because, if I remember correctly, another film offered more money. Eventually, we found this place in Salisbury. The house we'd originally hoped to use was just like something out of a Jane Austen novel, but when we approached the owners they declined as soon as they realised what kind of film we were making. I wanted this army colonel with this mad Garden-of-Eden idea to be living in a Jane Austen house, to symbolise everything he dreams about in England, the perfect paradise.

To which you added rape and pillage . . .

And all manner of carnage.

Before the quartet reach the house, they travel up the motorway in Frank's taxi. Was it a challenge to empty the M1?

Again, Tildesley set it up. People don't realise the importance of the location manager. Mark appointed this really good-looking guy, Alex Gladstone, who used to slouch around, but the places he knew about were brilliant. Alex went up to Leicester and made a deal with the police so we could film on the longest stretch of the M1 – there's a stretch of about fifteen miles between two junctions. He somehow managed to broker a deal in which two police cars drive towards each other on the M1 at 30mph with their lights flashing. The traffic in front of the first car clears quite quickly because it's all doing around 70mph. And everyone behind the second car sits there driving at 30mph because they daren't overtake a police car. So by the time all the other traffic had cleared, we were waiting with two taxis going both ways to ensure double footage. When it all cleared past us, we drove and it was empty. Meanwhile, what the viewer doesn't realise is that encroaching on the taxi at 30mph are all these cars. It's very effective.

We also put a camera on a bridge, on a crane and inside the two taxis. We put doubles in one of the taxis. I was in the taxi with the actors; Anthony was in the taxi with the doubles. It was so simple: Alex enticed a couple of bored cops on their night shift who love having bacon sandwiches at 4.30 a.m. There are lots of girls around. And Mark has presumably bunged their superiors quite a few quid to get them to agree to do it.

Once they've got up the M1, Frank has died and Jim, Selena and Hannah have moved in with the soldiers in the stately home, the pace and dynamic of the film changes. Some critics felt that the film lost its way at this point. Were you conscious of the potential problems it presented, given that you were taking the action away from the infected and into Eccleston's so-called Garden of Eden? Were you worried about such an obvious shift?

We were worried about it at the time, which is why we developed another storyline about the guy who might have a cure. Actually, when I look back on it, I think it was a good decision to take the Garden-of-Eden route. I find it much more plausible than them discovering a guy with a cure. In fact, I find Eccleston's vision chillingly plausible.

We had a couple of army people advising us. They took Eccleston and the other actors who were playing soldiers away on a boot camp. Army guys are different; they obey a different set of rules because they are in charge of our lives and our deaths. The apocalypse mentality affects their sense of self-importance. Especially the officer class. Which is why I thought Eccleston as an officer leading these slightly wayward soldiers was a really good idea. And then we had his hair dyed white in a slightly homoerotic way . . .

There's no electricity in this newly infected world until we reach the floodlit stately home.

We had to give the soldiers a generator because we were already massively behind. The bond guarantors came onto the set and took me for a walk in the country. They're supposed to pay the extra money needed if you don't finish on time, so they'll do anything not to pay up: they try to sack or replace you, to cut massive bits of scripts. We were already running over . . .

So the compromise was to provide the house with electricity?

It was one of the compromises, yes. Crude blanket lighting. That way we could pre-shoot and stuff like that.

Does such pressure from the bond guarantors invoke anxiety?

(*laughs*) You've got to love all that stuff. And use the anxiety to propel you forwards.

You couldn't wait to get home from Thailand when you were making The Beach. *How did you feel at the end of* 28 Days Later?

I don't remember it ending. It was very dissipated because we did some pick-ups and I shot that material in my garden.

And then, some months later, the film had a bad first test.

This anecdote is for everybody who's had a bad test. The first test we did was a tiny little pre-test. It's particularly important to test a genre film – in this case a horror film – because it's not only about unravelling the story, it's also about the relationship with the audience. It's about jumps, timings and so on. We did this test at what was then Mr Young's Preview Theatre in Soho. There were about ten people who'd worked on the film in some capacity and twenty supposedly random people. It turned out they were all from New Zealand; the person who'd done the recruiting had obviously got a quick job lot of Kiwis in a pub. God knows why they allowed such a big group in: if you have a group dynamic going on, they can feel each other's negativity.

They watched the film and declared it rubbish. It was the least scary thing they'd seen in their lives. They all hammered it. I remember it so well. It was so bad there was nothing you could do. There wasn't even a glimmer of hope. It was horrific.

I presume it's the worst test you've ever had?

By a long way, yes. And it wasn't that different to the version that went out in cinemas in the end. Peter Rice from Fox was there and he said we *had* to ignore them. He could tell it was better than their response suggested! They could have been watching *Amadeus* and still said it was fucking rubbish.

You were sitting in an intimate preview theatre with them: didn't they jump or respond in any way to the infected?

They didn't respond at all. Nothing. Apart from wandering in and out to the toilet. Films are weird. I've worked in the theatre and, in theory, it's not fixed – it changes every night. Whereas film is supposed to be fixed but really it's not: it depends who's watching the film, what mood they're in, what's happened to them that day.

Despite the job lot of New Zealanders, 28 Days Later *was a critical and commercial success. Which is not to say all critics embraced it. Let me read you part of a review from* Variety: *'a faux-low-budget zombie pic . . . that shows a rather arrogant disdain for its audience between occasional flashes of flair . . .'*

(*laughs*) So that was clearly written by an old-fashioned zombie fan! They all came out of the woodwork. There were people who hated it because it disobeyed all the genre rules. Andrew Macdonald had the very smart idea of showing the first twenty minutes to an audience at Screamfest at the Prince Charles in central London, and they really loved it. Buzz immediately began to build among the horror faithful. Andrew has an excellent sense of how to use a film. As a result of that screening, the *Sunday Times* gave away a DVD with the opening of the film on it. I remember wondering if it was a good idea to give away the best part of the film. Not any more! It got them in there. It was ideas like that which got the film to number one in the UK for two weeks. Number one in your own country is a lovely feeling.

Despite being a 'faux zombie pic', the film found great success in America, and you were quite literally staggered.

It opened here in the UK first and did very well. I've changed my mind about this, but I always used to believe we should open the films here first. Anyone with experience tells you not to do that, but I'd always believed in it. In fact, *28 Days Later* would have done even better here had it opened in America first. When you have a success in America, the mark that puts on it here is a big advantage.

It's interesting: the audience felt different from the other films, even though *Trainspotting* obviously enjoyed a big cross-over. It seemed to attract real genre fans, although it spread beyond that. It challenged some of the conventions of the zombie genre and freshened it up a bit. Then it went to America and took off.

Did you think UK success might translate into US success?

No. I never thought it would work in America. It's so specific. There are no Americans in it. But it was well told and so the fact that it was specific didn't create a barrier. We had a midnight screening at Sundance which went really well and was great fun. We'd done the same with *Shallow Grave*.

Americans love iconic images of London. Do you think that helped?

I didn't realise it at the time, but I think it really did help. Fans also want to see a good genre movie, a good horror movie with something new in it. There was repeat business in there too, with people going back to it. Not just for the other ending but simply to see it again. Fox Searchlight couldn't believe how well it went for them; it was a big hit.

What kind of promo material was there for 28 Days Later?

All sorts of things have spun off it, most notably the sequel. There was a prequel comic book – Alex and Andrew are more into that kind of stuff and they helped set it up. I didn't do much publicity in America because by the time it was released I was shooting *Millions*. I was working on this rather sweet-natured, semi-autobiographical film and suddenly I had to talk about carnage and blood lust. And this extraordinary idea of it having the alternative endings playing side by side in the theatres.

Did you choose not to shoot the sequel, 28 Weeks Later, *because*

you were committed to other projects? What was your input as executive producer?

I was deeply involved in *Sunshine*, which took way too long – three years. I loved the idea, and director Juan Carlos Fresnadillo was my main input into the film. I thought *Intacto* was an amazing film. The idea of someone coming in from outside was a really interesting way of approaching it. Anyway, I watched a couple of the cuts of *28 Months Later* and I gave them some notes.

Did you wish – just for a moment – that you'd directed it?

When I watched it with an audience, I'd forgotten how much pleasure there is in just watching a good story unfold. When I made *28 Days Later*, there was so much blood around; the details of making horror films are sometimes quite repulsive. You're literally standing around in entrails. But when you see the finished product and you're not involved in entrails, it's appealing all over again. I think I'd be quite happy to do the third part one day.

Shaun of the Dead *came out two years after* 28 Days Later *and messed with the boundaries of zombie movies even more.*

(*laughs*) That was awesome! Simon Pegg, Nick Frost and Edgar Wright are seriously good film-makers. That guy Pegg is a seriously cool actor too. Not so much in *Shaun of the Dead*, although he is excellent, but when I saw *Hot Fuzz* I thought, 'Fucking hell, he's a *really* good actor.' It's very hard to sustain that kind of acting in action sequences, but he nails it every time.

Then Alfonso Cuarón's Children of Men *came out four years after* 28 Days Later. *They make a nice pair of disturbing post-apocalyptic Garden-of-Eden films.*

I didn't think I was going to like *Children of Men* but I liked it very much. It's a brilliantly made film. I'd never have taken *Children of Men* on as an idea from a book. I'd look at it and say the pregnancy idea is never going to work. It's laughable. The only pregnancy on earth? Forget it! It's not my cup of tea. But as I say, it's great. And Clive Owen is superb in it.

Shaun of the Dead *obviously chooses humour above the fear factor, but both* Children of Men *and 28 Days Later are properly scary films, albeit in different ways. What scares you on screen?*

The Exorcist. I grew up in a very strict Catholic household, and I saw it just before I left home for Bangor University. I was in terrible digs in Penmaenmawr, near Bangor, and couldn't sleep at night because of the terror I felt after seeing that film. I saw it again recently and it scares me pretty badly even now. The feeling of dread in the movie is extraordinary. I think dread is what really frightens people, not sudden, unexpected movements that make them jump and then laugh. The feeling of dread in *The Exorcist* is terrifying. Everything is shockingly brown. It gets to your soul. Nic Roeg's *Don't Look Now* is a favourite too. A feeling of dread permeates the whole film. Of impending doom. Which we all feel, of course, about our soul, our future, our families.

Sheer, visceral dread is a brilliant cinematic device – as is unmitigated violence. I'm thinking specifically of the eye-gouging scene in 28 Days Later, *when the semi-feral Jim gets a bit King Lear with a soldier.*

It was fantastically well done by the actors. We had a dummy head when Cillian digs his fingers right in, but the rest of it was all done live. I'd say 70 per cent of it is sound acting. The soldier's scream is just blood curdling. There's some very funny writing from Alex in those scenes with the soldiers.

The music that accompanies a horror film is critical too: after working with him on Strumpet *and* Vacuuming Completely Nude in Paradise, *you asked John Murphy to compose the music for* 28 Days Later, Millions *and* Sunshine.

John is a Scouser who lives in LA. When you first meet him you can't help but wonder how much he knows about classical music because he's a proper tough Scouser. Classical prejudice, I suppose. But he just knows music. It seeps out of him. We did the music in Liverpool, where John had a small studio which he kept for a long time despite living in LA. He was a backing musician for Orchestral Manoeuvres in the Dark and Frankie Goes to Hollywood. I worked with OMD on a TV programme, so we had people in common.

I had a great time working with him on the opening scenes; we didn't want any back story as such, but we had this idea that communal hymns would stand for the culture and for the past.

Was it hard to convince Godspeed You! Black Emperor to let you use 'East Hastings' in the opening scenes?

They don't normally license their music or let their songs be used on soundtracks. Even though they agreed to let us use 'East Hastings', they still refused to appear on the soundtrack, which is a shame. You want people to have access to their music, because you can't get it on iTunes either. I understand them politically – they don't want to market themselves through global corporations – but it's such a shame that some of their music isn't more widely heard. Anyway, we went up to Newcastle to see them in concert – they were extraordinary, sitting on the stage on chairs, never looking up, playing this apocalyptic, driving music – and to try to persuade them to let us use that track, which they did. We showed them how we wanted to use the song at the start of the film, and they thought that was cool.

In fact, we did experiment with playing the opening sequence without any music, and it felt genuinely dangerous. It was *so* frightening. When Jim opens the car door and the alarm goes off, it's just terrifying. You couldn't do that in the cinema. People would have heart attacks. Pacemakers would short circuit. So we put 'East Hastings' on it.

How often do you encounter problems trying to secure songs for your films?

When Jim goes back home and discovers his dead parents – excellent prosthetic bodies based on real cadavers, by the way – the music we originally wanted to use was Laurie Anderson's 'O Superman'. 'O superman. O judge. O Mom and Dad. Mom and Dad . . .' But she wouldn't let us use it. She explained that it's what everyone identifies her with, and she wanted to keep it for a personal project.

You also wanted to use 'Hitsville UK' by The Clash. What happened?

I wanted to use that song right at the end, on the cut to black, and I was persuaded out of using it. I will never be persuaded again. I was very cross with myself. And then Joe Strummer died. Instead of 'Hitsville UK', there's a track by a group called Blue States, who were signed to the soundtrack label.

Is that you taking your eye off the ball for one second and then feeling pissed off for ever?

That's a very good way of putting it. It only takes a second . . . And yes, I'll be pissed off for ever. Joe Strummer died and I never got to meet him. I'll never get to say sorry for not using the song, even though I'm sure he wouldn't have given two hoots.

Cillian Murphy – 'His challenge was whether he could do the ferocity of the ending. He did it beautifully.'

Millions (2004)

Two young lads, Damian (Alex Etel) and his older brother Anthony (Lewis McGibbon), cycle through a field of bright yellow rapeseed somewhere in the north-west of England. Damian's voice-over explains that it will shortly be the UK's turn to say goodbye to sterling and hello to the euro. The brothers arrive at the bare plot of land where their new house will be built, close to a railway line. They argue over who will have which bedroom. The house is built around them – amid much excitement – using stop-motion and CG.

Later, as they pack up and leave their old terraced house, Damian talks earnestly to his dad, Ronnie (James Nesbitt), about saints. When no one is looking, Damian pockets the old house keys. On the drive to the modern estate, Damian's voice-over explains how Anthony says 'Start with the money', but he thinks 'Money is just a thing'.

The smart detached house signifies a new start – the boys' mother has recently died – and Ronnie is doing his best to move on, to give his boys another chance of happiness.

In a field adjoining the estate, the ethereal Damian builds a den out of removal boxes where his vivid young imagination may flourish. It shakes as trains hurtle past. Damian and Anthony start at All Saints, their bright and friendly new school: at one point the children spell out 'Welcome to our school, Damian Cunningham' with multicoloured magnetic letters on a white board. Damian rattles off a list of saints to his new teacher. Anthony warns him not to be conspicuous, or he won't fit in.

In a shop after school, Anthony informs the shopkeeper with just *the right amount of pathos that his mother is dead. He doesn't have to pay for the sweets.*

At a neighbourhood-watch gathering, a community policeman (Pearce Quigley) tells the Cunninghams that there is no community to speak of as yet and warns them that, living in a new house and with Christmas approaching, they will probably be burgled. They meet their neighbours, including three deadly serious Latter-day Saints in immaculate suits who say that if you give your possessions away, they can't be stolen. After eliciting the sympathy of a neighbour by telling him 'our mam's dead', Damian and Anthony gorge themselves on mint-chocolate biscuits.

An aerial shot shows Damian, used to sharing with Anthony rather than having a room to himself, padding around the house. Anthony sends him on his way, so he looks in on his sleeping dad, who is hugging the two pillows he's lined up under the duvet, and gets in bed with him.

Damian is alone in his den when St Clare of Assisi pops up out of nowhere, a halo hovering just above her head, and lights a spliff. A spiritual kid with an encyclopaedic knowledge of saints, Damian is surprised to see her, but accepting. As he listens intently, she tells him that 'You can do what you like up there, son.' He asks if she has come across a St Maureen, 'who hasn't been there long'.

As another train speeds past, Damian's den is crushed by a big bag stuffed full of cash. Worried that he may be imagining the money, he immediately shows it to Anthony. As they lug the bag back to the house, Anthony says they can't tell their dad for tax reasons – the government will take most of it away.

The brothers count the cash out – there is just under a quarter of a million pounds. Anthony shows a select group of friends part of the money, gives them a few twenty-pound notes and tells them to keep quiet about it. They give themselves some spending money. Damian decides the rest should go to the poor.

Damian frees pigeons on a hillside and sees St Francis of Assisi (Enzo Cilenti). He tells Damian: 'You could just help the poor.' Later, Damian hands a Big Issue *vendor money and then invites her – and her friends – to Pizza Hut, where he spends £168. Anthony, like most other pre-teens, is materialistic. He is already a consumer. As such, he is disappointed by Damian's philanthropy and thinks they'd be better off investing in real estate.*

Later, as Damian is stuffing money through the letterbox of the Latter-day Saints because he feels sorry for them – they have no white goods – St Nicholas (Harry Kirkham) appears to help him. Damian is thrilled to see him and asks him if he's come across a St Maureen who used to work on the make-up counter at Selfridges.

A festive advert shows Leslie Phillips (as himself) with a buxom beauty (Jo Hicks) announcing that it's twelve days till the euro is introduced and the pound is no longer legal tender.

At school, Anthony uses some of the money to bribe other pupils into being his bodyguards and considers investing in real estate. He appears at the school entrance with his posse, standing tall and wearing dark sunglasses. They walk, Reservoir Dogs*-style, down the school corridor.*

Anthony meets an estate agent, who reluctantly shows him around a loft apartment. He does deals – for Subbuteo figures – with fellow pupils in the school toilets.

Damian returns to his den to find the Martyrs of Uganda working the ground. One was beheaded and has bloody hands. They help him rebuild his den. One tells him that, where he comes from, people have to spend a tenth of their daily income on water. Water is so expensive, they cannot afford to wash their hands; Damian could build a well for as little as £100. He thinks it's a great idea.

Leaving his den, Damian finds himself alone. He notices a man (Christopher Fulford) watching him. Wearing a black jacket and black beanie hat, he is clearly a baddie. He is smiling, but in a menacing way. He tells Damian he's looking for money, and the boy asks if he's poor; he has, he says, got tons of money.

Anthony is suspicious. He gives the baddie a jar of coins.

The Latter-day Saints cycle up the cul-de-sac, their bikes laden with bags and boxes: they have clearly been shopping with the cash.

Damian knocks on Anthony's door; he is on his computer, looking at a lingerie website. Anthony, approaching adolescence, is excited, while Damian, still a boy, asks what nipples are for.

At a school assembly, the children learn about the impending euro. Dorothy (Daisy Donovan), a visiting charity worker, introduces a talking bin. It asks for the pupils' unwanted sterling, which will help provide water for the poor in Africa. Damian gives the bin a thick roll of notes, which turns out to be a thousand pounds.

In the school toilets, one of Anthony's friends tells them about a train robbery in which unwanted, used sterling was thrown out at every slow bend.

Damian storms out: he tells Anthony they have to give the money back. Anthony says: 'It isn't the money's fault it got stolen.' Damian, crestfallen, says: 'I thought it was from God.'

Damian's teacher (Toby Walton) hauls the brothers into his office. Ronnie has been called. Anthony says he stole the money from the Latter-day Saints. He bursts into tears: 'Our mam's dead.'

Outside the school, Ronnie gives them a team talk: 'Your mother would not want you to stand around crying. Or to steal things. She wants you to get on with your lives and do the best you can. Make her proud, son.'

Dorothy apologises to Ronnie; she didn't mean to cause any trouble. She says at least they gave the money to a good cause; he must be doing a good job.

Ronnie apologises to the Latter-day Saints for Anthony's behaviour. The community policeman asks them why they had so much money in the house. Standing next to a row of pristine white shirts, they tell him about the cash donation stuffed through their letter-box, which they thought was in answer to their prayers.

As Damian is putting money in envelopes for various charities, St Peter (Alun Armstrong) appears. Damian tells him 'the money is robbed' and wants to know if he can 'still do good with it'.

Anthony and Damian try to put the money in the bank but are too young. Anthony suggests they spend it. They buy mobile phones and continue to argue about what to do with the remaining money.

They arrive home to find Dorothy enthusiastically cooking them dinner; Ronnie has offered to mend the talking bin. They watch Who Wants to Be a Millionaire?

At school, a teacher (Frank Cottrell Boyce) is helping Damian express his lines as he pushes a model donkey along the stage: they are rehearsing for the Nativity play. Damian meets St Joseph (Nasser Memarzia) backstage, who gives him an acting tip. Ronnie brings Dorothy to the play. Anthony is carrying the money around with him but has to leave it backstage when he joins the play.

The baddie turns up, looking for the money. Damian escapes, taking the donkey with him. He sits at the front of the top deck of the bus, next to the donkey, his hood up. He lets himself into his old, empty terraced house, leaving the donkey outside. Hiding *in the loft, he is terrified when he hears someone come in. When his dad pokes his head through the trap door, Damian's relief is palpable. Father and son hold each other tight.*

Downstairs, Damian and Anthony show their dad the money, hidden inside straw sacks that were strapped to the donkey. Dumbfounded, he says they have to hand it in. He changes his mind when they arrive home and find it ransacked: now that Christmas has been stolen, he vows to keep the money.

Ronnie, Damian, Anthony and Dorothy – who has come to see if Damian is okay – look at the money piled on the kitchen table. When his dad goes to see Damian in his room, he tells the boy that no one is looking down on them, that his mother is dead and he will never see her again.

The baddie emerges from the trapdoor to the loft and instructs Damian to change the money into euros; he will pick it up tomorrow.

The next day, Dorothy teams up with Damian and Ronnie with Anthony. They have split the money and are to either change it into euros or spend it.

They return to the house with some euros and countless bags of shopping. They drink champagne and paste some cash to the bedroom wall.

In the middle of the night, the doorbell rings. Outside the door and snaking right down the road is a long queue of people begging for money for their respective charities.

Damian drags the bag with the remaining money to the railway track and sets it on fire. Meanwhile, the baddie gets in through the back door, sees the money pasted to the bedroom wall and is discovered by the community policeman.

Damian jumps out of the way of a train and, when it is gone, sees his mum (Jane Hogarth) on the other side of the track. Damian tells her that 'the money just makes everything worse'. She says to him: 'You are not to worry about me . . . Anthony has got a good heart, he just doesn't know where it is. He's going to need you . . . If you have faith in people, that makes them stronger . . .' He asks if she's really a saint and, smiling, she tells him: 'My miracle was you.'

Anthony turns up at the train track to find his brother and gets a glimpse of his mum. He is close to tears.

The next morning, Dorothy, Ronnie and Anthony – but not Damian – admit they've kept some money back and throw it on the table. All four crawl into Damian's den, a passing train makes it shudder and, rocket-like, it takes off into space. The family arrive in an African village and celebrate their water supply. Damian is happy, bright-eyed and soaked in water.

* * *

AMY RAPHAEL: *Not many directors follow a violent zombie flick with a warm family drama. As Manohla Dargis wrote in her review of* Millions *in the* New York Times: *'Mr Boyle is the sort of creative type in whom the milk of human kindness often seems to curdle rather than flow.'*

DANNY BOYLE: *(laughs)* Well, given my form until that point, I wasn't exactly the sort of director to be automatically associated with a family film! I was interested in the project because Frank Cottrell Boyce is a great scriptwriter. I thought the script and film of 24 *Hour Party People* was dazzling.

So I was excited when producer Graham Broadbent sent me the script for *Millions*, even though it was obvious that just about every director in the country had already been sent it. I was never top of the list and when I went to meet Frank and Graham, I got a pretty strong idea that they thought it was a joke I'd even turned up. They looked exhausted. They'd been everywhere to try and get it made, and no one was interested. I thought the script was beautiful. I could relate to the story; it felt very personal. Frank is a progressive Catholic, but was brought up like me in a very religious home.

We talked about making it as a musical, which, in a way, I regret not doing. We just didn't have the chutzpah. The truth is that we probably wouldn't have been allowed to make it as a musical; we wouldn't have been given the funding. But I still think the script was good enough to have worked as a musical. The storytelling had a freedom, a light touch and was about ordinary life. I love the fact that it was never arch. Frank is so bright – way brighter than me – but he's not one of those guys who's interested in showing off about it. He lets everyone access it through him, but in an entirely graceful and selfless way.

Did you discuss several ways of making Millions?

We also discussed making it as a period film; it felt as though it could be set in the same era as *Whistle Down the Wind*, which was made in the early 1960s. But, in the end, we decided to place it in the world no one deals with: today's lower-middle-class housing estates. We are only ever interested in crisis in *EastEnders* or in the 'evil poor'. But Britain is full of housing estates populated by decent people who are trying to make better lives for their kids, making them feel loved, trying to keep their lawns neat. We wanted the film to celebrate the sort of suburban estate that is usually sneered at.

Yet it's not quite the usual suburban estate: the Mormons are slightly out of place.

We had Scandinavian Mormons in one of the houses, and while we were filming some real American Mormons came round. They were proselytising on the estate. We'd seen them at the airport in Salt Lake City when we were filming *A Life Less Ordinary*; they were like the Third Reich with all these blond children running around. Frank's writing of those scenes is so witty. He trained on *Coronation Street*, which was a brilliant place to learn how to write dialogue. He'd sit in these writers' meetings and someone would come in asking for twenty-three seconds of dialogue about slippers. Frank can literally write about anything as a result.

The film is propelled by Anthony's mission to change the bag of money into euros. Did it feel like Britain was going to join the euro at the time?

I can't remember. I think that storyline came out of me saying it was inevitable that we'd join the euro. Of course, I was wrong.

What else did you bring to the script?

I had two big inputs. The first relates back to an extraordinary story I'd heard when working in Northern Ireland, but which I'd never figured out how to use in a film. No one who lived on the Falls Road could work out how the army knew so much about what was going on in their lives. Eventually, they found all these sponges soaked in urine in one of the attics and worked it out. The army would raid a narrow, back-to-back street and block it at both ends. Around 150 men would go into the houses and, when the raid was over, ten men would be secretly left behind in the attics. A week later they'd come back, raid the same street and, in the chaos, secretly collect the men. While they were in the attics, they ate food they'd brought with them, pee into sponges, etc. They were completely self-contained. So we used that idea in *Millions* with the bank robbery. They jump the train and, in an apparently unsuccessful raid, leave one man behind to carry out the real robbery later. The same idea is used in Spike Lee's *Inside Man*, during the credits of which I first heard A. R. Rahman's 'Chaiya Chaiya'.

The other input is one of my proudest moments. Frank was reluctant to write the scene with the boys' mum at the end. He's the most pliable guy and it was the most obvious missing link, but he wouldn't write it. I kept nagging him, but he wouldn't budge. Finally, I got this letter, which I opened in my garden. It was the scene with the mum. I cried and cried. Damian is talking to his mum about saints and miracles. She says: 'Don't you know my miracle was you?' It's genius writing.

Cottrell Boyce's script is brought to life by Alex Etel, who is a triumph as Damian. Was it an easy film to cast?

Gail Stevens was pivotal again. It was easy to find Jimmy Nesbitt.

Lewis McGibbon and Alex Etel as Anthony and Damian.

I loved working with Daisy Donovan, a piece of left-field casting that really worked. We got Leslie Phillips on board by telling him there'd be a beautiful girl to act alongside him. He was absolutely still interested in beautiful girls, so he was happy. We had a great supporting cast: Chris Fulford was very scary as the horrible guy jumping into Damian's bedroom from the attic. Someone hiding up in the roof was always one of my nightmares when I was a kid. Pearce Quigley is very funny as the community cop, one of those discoveries that the casting director makes sure you come across.

But finding the kids is what makes the film. Alex and Lewis McGibbon were fantastic. I met Alex the other week on the London to Manchester train; he looks exactly the same but is now six foot tall. He's drop-dead gorgeous and cheeky as anything.

How many kids did you audition?

Hundreds. We had a local casting director in Manchester helping us, Beverley Keogh. You get a little snapshot of modern Britain because few of the lads she brought in lived with their real dads. There are stepfathers, grandfathers, uncles, but a shocking amount of absent dads. These families are held together by women. Both Alex and Lewis had these great tough mothers. Lewis has the less showy part, but he has great comic timing; he just knows how to deliver lines. You'd never recognise him now. Total young man hanging out as a student.

Did you have a Kelly Macdonald moment with Alex?

I did; as soon as I saw him I knew he was Damian. I put him on a tape with some other boys, showed everybody and asked them to pick a boy. No one picked Alex. It was weird. I just knew it had to be Alex. I'd have done anything to get him in the film. There was another kid who was much more solid, reliable and conventional. Had we used him, I'm sure *Millions* would have ended up on television. When casting for a feature film, you've got to pick someone like Alex and take a risk. It was the same with Kelly in *Trainspotting*: we had to go with the risky person who has something, even if you're not quite sure what it is. It's not obvious; it's a mystery you're going to reveal over the course of the film.

Alex had never acted before, but he was so unique. The way he delivered lines was extraordinary. Completely off the beat; there was no way you could tell him how to say a line. You just had to shut up and let him do them. Frank and I used to stare at each other in wonder as the lads performed.

Unlike many child actors, Etel and McGibbon don't appear to be performing for camera and are instead naturalistic.

Kids feel vulnerable for obvious reasons, as do adult actors. You've got to try and set up a community feeling with both cast and crew. I have to give credit to Davey Johnson, who runs a youth theatre in Manchester and who was Alex's and Lewis's drama coach. We played good cop, bad cop: I was the good cop, and he was very strict. He was brilliant with the kids, gave them a really hard time and pushed them when necessary. But it's also about the way you set up the film. You tell the crew that everything has to be done for the kids. You can't allow the kids to be intimidated at any time; if they're intimidated, they're not relaxed. It helps that Jimmy Nesbitt and Daisy Donovan were delightful with them. Jimmy was very famous, which Alex and Lewis loved. Daisy was very funny, very warm, practising mumhood.

You mention the crew having to go easy on the kids; did you also have to step back and relinquish a degree of control?

I had to be really flexible and work out the best ways of getting a performance out of them. I only lost my temper once. The two lads were in one room and I was in another. They had to eventually come through to the room I was in, and they were mucking around. They'd been eating tons of mint-chocolate biscuits and were wired on the chocolate. I lost it and set out from that room to sort them out once and for all. Fortunately, Davey stopped me before I got to them, whispering, 'Remember, you're the good cop, okay?'

I assume all these experiences proved useful when you came to shoot Slumdog Millionaire: *as you learned from* The Beach *how not to film in India, so you picked up vital experience of working with kids from* Millions.

Millions is definitely the precursor to *Slumdog* both in terms of tone and story: in both films there's a brother who loves money and another who doesn't care for it, and there's a warmth in the story-telling. There are very tough laws in place to protect child actors in the UK, from time restrictions on the hours they can legally work to night shoots to on-set tutors. Learning to accommodate all those factors also really helped when it came to *Slumdog*. You can do what you like in India, but we took the UK rules with us; we didn't want to be seen as exploiting the kids in any way. I also learned about using child-actor doubles: with the time restrictions, you've got to be so crafty about the way you work. So I learned to call the child actors in the morning and the doubles in the afternoon.

You said that Millions *is a semi-autobiographical film. Did you relate directly to Damian?*

Yes, it certainly felt like that when we were making the film. I really loved it for that; I felt connected. I absolutely understood why he was talking to the saints. Frank and I both saw the film as being about a kid who is loyal to his imagination. When it came out, people thought it was a religious film, but the religious element was in fact almost anecdotal, with Frank having fun with the saints and so on. We were both brought up in good Catholic homes, and so I obviously recognised all the references. As I said, Frank is a progressive Catholic and not a slavish traditionalist in any sense.

Do you think it matters whether Damian is really seeing the saints or just thinks he's seeing them? The point is surely that they exist for him?

I don't mind how people interpret it. Because directors are all con-trol freaks, we imagine we can control the public life of a film. But it's impossible. An audience's response can hurt as well as delight, and I've had to learn that. Damian has a copy of *The Six O'Clock Saints*, which we put in because it's so beloved by Scorsese. John Woo was another practising Catholic who was meant to join the priesthood. There are a few of them around . . .

Was your parents' house full of saints?

It was! They were everywhere. I went to a Catholic school which had two patron saints, St John Bosco and St Dominic Savio. As soon as I became a teenager, I started to rebel and dismissed all the saints as crap and irrelevant. I should point out that our house wasn't like *Oranges Are Not the Only Fruit*. It wasn't austere at all. It was warm and welcoming but very religious. I remember my mum taking in a tramp once. The stink! I came home from school and she was giving him sandwiches. I was six or seven, and there he was in the kitchen. She didn't do it to impress anyone; she genuinely believed you should help people.

Damian is still at the age where all his touchstones are religious . . .

. . . but they won't be when he hits adolescence. They'll be music, girls, cars. But for now he's immersed in what his mum has taught him about saints. I don't have a brother, but I can relate to Damian in all sorts of ways; it's not just the saints – I don't really understand money either. Frank's like that as well. We found it very funny dealing with Anthony and his friends, all of whom are very monetary. These are kids who understand money and its power over people. They know how to work it around the school, they sell Subbuteo in the toilets, they 'employ' their mates as bodyguards.

Were you wary of making a film with a strong religious element in it?

No. I dedicated the film to my mum and dad. My mum died long ago but she would have loved *Millions*. She taught me about kindness and seeing the best in people. It doesn't make you weak, which is what survivalists would have you think. I believe it makes you stronger – as does Frank. I try as much as possible to bring it into my life and my work. It's not really a film about Catholicism or religion, not really. As I say, Damian's heroes will soon be music, Picasso, cinema, girls. He won't be driven by money like his brother; he'll still be interested in imagination and he'll turn into someone creative.

Did you enjoy working on a film that has an unashamedly big heart?

I think my other films have big hearts too. Frank's death in *28 Days Later* is emotional and proof of heart in the film. Renton's visit to Tommy as he's dying is an indication of the big heart in *Trainspotting*. Spud's got a big heart.

Is this your most life-affirming film?

Again, I like to think they all are. *Trainspotting* is really life-affirming.

It is in parts; I mean, from start to finish Millions *is warm and gentle.*

(*laughs*) Okay, I take your point.

Yet it avoids being overly sentimental and saccharine.

Frank and I tried to avoid it being either of those things. I think I could have done the film better. One of the reasons for doing films from different genres is that you do test yourself and you do learn. I didn't want to direct an exact replica of *Millions*, but as a result of making it I certainly understood more of a certain type of storytelling. So you make mistakes but – hopefully – you learn from them.

But you like this film on the whole?

Very much so. I'm very fond of it. I love the ending, in which they land on a beach with parachutes. I told Mark Tildesley that I wanted it to be like a NASA event, and he found all these red and white parachutes. We had great fun doing all that. We did the African scenes at the end on a beach in Formby, just north of Liverpool. The pick-ups for *Lawrence of Arabia* were done there. It's gorgeous. The sun shone for us and we had a glorious day out.

Did you really sell Millions *to Pathé as a combination of* Trainspotting *and* Amélie?

(*laughs*) I did! That's outrageous. I'm not sure how I got away with that. We wanted the light tone of *Amélie* and the surprising vivacity of *Trainspotting*. Anthony turns up to school wearing shades and escorted by bodyguards and The Clash are playing . . .

Given the bag of money, it's not Shallow Grave *for kids?*

Other people said that. I could only agree.

Despite the action often being motivated by money or drugs, all your films have a moral DNA running through them. How does it manifest itself in Millions?

You hear stories about people who make liberal message films and then behave towards their cast and crew like a plantation owner. If the means of production are completely at odds with the story you're telling, then it's hypocritical. Why shouldn't you try to treat everyone decently if you espouse these values? *Shallow Grave* has more moral standing than any number of liberal films which I am not going to name.

So I don't inject morality into my films; I let it emerge either in a positive or reflective way. It seeps into the film-making. For example, we behaved well in Mumbai but not in Thailand. I think you can feel the difference between *Slumdog* and *The Beach*. It's not only about the director's energy being discernible; you can tell when a director feels happy or at home on the film. It comes from everybody who passes through the film, either in front of or behind the camera, affecting it in an incremental way. And that's what film is: tiny increments that somehow add up to a whole.

Your attitude partly relates back to how you were brought up by your mother, partly to your Joint Stock experience and partly to what you've learned as a director both on stage and screen.

It's politics too. I've only ever been shocked a few times by people's behaviour and I usually don't tolerate it on set. You can also see it written on people's faces sometimes: they are waiting for you to shout at them. That's not my style.

Is Millions *a political film?*

Indirectly. My son and youngest daughter went to a primary school in Bethnal Green called Bangabandhu, which was very much like the school featured in *Millions*. It's one of those new schools that was set up and paid for by a Labour government keen to invest in education. It's full of really good teachers. Your vision of education comes from your own history of it. It persists for too long. Education is different now and some of it is wonderful. I loved doing the scenes at the school. Labour are criticised a lot, but the money they've put into schools and hospitals is phenomenal. Had the Tories stayed in power there would be virtually no National Health Service by now. The two-tier system would have been unbelievable.

The school we used in *Millions* was right in the middle of an estate in Widnes. The kids were great; they play most of the supporting parts themselves.

The film offers a valid celebration of new schools, but I was also thinking of the scene in which the children are asked to give their spare cash to charity – and the finale, which sees a celebration of water in a makeshift African village. You obviously wanted to make a point about the ever-increasing lack of water in the world, and particularly in developing countries – there's even a Water Aid leaflet in the DVD. But how do you make a humanitarian statement without it being clumsy or overly political?

For the final scene we had good actors, a beautiful location and a lovely soundtrack. It's a generous film and you go with that spirit of generosity. It's not a cynical film. It doesn't have that . . . I was about to say ugliness, but it's not quite what I mean. It doesn't have that sarcasm, that coolness. Everyone's on the front foot all the time, trying to make the best of whatever it is they've been handed.

The final shot of Damian, soaked with water, eyes bright, suggests the future might just be okay.

It's certainly a positive ending. The lad can take a close-up.

Were you pleased with the ending – from the transition scene in which they all admit they've kept some money behind to the den turning into a space rocket and the arrival on the beach?

Frank has such a light touch. We always had this idea of them tunnelling in the den for the lift-off. That's what everyone does as a kid in their den – pretends it's a space rocket. Because Frank was able to give those scenes a lightness of touch, I loved working on them. They were a joy to do, especially because I'm a violent film-maker.

Danny Boyle: visual, violent and . . . nostalgic.

Well . . . I'd say visceral. I had to work with a different set of rules on *Millions*. It's a really good exercise. I had to find my visual pleasure in something slightly more generous. It's not about bodily dysfunction or attack or regression. It's about huge flags blowing gently in the wind on the edge of the housing estate, giving the film an epic feel.

There is a wide open, epic feel to Millions, *but it's also intimate and even, at times, scary. I'm thinking particularly of the* Don't Look Now *scene with Damian and the donkey on the bus and then Damian alone in his old house. Was it hard to explain to Alex how to show fear when he returns to the attic in the old house and thinks the baddie has come after him?*

I could tell he'd never been hit. And he was brought up with so much love that he didn't understand fear. Or loss. His grandparents were quite young. I don't think he does now really, at fourteen, fifteen. I can see it in his face; he doesn't look as though he knows pain yet.

How did you teach him?

I've worked with kids on difficult scenes before. I did a film in Northern Ireland called *The Hen House* about these two brothers who find a kid their own age who's been brought up as a chicken. There was a scene where one of the brothers cried in the attic; he was very upset by the kid in the hen house. The lad couldn't cry. He couldn't access it at all. So we shot it by asking him to bury his head in his hands and then we added sound. He was about ten, so I asked a couple of girls on the set to do it, but they couldn't cry either. Then I asked my production manager, Jenny McAulfield, and, like many adults, she could access feelings of sadness very easily. So she cried and cried – for herself, I guess, but on behalf of the boy in the film.

The darkest moments in Millions *are generated by Damian coming to terms with his mother's death. He is excited by his new house, but also not used to having his own room. There's a lovely aerial shot of him padding around the house because he doesn't want to sleep alone.*

I remember moving to a new house as a kid; it was unbelievably exciting. You get your own room! But, as you say, Damian was a bit lonely and ended up going to see his brother and then his dad. John Rundle, the grip, built the rig above the set so we could get that aerial shot. It was amazingly complicated. Genius. I loved doing that shot. That was meant to be his mum looking down on him.

It's heartbreaking when his dad pulls the covers back to reveal that he's been hugging pillows.

It was Jimmy's great idea to recreate a body with pillows.

Damian also goes into his brother's room and finds him checking out a lingerie website. Anthony is excited, while Damian is slightly puzzled; it's basically the difference between the boy who's started masturbating and the one who hasn't.

The writing is so true that you barely have to direct the kids. The fact that Frank has seven children of all different ages is so apparent.

Despite the grief hovering over the family, Millions *is bathed in a positive light; it sometimes looks as though it was shot in Italy and not the wet north-west of England.*

Although we set the film in a netherworld between Liverpool and Manchester, most of it is shot in Liverpool, where we were based. But we wanted it to *look* Mediterranean and to have endless blue skies. We filmed in the summer, but it was set at Christmas. The kids didn't want to wear their winter coats on hot summer days – a nightmare for costume designer Susannah Buxton and her team. But it had to have those blue skies. So often the grey sky kills British films; it flattens everything. You are in competition with the Americans and they are obsessed with light – it's why the industry was set up in California. It makes a difference to your spirit as you watch the film. We tried to use Mediterranean colours all the time: the brothers cycling through the rapeseed field at the start, the bright school uniform.

Anthony and Damian in the rapeseed field.

Kids in coats in the summer sun is one type of challenge, but how did you get around not being able to film near railway tracks or use real money?

The railways are a nightmare to film on in Britain. They won't let you anywhere near them if the scene is anything less than picturesque. I remember filming an *Inspector Morse* in which there was a suicide on the railway line, and it was impossible to get near a track. You have to cheat and use private railway lines. Alex's den wasn't anywhere near the railway track, we just edited to make it look as though it was. We had this wonderful tiny guy Paul Lowe, a stuntman from Liverpool, whom we used in the scene where Alex burns the money and the train goes by. I learned why so many people are killed by trains: when they go past at speed there's a vacuum in front of the train that pulls you in. It's very scary. He was on a rope to stop him being pulled in.

I know all about fake money from *Shallow Grave*. These days laser printing is so phenomenally perfect that it's really worrying for the authorities. You're not even allowed to print fake money just on one side, but we did. It's illegal unless you put joke faces on it. You're not allowed to burn money either. But you find a way round it.

Tracey Seaward, our brilliant line producer, who normally works with Stephen Frears, took it all in her extraordinary stride and swept all objections to filming tricky scenes aside. Her dad, a Hull City fanatic, and mine were the same age, and it was lovely to have them visit the set.

Mark Tildesley had some interesting concepts to deal with as production designer, from the Nativity donkey to the talking bin and the saints' halos.

Mark and his team made this fantastic donkey; the look is borrowed from these beautiful picture books by Lisbeth Zweger. And Susannah, whom I worked with on *Mr Wroe's Virgins*, did the most beautiful job combining the El Greco world of the saints and the ordinary world of Widnes – another of my mini-directors. I got the idea of the talking bin from Disneyland, Paris. I took my kids quite soon after it opened and there was this talking bin. It was static and it talked back to the kids. No one could work out how it was done, including me. I eventually saw a guy in the distance who was talking to the kids through a hidden mic. It was mesmerising! The halos were done by Clear, a small CG house that helped us on *28 Days Later* and who have since gone bust. The halos have a slight delay on them which makes them both real and funny. Without the delay they were completely unconvincing. I first met Adam Gascoyne at Clear; he did all the CG on *Slumdog*.

How did you film the boys' new house being built from scratch?

I love animation, so it was great fun. Parts of it are stop-frame animation. We got the actors to green screen onto models of the house. Other parts we did on a real set. I wanted it to be Tim Burtonesque; he's a genius at that stuff.

Was it easy to persuade Cottrell Boyce to play a drama teacher at the school?

He was very nervous about doing it but he's actually a very good actor.

At what point did Cottrell Boyce start turning Millions *into a book?*

He wrote it as we were making the film. When we failed to make *Millions* as a musical, I suggested he write it as a novel. He won the Carnegie Medal and has now got a very successful career as a children's writer.

You added St Peter to the film after Cottrell Boyce put him in the book.

He sent me the book drafts, and I said, 'The bloody St Peter scene, why isn't that in the film?' We got Alun Armstrong to come in, and he learned the scene in half a day. It's a lovely little scene. Anthony [Dod Mantle] wasn't available do the reshoots, so Brian Tufano did this scene. Brian also shot some pick-ups at the railway-track scene at the end. I hadn't taken him to Thailand to do *The Beach*, but I rang him to ask if he'd mind shooting the pick-ups, and he was very gracious in agreeing to do them. In fact, Anthony is never available for reshoots! I've used different cinematographers for each of the reshoots and pick-ups. Grading is a wonderful thing. It plays an increasingly important role in movies now, equalising out the different effects of wildly variable weather in Britain, the different cinematographers or chasing the look in a particular sequence.

You worked with John Murphy again on the score.

It's a beautiful score. There's some pop music in it – The Clash, Nirvana, Muse – but most of the soundtrack is score. I used to find it very hard to use classical score; my instinct has always been to trust pop music. John taught me to trust score as well; he showed me how expressive it can be. We were inspired – and intimidated – by Danny Elfman's *Edward Scissorhands* score.

I could feel myself beginning to learn how to trust the score more on *Sunshine* and *Slumdog*. Pop music can't quite give you that invisible leadership you need sometimes to lead the audience somewhere emotionally.

A score also lends a film continuity.

It makes a film feel shorter. It's weird. A score that repeats themes lulls you into thinking it's shorter. The composer basically writes a theme, a counter-theme and one other theme. And then spreads them out through the film.

Were you disappointed when Millions *wasn't released at Christmas, given its appeal to family audiences?*

There was a lack of confidence about our ability to compete with the three big American movies released at that time. I remember thinking they'd be awful, and they were. They were shockingly bad Christmas movies, even by bad-Christmas-movie standards. Way worse than they normally are. It would have been a nicer time to release it, but it came out around Easter in the end.

Were you disappointed when it didn't do much box office?

It did nothing when it opened, yet it's had an afterlife as a family DVD in America. In fact, it got a few Christian storytelling awards in the US! Sadly, in Britain we've been bullied by the American market and the only family films we really watch are American. It's a real shame. I can't understand why we don't make better family films here. They're not expensive. I guess the world role model is the American suburban estate in *E.T.*

At least your DVDs always offer plenty of extra material.

I'm very conscious of offering value for money with the DVDs. I always try to do the director's commentary. You know DVD extras are going to be flogged shamelessly, so you might as well try to make them as good value as you can.

Is it reassuring to know that painfully cut scenes at least have a home?

You know they're going to be seen. You'd think it would have led to more cutting and running time being reduced on films, but of course it hasn't. Films have instead got longer and longer. Some wonderful scenes were cut from *Millions*, including one in which Daisy buys Alex a new coat in Manchester. You sense how much she wants a kid herself. It's just beautiful. I don't even know why I cut it! I think we were trying to concentrate on Jimmy's story at that point.

There's often extra space – especially on Blu-ray – where you can run someone else's short film. On *Millions* there's a short called *Badgered* about nuclear disarmament. It's a fantastic little film by Sharon Colman, who's now got a job at Dreamworks. That was the first time we did it. On the *Slumdog* Blu-ray disc there's a brilliant forty-minute film, *Manjha*, by this Indian film-maker called Rahi Anil Barve about a boy flying kites. A very savage film put together with no money, but brilliantly made and beautifully shot.

What do you feel when you watch Millions *again?*

The only film of mine I've seen recently is *Sunshine*. I saw about forty minutes of it over my daughter's shoulder when she and her mates were watching it for some reason. It's the only extended period of one of my films that I've watched. I genuinely thought it was quite good, and I don't always think that.

When you and Cottrell Boyce do the DVD commentary on Millions, *there are a few points at which you both sound as though you're about to cry.*

We were probably thinking about the opening weekend . . . I can't remember Frank and I being close to tears. Having said that, there are scenes in *Millions* that definitely make me cry. I'm sure I'm not supposed to cry at my own films but I do. I cried the first time I read the scene with Alex and his mum by the railway, and I cry now if I even so much as catch a glimpse of it.

Sunshine (2007)

A black screen with a pinprick of light cuts to the exterior of a spaceship, Icarus II. *A voice-over by Capa (Cillian Murphy), a nuclear physicist, informs us that the sun is dying and mankind faces extinction. Seven years previously,* Icarus I *was sent to restart the sun, but the mission was lost before it reached the star. Sixteen months ago, Capa and seven others left earth, frozen in a solar winter, with a nuclear payload the same mass as Manhattan island. Their mission is to reignite the sun.*

Searle (Cliff Curtis) asks the voice of Icarus (Chipo Chung) to refilter the Observation Room portal. His face is flooded with orange light: he is staring at the fiery yellow-orange mass of the sun. Icarus tells him that at 4 per cent brightness the sun would damage his retinas irreversibly; instead, he can observe 3.1 per cent for no longer than thirty seconds. The resulting brightness renders him breathless.

A lingering shot of a colourful photo of the crew of Icarus I *wearing Christmas hats as they float inside their spaceship. In the social area, Kaneda (Hiroyuki Sanada), the captain of* Icarus II, *sits down to eat alongside Capa, Searle, Corazon (Michelle Yeoh), Cassie (Rose Byrne), Trey (Benedict Wong), Mace (Chris Evans) and Harvey (Troy Garity).*

Searle describes his experience in the Observation Room. Kaneda says the solar-wind reading is higher than expected. Harvey adds that, within twenty-four hours, it's probable they may no longer be able to communicate with earth. The others fall silent. Kaneda says they are flying into the dead zone seven days earlier than expected; they should send a final message home.

Capa sends one to his parents. Emotional, he manages to make a joke about saving mankind. He deletes and records two more messages. Finally, he reminds them that it takes eight minutes for light to travel from the sun to earth: if their mission is successful, the sky will brighten up eight minutes later.

Corazon finds Kaneda in a startlingly bright Observation Room. She asks Icarus to filter out the sun.

Capa and Mace are fighting in the Communication Centre; Capa took an hour sending his message back and now the solar wind is too strong for Mace to send his. Harvey and Trey break them up. Searle, the psychology officer, talks to Mace and sends him to the Earth Room for two hours. Here, on a floor-to-ceiling screen, he watches girls dodging waves by the seafront. A moment later, he is in the middle of a misty forest.

Mace finds Capa in the oxygen garden; both apologise as Corazon, the biologist, looks on bemused.

Kaneda is alone in his room, watching old video footage from the crew of Icarus I. Pinbacker (Mark Strong) describes minor damage from an asteroid storm to Icarus I. As he describes its beauty, he has the same stoned look as Searle had earlier in the Observation Room.

Back in the Observation Room, the entire crew sit on the bench and Kaneda shows them a relatively small black disc travelling slowly across the front of the sun. It is Mercury.

Later, Harvey tells the others he heard a transmission: it's the distress signal from Icarus I. The crew conclude that they may still be alive. They realise they are going to pass within 10–15,000 miles of Icarus I. Mace is adamant they continue on their planned trajectory to the dying sun; Searle suggests they may have a higher chance of success if they have two payloads.

Kaneda says Capa, as the physicist, must decide. He says: 'Shit.' He is uncomfortable; it's not precise science, but a guess. Kaneda pushes him. Capa says this is their last chance, and two payloads are better than one.

Capa has a nightmare about falling into the sun. Cassie is in his room when he wakes up. She thinks he made the right decision.

An alarm sounds: Trey says he screwed up. He had to override Icarus to set the new co-ordinates for Icarus II's deviation to find Icarus I and . . . Capa jumps in: 'You didn't reset the shields to the new angle.'

Kaneda and Capa climb into heavy, reflective space suits: they need to inspect the damage to the exterior of the ship caused by Trey failing to reset the shields. Sweating profusely, they float outside Icarus II. They are pinpricks on the vast ship. The ship creaks; a turtle hanging near Cassie's computer suddenly starts to shake. Corazon says: 'It just sounds like she's tearing apart.'

Kaneda completes some of the work successfully before things start to go wrong. Mace orders them to continue with the procedure; Kaneda agrees. There's a fire in the oxygen garden. Corazon tries, unsuccessfully, to get in. Icarus says the fire will burn for six hours; there is a high chance of damage to life-support systems.

Meanwhile, Kaneda tells Capa to go back inside the ship. Kaneda continues working on the shield. He floats above the ship and stares into the sun. Searle, his face burned after being in the Observation Room, asks Kaneda what he can see. Kaneda falls into the sun. Trey is distraught.

Later, Trey is sedated and identified as a suicide risk. Harvey, as second in command, is now captain of Icarus II. The shields are now intact, as is the payload; the oxygen garden is destroyed. They no longer have enough oxygen to get them to the payload delivery point; they have to get onto Icarus I.

Corazon tells Cassie and Mace that there is enough oxygen on Icarus II to get four of the crew to the payload delivery point.

Cassie tells Capa that she knows they will die in space like the crew of Icarus I. She asks if he's scared. He thinks the new star being born will be beautiful, so he's not.

They are closing in on Icarus I. Once they are locked on, Capa, Mace, Searle and Harvey prepare to go aboard. They are not sure what they will find. As they investigate the dark ship, colourful images of the crew – from the Christmas photo seen earlier – flash onto the screen for barely a second.

Icarus I is dark, the air thick with dust. The four male crew are jumpy; there is a sense of menace on the ship. Harvey tells Corazon that the oxygen garden is overgrown; Corazon's face glows with hope.

Searle wipes the dust off the Christmas photo we saw earlier. There is food, he says, but no bodies. Mace, who is checking out the computers, watches a message from Pinbacker, commander of

Icarus I, *saying they have abandoned their mission: 'It is not our place to challenge God.'*

Capa reveals that the payload is fully operational. Mace says that without the central Icarus system – which has been sabotaged – the ship can't fly.

Searle finds the crew – or, rather, their burned cadavers resembling Giacometti statues – in the Observation Room. He says: 'Ashes to ashes, stardust to stardust.' Icarus I *moves suddenly: it has floated free of* Icarus II. *Cassie instructs them to return to the airlock immediately. She says they won't be able to join* Icarus I *again.*

There are two spacesuits on Icarus I: *as the payload operator, Capa takes one. Mace and Harvey argue about who will take the remaining one. Harvey, losing control, orders Capa to remove his suit. Mace and Harvey agree to fire Capa out of* Icarus I *in a suit and travel with him – without suits.*

Mace and Harvey cover themselves in padding. Searle points out that someone has to remain on board to operate the seal manually; he volunteers himself.

Capa, Mace and Harvey are propelled out of the airlock towards Icarus II. *Capa and Mace make it; Harvey floats away, frozen to death.*

Searle joins the cadavers in the Observation Room of Icarus I. *He is obliterated by the light.*

Capa, Mace, Corazon and Cassie discover deleted files on the Icarus II *computer. They discuss the possibility of Trey deleting the files, then realise that if they kill him, they will have enough oxygen to make the delivery point. Mace offers to kill him. He suggests a vote. Corazon and Capa are with him. Cassie, crying, stalls, then refuses to give her vote. When Mace overrides her, she says: 'Make it easy for him. Find a kindness.'*

Mace chooses a knife – we see that two are already missing – but Trey has disappeared from his bed. His body is slumped in a pool of blood in the Earth Room, his wrists slashed.

Icarus tells Capa that all the crew are dying. He doesn't mind, so long as they can live long enough to deliver the payload. She says they won't: she insists there isn't enough oxygen for the four crew members still alive on Icarus II. *Capa – slowly, quietly – asks where the fourth crew member is and is directed to the Observation Room. In the overwhelming light, he sees the silhouette of a figure,* who asks, 'Are you an angel? Has the time come?'

Capa recognises the burned figure as Pinbacker. Pinbacker, wielding one of the knives seen missing earlier, slashes off Capa's communication device. Capa locks himself in the inner airlock chamber.

As Corazon sees a green shoot poking out of the earth in her decimated oxygen garden, Pinbacker stabs her to death.

The lighting system shuts down. The ship is enveloped in darkness.

Communicating through a mic in a spacesuit, Capa tells Mace that Pinbacker is trying to stop the mission. The mainframe is suffering coolant failure. Mace jumps in the freezing coolant liquid and mends the malfunctioning panels. The lights come back on.

Cassie, who has been waiting in the dark, grabs a knife and tries to kill Pinbacker. Failing, she runs away from him.

Mace heaves himself out of the coolant and, before he dies of hypothermia, tells Capa to get the ship out of orbit by separating the payload.

Capa puts on a spacesuit, ties himself to the airlock wall and blasts the exterior door open: the whole ship decompresses. In amongst the debris, Corazon's body flies past.

Capa, weighed down by the spacesuit, walks slowly through the ship. He separates the payload on the flight deck. He heads for the payload bay itself: he has to fire himself from the main ship to reach it.

Discarding his suit, Capa stands on the vast surface of the bomb as it hurtles towards the sun. Capa asks Cassie, who is almost dead, if Pinbacker is there. She whispers, 'Behind you.'

Pinbacker wrestles with Capa, telling him that God told him to take them all to Heaven. Cassie slices his arm with the knife and slows him down. Capa leaves Cassie and Pinbacker falling down the side of the bomb.

Capa initiates detonation. He watches as the bomb starts to spark around him. The side of the payload melts away to reveal the sun. He closes his eyes in ecstasy then, opening them again, raises a hand to touch the sun.

Eight minutes later, back on earth, a mother and her two kids play on a dark, snow-covered landscape. It is Capa's sister, who watches her brother's message on a hologram photo. Moments later, the sun reappears, as if from behind a cloud.

Danny Boyle on the set of *Sunshine*.

* * *

AMY RAPHAEL: *Science-fiction films are notoriously tough to make: Arthur C. Clarke spent a long time co-writing* 2001: A Space Odyssey, *only for director Stanley Kubrick to announce later that the film was 'essentially a non-verbal experience'. What was your own experience of directing a sci-fi film?*

DANNY BOYLE: It's almost impossible to make science-fiction movies. *Sunshine* drove me mad. It was insane. I've never made anything like it; doing *Slumdog* in Mumbai was a breeze compared to trying to direct a science-fiction movie for $20 million. We were shooting in similar conditions to astronauts, sealed inside this studio for months on end. We arrived before the sun rose and left after it set. It was eternal night.

So it was the hardest film you've ever directed?

By a long, long way. It made me realise why virtually no one goes back to make a second sci-fi movie unless they have to because they're locked into a franchise. The real sci-fi films – not the fantasy ones like *Star Wars* that are populated by monsters – are a small discipline. It's quite a narrow corridor and you're always bumping into the other people who've been there. You can feel these directors' footprints trampling all over every decision you make. You realise very quickly that someone has been there before and made that same decision or a slightly different one. Or you're trying to avoid them and you can't.

Part of the problem is Kubrick – 2001 *was surely the best science-fiction film ever made – and there are limited storylines out there in space.*

So many sci-fi films are based on a signal or involve signals from elsewhere. You can't have a film in space unless there's a signal from somewhere that makes the crew consider changing course. It's such a cliché, but your story isn't going to work without it. Because we haven't been out in space en masse yet we can't actually write any authentic stories about it. The only stories are fantastical.

The fact that the stories are fantastical only seems to enhance our collective romance for space – from the 'Are we alone?' question to genealogy and space as the final frontier.

There's a fantastic book by Andrew Smith called *Moondust: In Search of the Men Who Fell to Earth*. There is some wonderful stuff about the tin can in which Neil Armstrong et al. go to the moon. You could literally punch a screwdriver through it because it was made out of aluminium to keep the weight down. They were very confident about getting them on the moon but really had no idea if they could get them back. The astronauts were prepared to take that risk, as, I think, most human beings would. It's *such* a frontier moment. I'd certainly go, even if there was no guarantee I'd get back.

Do you remember watching the moon landing as a kid? Did you want to be an astronaut?

I remember listening to it, but only vaguely. The limit of my world was wanting to be a train driver. Being an astronaut seemed out of our league.

Let's go right back to the genesis of Sunshine. *You were considering directing* Alien: Resurrection *years before Alex Garland ever wrote the script for* Sunshine, *so you obviously had sci-fi on your mind.*

I'd been very close to doing *Alien 4*, but had decided the CGI was beyond me. When I read *Sunshine* I wondered if I was ready to take the technology on. I decided that I was in fact ready to embrace CG – but only because we decided to approach it in a very particular way; we didn't want to rely on it. We wanted to make everything as real as possible for the actors because I hated the idea of them being in a green room.

It was a big factor in deciding to do *Sunshine*. I finally felt confident about the technical side. It isn't my forte, it doesn't come to me naturally, but you just learn to do it, you gradually pick it up. I'm always blown away when I go and watch the brilliant guys do it: *Avatar* is astonishing.

So Garland came to you with this very simple idea.

We met in a pub in Tottenham Court Road on either Christmas Eve or New Year's Eve in 2004. He gave me a ninety-page script. The concept was quite small. All the ideas were there but it was . . . I don't know how to describe it. For instance, at the end of the film the two remaining guys were playing chess as they were flying into the sun. There were gargantuan images. I became insanely obsessed with trying somehow to capture a bit of . . . scale isn't the right word . . . to somehow capture a *moment* of it. I didn't want to avoid this incredible setting by staying in a psychological world, which is what Alex's original script did. I wanted to make it into an event.

Alex is very much an atheist. I'm more agnostic really. He believes we would be able to restart our lives with science. He believes that science is our god. For me it was always a bit more complicated.

In what sense?

I'd just read J. G. Farrell's novel *The Siege of Krishnapur*. Farrell was a British novelist of Irish descent who drowned on a fishing trip shortly after winning the Booker Prize for that book. It gets closer to India and Britain than anything I've ever read. It's a proper novel; it's reflective in a way a film just can't be. This is what it has to say about religion: 'God has nothing to do with this sort of thing [designer of the world and all that's in it or not] . . . God is a movement of the heart, of the spirit, of conscience . . . of every generous impulse, virtue and moral thought.' But the guy who says it, the moralist, the man of modern culture, does not have the final say. Which is maybe why it's a great book.

So you brought a spiritual dimension to what otherwise might have been a godless film?

(*laughs*) I'm not sure Alex was very keen on that spiritual dimension. But once you start to consider the scale and the forces involved . . .

It's quite hard to stick rigidly to atheism when considering space.

Just the fact that we're so *small* . . . Alex's argument is, of course, completely dispassionate. It's just a question of scale. You're so small, but you can't be overawed by these forces. These forces are bigger than us but they represent exactly what we are. It's all part of a scientific universe. That argument is fine and I agree with it on a rational level, but part of what's interesting about us is that we don't only work on a rational level. There's this other side of us that science will never extinguish. Science may think it will make us more rational, but it won't.

So we started to work on the film without realising just how long it would take to make. The smallest element of it was the actors. Normally, I try to make the actors the most important part of a film, but on a science-fiction film they can't be. The actors were involved in the process for a limited amount of time compared to the amount of time we spent on it: it took a year to set it up, almost a year to film and then over a year in post-production.

We shot *Sunshine* at 3 Mills Studios, which is a tiny place to try and make such an ambitious film, but that was always the idea. I wanted to use a relatively small crew to make as big a film as possible.

Was your caveat always that you'd direct Sunshine *so long as it wasn't a Hollywood film? If Andrew Macdonald hadn't raised the money to do it here, would you have made it in Hollywood?*

When Alex originally came to me, he thought it had to be made in Hollywood. I thought we should make it here using our own film-making methods; in the end, Alex and Andrew agreed. It helped that 28 Days Later had been a big hit. Had it been like *Millions* and only had very limited success, I wouldn't have been able to make *Sunshine* on my terms. I would have been forced to use a big star who would have saved the world – and himself – at the end. We wanted to try and make a more intelligent version of that story.

And a more philosophical version?

I guess so. But we had a monster in it. I didn't really pull off Pinbacker in the way I should have done. I was arrogant. When we did 28 Days Later, I said, 'Leave the zombies to me.' I said the same with Pinbacker. I wanted to make him spectral, a part of the crew's minds; you'd never be sure if he was there or not. Ironically, I probably should have engaged in the new technology and made him truly spectral.

You should have created Pinbacker using CG?

Or based him on Mark Strong's performance but using CG. I tried to make him real and then, to try and take him out of the temporal again, we developed this amazing double-lens technique, which was fantastic. You shouldn't have known if he was there or not. He's this argument that's going on inside the crew's minds. He also needs to kill because he's operating as the monster. There are some wonderful scenes with Pinbacker, such as the one in which Cillian Murphy talks to the computer and is told there's another person on board.

That was a memorably chilling moment when I first watched Sunshine *at the cinema, although it was less effective when I saw it more recently on a television screen.*

Even though an increasing percentage of films are seen on television or DVD, *Sunshine* was uncompromisingly shot for the big screen. There was no point in doing it without shooting it for the big screen. In fact, we originally wanted to shoot it on 65mm! Ken Branagh did it with *Hamlet*, so that kind of ambition is possible.

The truth is that 65mm is no good unless you then watch the film on a 65mm print. You have these incredibly cumbersome cameras, and the film can only be processed in Paris or Los Angeles. And when people see it reduced to a 35mm print – because those are the only projectors in existence in this country – they can't tell the difference.

However, we shot some footage on 65mm and I saw it projected on a proper projector. It was awesome. It's like IMAX. You can not only make it much bigger and project it on any scale, but it's infinitely more detailed. Everything is more intense.

I guess you'd have felt like you were actually falling into the sun.

Can you imagine? Everything you experience visually, apart from IMAX, is called 2K resolution, and till that changes there's no point in filming on 65mm – other than for your own private pleasure.

That would be vanity film-making at its most extreme.

Sheer indulgence. So we tried to compensate for that by making it as visceral and electrifying as possible. To make watching the film about a physical and mental experience.

And if you'd shot it on digital, would you have lost the detail and the lush visuals?

It's very hard to tell. Until James Cameron's use of 3D in *Avatar*, we hadn't really progressed in the digital world.

Given that you usually direct on instinct, did you enjoy such an intense period of preparation, being locked inside a studio as though on a spacecraft?

I loved making *Sunshine*, but it did drive me mad. The major lesson I learned was not to spend so long in the edit. Chris Gill and I spent *way* too long editing *Sunshine*. We lost the feel of the film after a while. So when it came to *Slumdog* I told producer Christian Colson that we didn't need any more time in the edit. He was surprised; normally directors cling onto their work as long as possible.

I would now advise anyone working with CG – including myself – to shut down the cutting room for six months. Go off and make another film, go on holiday, write a book, anything. The CG is so incremental, the progress so tiny that you become locked into it. It's not particularly useful for you as director. You end up continuing to edit the film. The truth is that you don't improve it.

You literally couldn't leave it alone?

All this money is being spent on CG, so the film should be left alone. I believe the big directors, who really know what they're doing with CG, put up black slate saying 'image missing' if the studio insists on test screenings. It's a completely dissatisfying experience for a test audience – and also for the director watching it in the cutting room. I realised in retrospect that Chris Gill and I changed a lot of the film to make it work without the CG (*laughs*). It's in our nature; you're used to working in a make-do environment. Having said that, I was an experienced film-maker and I should have known to leave it alone.

Did you sit in with the CG guys at the Moving Picture Company? What sort of conversations did you have with them?

The guys at MPC did an extraordinary job: they made *Sunshine* look as though it cost $100 million. Michael Elson and Tom Wood ran MPC at the time. It was their ambition that actually allowed us to develop the film properly. Had they done it by the book, we wouldn't have been able to afford it. Anyway, we'd go and see what MPC were doing. We'd have conversations based on books and images. Here's a wonderful example of what we discussed: Mercury is always described as a massive planet, but I found this photo of it and it's tiny. It's surprising and gives you a much better sense of scale when it comes to the enormity of the sun. Having said that, it's almost impossible to get a real sense of scale. And, as I keep saying, the CG guys should really be left alone.

Tom Wood is one of those mini-directors who add unquantifiable quality to the film. Your job is just to keep them on your film and not let anyone poach them when they hear how good they are.

You usually avoid storyboards, but you can't make a sci-fi film without them.

Usually I find them restrictive but on *Sunshine* they were essential. And Brendan Houghton is a great guy to work with. We'd have discussions based on photographs, concepts, ideas. And then we'd start working with the storyboards. We had to storyboard both with traditional and digital artists, from the exterior of the space-ship onwards.

Did Mark Tildesley, the production designer, create the spaceship and then take it to MPC?

Yes. The spaceship was easy, in one sense, because there had to be a shield to protect equipment from radiation. The real shields up there in space are made of gold foil, but we couldn't work with it: the crew had to land on it and, because of gravity in our world, you knew it would just be shredded all the time by the crew, the actors. So we made the shield solid, which is bollocks. In the infinite light-ness and nothingness of space, it would be as thin a piece of gold foil as you could imagine. We've got some footage of a NASA satel-lite that uses gold foil. It's just beautiful. The only way we could have used it was by giving the whole thing over to CG, and we just didn't have the budget.

How did you come up with the design for the spacesuits, other than the obvious influence of Kenny's funnel-shaped hood in South Park?

(*laughs*) Again, so much of it was dictated by thinking about the sun – its power and its danger – in a practical way. Space helmets

Icarus II, the spaceship.

are interesting: the real ones are completely wrong for drama. They reflect everything. They don't let any light in at all simply because the light in space is so dangerous. But in a film you need to be able to see the actor. We couldn't have clear helmets because that would be ridiculous. When you look at Brian De Palma's *Mission to Mars*, the helmets look like goldfish bowls – although no more foolish than *South Park*.

So we made these helmets with slits across the eyes. I had this big idea that I wanted a camera inside the helmet to suggest a sense of the claustrophobia – and also so you could see who each crew member was. The overall look of the spacesuits was down to Suttirat Larlarb, who did the costume design on the film. She talked about them being like Japanese warrior suits, and her magical drawings are gems. In fact, designing the spacesuits was not unlike designing a car. There were so many people involved in making them that what we finally got in the end became very, very compromised. We also had to rely on available materials as we didn't have the budget to develop our own. Which is why you spend a year in prep.

Were the spacesuits prohibitively expensive? How many did you make?

We had two, and a third which was spare. They were a nightmare. Insanely heavy. You get into the suit and the top is locked. A stunt-woman fainted in one and I saw them trying to pull her out. These big men, full of panic, couldn't pull her out: although she wasn't big, her dead weight defeated them. They thought she was going to die. There was a design fault in the suit which meant she needed to release something inside to let herself out. They couldn't get the fucking thing off. It was terrifying. Another time Hiroyuki Sanada, who played Captain Kaneda, had to be taken to hospital. He'd been in a suit all day and even he couldn't take it after a while.

So when you see the sweat and spit it's totally genuine?

All that is real. It's brutal in there. Talk to anyone who's made a space film and they'll tell you how tough it is, because you're creating super-unnatural conditions all the time. The NASA and Russian spacesuits are phenomenally heavy. In space it doesn't really matter – everything is weightless – but filming in London for a year can be pretty cruel.

Especially when you want the action to look real. When Kaneda and Capa mend the exterior of the ship, how tough was it to make it look like they were working in zero gravity?

One of the biggest decisions we had to make was to have a centrifugal spaceship in which there is artificial gravity. You have to offer an explanation either visually – by showing something rotating – or in some other way to explain why there is fake gravity on board. It can look wrong *so* easily. Watch a sci-fi film done badly and you will immediately dismiss it as unconvincing. It's brutal. It kills you doing it because you can't afford to overlook the slightest detail.

There's also a great fakeness about sci-fi films. If you watch real footage of what happens in space, the astronauts appear to be moving too quickly. There's no gravity and, equally, there's no resistance of any kind. They move at the same speed as you and me. The tradition in film has always been to slow that movement down to alert the viewer to the fact that the film is set in space. It dates back to the slow-motion movement in *2001: A Space Odyssey*.

To get back to your question: yes, it was bloody tough! Richard Conway, an amazing special-effects supervisor whom I worked with on *28 Days Later* and *Millions*, flew Kaneda and Capa. It's so complicated . . . You have wires to fly the actors but they only work for a short period of time. You also need this pivoting dolly, a 'parallelogram' that attaches to their stomach so they can appear to float; you then exclude the mechanism in the shots or you remove it in CG. It just goes on and on . . . It makes me shudder to think about it. We spent *so* long inside that spacecraft trying to do those movements when the shield starts turning back to face the sun and its rays eventually kill Kaneda.

Did the minutes leading up to Kaneda's death – in what you've called his King Lear moment – take a week to film?

Everything took for ever. Hiroyuki was brilliant because, at the time, he didn't speak much English. He does now; we've stayed in touch and he's a friend. Those Japanese actors are very tough. They love a challenge – and he got one in that suit.

Top: Danny Boyle with Hiroyuki Saneda. Bottom: Michelle Yeoh in the oxygen garden.

Talk me through the cast. Was Michelle Yeoh the starting point?

She was actually. I wanted it to be an American–Asian mission. Even then it was obvious the next people on the moon would be Chinese, or the Indians might beat them to it. That's where it's shifting. It's all in Andrew Smith's book: western economies can no longer pay for space exploration, so it felt like it should be a joint mission taking place on behalf of all mankind. It would feel as though it was set in the future, and yet the film would still be able to open in America.

We got Michelle, who's Malaysian Chinese; Benny Wong, who's from Salford; Wong Kar Wai suggested I look out for Hiroyuki in

The Twilight Samurai – it's a brilliant film. I rang Hiroyuki up and we talked on the phone despite the fact that his English was almost as non-existent as my Japanese. We somehow trusted each other. He's a fantastic actor and a lovely man. We started to build the cast like that. Normally Gail Stevens casts my films but this time she did it in tandem with Donna Isaacson, the casting director at Fox. Donna introduced me to Chris Evans and Troy Garity, who's Jane Fonda's son but hides from all that famous-mom stuff. Gail brought in the enigmatic, beautiful Rose Byrne.

Cliff Curtis, who's a Maori New Zealander, had this really weird but wonderful idea of wanting to play Searle as an Indian officer. Normally I'd go with an idea like that, but it's an example why, in these films, it's not the individual actors who are important. Although you live everything through them, they have to fit in with the very specific confines of the film. So he did it as an American.

They were all quality actors: the scene where they agree to kill one of their own is one of my favourite scenes in all the films. Weird, disturbing, emotional, brilliantly written and performed.

All the actors had to be plausible scientists. Or, if not scientific, then a mechanic, an engineer, a Scotty. We couldn't cast randomly. It's like those moments in Bond movies where a beautiful woman steps forward and declares herself a nuclear physicist: no, you're not!

The crew of Icarus II *are still extraordinarily good-looking.*

I suppose they are. I think you buy into them in the end because of their skill.

Cillian Murphy had to be American because his native Ireland doesn't have an active space programme.

Not yet! Cillian has a wonderful otherness about him. He had an extraordinary time with Professor Brian Cox, the young particle physicist from Manchester. When you mention a physicist you hardly expect this slightly feminine, rather beautiful-looking man to emerge. He'd been a backing musician in D:Ream while studying physics at Manchester University; he played on their Labour Party anthem 'Things Can Only Get Better'.

So Cillian and Brian went off to the particle accelerator at

CERN, in Geneva, Switzerland. We all had lectures from these amazing concept guys who imagine the future. Clare St John – post-production supervisor extraordinaire on *The Beach*, *28 Days Later* and *Sunshine*, who runs the films behind the scenes and who is the very definition of an unsung hero – introduced us to Richard Seymour, a friend of hers. He had invented the cordless kettle and was working for Ford on concept cars and motorbikes.

Did you enjoy the research?

It was great fun. It was also part of popping the bubble of the cast – and my own too – and putting ourselves in this new, extreme bubble. It has to be airtight and sealed before it can go off into space. We had to be a team!

The actors experienced zero gravity, went scuba-diving, crash-landed a plane on a simulator . . .

I experienced some of those things too, including the simulator at Heathrow. The stunt guy, Julian Spencer, was fantastic. The cast went up in an acrobatic plane to experience zero gravity. I later went on the proper 747 in Florida for press and publicity, which was amazing. It's like a soft cell in a mental asylum because it's all padded and you can't see anything outside. But the acrobatic plane was incredible too: they put a glove in front of you and at a certain point it just floats in the air. You can feel all your internal organs lift.

Did you try, unsuccessfully, to get onto an oil rig?

We couldn't get onto one, but somehow Andrew got us onto a nuclear submarine in Faslane. It was fantastic to get an idea of confined living conditions. The silos where the missiles are held run virtually the length of the sub. They have a running track between the silos where they exercise. They obviously won't let you in the back of the ship where the nuclear reactor is.

Did all the cast do everything?

They did the acrobatic plane, they did deep-sea diving. One of them got in a panic and didn't do the diving. Such experiences do affect

The team in the communication centre.

the acting in a tiny way: they make it plausible or just this side of convincing. The acting has to be plausible otherwise the cynics – including me when I watch other directors' sci-fi films – will just pull it apart. You have to keep just on the other side of the convincing line. You use any techniques you can to keep them there. It felt as though the actors were on a crash course, trying to pick up as much information as possible to make themselves feel plausible.

Did making the cast live together before the shoot help them to bond and begin to feel like a team?

I think so. We kept them in a student dormitory in Mile End for two weeks. Living together was weird for some of them, I think. Hiroyuki didn't speak much English, but he played a mean guitar. Music is, of course, the universal language. Everybody knows a Beatles song!

There are all those interesting stories about Ridley Scott not speaking to any of the actors in the first *Alien*. Any commands came through loudspeakers or assistant directors. So the cast felt isolated from central command. I've no idea if it's true – I doubt it is – but it's certainly a good guess at how he got the results he got. The acting is fantastic. It's great in the second *Alien* – directed by another genius, James Cameron – but in the first one it's on a special level across the whole cast.

When the cast were locked away in their student dorm, did you feel as though you'd chosen them wisely?

I never think otherwise. You can't look back.

Did you have religious discussions with any of the actors?

Mostly they were talked at by experts: science is intimidating. We only discussed religion at length with Cillian. His Irish background definitely helped him to understand what was going on at the end.

What was going on at the end?

(*laughs*) Indeed. What *was* going on?

Does Capa see God just before he dies?

We define God in such limited ways. It's something beyond ourselves.

Capa (Cillian Murphy) sees infinity.

And that's what Capa sees: infinity and possibility after being so temporal. You hope when you die that's what you'll see. It resolves all the contradictions we are saddled with. That's what the ending was for me anyway. Not a narrow idea of God. It's not an Old Testament thing. For a nuclear physicist to die in the firestorm of a nuclear-energy force is a scientific nirvana, even if it's nothing else.

If you're going to take it seriously – and it was a very serious film – you have to poeticise the ending. Otherwise, no matter what the technology, you can't go a quarter of the way towards believing you could fly into the sun and still be alive. So either you are poeticising it or you're not. That was always my argument: we're now in poetic territory. It's about feelings beyond knowledge that we have now. It has to be about that.

I can't imagine watching the ending without having a strong emotional response.

For me it was always very emotional. I wanted Capa to cry at the end, but Cillian had a stinking cold that day. Every time we stopped filming his eyes were streaming, but every time he got in front of those lights it was like being inside a hairdryer. His tears just dried up.

Did shooting Sunshine *make you feel more spiritual?*

We tried using that great Coldplay track 'Fix You' at the end, when the sun bursts through and Capa holds up his hand. It felt too cheesy in the end, but boy did it make me cry. Oh my God. We used score instead but we probably should have gone cheesy. You're not meant to like these songs, but they work. When 'Fix You' was at the end of *Sunshine*, I certainly felt like I'd been moved somewhere else.

Meanwhile, Cillian Murphy was suffering in front of all those disco lights.

Alwin Kuchler, the cinematographer, and his gaffer Reuben built the most amazing rig: a scaffolding structure on wheels, the full height and width of the studio, packed with hundreds of lights. Mark Tildesley came up with this idea of using disco coins con-

Icarus II enters the heart of the sun.

nected by string which could twirl. He created a curtain of these coins as big as the side of a large building. We wanted to see the effect of infinite light on the actors' faces, so Mark effectively created an infinite, abstract curtain which Alwin then blasted these huge lights onto. At the end of the film a disco wall is travelling towards Cillian that wouldn't look out of place at a huge U2 concert. The wall of fire is then ultimately created by CG. But the effect of the lights was Alwin's – the cinematographer as God!

We also did a series of these tests with Richard Conway on 65mm film. We photographed different fire elements he created for us, which was wonderful. Abstract, liquid, changing – it was beautiful. And very like the surface of the sun when you look at it. It's very hard to know what to trust in the images we have – the images of the sun have all been computer-enhanced and colour-field corrected. So you've no idea what is really there, and it would, of course, be impossible for the human eye to take it in as it would obliterate your vision straight away.

If Murphy was in a green room rather than in front of U2's disco lights, would it have been the wrong side of the plausibility line?

For me it would have been, yes, no matter how great an actor Cillian is. I think I can tell how genuine an actor is when he's screaming, 'Oh my God, look at that dragon! There's a huge dragon coming straight at me!' Actors will always compensate – they will overact. Or do nothing and look bored. Whereas if you create something that's truly fearful for them to look at, something that frightens them in their gut, they'll have an appropriate response. We talked endlessly about ways of giving the actors real things to look at.

The Earth Room is pretty impressive, with its images of the forest and the sea. Is Chris Evans looking at real images?

Instead of putting Chris in front of a green screen, we actually took him to a forest (*laughs*). I could see people thinking, 'This isn't the way to do it.' I think it makes all the difference. The image of the rough sea is based on an old photograph taken in Scarborough of these three girls chasing the waves on a stormy day. We recreated it in the Docklands in east London. Richard Conway got hold of the bottom of a transport container that weighed tons and tons and suspended it on a crane above the Thames. He then dropped it into the water in front of a wall we'd created. The water came up and over these stunt girls, and Chris was standing there too. So, yes, we did it for real.

Richard set up the Technicolor photo of the crew of *Icarus I* waving at the camera in weightless conditions. It was an act of genius: he built eight very narrow racing-bicycle seats on stands that swivelled and put them in a hole; the crew sat on the bikes in the hole and looked up to the camera. The illusion is that they're weightless. Brilliant.

Keeping it real even extended to immersing Chris Evans in a tank full of freezing water. Weren't you tempted to use warmer water and to add frozen CG breath?

The CG budget was spoken for, and anyway Chris wouldn't have started to shiver involuntarily. Once he started, he couldn't stop. He felt the cold, the pain – which was great. I thought he was very good in that scene.

When you shoot scenes like that, I don't suppose you can have much regard for the actor who is freezing almost to death?

You have to keep going. They thank you for it afterwards. The kind of actors you hire usually want to see it through anyway. There's no room for being sentimental on a film like *Sunshine*.

Given that you were shooting as much as possible without CGI but were still hugely reliant on it, did you feel as though you were making two films?

In some ways I did, yes. But we brought the two worlds closer together than usual. For example, Alwin building the lighting rig for the final scenes gave the CG people a head start. He worked closely with the CG guys, who were upstairs at 3 Mills while we were shooting, so they could watch and advise us as we were going along. You have to make it as much like a family as you can. There's a danger with CG in that it tends to get a bit separated and left till later. But the more you include the CG guys early on, the better it is in the end. CG is still not a world I fully understand, but sometimes these guys show you what they can do – and it's incredible! I remember the first time I saw the wave of fire coming up the shield to kill the Japanese captain, and I was gobsmacked. Yet, however impressive CG may be, it's still a weird, dislocating process.

Kuchler has shot some interesting films, including Lynne Ramsay's Ratcatcher *and Stephen Frears's TV film* The Deal. *What did he bring to* Sunshine?

Many things. Alwin did a wonderful job of lighting *Sunshine*. He has an excellent working relationship with Mark Tildesley; their understanding of each other is so complex it's as though they are married. They built all the lights into the spaceship itself, which helped enormously in terms of time. It was always a pre-lit set.

Alwin and I are both very puritanical. We were very careful about how much anamorphic flare we used on *Sunshine*, and then I went to see *Star Trek* and every single shot was covered in it! I sent him a text afterwards joking about it. He's a great cameraman. He did the pick-ups on *28 Days Later*; he embraced digital even though he knew very little about it. He's a very good combination of classical and modern, steeped in 35mm but open to new ideas too.

Sunshine *is shot in a more classical way than your previous films.*

Space films have to be shot classically. Alwin was perfect: he's got the necessary restraint and control. You can't grab stuff. Which is why doing *Slumdog* after *Sunshine* was such a contrast: it's a complete other world because Mumbai is teeming with life. You've just got to try and grab a bit of it. Whereas in space you have to create every single moment and do it plausibly. In the most hostile environment for mankind.

Did you worry about style over substance in Sunshine, *as you had in previous films?*

Not in *Sunshine*. Absolutely not. Anyway, style is an interesting way to get at substance. On *Sunshine* the style is classical. Long shots, deliberately controlled pace. As controlled as the ambient temperature in the ship.

You refer to 'deliberately controlled pace': the start of the film is unusually slow for a Danny Boyle film.

There was no other way of doing it. If you do big gestures in space, people don't believe them. If you do anything too fast, they don't believe that either. It's the only genre in which the tempo *has* to be slow. The shots have to be long, so that people can self-select inside them. Which is why it's so critical you get everything right. Everybody is scanning your spaceship to check it looks right.

Well, I thought the spaceship looked very convincing. And at least you didn't cut back to shots of earth to supposedly heighten our emotional response.

I was adamant about that. And that there would be no shots of all the crew marching towards camera. Of course, when the poster came out, there they were marching towards the camera. The public gets what the public wants, or rather what someone thinks they want! I'll bet they use the photo of me outside the Taj Mahal for the cover of this book!

Let's talk about Garland's inspiration for Sunshine. *He has said that the initial idea came 'from an article projecting the future of mankind from a physics-based, atheist perspective'.*

That's the kind of stuff Alex loves. At first we thought no one had ever made a film about the sun. We were very excited because the sun is so important: it has to pulse just once and we'll all be

The interior of *Icarus II*.

finished. Then we found out about this Japanese film called *Solar Crisis*, which is about the same subject – trying to mend the sun. I still haven't seen it.

But you've seen most other sci-fi films; you and Garland are both huge fans. Unlike on 28 Days Later, *when he was the zombie-film expert and you were just dipping into the genre.*

And I think it's better if one of you isn't quite as keen. As you say, we are both crazy about sci-fi films. He's from the *Stars Wars* generation, while I'm older and not a big fan of the series. I've never been into that slightly more fantastical side of sci-fi. I'm hardcore sci-fi: the rules are as on earth. Except we defy them by going out into space.

And the 'hardcore sci-fi films' will orbit for ever around the Holy Trinity of Kubrick's 2001: A Space Odyssey *(1968)*, Tarkovsky's Solaris *(1972) and Ridley Scott's* Alien *(1979)?*

And it's so difficult to step out of their shadow, but everybody should keep trying.

I first saw *Solaris* at a film festival in Spain. I was there for either

Shallow Grave or *Trainspotting*. I got up early one morning and went out into the town, where there was a screening of this Russian film with Spanish subtitles. I don't speak much Spanish and I certainly don't speak Russian, but what turned out to be *Solaris* was *amazing*. When we came to do *Sunshine*, I read the original book, written by Stanisław Lem in 1961. It's interesting that an American in Europe and a Russian in Russia – Kubrick and Tarkovsky – were both tackling space before we even got up there.

Kubrick had more money than Tarkovsky and, more importantly, the time. He was working in his idiosyncratic way, using a small crew and painstakingly working through technical problems. He pretty much laid the groundwork for sci-fi films until CGI was introduced; the tricks he used were appropriated by subsequent sci-fi directors. It was wonderful to think of Tarkovsky at the other end of the scale having no money; what he did instead was to inhabit Lem's visionary book. He depicts space travel as this road trip through Moscow, for God's sake, and it's just dazzling!

Did you set out to create another definitive film? Did you want the Holy Trinity to become a quartet?

(*laughs*) Oh yeah, why don't I say that? No! Not at all! You just get hooked on a story and an idea; you become obsessive about it and you chase it and chase it. For good or bad. You lose sight of it in the end. When you come out the other side, people start talking about other movies in the genre. They use these to flatter or condemn your work. Or, sometimes, they accuse you of ripping off another director. You have to deal with it as part of that process.

So the film is defined by the media?

But you feel it on set too: you suddenly realise you're shooting a scene that's been done before by another director. It's what I mean when I say you can't help but stand in the footsteps of Kubrick et al.

Sometimes you openly acknowledge the influence of other films: in Sunshine, *Pinbacker's name is taken from Sgt Pinback in John Carpenter's Dark Star. Is that okay because it's a nod to what's gone before?*

Sure. It's fine. It's open. It's not attempting to copy; instead, you acknowledge all your sources and inspirations and you try not to forget where you've come from.

I bet you've even been asked about the 1968 Pink Floyd song 'Set the Controls for the Heart of the Sun'.

I have! I got a letter from this guy who worked for 20th Century Fox asking if I'd heard of that song. And other letters saying it should be on the soundtrack! I was even sent a compilation of Pink Floyd songs culminating in 'Set the Controls for the Heart of the Sun'. Using Pink Floyd would have been wrong in so many ways. *Sunshine* isn't that kind of film. It's a small-scale sci-fi movie made in east London. And it's *so* important to keep making such ambitious films on a relatively small budget – otherwise all these films will become the preserve of directors with huge budgets. Duncan Jones's *Moon* was made for a few million quid but has ambition. Kevin Macdonald has made a gladiator film – *The Eagle of the Ninth* – on a tight budget. These films shouldn't only be made by huge-budget directors. We've got to keep making lower-budget forays into everything.

Are you saying that British film-makers in particular should be ambitious?

Yes. You don't just make standard social-realist films, valuable as they might be. You should try and make every other kind of film possible. Otherwise we'll disappear very quickly. We've always got a crisis in the British film industry, but there wouldn't be one if we kept making films like *Sunshine* or *Moon*. Or Roman epic films. The kind of films where everyone laughs at your crappy budget. Fuck you! Let's try! It's *really* important to keep trying. I think film-makers should have *ludicrous* ambitions. To keep the sense of the impossible is really important.

It's not, of course, just about a director's ludicrous ambition. Bernie Bellew, who co-produced *Sunshine*, is yet another mini-director. His speciality is unravelling the schedule and budget so that they seem independent from one another. What he does is anathema to the bond people, who believe everything has to be quantified. Bernie somehow manages to give them – the money people – the impression that he is quantifying everything, while giving me another impression entirely. It's as though, through his love of movies, he's created some kind of magical software onto which can be programmed diminishing time and money alongside ever-increasing ambition – and out pops freedom and all your dreams.

As a producer, Bernie is supposed to represent the brick wall into which my blind optimism must run at some point, but he's the only person I've met who's more hopelessly optimistic than I am. The UK Film Council should hold masterclasses with him; young film-makers would get more in ten minutes from him than from hours listening to 'favourite' directors.

I like the idea of Bellew's dream machine . . . It's interesting, I think, that Sunshine *looks as though it could have been made in Hollywood – it certainly has that ambition, as you say – and yet it still* feels *like an indie film.*

Nobody goes to see movies because they cost only £5 million. Nobody ever turns up at the cinema and thinks, 'I'm going to see that because it cost a lot less than all these other ones.' Quite the reverse often, unfortunately. So you have to find clever ways of telling the story and of making films which can contend with all the big-budget films.

What was the most expensive element of making Sunshine? *I assume it was the CG?*

Actually, it wasn't, simply because of the extraordinary job done by MPC. They were also working on the Roland Emmerich film *10,000 BC*, the type of movie for which they are paid staggering amounts of money. For morale they try and take on a project like *Sunshine*, which is an aesthetic challenge and which allows them to not only chase staggering budgets from Hollywood, but also to chase the impossible. So, the most expensive element of *Sunshine*? I don't know how it would break down. Cast and crew weren't very expensive. We didn't pay ourselves a lot of money.

Did you dip into some of the profit from 28 Days Later?

I'm not quite sure how that works. I certainly used some of the goodwill from the success of *28 Days Later*. But it only lasts for one film (*laughs*).

So who made the decision to have Chipo Chung, as the voice of Icarus, on set every day? It would surely have been cheaper just to pre-record her voice rather than insist she play the scenes live with the rest of the cast?

I automatically make that kind of decision. Chipo is a fantastic actress. I felt that it was particularly important for Cillian to be able to play scenes with her one on one, so that they would pick up a rhythm and routine with one another, which they did. We didn't have to edit round it to make it work, which is what you'd normally have to do.

The oxygen gardens look fantastic, but I'm sure you're going to say that Mark Tildesley created them on a shoestring budget.

Tildesley! It's a great example of a mini-director at work. You say to Mark, 'We haven't got any money but we want this!' We drew pictures of how we wanted the gardens to look. Incredible research is being done about what we're going to be able to do fifty years hence, how we're going to be able to live in space . . . I discovered this amazing list of the things they're already doing: one of the

Rose Byrne as Cassie.

Shuttles includes pig sperm to inseminate pig ovaries in space. Then they bring it back to earth and see if there's any difference, if there are any abnormalities given that the process has taken place in weightless conditions. They are clearly thinking that in fifty years' time a human will be conceived in space.

We had a great time researching the gardens. The space guys we talked to said the idea everyone has about eating dried food in space was baloney. It's nothing to do with the food itself; it's to do with the psychology of the people: if you don't grow food you'll go insane. They try to keep the same pattern of meals and sleep in space because both are so deeply ingrained in us. We also discovered Robert McLeod, a German conceptual artist who created pods with grass growing inside them, and Mark got his permission to recreate the pods. So you look everywhere for ideas.

Weren't you tempted to put more action in the gardens?

At one point a sex scene was going to happen in one of the pods, but few films set in space have any romance or sex in them.

Why not?

It just doesn't work. What's going on is so awesome that you find interpersonal relationships a bit trivial.

Even though there's sexual tension between Capa and Cassie, it doesn't have to be acted upon?

The frisson is enough. Actually, I don't really know why sex in space doesn't work. I looked carefully at the history. Helen Mirren and another actor try it in the Peter Hyams film *2010*, and it just doesn't work. It's weird. There are all these rules attached to making sci-fi films. Presumably, someone will come along and break the rules brilliantly. You always wait for that moment.

So no sex in space but a terrific fire in the oxygen garden: how much of that was filmed and how much done later on CGI?

We couldn't set the actual garden on fire – it would have burned down the studio – so it had to be re-dressed as though it had burned down.

Fire in the oxygen garden.

How big was it? Like a section of Kew Gardens?

Yes. They went to Kew and the Eden Project. Michelle Yeoh went and worked at the Eden Project for days. That was her task. Again, it's that guy Richard Conway who creates and controls fire. We built a cubicle for Michelle and surrounded it with fire. We made it as real as we could for her. The fire was then supplemented with CG. If CG is based on realism, then it feels authentic. At least, that's the way it works for me.

It's amusing that, given the fact you couldn't afford to build a second space ship, Icarus I *is* Icarus II *covered in Cornish-pasty dust.*

I'd forgotten about the Cornish-pasty dust! That is really what we used! Cliff Curtis was very brave to film in all that dust. He gets blasted by it at one point, which really wasn't very pleasant.

And he has to sit on Icarus I *with the dead crew looking like Antony Gormley figures.*

They were amazing prosthetic figures made by one of those guys who are fixated by the skin texture and deathly pallor of cadavers, and who spend most of their time recreating the dead.

The prosthetics guys made a scarily lifelike dummy of Corazon too.

They did a body cast of Michelle, which was pretty convincing. It's weird for an actor to come in and see a dead version of herself. And even weirder to see a bunch of guys chucking the dummy in front of a camera. We were inspired by the great Australian sculptor Ron Mueck, who did *Dead Dad*. His stuff is just incredible.

Were you determined to make Sunshine *aesthetically dazzling, despite the relatively small budget? Who decided to contrast the blazing sun with the monochrome colours of the cabin and the crew's costume?*

Mark, Suttirat Larlarb, Alwin, Tom Wood, me: we did everything we could to make it dazzling. Everything had to contrast with the sun. One of the toughest jobs was designing the crew's T-shirts. It was so weird thinking about what they're going to wear. *Star Trek* the television series kept sticking in our minds. Suttirat put a huge amount of work into the design of the T-shirt and the badge, but it's crucial that you don't in fact notice them, that they don't stick out and somehow look wrong. What a job for a designer, creating something so that it's not noticed . . .

'We did everything we could to make it dazzling.'

Who designed the clackers the crew wear around their necks to communicate with one another?

That was Suttirat again. It was the early days of the iPod and it obviously had to be carried on a lanyard. It was close to the heart, so it monitored their biometrics at the same time.

Were the clackers functioning?

Of course! We had to make them slightly bigger than we wanted to in order to fit in a speaker as well as a light.

Space is eerily silent and so you added the sound of the spaceship creaking. Does sound weigh down the CGI too?

Sound gives CG weight, yes. Recreating space and actually having no sound would have been impossible; even the films that you think have no sound actually do. If there is no sound, you think something's gone badly wrong. So spaceships have a hum or drone. Even a visual film like *Sunshine* is only going to work for about five minutes without sound. The whole idea that film is

Searle (Cliff Curtis) in the
Observation Room.

visual is just nonsense. Cinema is about sound; it's about hearing dialogue between people or, if there's no dialogue, a whole universe of sounds.

'Without sound there is no light' is what I always say when I'm trying to persuade Glenn Freemantle to work for our relatively low budgets. He's one of the group of mini-directors who arrives last of all to create the sound.

When Capa is on his own at the end, bathed in sweat, there's no sound for a few moments, and the silence is very conspicuous.

Mapping out Capa's journey was great fun. Cillian was fantastic at the end of the film, but it was very tough for him. John Murphy added an amazing orchestral track which is proper big scoring. I think he had had that tune for a long time and was waiting for the right moment to use it.

Music is obviously important in all your films, but a bold score is so central to sci-fi films – probably because of Kubrick's inventive use of classical music in 2001.

Kubrick again! I decided to use both John Murphy and Underworld; it was really interesting putting them together. John was hardly able to come to England, so I worked with Underworld in London and then flew to LA to play their music to John. I ended up flying back and forth with all this music. I love that kind of process. It allows you to do so many different things. And I was *really* pleased with the music.

You say that mapping out Capa's journey was great fun, but were you happy with the finale of Sunshine*? With the emergence of Pinbacker the film moves into horror territory: did you want to mix up the genres, to make it genuinely frightening?*

That section was criticised because of the execution of Pinbacker. Not Mark Strong's performance, but the way I directed it. People thought it was a shift into something *too* much like a horror film. Whereas the first two-thirds of the film is actually procedural, hardcore sci-fi, with realistic deaths and issues. I love doing that. We did something similar in *28 Days Later*.

And in both films you've been criticised for a weaker third act.

I never know where the third act starts, but I didn't execute Pinbacker as well as I could have done. It's what I said earlier: I had too much arrogance from 28 *Days Later*; I thought monsters were no problem. 'I know how to do those!' If you start to think like that, then you're not pushing yourself enough. You must never assume you can do something with the minimum of effort, in an almost offhand way. You should always be at the point where you don't know what you're doing. It sounds facetious because obviously you *do* know what you're doing, but you really should be at the point where you're thinking: 'How the fuck do I make this film?'

What would you have done differently with Pinbacker?

I should have recorded Mark's performance throughout in motion-capture and then worked with it. I tried to control him through the 50–50 lens: you get two images of him and you can distort one. We went to laborious lengths doing that and it was fascinating to shoot, but not as effective as I'd have hoped.

You wanted Pinbacker to be genuinely frightening?

Yes. I love Alex's idea of a man burning himself. You can barely believe he's still alive. Pinbacker's philosophy about why he was stopping the crew from delivering the payload was pretty difficult to take on board: why, in some way, he felt that nature had to be allowed to run its course and destroy humankind.

We reshot the scene where Pinbacker grabs Capa on top of the bomb at the end. The bomb is so vast – the size of Manhattan – that you can't do human drama on it. We spent for ever fiddling with that scene.

So were you happy with the end?

I was. And not just Capa's demise, but the very final scene in which his sister and her kids watch the sky from a snow-covered field in Sydney. We didn't fly to Australia to shoot that one scene, of course; the Opera House was added on afterwards. After doing a test shoot on digital cameras in Victoria Park in east London,

Peter Rice from Fox secured more money for us to shoot the scene properly in Stockholm. It was the most reliable place to get snow in a park, near a city, at that time of year. Wow, it was cold. Alex Garland's partner Paloma Baeza played Capa's sister, and the kids were two of Andrew and Rachael's – they got together on *Trainspotting* and have now had five children together. It was very cold for the two kids. The only thing that stopped our feet from quite literally freezing were reindeer mats.

If you're asking specifically about Capa, though, I was sure about him giving up his life.

He is quite happy to die to save the human race?

Any physicist would be. To be able to touch this engine that drives the whole universe.

It's metaphysical but also very trippy.

Our physical capabilities are nowhere near what the mind can imagine, with or without stimulants.

Most frightening things happen in the dark, whereas the finale of Sunshine *takes place in the ultimate light source.*

That was one of the great ideas about the film.

Capa travelling into the heart of lightness?

Yes. There was so much light everywhere. Though when you get Pinbacker running around you have to turn the lights off because things can only be really frightening in the dark. That way he is always behind you.

Did you have fun killing off the characters?

Corazon's death was fantastic – just as she discovered the green shoot. I remember when we showed it to the studio in America, they said we couldn't offer hope in the form of the green shoot and then kill her. They were adamant.

Obviously you won the argument. Were you simply dogmatic?

I have final cut on my films, which not many directors have. But it's a nonsense really. People make such a fuss about getting it. But the real final cut is how many screens the studio will put it out on. They can put it out on one screen or 600 or 3,000. They can advertise it or ignore it. The studio found *Sunshine* too bleak. But I think sci-fi always has an edge of intense bleakness. Space is a machine waiting to kill everyone. You expose yourself to it for a millisecond and it will kill you. It has an edge of hopelessness. Having said that, it's actually a very hopeful film: it says they succeeded. They saved earth. Our destiny is in our hands now. Entirely. Up until a hundred years ago it wasn't.

The studio found Sunshine *too bleak, but what about the public? Why didn't more go and see it?*

At the time you make up what are actually feeble excuses. The classic one was the weather – you regularly hear we film-makers relying on that as a reason for low attendance. It was so hot/cold/wet no one went to the cinema for weeks! None of those factors make any difference at all. If you've made a half-decent film, the truth is that it will either catch or it won't. That process by which films do or don't is just extraordinary.

You can make a blockbuster or franchise film catch by spending staggering amounts of money and making the film virtually unavoidable. Even if you hate the idea of it, hate it the whole time you're watching it and still hate it afterwards, you've been sucked in. But that kind of event cinema often doesn't make much profit because of the millions spent getting everyone into the cinema. If millions aren't earmarked for publicity and it's about a film catching or not, then I don't understand it at all. I did the requisite publicity for *Sunshine* and *Slumdog*: you couldn't make people go and see the former, and you couldn't stop people seeing the latter.

Films are just like that. You watch them at different times, they appeal in different ways. They are completely fixed, yet they're not. People watch them and forget whole chunks of them – and perhaps remember a scene the director wasn't fond of. It's really fluid. Film has this weird, semi-spectral life that kind of lives in your mind.

Whatever the logic, I'm surprised a really good sci-fi film didn't have a ready-made fanbase.

There's a theory that the audience will always be there. I'm not sure. *Sunshine* did all right in the UK but not as well as it should have done. It did absolutely nothing in America.

Yet there were positive reviews: Manohla Dargis in the New York Times *wrote that '[Boyle] is wickedly good at making you jump and squirm in your seat, which he often does in* Sunshine', *while Peter Bradshaw in the* Guardian *described the film as 'a thrilling and sensual spectacle'. I also found a great quote in* Vanity Fair: *'Boyle keeps saving the world with his movies. He's the Sir Bob Geldof of cinema.'*

(*laughs*) Oh God. There you go. That's why no one went. They didn't use that on the poster . . .

I know I keep asking, but despite the slog did you enjoy making Sunshine?

I really did love doing it. Despite the fact that, long before it was released or reviewed, I swore I'd never make another sci-fi film. I certainly feel every film-maker should make a sci-fi film. If nothing else, it will make you realise just what Kubrick achieved forty years ago. And, although *Solaris* was made in a completely different way, what Tarkovsky achieved on a metaphysical level is just mind-blowing. You'll be in that corridor watching the giants, always so far ahead of you.

Slumdog Millionaire (2008)

Titles on the screen tell us: 'Mumbai, 2006. Jamal Malik is one question away from winning 20 million rupees. How did he do it? A. He cheated B. He's lucky C. He's a genius.' We see snatches of Jamal (Dev Patel) on the Indian version of Who Wants to Be a Millionaire?; *Jamal in a police station with Sergeant Srinivas (Saurabh Shukla) blowing smoke in his face; thousands of rupee notes being scattered in a bath.*

Prem (Anil Kapoor), the Millionaire *presenter, introduces nervous teenager Jamal as the first contestant of the evening and a local from Mumbai. The action keeps cutting back to the police station: Srinivas slaps Jamal around the head, then repeatedly dunks his head in a bucket of water. Between the two locations – the studio and the police station – we learn that Jamal is a chai-wallah in a mobile-phone call centre.*

Prem, fully expecting Jamal to go out in an early round, preens and sneers.

At the police station, the police inspector (Irrfan Khan) turns up and asks Srinivas why Jamal has yet to confess. He adds: 'A little electricity will loosen his tongue.' Jamal's body is dangled from the ceiling. The inspector asks if he was wired up in the studio or perhaps had a microchip under his skin; he asks Jamal to stop wasting time and come clean about how he cheated. Jamal says nothing; his body spasms with electric current; he falls unconscious.

Srinivas timidly says to his boss: 'Maybe he did know the answers.' The inspector is incredulous: professionals never get beyond 16,000 rupees, and Jamal is one question away from winning 20 million. He angrily concludes: 'What the hell can a slumdog possibly know?'

Jamal, coming to, mumbles: 'The answers.' Spitting blood out: 'I knew the answers.'

On an airstrip, seven-year-old Jamal (Ayush Mahesh Khedekar) and his nine-year-old brother Salim (Azharuddin Mohammed Ismail) play cricket with their friends and shout to each other in Hindi. Security guards on motorbikes chase the skinny kids – barefoot, in shorts and T-shirts – off the airstrip. The kids run and run through the endless narrow alleyways of the Juhu slum; the guards pursue them on foot. Jamal and Salim come to an abrupt standstill: 'Shit, it's mum!' She promises the breathless guard she will sort them out.

Their mum (Sanchita Choudhary) changes them into their school uniform and shoves them into a crammed classroom. The pupils are reading The Three Musketeers. The teacher says: 'Ah! Here come our very own musketeers.'

Back in the police station, the inspector is now at his desk, with Jamal facing him. He plays back a videotape of Jamal on Millionaire. The first question for 1,000 rupees is: 'Who was the star in the 1973 hit film Zanjeer?'

The action cuts back to the young Jamal and his brother: Jamal crouches over a hole in a wooden shack at the end of a wooden pier; Salim sits on a chair outside. Prakash (Sharib Hashmi) rushes along the pier, bucket of water in hand, desperate to use the toilet. He gives Salim some money. Jamal, refusing to budge, says: 'It's a shy one. Since when was there a time limit on a crap?'

The toilets are adjacent to an airfield. Amitabh Bachchan's helicopter is arriving. There is much excitement about the Bollywood superstar. Jamal pulls up his trousers; Salim jams the door shut with the chair. Jamal, desperate to join the hordes running towards the helicopter, looks at his creased photo of Bachchan and, in desperation, jumps into the human waste.

Bachchan (Feroze Khan) is confronted by a group of fans and ... Jamal covered in shit. He signs the photo. Jamal cheers.

As Jamal is being scrubbed down by his mum, Salim sneaks off and sells the signed photo. Jamal is utterly despondent.

Back in the Millionaire studio, Jamal gives his first correct answer: Amitabh Bachchan.

The next question: 'A picture of three lions is seen in the national emblem of India. What is written underneath it?' Jamal asks the *audience. They – and he – get the answer right: 'The truth alone triumphs.'*

The third question comes up on the computer: 'In depictions of the God Ram, he is famously holding what in his right hand?'

In the Juhu slum, clothing is drying by the railway track. Clothes are being scrubbed in a large outdoor concrete bath. The young Jamal and Salim play around in the water as their mum does the washing. There is a distant commotion; suddenly rioters appear. She tells her boys to run. As they climb out, Salim turns to see his mum being repeatedly hit by rioters, who are shouting, 'They're Muslims, get them!'

As Jamal and Salim run through the slum, they see a man burning alive and a young boy painted bright blue and holding a bow and arrow. A young girl follows them tentatively. The police tell the boys to get lost. We see their mother's body floating in the pool.

Back in the police station, Jamal says: 'I wake up every morning wishing I didn't know the answer to that question. If it wasn't for Ram and Allah, I would still have a mother.' In the studio, he says: 'A bow and arrow.' He wins 16,000 rupees. As the show takes a break, Prem says to Jamal: 'Got lucky? I'd take the money. You're not going to get the next one.'

Young Jamal and Salim watch their slum burn from a hillside. At night, they shelter from torrential rain in an empty lorry container. The girl, who has followed them, stands in the rain. Salim tells her to piss off. Jamal says she could be the third musketeer – although neither of them knows his name.

When Jamal thinks Salim is asleep, he invites the girl in. They introduce each other: she is Latika (Rubina Ali).

In the Millionaire *studio, Jamal is onto the next question: 'The song "Darshan Do Ghanshyam" was written by which famous Indian poet?'*

A long shot of Garai Beach dumping ground, which is the size of a small town. People sift through the waste. Young Latika, in a filthy yellow dress, hauls a bag around behind her. She watches a yellow orphanage van pull up. Jamal and Salim sleep in a crude plastic tent. A well-dressed man – Maman (Ankur Vikal) – gently wakes them up and gives them a fizzy drink.

Jamal, Salim and Latika are settling into the orphanage on the outskirts of Mumbai. Sitting amongst kids with limbs missing, they wolf down food and remark that Maman must be a saint.

In central Mumbai, under a flyover, the yellow van is parked up. Salim, who has been put in charge of the other kids, grabs a baby off a girl and forces it upon Latika: he says that babies earn double. The kids disperse into the streets to beg.

That night, Latika and Jamal slip chillies beneath Salim's sheet: he is in agony, but they have made their point.

Later, Maman is 'auditioning' Arvind (Chirag Parmar). The small boy sings a bhajan – an Indian devotional song – written by Surdas, an Indian composer and poet who was born blind. Maman declares him ready. Punnoose (Tiger), one of Maman's men, drugs him; he is blinded with hot liquid. Salim, looking on, vomits. Maman instructs Salim to bring Jamal over. Salim is frozen. Maman says: 'You want the life of a slumdog or the life of a man? . . . Your destiny is in your hands, brother.'

Meanwhile, Jamal is telling Latika how his singing will bring them enough money for an apartment for the three of them – the three musketeers. As he is dancing for her, Salim comes to collect his brother. He leads him to Maman and, for a horrific minute or two, it looks as though Salim is going to choose the life of a man.

Suddenly, Salim throws the hot liquid at Punnoose and the brothers, with Latika in tow, run for their lives. Jamal and Salim pull themselves up and onto the back of a train; Salim lets go of Latika's hand and she is left behind. Jamal is desperate to go back; Salim says they'll be killed.

Back in the Millionaire studio, Jamal gives his answer: Surdas. Prem, increasingly disgruntled, says he's right.

It's now morning and Jamal and Salim are sitting on the top of the train, which is travelling through stunning countryside. Jamal is clearly thinking about Latika. The brothers are thrown off the train but climb back on with a rope. Salim dangles Jamal down the side of the train with the rope; he steals food from a wealthy family with a noticeably chubby son.

The brothers tumble off the train and, when the dust settles, we see the now twelve-year-old Jamal (Tanay Hemant Chheda) and fourteen-year-old Salim (Ashutosh Lobo Gajiwala). Jamal thinks they are in Heaven; they have arrived at the Taj Mahal. They quickly work out how to make money from tourists by posing as tour guides, talking English instead of Hindi and making up wild stories about the Taj.

Jamal shows a middle-aged American couple – who are being driven around by a local – India's largest dhobi, where acres of women are washing and drying brightly-coloured clothes. They return to find the Indian driver's car stripped bare. The driver pushes Jamal to the ground and kicks him; the American couple are concerned. Jamal, clutching his eye, says: 'You wanted to see the real India: here it is.' The man says: 'Well, here's a bit of the real America, son' – and hands him a hundred-dollar bill.

That night, Jamal sneaks a look Gluck's opera Orfeo ed Euridice, set in front of the Taj. As other kids pickpocket the tourists and wealthy Indians, Jamal is entranced by the love story and thinks, once again, of Latika.

In the Millionaire studio, Jamal's next question: 'On an American one-hundred dollar bill, there is a portrait of which American states-man?' He pauses. Prem asks if Jamal gets many hundred-dollar bills in his line of work. Jamal shoots straight back: 'The minimum tip for my services.' Then gives the correct answer: Benjamin Franklin. He wins one million rupees.

The middle Jamal and Salim arrive back in Bombay – now Mumbai and a city changing at a rate they barely recognise. Their slum has gone and in its place are high-rise buildings. Jamal starts an exhaustive search for Latika. He works with Salim in a kitchen. Salim refills old mineral-water bottles from the tap and, gluing the top back on, derides his brother's naked emotion.

Jamal comes across Arvind (Siddesh Patil) singing and begging in an underpass, blinded and scarred by the hot oil. Jamal gives him the hundred-dollar note. Arvind asks what is on the note; he recog-nises Jamal's voice and warns him to stay away as Maman doesn't forget. He reveals where he can find Latika, now known as Cherry. Men come to flush the underpass out with mosquito repellent.

Jamal and Salim look for Latika (Tanvi Ganesh Lonkar) in the brothel. They find her dancing; she is stunned but ecstatic. As they pack her bags, Maman and Punnoose turn up. Salim produces a gun, asks Maman for money and kills him. The three musketeers escape.

In the studio, Prem's next question: 'Who invented the revolver?' Jamal answers immediately: Samuel Colt. He wins 2.5 million rupees.

The middle Jamal, Salim and Latika camp out at an empty hotel.

As Jamal and Latika reconnect, Salim walks the streets. In a balcony bar, he tells a group of men he has killed Maman and is looking for Javed (Mahesh Manjrekar); Javed appears and recruits Salim.

Jamal and Latika lie on a mattress in the hotel, tipsy. They agree it was their destiny to meet again.

Salim wants to take Latika away; the brothers fight. Salim points his gun at Jamal: 'The man with the Colt 45 says shut up!' Jamal is forced to leave.

In the police station, the inspector asks how he got on the show. We see the eldest Jamal in the call centre, where the phone operators are quizzed about British culture: they talk about EastEnders, Edinburgh and Ben Nevis. Jamal sits at a colleague's desk as everyone in the office, desperate to be a contestant, tries to get through to Millionaire. He looks Salim up on the computer, rings him and they talk, briefly.

In the studio, the next question: 'Cambridge Circus is in which UK city?' Jamal remembers the lessons on British culture at the call centre. He chooses London. He is now up to 5 million rupees.

Jamal meets Salim (Madhur Mittal) at the top of a tall building: it is the first time they have met as young adults. Salim heads for an embrace; Jamal punches him. Sitting on the edge of the half-built tower block, they look down at where their slum once was.

Salim, who is expensively dressed, says that India is at the centre of the world now; he explains that he works for Javed Khan, the gangster from their slum. Jamal is suitably horrified but agrees to stay in Salim's apartment.

The next morning, Jamal secretly follows Salim to Javed's house, which sits proud amongst the frenzied building work surrounding it. Jamal has a glimpse of Latika (Freida Pinto), now a stunning young woman. Posing as the new cook, he gets into the house. They embrace; he sees a scar on her face. Javed returns; Jamal pretends to make a sandwich. Javed scorns Latika for having Millionaire on in the background and turns over to the cricket.

Jamal urges Latika to come away with him and live on . . . love. Javed orders Jamal out. Before he leaves, Jamal whispers: 'I'll be waiting at VT station at five o'clock every day until you come.'

In the studio, Prem is increasingly exasperated. He asks the next question: 'Which cricketer has scored the most first-class centuries in history?'

Meanwhile, we see Jamal waiting faithfully at VT station. On the verge of losing hope, he spots Latika in a yellow top. They exchange smiles but Salim is heading straight for her. He grabs her violently by the hair and drags her out of the station.

A commercial break in the studio. Prem and Jamal are in the toilets. Prem says he is the only person to have left the slums and become a millionaire. Jamal says he won't become a millionaire; he doesn't know the answer. Prem washes his hand and writes 'B' in the steam on the mirror.

Before they start filming again, Prem whispers to Jamal: 'From rags to raja, it's your destiny.' After a torturous pause, with Prem pressing him to choose 'B', Jamal says 'D' – Jack Hobbs. He wins 10 million rupees. Prem does a little dance to hide his fury.

The final question, for 20 million rupees. The horn blows to signal the end of the evening's show; the audience will have to hang on till tomorrow. As Jamal is leaving, Prem directs him to the back door, where a blanket is thrown over Jamal and he is taken to the police station.

Fast forward to the present: the inspector, surmising that Jamal is incapable of lying, lets him go. Before he leaves, Jamal says he only went on the show because he thought Latika would be watching.

At Javed's new place, Latika and Salim watch the news, about a slum boy on the verge of winning the top prize on Millionaire. *Salim gives Latika a set of car keys and his mobile, asks for forgiveness and tells her to go.*

As Jamal is driven back to the show – with the public giving their blessing en route – so Latika drives through gridlocked traffic to find him. The whole of India, it seems, is about to watch Millionaire.

The final question: 'In Alexander Dumas's book The Three Musketeers, *two of the musketeers are called Athos and Porthos. What was the name of the third Musketeer?' Latika has jumped out of her car and is watching the show on a television in the slums. Jamal doesn't know the answer. He stands to lose everything, but decides to play.*

He phones a friend: Latika's mobile rings. Salim fills a bath with cash. Latika, grinning, doesn't know the answer. Jamal guesses 'A': Aramis. It is, of course, the right answer. Salim lies in the bath. When Javed walks in, he shoots him. Salim is shot dead by Javed's men.

Danny Boyle on the dumping grounds beside the Juhu slum.

Jamal waits by the statue of Frederick W. Stevens at VT station. He sees Latika in a yellow scarf and crosses the track to reach her. They embrace and he tenderly kisses her scar. Jamal says: 'This is our destiny.'

As the closing credits come up, Jamal, Latika and a host of others dance to 'Jai Ho' on the platform at VT station.

* * *

AMY RAPHAEL: *Is it true that you almost didn't read Simon Beaufoy's script of* Slumdog Millionaire?

DANNY BOYLE: Christian Colson, who produced the film, sent me the script. I'd never met him. I'd heard he was a gambler, that he was out of the Miramax camp and that he'd been trained by Harvey Weinstein. That was all I knew about him. I was told it was a script about *Who Wants to Be a Millionaire?* – no one even mentioned India! This is the God's honest truth: I didn't think I'd read it. Why would anyone want to make a film about Chris Tarrant? Then I saw Simon Beaufoy's name on the cover. I didn't know him personally either, but I obviously knew his name as the writer of

The Full Monty. I thought I'd better read some of it and then thank him for sending the script.

Did you like The Full Monty?

Big time. In fact, I very clearly remember going to see it when I came back from making *A Life Less Ordinary* in America. It hadn't had particularly good reviews and yet, when I went to see it, I thought it would still be a big hit – which it was, of course, but it built very slowly. So I started reading *Slumdog Millionaire* and after less than twenty pages, once I'd read the scene set in the outdoor toilet, I knew I was going to make the film. I was seduced by the whole set-up with Amitabh Bachchan as the star and the two boys doing anything to get to him, to get his autograph.

I've made snap decisions about scripts before. In retrospect, it seems ridiculous, because of course on previous occasions I've then gone on to read the next eighty pages and been disappointed. But sometimes something happens where you just fit with a script.

You've talked of it before as your 'giddy moment'.

And in that moment no sense prevails at all. *Sunshine* had not done well. From a career point of view I should have been directing *28 Months Later* with a big American star in it.

Were you seduced by Beaufoy's script from start to finish?

I had a very strong emotional response. I cried and cried at different elements of it. Another good sign was that I only had one or two very clear notes. So I met Christian and liked him very much. I then met Simon and we talked – it was exactly the same experience as speaking to John Hodge about *Shallow Grave*. Simon took my notes on board and carried them off brilliantly. I always say to young film-makers that they shouldn't be frightened of telling someone how good something is. If you think something is fucking brilliant, then say it. Speak with your heart.

Do you remember your specific notes?

Christian and I told Simon that he had to put a break in the show to force the idea that Jamal might not get back on it. The audience is then going to be desperate for him to get back on the show. The second note was about Prem, the host, giving Jamal the false answer in the toilet. And the final note was about the dance at the end, in the station. Actually, I think the dance wasn't in the first flush of notes; it came later, after we'd been to India.

Had you ever been to India at that point?

Never. My dad was there during the war and often talked to me about it. When I was young it bored me. But his stories stuck: he'd been in Bombay for eighteen months as part of a huge Allied presence being trained to invade Japan. Had they invaded, they would certainly have died. My uncle John, his brother, was also there. And some of the guys he still drinks with at the club in Radcliffe. They met by accident on the Colaba Causeway. The Americans dropped the bomb on Japan, and ten days later they were on the *Queen Elizabeth* going home. My dad talked about the poor people being driven off the streets in India. He talked about how clean Indians were despite how dirty their environment was. He used to go on about how they took a bucket of water to the toilet with them . . .

Was he in awe of India?

I think he was. We'd watch Alf Garnett at home – this was in the 1960s – and he'd object to the racism directed at Indians. He'd shout at the telly, saying Indians weren't dirty; in fact, they were much cleaner than us.

How was your first trip to India?

I went with Simon; we got on very well. He had been twenty years earlier as a student backpacker. I never had anything like a gap year because I was always working; it's only as an adult that films have allowed me to travel. India is overwhelming. It's obvious how most people respond: you either hate it or you love it. I personally found the cacophony irresistible. I loved it. There's life teeming everywhere. I thought Simon's script was deadly accurate; it just got India. Well, Mumbai anyway.

I read Beaufoy's script after seeing Slumdog; *it was surprisingly muscular given the contrived nature of the story.*

It *is* totally contrived. I wrote in the introduction to the script that Simon is an architect. I've never worked with a writer who understands so well that you build a script from the inside. But an architect builds a structure that's incredibly manipulative and – if you're cynical about it – deeply implausible. In fact, I remember doing a Q&A in London with Simon and Christian just before *Slumdog* opened, and that guy Toby Young was in the audience. He got up and made a speech about how implausible the story was, and I wanted to punch his lights out. I was just about to stand up and call him a twat when Simon gently stopped me and was incredibly gracious instead.

Of course you could unpick the story in *Slumdog*; you could unpick most film scripts if you really wanted to. Simon makes writing look easy, but it ain't. It took him ten years after *The Full Monty* to produce a script like this. Christian, who knows Simon better than I do, says the delay was a lot to do with his bitterness at the way *The Full Monty* turned out. He was the guy who dreamt it all up and yet he got no money out of it because he sold his rights. It's a famous story: he had points and he gave them away for an insubstantial amount of cash. *The Full Monty* then became one of the most profitable films ever. He appealed when it became a hit but got nowhere. Christian thinks Simon's bitterness affected him for a decade. Thankfully, his innate generosity returned on *Slumdog*.

So when Tessa Ross, head of Film4, asked Beaufoy if he'd be interested in adapting Vikas Swarup's novel Q&A, the timing was right?

Simon knew India and he thought there was a story worth telling in *Q&A*. The fact that Tessa has an impeccable track record obviously helped. Simon approached Swarup's book in a brilliant way: he kept the structure, in which a poor kid can answer increasingly difficult questions on the show, but he made up all the incidents that tell Jamal's story. He didn't have to look far; India is teeming with amazing stories. The novel belonged to Britain up till the Victorian era, it belonged to America during the last century and in this century it will belong to Asia. The immediacy of life is there for writers to feed off. We are suffocating in relative comfort elsewhere, but in India the rich are face to face with the poor. It's the most extraordinary place.

The vibe in India is intoxicating for a film-maker – and particularly for me, coming off a sci-fi film like *Sunshine*. India was oxygen. I couldn't get enough of it.

There are eight producers on Slumdog – *from Christian Colson as producer to Tessa Ross as executive producer to Pathé's François Ivernel as co-executive producer – but no Andrew Macdonald.*

I guess Andrew didn't want to do it. He sent me a note saying he thought it would make a great film, but he obviously didn't want to be involved. He was very gracious, though, when he saw the film, and especially when it took off, wishing us all good luck and writing that he was a mite envious now! I think I always wanted to be closer to Andrew than he did. Still, we had no shortage of good producers. Tessa Ross has reinvented Film4, despite continual and hereditary financial problems. She sets up great material and her attention to detail and her care for the project is intense and yet non-possessive. She's astute at picking people and then, like all great producers, lets them take charge.

Paul Smith was another executive producer. When he sold Celador – the production company behind *Who Wants to Be a Millionaire?* – he ensured there was a clause in the contract allowing him to use *Millionaire* in a feature film for nothing. There's a reason why he's a very successful businessman! On our budget we'd never have been able to afford the image or music rights of the show without that clause. Apparently he spends all his time these days dealing with people trying to sue him for money owed in relation to *Millionaire*.

François Ivernel, who had taken a risk with *Millions*, was the bedrock upon which everything was built. During all the shenanigans, all the ups and downs, his faith in us, and his co-executive producer Cameron McCracken's, never wavered. They were eased aside by the media and the success of the film in America, but I've never forgotten how much we owed them.

So how did you get Warner Brothers and 20th Century Fox to take a risk on a film set in India with no A-list Western actors attached to it?

Christian used his experience at the poker table to get us an extra few million. He did a brilliant piece of gamesmanship in which he played Warner Independent by saying another studio was interested. I believe the technical term is 'phantom bidder'! Of course, the other studio turned out to be non-existent. Being a gambler, Christian knows how to play such a situation. It's a great skill because the market is usually pretty astute. The cap should have been $10 million for the kind of film *Slumdog* appeared to be at development stage. And somehow he got Warners to bid $5 million on a film nobody else wanted – for which we have to thank Polly Cohen and Paul Federbush for pushing for us at Warners.

Anyway, the reality was that the only other offer we'd had was around $2 million from Fox. Warners were quite interested in the fact that I was directing a Simon Beaufoy script. Maybe. Kind of. But not the story itself because it was set in India. And, as you say, there was no one famous in it – not as far as the West was concerned, anyhow.

The initial lack of interest in the story is fascinating: I noticed in interviews you gave to promote Sunshine *that no one really bothered to ask you about this film you were planning to make in India, even though you kept enthusing about it.*

I remember. But I didn't mind. I was infected by India at that point. As well as the $5 million from Warners, Christian managed to raise $8 million from Pathé. We ended up with between $13–15 million, depending on the exchange rate and who you listen to.

With the budget in place, were you raring to go?

God, yes! Instead of bringing most of the crew over from the UK, as I'd done on *The Beach*, I wanted most of the crew to be local. We started visiting production companies in Mumbai and finally signed up with India Take One. We met a series of casting directors, one of whom was Loveleen Tandan. But it was impossible to hook up with her because, like everybody in India, she seems to be busy all the time doing multiple jobs. It's just incredible; it's one of the things that gives the place its energy. In fact, we didn't meet Loveleen at all before giving her the job; we ended up speaking to her on the phone and appointing her to search for the cast. She started sending us auditions via the internet. The number of auditions we saw . . . it was endless.

Jamal (Ayush Mahesh Khedekar), Latika (Rubina Ali) and Salim (Azharuddin Mohammed Ismail).

The kids you were looking for to play the youngest Jamal and the youngest Salim were originally going to be English speakers.

The whole script was originally in English. Initially, we thought we'd just throw in the odd word of Hindi. '*Mader chod*', which means 'motherfucker', and '*bhen chod*', which means 'sisterfucker'. Loveleen tentatively hinted early on that it wouldn't be very accurate if the young boys spoke English. We dismissed it as being an obvious thing to say. And we were making a film for the world market; it had to be able to play. We slowly changed our minds as the auditions came in; we could see evidence of what she was talking about because the ones who spoke English were all chubby McDonald's kids.

Meanwhile, I was going round the slums location-spotting and seeing kids running around without an ounce of fat on any of them – there's more meat on a bicycle, as they used to say. I finally asked Loveleen how we could get access to those kids, and she said we'd have to be prepared to do the film in Hindi. Not just let them audition in Hindi, but perform in it too. The older kids could then move on to English, because most pick it up in their teens when they become absorbed with popular culture. It's only the very rich kids who speak English so young. At which point we gave Loveleen permission to rewrite some scenes in Hindi. She'd explained very carefully that you can't just do a direct translation; you have to adapt the vernacular too.

Did doing auditions for Hindi-speaking kids feel like a risk? You must have been concerned about alienating part of your potential audience simply by the presence of subtitles?

I was aware of it but I was mad; I was so into the whole experience. I knew people would think I'd gone native. They fully expected me to turn up in a kurta. But I also knew it wasn't working with the McDonald's kids and it felt horrible. The script is so savage early on that you couldn't pretend those kids were from the slums if they weren't; chubby-cheeked kids couldn't realistically be living in desperate poverty and watching eyes being gouged out. The kid who plays the young Jamal, Ayush Mahesh Khedekar, was from a more middle-class background and was carrying more weight; without allowing him to have a food crisis we encouraged him to slim down.

I remember very clearly the moment we started to audition this bunch of Hindi-speaking kids. Loveleen translated the scene where Salim is banging on the toilet door, telling Jamal to hurry up because Prakash wants a shit urgently. You realise how natural acting is for Indian kids because they all go to the cinema from an early age and they all love movie stars. They all want a chance to show off. There's no hesitancy, no shyness. They're not interested in the camera; you just have to stop them from posing sometimes.

It was harder with the young female actors because of the role of women in India. We had a big problem with the middle Latika because the implication is that she is raped. The first girl we auditioned didn't want to do it. We were very lucky to get Tanvi Ganesh Lonkar, because she was a classical dancer and had a physical confidence lacking in many of the others. But her parents had deep reservations about doing it. Her father was there all the time, watching me. I knew he was suspicious about what I might ask his daughter to do. I was very careful to show him everything, to let him know in advance what we were doing.

We were also casting in London, New York, Toronto – virtually everywhere with a big Indian population. We were looking for all the cast but principally the grown-up Jamal, Salim and Latika. We tried to cast Jamal and Salim in India, but the young guys were ridiculously musclebound; they looked as though they'd been going to the gym for ten years. They were like Michelin men with tiny pinheads. They appeared in ripped T-shirts, their bulging arms hanging away from their sides. Shaved chests. Heavily perfumed.

In the original script Jamal, Salim and Latika were considerably older. Why did you decide to make them younger?

It's quite complicated. At one point there were only two ages, but I was adamant there had to be three. Everyone was sceptical: how would we incorporate three ages into the film? There are certain rules in studio film-making that I always try to avoid. For example, they believe that in order to generate that awful word they love, 'emotionality', the audience has to invest in the actor. On the way, plausibility will often be sacrificed – a twenty-nine-year-old will be cast and then, when there's a flashback, he is supposed to look fourteen. I've always found that cringeworthy. You can tell a beautiful thirty-three-year-old isn't a teen virgin.

So I insisted on three different ages and three different actors. I always had this image of Jamal and Salim tumbling off the train and being transformed into older versions of themselves: when they readjust from the fall, Jamal, now twelve, and Salim, now fourteen, find themselves looking at the Taj and thinking they're in Heaven. Theatre teaches you to take risks like that: just do it with brio and people will buy into it. They will applaud it. Whereas in America they distrust using theatrical devices.

The three age groups were initially going to be ten and twelve, fourteen and sixteen, twenty-three and twenty-five. We made each group several years younger partly because we found seven- and eight-year-old actors to play the little kids, but also because Dev Patel and Madhur Mittal, as the older Jamal and Salim, were far too young to play men of twenty-five. Making everyone several years younger was a big risk. Simon was very concerned about the middle ones and their implied sexuality at twelve, thirteen. But we all know that kids can be sexualised at that age. It gave the film more edge. It also made the oldest Jamal less likely to succeed on *Millionaire*, which created a good tension.

Finally, India is a very young country. It's teeming with young people; 75 per cent of the population are under twenty-five. Twenty per cent of the world's children live there! China's one-child policy put a brake on its population, but there's nothing similar in place in India. So the population is surging and will surpass China to become the most populated country on earth by 2020. And there still isn't much infrastructure in India! I doubt it will change much: they'll have the most sophisticated mobile-phone network in the world but no public toilets.

So you struggled to find Jamal in India and instead discovered him virtually on your doorstep, in London, thanks to a tip-off from your daughter.

(*laughs*) Caitlin said to both me and her mum Gail, who was casting the film in Britain, that we should watch this guy Dev Patel in the television series *Skins*. I was a bit alarmed at what Caitlin was watching – it was a bit racy – but he was genuinely funny. When I met him, he wasn't funny at all. I liked that. I'd seen that before with

Dev Patel as Jamal.

real comedians. Keith Allen's younger brother Kevin is like that.

Did you have to talk the producers of Skins *into letting him go?*

Dev was tied up with the show, but fortunately Gail has a good working relationship with one of the producers. Otherwise we may never have got him. We didn't have him for the whole shoot, as we would have preferred, but he was clearly so exceptional that he was worth the sacrifices we had to make in terms of scheduling and continuity.

When you met him did you think, 'He's the one,' or did it take some time to come to that conclusion?

He wasn't as conventionally good-looking as we'd imagined Jamal to be, and I'd always imagined casting the part in India. But there was something about him. The most amazing thing about Dev is that he was seventeen at the time, the *only* piece of acting he'd done before *Slumdog* was a small comic turn on *Skins* and yet he had the Russell Crowe approach: he had a very clear opinion about how things should be.

But it wasn't easy for him. He left behind his mother, who came to every single audition with him – you could tell he was both loyal and embarrassed, like a good Indian lad. He turned up on set, where he was the only cast member not born in India – he knew more about Harrow, north London, than Mumbai. He was constantly advised about accent by his fellow actors, who were not frightened to tell him how it should be done.

Despite all his limitations in terms of experience, Dev had that certainty of how to play the part. Despite the sneering of the chat-show host, despite Jamal's lack of education, his poor background and his poor job prospects, Dev knew how to give him dignity. Madhur – a wonderful actor – was pivotal in giving Dev confidence. He guided him through the local world and thus bedded him into Mumbai better than anyone.

Dev had no hesitation in making it quite clear to me that he disagreed about certain things. Your initial impulse is to think, 'You cheeky little fucker!' But then you stop and realise that's exactly what you need in a lead actor. Films don't work unless your lead quite clearly has a vision of how he's going to do it. As a director

Madhur Mittal as Salim – 'a wonderful actor'.

you can give yourself a false impression of doing a lot. In fact, as I said about the guys on *Trainspotting*, when actors are good you're not directing them at all.

We used to fight because Dev didn't want Jamal to turn into a smiler. He didn't want to earn people's love for him in an easy, cheesy way. If you've got a cracking smile, as Dev has, it would have been an easy option. Yet he wanted to play Jamal honestly and simply, which meant he held the centre of the film with great dignity. You can't teach people that. You can talk about it, but they can either do it or they can't. It's what makes a great star.

Do you think he's a movie star rather than an actor?

He's both. His presence transformed the film. His gravity and his determination gave a surprisingly young yet solid centre to a film of increasing chaos. He holds the centre of *Slumdog*, just as Ewan did in *Trainspotting*. Sadly, however, he may find that there are not enough roles to nurture his talent in the world of film. There is still, unfortunately, a sense of colour in film casting, so he won't be up for everything. You couldn't cast Dev as a white Mormon from Utah, unlike in the theatre, where colour is wonderfully irrelevant. I don't know if he'll move into theatre; he's still young enough. He

275

should try it. He will need to be fed a diet of great parts to keep stretching himself.

Was Freida Pinto, a model, the obvious choice as the older Latika?

Not to everyone. When we cast her, people said no one in India would like her because she's not voluptuous enough. That is no longer seen as an issue; since the release of *Slumdog*, she's picked up a big cosmetics contract.

She is stunningly beautiful and a pleasure to look at on screen, but she had never acted before.

She got much better even while we were making *Slumdog*. After the film came out, Julian Schnabel asked me to audition Freida on tape for him as he was about to start shooting *Miral* in Israel. He sent some scenes over; I rehearsed them with her and then shot them. She's a different actor now. So much of it is confidence. It's not uncommon for beautiful girls to find a way of acting, mostly by being truthful and – to be honest – letting the way they look do the work for them. But she had improved tenfold. I was amazed. And she got the part.

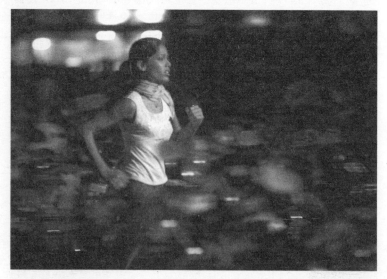

Freida Pinto as Latika.

She's not actually in Slumdog *that much, given that Jamal's love for her drives the film.*

She wasn't in the film as much as people might think, but the public scenes she did were very courageous. I was surprised at how brave she was. It's very hard for women to film in public places in India. Not only did she have to kiss Jamal, but she also had to be dragged away kicking and screaming in the station. She was so convincing that people kept asking if she was okay – thereby ruining the take!

Jamal and Latika's relationship isn't electric like Cameron Diaz and Ewan McGregor's in A Life Less Ordinary, *but you do believe in Dev Patel and Freida Pinto as star-crossed lovers.*

I think that's because of Dev's innocence, which was one of the advantages of making the characters younger. He was young enough to fall in love with someone and not be able to see anyone else in the world. Her beauty and grace haunted the film. He was devoted to her on screen. And, of course, they went on to become a couple, but only after the end of the shoot.

Dev Patel is a geeky guy with big ears, but as the film progresses he becomes increasingly attractive. Was he growing up on screen or were you working on him?

Dev was slowly beginning to realise he mattered; he wasn't just a spot-ridden teenager, which is what you can feel like at seventeen. Actors don't carry the same burden as a producer or director – they're not interested in the fact that a film costs a certain amount of money and therefore has to have an audience. And rightly so. Dev had a mind of his own. I was old enough to be his dad, but he often wouldn't back down! Which is a good sign: he was taking it seriously, he was thinking about it, he wasn't just doing as he was told. He had his take on it. It's why you believe the relationship with Latika. His motor is generating it.

He also has some emotional depth, as illustrated by the scene where he is reunited with Salim at the top of the tower block.

This will amuse you. The two brothers are sitting on the floor in the unfinished tower block and looking down on the area where their slum used to be. I thought Dev was playing it like he was a *Guardian* reader, feeling sorry about the slums disappearing. I said to Dev: 'Jamal was from the slums, he'd be delighted that the slums are going and in their place are shopping malls, bars. All this consumerist stuff that the *Guardian* despises, Jamal would be delighted about.'

We fought very hard. I accused him of being desperately, hopelessly liberal. He was definitely going to play it as a tragedy – his old life being replaced by America. I said it was a political point of view that was just and proper, but Jamal simply wouldn't be feeling that. He'd be embracing the progress. Immediately after our row, Dev did the scene where Jamal loses it with Salim, calling him a liar and saying he will never forgive him for disappearing. Dev got on really well with Madhur – the anger came from the argument Dev had just had with me.

How heated were these arguments with Patel?

Very heated, but not to the extent that anyone stormed off. The atmosphere would linger on into the scenes. However, because you all stay on the same playing field, what comes out of it is a good scene. And the scene in the tower block is a powerful one. Madhur was more than good enough to deal with Dev's anger.

How many young kids did you audition for the youngest Jamal, Salim and Latika, and where did you find Ayush Mahesh Khedekar, Azharuddin Mohammed Ismail and Rubina Ali?

Thousands. We found Azhar and Rubina once we started to look at slum kids. It was harder to keep track of them because they generally don't have home phones. They have a reputation for being unreliable because their lives are harder to regulate, but in fact we used fixers and it worked out perfectly. Azhar was in the first bunch of kids who came in, and he was outstanding. I remember his impatience to get on with the scenes vividly. Loveleen was guiding him, and he was comfortable because he was acting in Hindi.

Was finding the two middle actors, Tanay Hemant Chheda as Jamal and Ashutosh Lobo Gajiwala as Salim, your biggest casting challenge?

Two weeks before the shoot, we had only found Tanay. We couldn't find a middle Salim who looked at all like Madhur and Azhar. We were incredibly lucky: Tanay suggested we see a friend of his from school. He literally said, 'Meet my mate Ashutosh, he's good.' So we met him in the Marriott and cast him with virtually no time to go.

The middle Jamal and Salim are certainly the least rewarding parts, and those two actors have been the least championed since *Slumdog* came out. Yet their roles were quite demanding: they were involved in scenes about transgression and transformation, with guns and girls. And loyalty. Tanay is a seriously brilliant young actor. He's like Ayush: both are technically able to do anything. Like Freida, Ashutosh had never acted before, but his learning curve was so sharp that he was pretty skilled by the end. And Tanvi, being a dancer, was able to cope with the physically demanding nature of being the middle Latika.

Did you do dumb shows with the youngest kids, acting out the parts for them?

You develop a vocabulary with them which is not always based on language. But they pick up English pretty fast – and they torment you with it if they can. They're just the same as kids anywhere: they're cheeky, they want warmth and affection. You also have to set a strict line which they can't cross. You play good cop, bad cop. I did it on *Millions*, where I was the good cop, and I did it again on *Slumdog*: Loveleen was very strict with the kids, whereas I'd instigate play. They respond to that because there's discipline, but it stays fun at some level.

The kids who weren't cast as the three main actors were used in the orphanage scenes.

It's quite a nice way of letting them down; they are still involved in the film.

Once you'd got to grips with the kids, did the adult parts follow quickly?

In a way, yes. But all the actors in Mumbai are busy doing two or three films at the same time. Bollywood actors work very differently:

they don't read the script. You audition the film for them, in front of them. You present and pitch the story to these huge stars. They either see something in it or they don't. It was slightly different with Anil Kapoor because his son was fanatical about Western films and loved *Trainspotting*. When I went to Anil's house, his son's room was covered in *Trainspotting* posters. He urged his dad to do it. Playing the host of *Who Wants to Be a Millionaire?* was an unusual part for Anil because he normally plays the lead. And in a Bollywood film he might reasonably be expected to play the eighteen-year-old romantic lead. Well . . . maybe not quite.

Anil was a very famous actor. Then his star waned for a while, but he's since experienced a comeback. He deals with the fluctuating nature of fame in a very interesting way. He's so gracious with his fans. His patience is incredible. And, most importantly for us, he liked the idea of playing a supporting part. Although his English is fantastic, he was incredibly nervous about actually acting in English. Bollywood stars are all like that. Suddenly they are in the territory of the movies and stars they worship: Pacino, De Niro, Hanks . . .

I think Anil was very brave to take on the role of Prem. Loveleen guessed that he would be tempted by the role and have the balls to go through with it. He wanted to rehearse, so we rehearsed separately as much as we could to facilitate him with the language.

Anil Kapoor as Prem.

He did extensive research on both Chris Tarrant and Amitabh Bachchan – the latter originally presented the Indian *Millionaire*, which is called *Who Will Become the Owner of 10 Million?* He watched the idiosyncrasies of these guys, the little mannerisms. Anil is such a clever actor; he insisted on having the chair at home so he could practise sitting on it. When a Bollywood star insists to the props department, the chair is instantly there. When we were filming, Anil helped Dev, but he also tested him quite a lot.

Was there a danger of an actor as experienced as Kapoor upstaging Patel?

Anil wanted to see if Dev could deal with being upstaged. I'm not sure how much was natural enmity between him and a younger guy and how much was actually useful for the dynamic of the two characters. Of course, that's the sign of a great actor: using elements of a real dynamic, infecting those with the story dynamic and then bouncing back and forth between the two. I liked Anil very much. If you watch some of his films in Hindi, he's a major actor. It was a great plus for us to get him.

You were very keen to get Irrfan Khan as the police inspector.

I remember Peter Rice at Fox Searchlight saying early on that if I was going to make a film in India, I should get Irrfan Khan on board. I realised I knew his work because he's acted in a number of Western films. But initially Irrfan didn't want to be the police inspector in *Slumdog*; it's not a very big part and he had already played a police officer in *A Mighty Heart*. I lied, as you do, about how good the part would become. I'd have done anything to get him. Eventually we got him, but not for a whole lot of time; we had to shift the schedule around to fit him in. But it was worth it. There's a warmth about him, despite the fact that he instigates the torturing of Jamal. He really pulls you in; you kind of float into him. He's a great vehicle for a series of tricky 'Why did you do that?'-style questions. He makes the story his own.

We got this guy Saurabh Shukla to play the fat torturer, Sergeant Srinivas. He's awesome. He's a writer and director too; in fact, he was directing a film while we were shooting. He wrote *Satya* with Anurag Kashyap, which to my mind is one of the great Indian films. We were lucky to get those guys – a lot of which was once more down to Loveleen.

Did you direct the Bollywood actors differently?

Apart from Irrfan, most of them wanted me to keep an eye on them. They know their acting is richer than the conventional Western menu. I generally like big performances, I like actors to be bold. I don't like actors to mutter their way through parts. I'm not an advocate of 'mumblecore', those American indie films which embrace low-volume chatter. So we found quite an easy meeting point. I didn't have a problem with egos either; they weren't playing on being the big Bollywood stars, although they could easily have done.

Did you already have a reputation in Bollywood?

Only from *Trainspotting*. One or two knew about it, other than Anil's son.

Was being relatively anonymous an advantage?

It was in the sense that you need people to speak without fear. It's essential to create a climate of frankness. Everyone was encouraged to tell the truth about the script – things that would never happen, that were insulting or factually wrong. You accept some of those criticisms and others you ignore because that particular moment is about drama rather than historical or factual accuracy.

How did the Indian crew work out?

Raj Acharya, the first assistant director, was very, very important to me. All the street scenes were done by Raj. I wanted to film in real places, and I made that clear to him. He said it would be very difficult to film in the slums but he'd do it.

You were under pressure to recreate the slums of Mumbai. The studio fully expected you to do so, while Acharya knew from experience how hard it would be.

All the Indian crew assumed we'd build our own slums. They kept shaking their heads at the idea of filming in the real slums. But

India is the country of the no. There's a whole chapter in Suketu Mehta's fantastic book *Maximum City: Bombay Lost and Found* about the use of 'no' in India. It's a very funny chapter. The first thing you've got to learn is that you don't accept the no. So I said no to the no! The Indians love all that banter.

Anyway, I got to know the guys I came to call our Three Musketeers – Tabrez Noorani, line producer; Pravesh Sahni, production supervisor; and their sidekick Sanjay Kumar, unit production manager – very well. I really liked them and we thrashed things out together.

And then I had Raj, who has worked his whole life in Mumbai and can shoot on the streets. It used to drive Anthony Dod Mantle, the cinematographer, mad. Raj was never around, and the cinematographer relies on the first AD as a conduit to the director. But I always knew where Raj was. He's no good at delegating, but actually it's impossible to delegate in India anyway; you've just got to get stuck in and get on with it yourself. And I used to love that.

Raj is an extraordinary guy. Usually on his days off he works in street schools, where kids sit on the pavement and learn. The teachers are people like Raj who give their time to the kids. Raj and I ended up working on our days off. I couldn't understand why you would be in India and want to lie by the pool. I used to get up every day and just look out at the Juhu slum. The people have nothing, yet are so hospitable.

Did you want to shoot Juhu endlessly in an attempt to capture its energy on film?

Oh God, yes. But you can never fully capture it. You might get odd moments when you think it's like that, a bit. It's beyond capturing.

So you were captivated by Juhu and you liked Raj. What about Loveleen Tandan: at one point did she become 'co-director (India)'?

As the film progressed, Loveleen said she had to go and work on another film. Everyone in India does it; it's a bargaining tool to get more money. Loveleen was important before we started shooting in the way that Raj then became important during the shoot. She was basically educating me all the time, in terms of films to watch, crew to pick up on, actors to see, culture to understand, working practices to get my head round. Everything.

I knew she'd done similar work on other movies but had never been properly credited. So I suggested she be given a co-director credit. The studio weren't very keen because they didn't want to split the director credit; they had nothing to sell the film but my name as director. But I insisted. Once we started shooting, I gave Loveleen second-unit work. She wants to be a director and, although it's tough for women in India, I think she could do it. In fact, I wanted to credit Raj as a co-director too, but they wouldn't let me. That was for Guild reasons.

What would Slumdog *have been like without Raj Acharya and Loveleen Tandan?*

A quarter of the film it is. I'd have made so many mistakes. It has nothing to do with skill and everything to do with understanding the country. They made the biggest single difference to the film. And Resul Pookutty, the sound recordist, became equally essential to me. They became another set of Three Musketeers in my mind. I checked everything with those three constantly. I found my access to them as important – if not more important than – the traditional access you get to your designers and your cameraman.

Anthony Dod Mantle did an incredible job: Slumdog *looks amaz-*

Danny Boyle, Loveleen Tandan and Anthony Dod Mantle.

ing. It's almost as though you can smell the country.

He's fantastic. He's the only cameraman in the world who could work under those ludicrous demands. He's a brilliant, inventive cameraman with balls and soul. Thomas Neivelt, the gaffer, was working with him, as was a brilliant Indian gaffer, Mulchand Dedhia. Thomas is like a second Anthony; they are so symbiotic that he can read Anthony's mind. Anthony is the best digital cameraman in the world. He's peerless. Yet there was a lot of panic about what digital looks like; no one really understands it. There was also a lot of trouble with the bond people here in the UK who were concerned when they heard it was digital. You just have to fight all those battles.

Why were they specifically concerned about it being digital?

There had been some quality issues with other 'digital films'. I said there are never quality issues with Anthony Dod Mantle!

How much of the film was shot in digital in the end?

Roughly speaking, we shot 75 per cent of the film on SI-2K cameras, which use a digital system recorded onto a hard drive. We shot about 20 per cent on old-fashioned celluloid. The other 5 per cent we shot on CanonCam, a stills camera that takes twelve frames a second. These stills can then be blended in a computer to create a slightly halting but incredibly rich, crisp, deeply saturated image. The SI-2K records at 2K resolution and celluloid at just above 2K, whereas the CanonCam records at 8K. The CanonCam was very good for us. It's a technique that in cinema language we tried to associate with memory. It's really just a nicer way of doing slow motion.

We used the different cameras for different reasons. The SI-2K was wonderful in the slums because it's small and flexible. It's very good for handheld work because the cameraman can strap the main body of the camera – which is the hard drive – on his back and then hold the camera itself. A film camera has to either sit on the shoulder or the hip and, although you can run with it, it tends to stay in one of those two positions. The SI-2K is lighter, so you can not only run with it, but also hold it in your hand. Initially, when we did test shoots, there was a juddering or flickering on it. So Anthony and his team developed a giro to be fixed underneath it, which effectively created a poor man's version of a Steadicam. The giro system takes a few minutes to warm up but it stabilises the image so you can hold the camera in the hand. But then the giro was humming constantly, which drove the sound department mad. So Anthony had to build a blimp for the giro, which made the SI-2K bigger! But it still wasn't as big as a film camera.

Did Dod Mantle discuss the various cameras with you?

The first thing we talked about was wanting to use digital; I assumed we'd work on a slightly more sophisticated version of the system we'd used on *28 Days Later*. Then Anthony came up with the SI-2K system and the CanonCam. He thought the latter would be a wonderful way of recording or documenting fleeting memories. Anthony knew how vibrant India would be and he wanted a system whereby he could capture it at a moment's notice. He gave me the camera and I shot footage too. It was a joy to be able to capture life as it passed us by. Had we used a traditional camera and spent time setting up a crew for each supposedly random shot, either the moment would have gone or it would have looked self-conscious.

We used celluloid for night shoots. And I loved the SI-2K for footage of the kids because of its potential for spontaneity.

I presume you used the SI-2K for the runway scene at the start of Slumdog?

Yes, because the kids could do what they liked and it was up to Anthony to follow them. You had to hope and pray he didn't pull a hamstring as he was chasing them! Anthony is an absolutely brilliant handheld cameraman. He's in a league of his own.

Were the Indian crew committed to the shoot, or were they distracted by other jobs and other job offers?

I often noticed that a crew member would turn up looking a bit different. And it would be a brother or an uncle who'd been asked to stand in for a day or two. Saurabh Shukla was doing two other jobs while working on *Slumdog*. He'd be with us for about eight hours, go off and act on another movie, and then direct a third through the night. He'd be fast, fast asleep on the *Slumdog* set by the morning – we often had to wake him to do his scenes. Other actors were off doing whiskey commercials in Malaysia. You can't get frustrated, you can't shout and scream. It's bigger than you. Way bigger. It'd be pitiful to shout and scream. You have to get stuck in there and start enjoying it.

Did it make your impressive energy levels seem low by comparison?

I enjoyed every moment of it – even when we got hounded out of Agra because we were shooting scenes around the Taj without permission. The Mafia-style tourist guides were really heavy. There were punch-ups. Sunil, the Steadicam guy, actually got into a fight and was throwing punches!

What happened?

We were filming 'disrespectful' scenes; the boys were stealing and living on their wits.

Did you have permission to film?

We applied for a kind of permission. You send in a version of the script, one which isn't in any way provocative. Of course, they twig eventually that you're actually working from a different script. Basically, the tourist guides didn't like us being around because it was their turf and it's obviously big business. Finally this fight started and they threw us out.

And you had to send another crew back to finish off the scenes?

We sent Mrinal Desai, our second-unit cameraman; he hadn't been with us the first time. He pretended to be shooting for a German documentary crew. We'd edited the material we had and knew exactly what we needed to make a coherent sequence. There's a time-lapse shot to stitch it all together. We couldn't send back any of the actors because they were in the local papers. People had been told to watch out for them!

Were there endless escapades?

We only got into trouble at the Taj, but there were stories every day! Which is where Simon Beaufoy initially got his impetus for the script and it's what we fed on when we were there. There's a good snake story. We could only find one place to film the transition moment, from the three little kids running away from the bad guys to Jamal and Salim jumping on a train and leaving Latika behind. This place was a goods yard populated by cobras. There were shrines to cobras everywhere; the people who lived there worshipped them. The kids had to have bare feet and there were snakes everywhere, but there was no question of smoking the cobras out. This was their territory, and you had to respect that. Finally, we used snake charmers to entice the cobras into baskets. When we'd finished shooting, they let the snakes go.

How did you film the kids hanging off the train? It looks as though it's done for real.

It was. We went to a place called Penn outside Mumbai to do the train scenes. It's quieter there and you can control the trains on some of the tracks. It was complicated doing those long scenes on trains. It was a bit scary in terms of making sure the kids were okay, as they were tied to ropes, hanging off the roof and down the side of the train. The stunt guy Sham Kaushal was amazing. A proper godfather: he has this thing that if anybody dies or gets injured, he looks after their family. There's no medical insurance, so he takes responsibility. And, in turn, they're devoted to him. He's made so many films, he's seen everything. Especially overexcited directors!

Let's go back to the Taj Mahal: how did you feel seeing it for the first time?

It's certainly one of the wonders of the world. The light on it changes constantly, making it infinite. It's so beautiful, so romantic. I'm not a terribly romantic person but it's . . . incredible. It's vast. You're so familiar with images of it, but you have absolutely no idea of the scale. The story – of Mughal Emperor Shah Jahan building this magnificent monument in memory of his wife the year after she died giving birth to their fourteenth child – is both desperately romantic and sad. During both the Second World War and the Indo-Pakistani war in the 1970s, scaffolding was erected around it and it was covered in tarpaulin so bombers couldn't find it at night, because it shines in the

Salim (Azharuddin Mohammed Ismail) and Jamal (Ayush Mahesh Khedekar) leaving Mumbai as young boys.

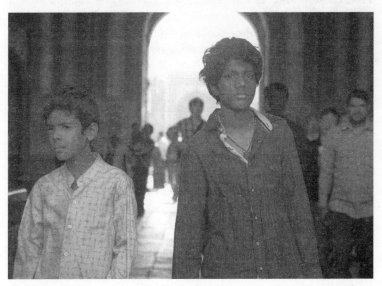

Jamal (Tanay Hemant Chheda) and Salim (Ashutosh Lobo Gajiwala) arriving at the Taj Mahal as teenagers.

dark. Building something as huge as the Taj is a staggering feat. To cover it in tarpaulin just beggars belief – welcome to India.

Did you feel like a tourist while wandering around the Taj?

I kept repeating this mantra in my head: 'We're *not* tourists. We're not here to stare at the sights. These kids, these actors are here to make some money if they can.' The crew couldn't believe it when we said we didn't want to film the Gates of India in southern Mumbai, because they're such a big tourist attraction. But I didn't want any of the tourist icons. I deliberately avoided all touristy ideas of India until Jamal and Salim turn up at the Taj. And then you see tourists being ripped off and the two lads being beaten up. The idea of the American tourist offering a hundred-dollar bill to Jamal when he's just been beaten up by the driver is brilliant. Jamal says to the American: 'You wanted to see the "real India", Mister David. Here it is.' And the American replies: 'Well, here's a bit of the real America too, son.' They love that moment in America. Not in the Warner Brothers screening, as I remember, but in every other screening.

Shortly after the 'real America' scene, Jamal watches Gluck's opera Orfeo ed Euridice. *Did you and Beaufoy disagree about this scene?*

We did have a big disagreement. Simon loves *Orfeo ed Euridice*. I'm not a big opera fan. When I was directing *Morse*, John Thaw took me to the Royal Opera House. I was fast asleep inside forty minutes. He was a Salford lad, but he liked sitting there among the hoi polloi and being the centre of attention. Simon loves opera too. I always felt it was the only scene in the whole script that was basically colonial, in the sense that we were dispensing our highly rarefied Western culture to these Indian kids.

I told Simon my John Thaw story and said if Jamal went to see the opera, he'd be so bored by these ridiculous people. But Simon's heart was in the emotion of the music and the connection between Orpheus looking for Eurydice and Jamal looking for Latika. This dates back to my Royal Court days, but if the writer really digs his heels in and I've done everything to get him to change his mind, I've tried to humiliate him and nothing is working, I shoot the scene. Because I might be wrong. I'll only find out in the edit. So I shot it and, in the end, we kept it.

Was that the only major disagreement between you?

No, I was also worried about the motif of the Three Musketeers. I thought it was another hint of the old colonial. I didn't think Hindu kids would be reading about the Three Musketeers. So that went back and forth between us all. In the end Simon was proved 100 per cent right. It doesn't feel colonial at all. And as we were filming we met more and more Indians who knew the story. Later, we felt audiences react to it; they like the idea of it.

During the process of making the film, Christian, Simon and I were like the Three Musketeers. As were Pravesh, Tabrez and Sanjay, our three main guys from India Take One, then my touchstones Loveleen, Raj and Resul. They love all that symmetry in India. You see? You can't rationalise everything!

Nor can you hurry things up. India has a unique, seductive energy, but things also happen very slowly . . .

. . . or not at all. But you'd get into the groove of it and know you were going to get there eventually. Because Mumbai is a very generous place. The right-wingers think it's too open, too welcoming. People from all over India charge to Mumbai because it's the country's dream factory. Not just because of Bollywood being based there, but also because it's slightly more progressive. It's the only place you can really be homosexual with any kind of safety at all. Calcutta was always the big city, until they opened the Suez Canal and access to the West suddenly grew. Bombay was that gateway. Mumbai is a great cosmopolitan city, but it doesn't quite have the infrastructure to be like Barcelona or London – they have a lot of building to do. But, boy, are they getting on with it.

Did you learn what you could about India before you went – from books such as Suketu Mehta's Maximum City *– and then basically accept the fact that the only real way of learning about the country was on the job?*

Usually it's hard to read a book about a country you have yet to visit; you don't know what is and isn't true. But *Maximum City* felt completely convincing. And then I got to India and it felt ten times truer. A work of true genius. Eventually, I was told to stop mentioning *Maximum City* in interviews because of potential legal problems – I was making it sound as though we'd adapted Mehta's book and not *Q&A*. I also watched some of the more controlled, restrained Bollywood films, and they're brilliant. Like *Satya*, a 1998 Hindi crime film directed by Ram Gopal Varma, and another of his films, *Company*, made in 2002. Anurag Kashyap's *Black Friday*. Aamir Khan's *Taare Zameen Par*.

I think *Slumdog* has started to change people's attitude to Bollywood. For a long time we'd watch ten minutes of a Bollywood film and have a good laugh. We'd sneer. But in doing so we are seriously underestimating the quality of the actors. They make so many movies and, as a result, are incredibly confident. I think the business side of Hollywood realises that Bollywood may well prove to be their saving grace, their chance to be reborn. The Indian film industry may well be their way out of the maze. They are all over there already, trying to set up companies.

I always tell a story that appeared in the gossip papers while we were making *Slumdog*. Will Smith was in Mumbai twice while I was there, but he wasn't shooting, he wasn't on holiday and it's as far away from Los Angeles as you can get. Of course, he was working – setting up a company to co-produce films. He's a big businessman, a very smart guy. He's the kind of figure who will cross over. All the big Western films are released in India now.

Having said all this, you can't deny that it's a completely different environment to work in. When you're there, shooting a film, you have to accept India for what it is. You can't half-trust the people around you; you have to go all the way. It's a very proud country. It's the biggest democracy in the world, so you have to be careful not to go in thinking you're bringing civilisation.

I guess you'd do it without really thinking.

You have to consciously stop yourself. That kind of Western superiority complex, however wrong, is innate. And if you're surrounded by the comfort zone of your own people, you'll never lose it.

So you're out of your comfort zone in an insanely chaotic country, trying not to be remotely colonial. How did you deal with the bureaucracy as well?

We got detailed advice about how to negotiate that. It's interesting because there are still visible remnants of British rule. We'd go into offices overwhelmed by paperwork – Dickensian, Kafkaesque walls of files. Yet there's an order to everything too. As a result of Indira Ghandi's relatively close relationship with the Russians in the 1970s, there's this Stalinist, state-controlled mentality. It exists almost ludicrously within the chaotic world of India. There's still a sense that everything has to be done properly: 'Oh no, sir, that has to be stamped – by twenty different people.' So you have to be taught how to negotiate your way through those different strands of British and Soviet bureaucracy. Which means lying sometimes. But it's like the infinite no we talked about: it's not really lying because everyone knows you're lying. It's not really the point.

Did you have to be particularly inventive? For example, you needed an aerial shot of the city, but it would have taken months – years, even – to get permission. So you found a way round it.

The first thing you have to do when you want to film in India is submit a script. I never saw the submitted script, so I can't tell you very much about it. This was deliberate so I never had to lie, but I've a pretty good idea of what was and wasn't in it. When we needed the aerial shot, we didn't even bother to try and get permission. We just went up in a helicopter with a stills camera; nobody was any the wiser and by the time the film came out nobody cared. There were other occasions when we wouldn't dare be so cheeky. There's a famous bay in Mumbai called the Queen's Necklace; it's very romantic and full of ordinary people who have nowhere else to court. On the other side of the bay is the so-called Slum Necklace. It's an extraordinary slum attached to a fishing village, and everyone shits on this necklace of stones because it goes out to sea. It's a huge toilet, but visually it's fantastic because it faces the Queen's Necklace.

I said, 'We've got to film there!' But nobody is ever allowed to because they can't get permission: next to the village is a closely guarded naval bay. It's where the remnants of the Soviet bureaucracy come into play; anything to do with national security is out of bounds. So you might be able to get up in a helicopter if you're crafty and film furtively but, if you shoot near that naval base,

293

chances are you'd be shot down. It's that weird, sharp-edged state line. The infinite flexibility of Mumbai stops for a moment.

At least you got the aerial shots of the slums without getting into trouble.

That's true. The day we went up, it was pouring, and we had to land in the backyard of a factory until the rain eased off. The rain is so fierce that helicopters can struggle. We used the CanonCam; because it's a stills camera, we knew that if it came to it, we could argue that technically we weren't actually filming because you're allowed to take reference stills. And the CGI guys, Adam Gascoyne and the team that had worked on *Millions*, cleaned it up really well.

What did the slums look like from the air?

It struck me that there's no separation between sophisticated and prosperous buildings and these enormous slum areas around them. India doesn't have the Western habit of ghettoising its poorer population. The poorer people tend to live next to the buildings they service. They are not bussed in to work in the big apartment buildings. Life is interconnected in a surprising and yet wise way. No matter how rich you get, you are still dependent on your driver. Although some of the tasks are very menial, it's not a slave-and-master relationship. The rich have a responsibility not only to create work, but then to look after people for most of their lives.

What were your most basic thoughts and feelings about the slums? Are people happy enough in their slums, as Mehta describes in Maximum City, *or should they be torn down in favour of standard housing?*

It's not that black and white. The first thing that hits you when you go to India is the fact that, as I just pointed out, there are no geographical ghettos. Mehta is very specific about the situation in *Maximum City*: the slum dwellers' greatest fear is living in a lonely room on the edge of the city. Most would be very happy to stay in the slum if they could go to the mall too. The Dharavi slum is full of people who are holding down quite decent jobs in nearby IT centres.

Our image of Dharavi is of hopeless poverty. I almost wrote to the *Guardian* after reading an article about Dharavi having no schools in it. We'd filmed in the schools there! They are extraordinary. Of course they are overcrowded and chaotic – but they are there, run by dedicated people against all the odds. People work hard so they can pay a few rupees to get their kids into them. It's worth it because everyone believes in education. The only way they'll break the cycle they're in, coming from a poor area, is through education. In Mumbai it's all about learning English and IT because then your job prospects shift completely.

And will those who are educated then leave the slums?

Not necessarily. It's very difficult to buy property because land is scarce and therefore it's incredibly expensive. Property is, in fact, the same price as in New York. Most of Mumbai is still mangrove swamp, limiting the land that can actually be built on. Which, of course, makes Dharavi, in the heart of the city, very valuable. If property developers could get the 2 million living there out, it would be worth a fortune. But the people won't go. They all have a vote, which makes them pretty powerful. Local politicians only have to say, 'Vote for me and I'll make sure you don't have to move.' And it does feel like you're at the centre of everything there. It would be hard to break the cycle.

Everything in India seems to be constantly evolving. Nothing stays the same. Nothing is simple. Every day you hear extraordinary stories. They say virtually everyone in the police force is corrupt. There are so many bent cops who earn extra cash by, for example, fining a driver for shooting through a red light when the driver has done no such thing. If the cops were well paid, they wouldn't have to resort to such tactics.

People do need to fight to make sure that the exploitation of people's rights doesn't become more than casual. It's maybe okay to be clipped round the head by a cop as you're walking down the street – like it was here in the 1950s. But more serious crimes by cops – casual torture, extortion, even murder – are being clamped down on. If you want your prime minister or president at the G8 summit, you can't keep operating under your own rules only.

What did you find when you were looking around police stations to research the torture scenes with Dev Patel, Irrfan Khan and Saurabh Shukla?

They showed us everything. You see the handcuffs on the wall. We even saw these huge kind of doorstoppers made of leather and wood and flexible at the end. They were used for hitting people; they must have really hurt. There we were, a Western film crew with cameras, and they were quite happy to show us around. The Indian crew told me that if you came from a certain kind of background and you were picked up, there was a 50/50 chance you'd be beaten up a bit. If it was anything serious, the electricity would be out straight away, as it is in *Slumdog*.

You have to get permission for anything involving the police. We were very nervous about submitting the torture scene; we were expecting to get a knockback, and I was planning to film the scene outside India and cut it in. In fact, the reply came that the torture scene was fine so long as nobody above the rank of inspector was involved. Which just confirmed what the Indian crew had told me: people from a certain social class get knocked about quite freely. And the police don't even try to hide it!

The torture scene.

Despite the torture scenes, Slumdog *isn't a political film. How did you approach filming the scene in which Jamal and Salim's mother is brutally killed at the start? I presume you had to be pretty sensitive?*

We couldn't film those scenes in the actual slum. They were the only scenes we recreated elsewhere. We were told a real riot might start if we filmed in the slums. You can't control that infinity of people. Anything can happen: a bicycle can be knocked over and a riot can begin. I'm not exaggerating; when we were filming on the balcony outside a cinema there was almost a riot on the street because too many people were watching us film. Somebody knocked a motorbike over and then a fight started which spread contagiously along the street.

So we shot what we needed in the real places. We filmed the burning man running in the street in the Dharavi slum. It was an insane idea, but Raj, the first AD, and Sham, the stuntman, were both amazing. They made it happen. I was shocked by Dhobi Ghat, the place where people wash their clothes by the railway line. So many people are killed by trains as they dry their clothes next to the tracks. The clothes, which are all saris and other very light clothing, have to be held down with stones. The trains are like a tumble drier, blasting the clothes with warm air every ninety seconds. The women's heads are ducked down, laying the clothes out, as the trains whizz past.

The riot took place in a studio in Penn, which is a long way outside Mumbai. There's a much longer version of the riot scene that's incredibly brutal – and accurate – but we cut it right down because it felt out of tone with the rest of the film. To answer your specific comment about *Slumdog* as a political film or not: as a Westerner you're not commenting on those riots because you don't know enough about the history; they are used in the story to show Jamal and Salim's personal loss. The political perspective on them can only be tackled by local film-makers.

How much did you talk to the young actors about what was going on with the riot or, later, the kids' eyes being burned?

We talked about how it would affect them in terms of the story. You wouldn't expect seven-year-old kids to understand anything other than their mother being killed in front of their eyes and how upset they would feel. They rush to the police; the police don't help them – which is how it was: the police didn't go into the slums initially. I think it allowed us to touch on those issues, because you view them through the eyes of a child who doesn't have any politics or an axe to grind.

I thought the riot scene would cause trouble, but because it wasn't exaggerated and it wasn't ultra-violent there was no trouble. It was more a case of 'How dare they call us slumdogs, what does this word mean?' Simon made the word up and it was meant affectionately. Yet, for Indians, 'dog' has colonial connotations.

When you were filming the eye-burning scenes in the orphanage, Azhar throws up for real. How did he do it on command?

The two boys – the youngest Salim and Jamal – are brilliant in different ways. Ayush is an incredible professional. For a kid of that age he understood story structure straight away. Azhar, who isn't remotely interested in acting as an intellectual pursuit, relies on instinct. If he's up for it, he's great; if he's tired, forget it. The lads in *Millions* were exactly the same; if they were tired they just fell asleep. You just have to wait or send them home. It's not like a grown-up actor who can be bribed with coffee or threats or extra cash.

There are no laws protecting child actors in India, but were you careful not to overuse the kids, even though it must have been tempting to do so at times?

I'd made it work on *Millions*, so we tried to apply the same rules. I'm not making myself out to be a saint, because the reality was long, long hours for everyone, including the kids. Travelling in Mumbai is so time-consuming that it could take two or three hours to get to and from set. It was less gruelling for me than for the kids, of course: I ate in the cab on the way home and I set up mobile broadband so I could take conference calls and do emails. Sometimes I'd leave the set at 7 p.m. and yet not be back at the hotel till 10 p.m. And the hotel was only a few miles away. There's no point in shouting and screaming about the traffic; you have to organise your work life around it.

Although you obviously fell in love with Mumbai, there must have been aspects of the city that shocked you. Even the crew were upset when you filmed on the landfill sites.

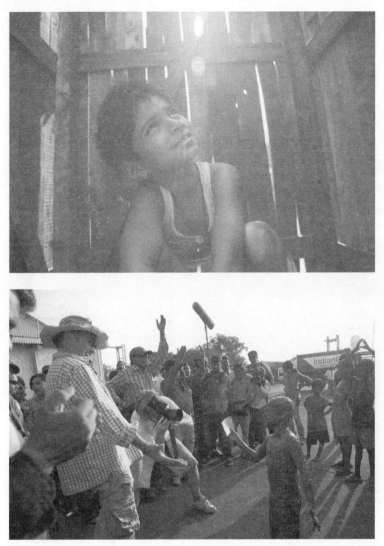

Top: Jamal in the toilet . . . Bottom: . . . and covered in human waste.

I said we were going to shoot there all day, and the crew thought I was mad. People live there, although not in the same numbers as in the slums; it's a hive of activity with people recycling whatever they can find. They started recycling way before we discovered the ozone hole. It's just part of life; it's the way society is organised.

Everything that is thrown away is sifted through by gangs of people who recycle it for money.

We went to two tips. The first was Garai Beach, and I've never seen anything like it in my life. We went on a rainy day, so it looked particularly apocalyptic. We were driving through 30–40ft canyons of sheer banks of rubbish. We took loads of photographs before getting caught; we only had dodgy permission. They are not very proud of Garai Beach as it's pretty horrific; they certainly don't like anyone taking photos of it. Before they threw us out, they inspected the car we were in. The local guy who was with us urged us to delete all the photos. Which we did, sadly.

Then we found another landfill site which wasn't quite so bad. You can't capture it on film, but the ground you stand on is actually towers of rubbish rocking gently from side to side. Standing on the rubbish was like balancing on a fishing pole at sea. Some crew wanted face masks, but I didn't think it was respectful given that people actually lived there.

How tricky was it to recreate the scene in which middle Jamal and the blind kid Arvind are smoked out of the underpass by some kind of mosquito repellent?

That really happens in Mumbai: they hoover the drains and underpasses with this incredible machine. We tried to use non-lethal smoke, but of course it doesn't look anything like the diesel smoke they use. So we ended up using diesel smoke and telling everyone to hold their breath as they ran through. You see so much stuff like that – which is why it's such an inspirational place to work. The blind kid was amazing. Loveleen found these brothers who were both born blind and who were singers. Siddesh Patil plays the older Arvind; there's another version of the scene with his brother playing the harmonica, but we didn't use it in the end. We wanted the scene to be more intimate. I'd never worked with a blind actor before. He spoke no English, only Hindi, so I couldn't communicate with him that much, but he was amazing. Loveleen did a lot of work with him.

With the wobbling landfill sites and the smoked-out underpass, you must have felt you were capturing at least some of the DNA of Mumbai on screen?

Maybe a tiny bit. You've also got to find a way of portraying the city that fits the story.

Not even in the discombobulating yet breathtaking opening scene? From the airstrip to the chase, it undeniably captures something of the spirit of Mumbai.

It was certainly amazing to shoot. It was exhausting for the crew, but I loved it. Again we had the support of the people in the Juhu slum. We were there so often, and they were fine about it. All the shacks have got a telly, so they're watching it the whole time and are quite savvy about it. Anyway, they are busy people. At certain times the cows are driven through, and you have to get out of the way – it's like Pamplona in slow motion. The crew were always teasing me about having cows in *Slumdog*. Westerners always do, they said. So I refused to include them; it would have been *way* too obvious.

You talk of finding 'a way of portraying the city that fits the story'. It's apposite that, in such a frantic city where everyone is doing several things at once, you had to deal with five timelines in Slumdog.

This is a slight detour, but I remember going to VT station – which is now called Chhatrapati Shivaji Terminus – when I first arrived in Mumbai and feeling surprised when nobody even glanced at me. I was expecting some kind of response to my British, colonial background – these trains were built in Crewe! But Mumbaites have so much to do, so many people to get through to do it, so little time to do it.

So yes, the multiple timelines suited the frenzied complexity of the city. But they were tricky to execute. They seemed to work in the script, so my job was to make the three kids at different ages feel like the same person, although not to a ridiculous degree. And then you just trust the structure. You have to film the script and not your red herrings, the little things you think are fascinating at the time. Experience tells you they are often not. When you're a story-based, narrative-based director, always make sure you shoot the narrative. That's your first and foremost priority, even though you may doubt it sometimes when you're in the middle of filming. Because at that point you're not a rational person. You're a hormonal imbalance of self-importance, exhaustion . . . all these stupid things are going around your brain as you're trying to organise it all. Ironically, it makes you not the best judge of the film. You become a far better judge, hopefully, in the editing room. It's weird the way the scales fall from your eyes. I might think I've had a genius idea on set, but when I see it in the edit I'm embarrassed.

Shooting the narrative – almost at all costs – allows you to film for a certain amount of money. It makes you brutal with your own fantasies. I always have fantasies: I'd love to do it this way, that way. I'll have a wish list, but I know I'll have to abandon it eventually. I might come back disappointed sometimes, but I will have the film in the end. Not that everyone else will be watching the same film; it's amazing talking to people after they've watched a cut and realising how little they've actually absorbed. They take in virtually nothing other than the big scenes. And there you are, waiting in silence for them to mention all this peripheral work you've done!

Given that no one seems to notice detail, I do sometimes wonder if it would be enough simply to hit those big points. Or if the stuff they appear to not notice really does let them access the big things . . .

But detail is, surely, everything; a film that hit only the big points would be empty and one-dimensional. I don't believe you could make such a film even if you tried.

Maybe. Interesting idea, though. Anyway, it's always best to end up in the edit with too much material, too much detail. We decided early on to shoot too much material on *Slumdog* and then edit it very carefully simply because it would allow us to work very freely with the young kids who hadn't acted before. We ended up with a very long cut, as you'd expect on such a picaresque film. Editor Chris Dickens and I had to be tough. You've got to be open to what others suggest in editing. But you need a great editor to absorb everything that is chucked at him and then paint the fine watercolour.

I remember inviting M.I.A. – or Maya – to watch an early cut because we wanted to use 'Paper Planes'. My daughter Grace introduced me to the track when it was first released and it always stuck with me. Maya was very complimentary, which was obviously very nice, but more importantly she had a couple of really good notes. One was cracking: how did Jamal get on the show in the first place?

She said some kind of explanation had to be offered as it's not that easy to get onto these shows. The scene in which Jamal tries to get through to *Millionaire* while he's in the call centre had been cut from the version she saw. So I put it back in. It was an incisive narrative note that you would normally only get from really good producers. I was impressed. She's a very smart girl.

Maya worshipped A. R. Rahman; they share a Tamil background. I'm pretty sure one of the reasons she came to see the film was not to endorse the use of 'Paper Planes', but because she wanted to work with Rahman. Which of course she did. They came up with a lovely piece, 'O . . . Saya', at the beginning of the film.

A. R. Rahman is a megastar in India. How did you get him on board?

I met him a few times in Mumbai. The so-called Three Musketeers from India Take One were crucial in setting up such meetings. It still took for ever to meet up with him as he's always so busy. But he's done everything he can in India, where he's like a god. This was a different sort of challenge.

I showed him the film with a temporary soundtrack. I used some of his songs but most of it was Western music that I'd been listening to. So he saw the film, went off and started work. He has an amazing micro-studio in the middle of a suburban maisonette in Tufnell Park, north London. I was constantly travelling across the city to see him, and we spent many a late evening listening to music. He welcomed endless late-night visitors – singers and musicians coming to record bits for the film after they'd performed in the West End that night in *The Lion King*, *Chicago*, etc.

I encouraged him to be really bold. There's a big connection between Bollywood and Disneyesque songs, but I didn't want any of that. I wanted something that would shock people. I wanted the music to be part of the appeal of the film. I didn't want it to sound Bollywood. I got to quite like Bollywood music, but it was a barrier when I first heard it. Initially, I thought only a Western composer could play around with it. But when I met Rahman, I really thought he could do it, provided I gave him the space to do it properly.

Surely we're done with *Slumdog* now (*laughs*)?

We've barely started! You wanted the ending to have the spirit of Sebastião Salgado's 1995 photo Mumbai, *a black-and-white image of men in white kurtas streaming through Church Gate station.*

Oh yes! It's always been one of my favourite photographs. I've got it up in my house, and I gave it to my daughter Grace for her eighteenth birthday. It's also on the cover of *Maximum City*. I went to the window Salgado shot it from, but the view has changed so much because very few wear the kurtas now – it's more Gap and Abercrombie & Fitch!

You took inspiration from more than one station: you particularly enjoyed shooting the dance scene in VT station.

Oh God, I *love* VT station. It's the heart of the city. When the terrorists attacked it in November 2008, we wondered what was going to happen, because the film had yet to come out. I was really pleased we'd shot the dance scene there because it's about love. It's unashamedly romantic and ludicrous, in a sense. They dance, and you think it's a great celebration. I went back there shortly after the terrorist murders and it was already back to normal. It's like New

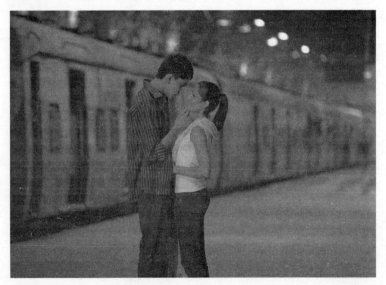

Jamal and Latika in VT station.

Jamal and Latika lead the celebratory dance.

York, London and Madrid: it doesn't matter what terrorists try to do, these cities will just carry on.

In the same way that you shot the empty streets of London in 28 Days Later just before 9/11, you were fortunate to film in VT station before the terrorist attacks; you may not have got permission otherwise.

That's true. Films *are* blessed or cursed. So we got chased out of the Taj and came home for Christmas. On Christmas Day I suddenly realised we hadn't even started to rehearse the dance. Nobody had really thought about it. Normally the line producer would be banging on at me, but in India everything is left until the day itself. They don't prepare stuff. I didn't quite panic, but I did realise Dev and Freida had to start working with the choreographer Longinus Fernandes, whom we forgot to credit in the film. It was clear that given Dev's skill level and how much time we had, it was going to be fairly basic. So we did it simply.

We had limited time in the station: for three or four nights we could close it down between 1.30 a.m. and 4 a.m. We didn't have time to stop and do the next bit, stop and do the next bit; we had to do the whole dance and any mistakes, Dev, we'll just have to forget them and cut them out. So we did the whole dance two or three times each night using loads of cameras.

I originally wanted 5,000 people in the dance sequence. That shrank to 3,000 then 1,500 . . . in the end we only had a few hundred. I thought about having Ayush and Rubina in the scene quite late on. It was one of the few occasions we used them after midnight. Their homes weren't far from the station, and we'd finished with them by 2 a.m. They had no idea what we were doing. We just told them to watch and copy. Dancing is so natural in India, even for kids of seven.

The trains were different each night; I think one is a completely different colour at a certain point. With all that going on, the only option was to create a blizzard of movement. We had to cut a wonderful scene in which a statue of Frederick Stevens, who designed VT station, joins in the dancing. I asked Suttirat Larlarb, the costume designer, to make the choreographer's assistant look like the statue with a day's notice. She did this brilliant costume that looks like stone. And then we cut the scene . . .

Let's talk about costume and make-up.

Suttirat was a young assistant in the art department on *The Beach* and she really stood out. I've tried to use her in various capacities in every film since then. I think it's harder for women in the art-department world to ascend to the top job, but it's what she deserves. She's super-bright. I want to design a whole film with her eventually, not just costumes. She's a visual artist, so she doesn't think of costume in a rigid way. She thinks of it much more fluidly.

Suttirat had done the costume on *Sunshine*, so I asked her to come to India. She had a great time, I think. She had to deal with the very male-dominated crews, but she's pretty tough. She was working closely with Riyaz Ali Merchant, who's usually a costume designer in his own right. He had to accept he was working under her but he showed her round town, showed her all the things she needed to see. There's no fuss with Suttirat, so no one else fusses either.

Suttirat got some great suits for Anil, which he wisely kept. I remember her explaining how she was going to associate Latika with yellow. She'd already read *Maximum City* and knew picking out individuals in India is very difficult, so Latika needed to wear a visible colour. She said that when Dev comes across the railway track at the end, he should wear a *Die Hard*-style vest underneath his shirt. 'You've got to sex him up. You're a bloke, you don't realise, but we want him to be hot!' So she put a black T-shirt on him and she tells me he looks a bit like John Travolta in that scene.

We had two amazing people in the make-up department too: Virginia Holmes, a Brit who moved to India years ago, and Natasha Nischol, who's part of a big film dynasty in Bollywood. These two live half in the world of Bollywood and half in the Western world. Of course, they represent the way that industry is going to go. You can see the hybrid thing that will emerge, that's able to access the skills and traditions and flavour of Bollywood, but also has this Western sensibility in terms of prep and detail.

Sometimes Virginia and Natasha alerted us to the rules of how and why things do or don't work in India, which was incredibly useful. Probably their biggest challenge was applying a very tricky scar day after day onto Latika's face. It's not the scar itself that's tricky, but the damage done to the skin; the next day she may not need the scar and her skin has to be perfect.

Production designer Marco [Mark Digby] and Suttirat got some acknowledgement in America, but they didn't get as much as the rest of us. It's a shame because although their work is often not as flamboyant as, say, the camera work, it's of equal importance in the end. Marco certainly deserves a lot of statues for what he went through.

What did Digby bring to Slumdog?

The designer is on the front line, so Marco and his team – Michelle Day and Arwel Evans – were always one step ahead of us, slowly negotiating the Indian system. They were out there first, learning all the painful lessons and protecting us from having to do the same. Marco brought great flair to the job but his effect on *Slumdog* is partially invisible: he was constantly manipulating locations to make them more visually stimulating for both the camera and the story. One more obvious example of his work was his creation of the outdoor toilets. The original ones that Simon spotted had been torn down, so Marco built several weird, private forts at the end of these piers. He may not have had as many awards as he was due, but he did us a great job.

Are you suggesting Slumdog *should have won more than eight Oscars?*

(*laughs*) No! It's just that not everyone gets the awards they deserve.

We'll get round to those Oscars, but first I'd like to know if the experience of working in India eclipsed any award going?

That's a good question. Way before anyone started to fuss about the film, I remember thinking: 'I just learned so much from being in India. About myself, about directing, about using the camera. If only I could have such an incredible learning experience on every film.' It's why I contrast *Slumdog* so much with *The Beach*: I could possibly have had a similar experience on *The Beach* but I didn't even know enough at that point to be able to operate properly.

Were you itching to get back to India as soon as you left?

Oh yeah! I couldn't stop shooting on my days off and, even when Christian and Anthony had left, I just carried on. Christian decided the only way he could stop me was to shut the bank account. I was reluctant to come home even after eight months out there. So yes, I'd love to work on another film in India. There are several ideas floating around. I'd love to make a film about this incredible bridge linking two sections of the island of Mumbai. They were building it for ever and it's only just opened. You just know the level of corruption that is taking place. It's visually stunning, like the George Washington Bridge in Manhattan. In *The Great Gatsby*, F. Scott Fitzgerald writes that the city seen from the Queensboro Bridge is the city seen for the first time. It's how a city declares itself. I want to make a film about someone who was living under that bridge when it was first being built. There are all sorts of rumours about people being buried in the concrete underneath it and so on.

I'd also love to make some kind of thriller in India. While we were making *Slumdog* – which is more a picaresque film with thrilling elements in it and, in the end, a feelgood journey – I kept thinking about making a thriller. Corruption is so endemic. There's such a close connection between the movie world, the police and the underworld that makes it feel like 1930s America.

We bought the rights to *Maximum City*. We met Suketu Mehta in New York, and he was lovely. The most obvious way of approaching the book is to use it as inspiration for another film rather than make another adaptation.

The relationship of the crowd to the individual, as described so brilliantly in Maximum City, *is interesting too.*

There are a billion people. You've got one chance, you've got to take it. It was extraordinary watching it happen to people around us. As I just said, it's infinite what you learn in India, both about other people and yourself. Actually, you learn nothing about India really. What you learn is about yourself.

I imagine you had a spiritual experience in India?

It's a very spiritual country. Everybody prays – Raj went into every temple we passed by to pay his respects – but I'm not sure Mumbai itself is that spiritual. We had a ceremony invoking Ganesh, the elephant god, at the start of the shoot to bless it . . .

Well, that clearly worked.

It certainly did! Apart from the film's success, we didn't have any near-death experiences, whereas we had three in Thailand. I am still amazed.

In a wonderful example of life imitating art, Slumdog's *behind-the-scenes tale was a rags-to-riches story every bit as tense as Jamal's. It was no small miracle that the film was ever released theatrically: having finished it there was a real possibility that it might have gone straight to DVD. What happened?*

Basically, it looked like the film wasn't going to be released in America. We knew we had the support of Pathé to release the film in the UK and Europe, but it looked like its fate in America was sealed by Warners' indication that they may only put it out on DVD. They shut their Independent division in May 2008 and, alongside many other films that didn't get out of jail like we did, it looked as though

Slumdog wouldn't get a theatrical release in the States. Then my American agent, Robert Newman, showed it to Peter Rice at Fox. Peter wanted to buy it but he didn't want to reveal to Warners how much he was prepared to pay. Obviously he wanted to pay as little as possible. Then, of course, Warners realised it might be a good film and didn't want to give it away!

To cut a very long and complicated story short, the collective genius of Robert Newman, Peter Rice and John Horn, a journalist at the *LA Times*, was absolutely pivotal in *Slumdog*'s story. Horn was a big supporter of earlier films such as *Sunshine*, and he used his newspaper – which is very powerful in the enclosed world of Los Angeles – to support the film. And, in the end, *Slumdog* got a proper theatrical release in America: Warners and Fox Searchlight agreed to share distribution and Fox bought 50 per cent of Warners' interest in the film.

How did the Telluride and Toronto film festivals then help your cause?

By the time *Slumdog* went to the festivals it was with Fox Searchlight. The deal may not have been legally signed, but we had shaken hands. However, festivals such as Telluride and Toronto run on small budgets and in difficult circumstances. They are key to the success of films like *Juno*, *Slumdog* and *Precious*. Toronto has now become the crucial festival from which you launch your Academy campaign.

Warner chief Alan Horn – no relation to the journalist John – told the LA Times *on 14 August 2008 that* Slumdog *was for sale. 'We're not going to give it away . . . I like the movie. I just don't know how big the audience is for it.' How did such a comment make you feel? Did you instinctively sense that it* would *have an audience?*

I wouldn't pretend to know the American audience better than Alan Horn. And Warners are, of course, very successful at what they do. But I did know by then that there was a genuine appetite for the film among like-minded people. Just as Warners were reluctant to give *Slumdog* away, we were determined to ensure that they eventually did! And they made a lot of money out of it in the end. I think everybody came out of it well finally.

What was your reaction when you thought, however briefly, that Slumdog *might not get a proper release?*

I remember talking to Robert Newman, who was the first to mention the dreaded 'straight-to-DVD' phrase. I'm not just making this up because it sounds noble: I learned a huge amount from India and thought that if the film's fate in America was a DVD-only release, then I had to let it be. At the same time, I knew we wouldn't let it happen in Europe; *Slumdog* would definitely have a home there. Part of me was thinking that America always felt a long, long way away from this story, whereas Europe didn't, if only because of our colonial history with India. I knew we'd done a decent job on the film; we'd done our best. So I kept thinking, 'What will be, will be.'

You genuinely thought that?

Genuinely. I know exactly where I was standing in my house, with the phone at my ear, when Robert told me the bad news. Listen, I'd just been through *Sunshine*, which might as well have gone straight to DVD in America. So it wasn't like I thought, 'How dare they?' And India had, as I say, deeply affected me: things play out in the way they play out. There's something you can't understand about it. You have to try your hardest to work it the way you want it, but part of you has to accept that things are written. Thankfully, Robert Newman, Peter Rice and John Horn were determined to write it a different way.

At what point did you realise you had something really special?

At an early screening in a very narrow cinema in north London. We were testing it for ourselves at that point. I remember thinking, 'The story works.' You could tell by the guys off the street who were down the front and who'd turned up to make trouble: the film just shut them up. People's reaction during the running of a film is often much more important than what they say afterwards. You can feel their response to certain scenes or sequences. 'Fuck, that's too slow! We don't need that scene!' You learn about the rhythm of things.

I used to be very anxious and defensive about tests. Now I'd encourage anyone to do it. You learn so much about your film.

It gives people ammunition to attack you with, but none of that matters: listen to the vibe in the room.

You pointed out earlier that you'd done the deal with Fox Searchlight by the time you got to Telluride, but the film festival was still a huge turning point. When Slumdog *was screened on 30 August 2008, John Horn wrote in the* LA Times *that 'the response inside the sold-out theatre could not have been much more enthusiastic'. He was clearly on your side, but he was also simply reporting the audience's response.*

We went to Telluride and the first screening had this terrible sound problem. The sound played twice. It was like having two televisions on simultaneously. When it got really loud, it distorted hideously. I remember sitting there at the end of the row thinking, 'Shall I stop the film?' I was *so* nervous. It was *Slumdog*'s first proper outing. And after all the problems we'd had with Warner Brothers . . . I thought it was best to keep it running, but it was absolute agony for me to watch. Luckily it didn't matter in the end. Which just shows you all the things you obsess about . . .

What was the atmosphere like during the screening from your perspective?

It was good. You could tell the audience thought they'd discovered something. I was super-tense from the sound being so distorted and my shoulders were up round my ears. Mike Leigh was the first person to come up after the screening and try to relax me with a bit of his best Salford: 'Well, you've certainly done it there, lad!' After that screening it just went mad. *Then* you can tell. They started putting on all these other screenings. It's only a tiny town, but all the screenings were sold out.

How did that *feel?*

A huge relief. It was largely down to Peter Rice at Fox. If we could get *Slumdog* ready on time, he wanted to get it into Telluride and Toronto. He knew the routine from *Juno* the year before; he knew the way the trajectory can work. You launch something unprepossessing into a market that's desperate for it. Which is how they see it. It's the end of summer, all the big blockbusters have been and gone; they want something idiosyncratic to take them into the awards season. So we took *Slumdog* to Toronto. You begin to hear the buzz around it. You start to do interviews. You meet people who really like it.

Alongside being pleased for your entire cast and crew, is there an element of ego for you?

I can't reiterate this enough: ego hovers over everything. It threatens to destroy everything and every relationship in the film industry. As in any world of achievement and acknowledgement, I'm sure. It's always there: jealousy, resentment. Having said that, there wasn't much sign of negativity at all. But then we'd made it against the odds. We tried to do everything together, and it paid off. If you stick together, you're stronger and wiser. It occasionally looks like you and the producer are lovers but, that aside, it's the best way to go. Christian and I did make a couple of good decisions. We wanted to present everything as a group. It was hard to do with the actors because there were so many of them. Dev and Freida were obviously the loving couple in the middle of it. Madhur was left out quite a lot. He proved himself the most gracious of all the cast in dealing with that situation, so we owe him one. Anil became a spokesman for the Indian community. He gave them access to the film. He did an amazing job and he benefited from it himself too because he wanted a better profile in the West.

Going back to the very early film festivals for a moment, I remember having a discussion in Telluride with Angela Johnson, the Vice President of Publicity at Fox Searchlight. They had received a screenwriting Oscar nomination for the past five years and promised to try for *Slumdog* too. It was the first time anyone mentioned an Oscar. Our initial hope was Simon. And then the fuss about the music started.

There was another kind of fuss too: although Slumdog *proved to be the third-biggest opening film in India, after* Spiderman 3 *and* Casino Royale, *it wasn't universally celebrated by the Indian community.*

Bollywood as an entity certainly felt ambiguous about *Slumdog.* It loved the attention that was coming its way; there was proper respect from America pretty much for the first time. On the other hand, the top ten people involved with the film were Brits. We had an upset with Amitabh Bachchan, who condemned *Slumdog* on his blog. It was definitely unsettling because he's such a powerful figure in India. Thankfully, he withdrew his criticism after many of his younger fans suggested he was wrong. There was something they liked about the film – perhaps the fact that it was a bit more challenging, a bit more truthful, not so confectionery.

There's a growing middle class in India, estimated at around 350 million people, that is driving the economy now. They have good jobs. As they make their money, they want this kind of car, this kind of movie. They don't want to accept *any* kind of movie; they want to be challenged. These super-bright kids have seen *Trainspotting* and *Fight Club* on DVD. They don't want the confectionery their parents liked. Young Indians no longer just go to the cinema with their families; they go to multiplexes with a date and some popcorn. We bumped into this guy from the UK who was on a two-year mission to install sixty-five new digital projectors around India.

Bachchan may have felt left behind by Slumdog, *but a small number of Western critics accused the film of being poverty porn. What do you plead?*

(*laughs*) I don't plead anything really. I found the places we were working really inspiring both in terms of the people and the way they lived. Although you can regret the conditions in which they live, you must not patronise these people. They are so resilient, so resourceful. It's breathtaking what they achieve with their lives, given they have so little. The idea of the film is to celebrate such achievement: Jamal goes on the show without any real formal education and he wipes the floor with the sneering host. *Slumdog* is saying that no matter how impoverished a life might appear, it is just as valid as the next person's.

I definitely didn't want to make a film where we dwelt on how moved we were by these outrageous living conditions. That was never the point. *Slumdog* is not that kind of film.

But do you think Slumdog *glamorises poverty?*

I only wanted it to reflect the energy I found in those places. Which is in itself a huge challenge: can you simply observe and capture a foreign country without passing any kind of judgement? People go to Africa and say the energy of the place is incredible. The people seem, by and large, happy. How do you square that with their living conditions? But *Slumdog* isn't an outsider looking in and trying to challenge the Indian government on its strategies for dealing with poverty; it's a story about a guy succeeding on his own terms. So you try to make it from that perspective.

I don't think it helped that the poster in the UK had 'feel-good film of the decade' emblazoned on its white background. Jamal may, as you said, have made a feel-good journey, but the movie itself is far darker than the newspaper quote suggests.

If it was up to me, I'd have chosen a black poster without the quote and with a different image of Dev and Freida. I argued my case with John Fletcher at Pathé, and his case for the white poster and the quote were simple: nobody will go and see the film if we put out the black poster. He suggested I imagine it at bus stops in Leeds at 10 p.m. It needed that triumphant element to it. I did my best to argue against John, pointing out that white is the colour of death in India. But, quite rightly, he didn't care about any of that; he was only concerned with bus stops in Leeds. People like John Fletcher know what they're doing and do it for the best of reasons – to get people into the cinema to see your film. Thanks, John.

But you still have to defend the feel-good quote.

And the fact that Dev is punching the air on the white poster. It's a completely fake image. He didn't even do that when he won *Millionaire*, which was very deliberate; he wasn't interested in winning, only in finding the girl. However, having said all that, I'd never trust myself to market my own films.

Returning to the poverty in India, you were determined to give something back to the country – driven, I presume, not by guilt at the huge sum of money Slumdog has made, but by a warm heart – so you set up the Jai Ho Trust. What was its fundamental aim and how successful has it been? Have you been disappointed by the endless reports in the international press about some of the kids' parents wanting more money?

We initially set up provision for the kids while we were still shooting. We thought it was only right that if we were to introduce them to this world, then they should get some benefit from it. We made it clear from the start that they weren't going to get much immediate financial gain from the film. Obviously the best way to benefit the two poorest members of the cast – Azhar and Rubina – was to give them the opportunity of an education. So we set up the Jai Ho charity as a trust fund to see them through to eighteen and beyond by providing school, some basic social support and decent accommodation which they will eventually inherit. They will also receive a lump sum, either when they reach eighteen or when the trustees feel they are ready.

Christian and I made the decision to buy an apartment each for Azhar and Rubina once the film became a commercial success. Each apartment has one room with a kitchen attached and a toilet. They are pretty basic – actually, Azhar was disappointed because it didn't have a swimming pool! Property is so ridiculously expensive in Mumbai; we've been told that some of the members of the regular *Slumdog* crew wouldn't be able to afford these basic apartments. Although it was only right to give Azhar and Rubina as much of a head start as we could, it's a bit unfair on their old neighbours in the slum, the people they've grown up with – but you can't help everyone. We are, however, trying to help more kids by putting some of the profits from *Slumdog* into Plan India and a project they've set up in the Garib Nagar and Behrampada slums in East Bandra, central Mumbai. Over the five years of the project an estimated 2,000 families and 5,000 children will benefit directly through job training, education and health awareness.

The Jai Ho Trust has faced challenges. Christian and I had a ruck with Azhar and Rubina's parents a couple of months ago about their very poor attendance at school. It's partly because the parents are using the kids to make appearances and earn money. We made it very clear that unless they used the opportunity in the proper way and took school seriously, we would withdraw the money. Since our visit, their attendance has improved.

We are committed to Azhar and Rubina until they are adults and can make their own decisions. We benefited a lot from them and we're trying to give something back. Not everybody, however, wants to be lifted out of their circumstances. Azhar's father, who sadly died of TB recently, didn't want to leave the slum and move into the apartment with his wife and Azhar. We tried to at least help him with the TB, but it was too late. It's an ongoing situation.

And will you have to keep going back to India to see how Azhar and Rubina are progressing?

Yes, but I don't think of it like that. It's not a chore; it's a treat for anybody to visit India. The parents of all the young actors deserve a mention here too: Ayush's mum and dad; Azhar's mum; Tanay's mum and dad; Ashutosh's mum and dad; Tanvi's mum and dad. Their support of the kids and their balanced appreciation of the demands of film-making and school and their support of us as film-makers and of the film on its release has been exemplary. But also typical of that city. It's crazy – no one can get anywhere very quickly but it has a mighty heart which pounds away on your behalf.

No amount of criticism or bad blood could stop the awards, which started with the People's Choice Award at the Toronto Film Festival. On 1 February 2009, you picked up the prestigious Directors Guild of America (DGA) award for Outstanding Directorial Achievement in Feature Film.

The DGA awards are seriously nerve-wracking. They do it beautifully. They have a breakfast in the morning with all these serious directors swanning around. Then David Fincher, Ron Howard, Chris Nolan, Gus Van Sant and I sat around discussing our craft for literally hours. The awards ceremony itself is in the evening. I took Raj Acharya, the first AD, and when I won I got him up on stage too. You get one plaque for being nominated and another fucking huge gold one if you win. Raj went home with one and me with the other. We did all the stuff you do the first time you visit Los Angeles: photos under the Hollywood sign, paddle in the Pacific Ocean. First ADs are never properly acknowledged, but on a film like *Slumdog* a guy like Raj was everything to me.

Anyway, the award is presented by the previous year's winner, so the Coen brothers gave me mine. That was pretty cool. I made a speech that acknowledged how much I'd stolen from their films and how happy I was to actually be *given* something by them.

Christian got the PGA producer of the year award. That was

a big sign of what was to come at the Oscars. Most of the films in contention have multiple producers; there is often squabbling about how many producers can be eligible. And there's Christian all on his own and they've never even heard of him. I was *really* proud of him. That was pretty special. It's what they call the money award. Producers take account of the film's financial legs: has it earned its way in the world?

I'll embarrass Christian here, but he was extraordinary throughout. He had great support from his team – Paul Ritchie, Diarmuid McKeown and Gaia Elkington (God knows where we'd be without Gaia!) – and, in turn, he gave me great support. We met every day to deal with whatever crisis was critical that day. He calmly dealt with all my needs – and directors are a pain when they're shooting – while all the time trying to squeeze this film through the sceptical eye of the film-financing world on his own. We never had to sell any of the furniture – as Andrew Macdonald and I had done all those years ago on *Shallow Grave* – but it was touch and go at times. And Christian is a genius in the edit room. He drifts around, looking chaotic, puffing away out the window, but put him in front of an edit of the film and he goes right to the heart of what you need. I never got the chance to voice my appreciation of him in all those endless speeches as there were so many others to mention, but in the rankings of 'All the things to be said or left unsaid', he's in the 'left unsaid' column all on his own.

You certainly made endless speeches, as Slumdog *went on to win over a hundred awards across the world. What do you remember of that protracted frenzy?*

It all blurs a bit because I was literally skimming around the world as the fever built. I'd done it before for films that no one was interested in. I could have pirouetted in a nightgown and nobody would watch my film. Then the opposite happens and there's nothing you can do to stop people watching it. Like they say, remember what this feels like because nothing else will feel the same. Having said that, I got to the point where I wanted to get back on the bicycle. I wanted to enjoy it while it happened, but I want to get hurt again because it's part of it. Only a fool believes it's all about awards and recognition.

By the time you reached the Academy Awards on 22 February 2009, did you think you were in with a chance of winning at least several Oscars?

We heard about the nominations in India. Everyone told us not to open the film there. They said it would provoke a row, that it might puncture the campaign in the US. But we didn't listen: for God's sake, we made the film in India! We had opened it in America and Britain, so why not India? There we were in India, doing a live interview on America's *Today* programme. They would never normally feature a film like *Slumdog* as it's all about middle America – but they ended up giving us tremendous support.

Anyway, the Oscars were announced on this live broadcast. Dev and Freida were so excited they started Bollywood dancing. It was incredible: ten Oscar nominations! We knew we had a chance then. Yet, as Simon pointed out, *The Full Monty* had several nominations and they walked away with no awards. But they made sure they had a great evening, so we started to plan for one. We wanted the kids to be there, to get as many people out to Los Angeles as possible. In the end Fox Searchlight paid for forty-two plane tickets and put everyone up in hotels. We all got caught up in the spirit of it.

Did you enjoy the Oscars or were you nervous?

It's so logistical. All my family were there, so I had to look after them. Then the family of the film. You have to do a staggering amount of press. You have to be gracious about your presence at the awards, and about your fellow nominees.

There's this idea that you have to be on best behaviour because it might help you win. But, if you believe what some say, it's already been decided and is in a sealed envelope. In which case you should say what the hell you like – it's not going to change anything. I'm sure that one day some outrageous personality like Sacha Baron Cohen will defy the convention of being there by behaving in an appalling manner. That would be pretty interesting . . .

Before you know it, you're in the theatre and the ceremony has started. The fact that it was a live show made it feel very quick. Quite the opposite sensation for those watching on TV, of course!

We had one heartbreak early on where Glenn Freemantle and Tom Sayers, who'd done so much, didn't win for sound editing. I really felt for poor old Glenn and Tom. When that happened, we all thought, 'Oh well, let's see how we get on.' We'd got one Oscar at that point. Then the others started happening and I kept thinking about Glenn and all the extraordinary work he'd done. Everyone else who was nominated won – A. R. Rahman was nominated three times and won twice.

And then it just accelerated. Suddenly I was up there. I decided what to say almost there and then. Seriously. I had a few ideas about what I might want to say, but they just simmered in my head on the night. It's the best way to do it. I'd done so many public appearances at that point. But I was still nervous, obviously. I mentioned my dad, my sisters, my kids and their mum. But I left people out – I forgot to mention my agent, Robert Newman – because it was a blizzard. I wasn't aware of what I was saying. In fact, I

Christian Colson, Danny Boyle and Simon Beaufoy at the Academy Awards® ceremony. (Photograph courtesy of Getty Images. OSCAR® statues are the copyrighted property and registered trademark of the Academy of Motion Pictures Arts and Sciences.)

watched it back at my sister Maria's house four or five months later and I couldn't remember any of it.

It was a fantastic evening. But the glory is temporary, believe me.

If you didn't believe the glory was temporary, you'd be in danger of stagnating.

You've got to be so careful. It must be very difficult to deal with that kind of attention if you're young. Most of us had a few years under our belts. We'd seen quite a lot already, and that's got to be good for you.

You have to accept that you'll never make another film that wins so many awards, earns so much money (nearly $400 million internationally and counting) and is so widely loved. It's the film that wouldn't die; a year after its debut at Telluride it was still generating stories in the international press. None of which is relevant if you keep on making films to please yourself, as opposed to chasing those which might be hugely successful.

You should never chase success. You look desperate very quickly.

And there's little way of knowing what will be successful thanks to the alchemy of film-making.

You can never predict how a film will turn out. So you go with your nose, and if the stars are in alignment for you then it will work out. It's an old cliché: you want to make something with your heart, so you make *Millions*. And no one goes to see it. But because you made *Millions*, you get to make *Slumdog*. That's what an Indian would believe: it is written. They'd do the head wobble and see the connection. We shouldn't try to understand it, but we should perhaps trust it.

2009 has been a fantastic year. We've been trying to set up work, which is good. You get crazy propositions, including offers of outrageous money to direct Chanel adverts. Ludicrous stuff. I don't want to do any of that. But the attention *is* just temporary. You get to keep your Oscar – it's not like the World Cup, which has to be passed on – but it will be someone else's turn soon. As it should be.

I'll be happy enough to take my place back in the audience for the next round of this madness.

You certainly seem ready to move on, to face the next set of extreme challenges offered by 127 Hours. *Are you able to describe your journey on* Slumdog *in a few simple sentences?*

This kid from the Juhu slum in Mumbai, his story is worth as much as anyone else's; in fact, thanks to the efforts of a miasma of people, his story shines for a moment. Not a bad philosophy for a film.

127 Hours (2010)

A series of triptychs show generic crowd scenes: a marathon, a triathlon, commuters packing out pavements, Muslims at prayer. Aron Ralston (James Franco) appears in one of the triptychs at home, alone, wearing a baseball cap, shorts and trail shoes. He is packing his rucksack with climbing gear. We see a close-up of a water bottle being filled from the tap in the kitchen. He glances in the fridge, grabs some pre-prepared food. The answer machine clicks on and his sister Sonja (Lizzy Caplan) leaves a message. She is slightly exasperated that he hasn't returned any of her calls.

Meanwhile, from a shot set up at the back of a high kitchen cupboard, we see Aron's hand fishing around for a penknife. He misses the Swiss army knife and makes do with a plain black multi-tool.

Aron drives through the night slurping Gatorade. His headlights illuminate a sign: 'Next service 100 miles'. Another indicates he's in the vicinity of Blue John Canyon in Utah. With one hand on the wheel, he flips open a video camera. 'Friday night, April 25 2003. I'm just entering Canyonlands.'

He arrives at a makeshift car park cum campsite with two small tents. He beds down in the back of his battered wagon.

Saturday morning. Aron, his rucksack on his back, sets off on his bike. He hurtles across the bumpy terrain at full speed. He is exuberant. He pauses to slug at his water and record a message: 'Blue John Canyon. The guidebook says four and a half hours to the Big Drop rappel. I aim to take forty-five minutes off that.'

He goes flying off his bike, groans, laughs and takes a photo of himself lying on the rich orange earth. After seventeen miles, he padlocks the bike to an old tree, wolfs down a pie and sets off on foot, with a bandana protecting his mouth and nose from the desert dust. He listens to his favourite band, Phish, on his Discman.

Spotting two girls who say they are lost, he says he's a guide, helps to locate them on the map and offers to take them to a hidden pool. Megan (Amber Tamblyn) and Kristi (Kate Mara) hesitate only briefly. Displaying an easy charm, Aron says: 'Guaranteed best time you can have with your clothes on.'

Aron, Megan and Kristi are forcing their way along a narrow ledge in a tight space between two slabs of rock. Aron admits he's not a guide, but an engineer. He lets himself drop and makes a dramatic plunge into a natural pool. Both girls follow. They all jump time and again, stripped to shorts and, in the case of the girls, bra tops.

Aron asks if he will ever see them again. They tell him about the party they will be throwing that evening and how it will be impossible to miss because of a giant inflatable Scooby Doo. It's time for him to go; he starts his timer again and runs off. Megan and Kristi wonder if he might show up at the party later and conclude that they probably didn't figure in his day at all.

As he progresses along the canyon, Aron takes more photos, runs his hand along the smooth walls of the canyon, manoeuvres athletically through the narrow space. He barely hesitates before a long, steep drop. As he descends, he dislodges a chockstone and finds his right forearm lodged firmly between the canyon wall and the rock.

Aron is confused. Shocked. He glances up at the blue sky and sees a vapour trail. Propelled by anger, he tries with all his might to pull his arm free. He shouts: 'This is insane!' He tips water into his mouth, letting it spill down the side. He removes his digital watch: it's 3.14 p.m. He shouts again: 'Kristi! Megan!' He voice is lost in the silence.

He empties his rucksack, placing each item carefully on the chockstone: the watch, sunglasses, the Discman, a small amount of food, limited climbing equipment, the video player, keys, a camera, a head torch and the basic penknife. He tests the sharpness of the blade: it's almost totally blunt. He hacks, pointlessly, at the boulder.

The next morning, when the sun passes through the canyon Aron rips off his shoes and socks and heats up his bare feet. It's a small moment of pleasure. A flashback shows a young Aron watching the sun rise in a canyon with his father (Treat Williams).

Aron records a message. It's 2.05 p.m. on Sunday 27 April 2003. He's been trapped for twenty-four hours. He gives his name and his parents' names. He urges whoever finds the video recorder to give it to his parents. He explains how the chockstone came loose.

A quick check of his food and drink shows he is low on both. 'I'm in very deep doo here . . . Don't lose it, Aron. Do. Not. Lose it.'

The temperature drops, and Aron winds a climbing rope round his legs in an attempt to stay warm. Dehydration is setting in. He thinks of the giant inflatable Scooby Doo, of everyone drinking beer. He cleans a contact lens with spit. He regrets ignoring his mother's (Kate Burton) phone calls. He recalls photocopying the map in a mountaineering shop and saying he doesn't know where he's going yet.

Monday. Aron's video diary is less exuberant. He's peed twice, the second time into the CamelBak hydration pack: 'It smells really bad. I'm sure it will settle. It's gotta be chilled, like Sauvignon Blanc.' He chips at the chockstone. He's made a tourniquet for his arm. He makes a first, unsuccessful attempt to break the skin below the elbow. 'Lesson: don't buy the cheap, made in China multi-tool. This thing came free with the flashlight.'

A flashback shows Aron filming his sister as she plays piano when they were both kids. Another shows a bunch of his friends and his girlfriend, Rana (Clémence Poésy), frantically getting naked to Plastic Bertrand's 'Ça Plane Pour Moi' in a truck in a snow-scape. The scene switches to Aron and Rana lying in the back of his wagon. She caresses his chest and asks: 'How do I get in?'

A dramatic, violent storm interrupts. Aron holds his tongue out as the rain lashes down. The water rises until he is submerged. His right arm comes loose. He returns to his car, drives to Rana's house, bashes on her door. Then he wakes up, shouting: 'Please!' His body heaves with sobs.

Tuesday. Aron is in better spirits. He records a funny, self-deprecating sketch in which he plays both an overenthusiastic talk-show host and himself. 'Good morning, everyone! It's seven o'clock here in Canyonlands, USA. And this morning on the boulder we have a very special guest: self-proclaimed American superhero Aron Ralston.' As Aron, he apologises to his mom and acknowledges that if he'd told her where he was going, 'Well, I probably wouldn't be here right now.' Aron's chat reveals that he won't officially become a missing person till Wednesday at the earliest. 'Which means . . . I'll probably be dead by then.'

Ending the talk show, he records a message to his mother and father that is as loving as it is apologetic. He builds himself up to stab his arm with the penknife, pulls it out and shakes his head.

Wednesday. Aron drinks his own urine, retching as he does so. At night he watches video footage of Kristi and Megan in the pool, freezing the shot of the girls in their bra tops. He considers masturbating, then scolds himself. The hallucinations begin. He sees the giant Scooby Doo in the canyon. His mouth is dry and discoloured. He is losing weight. A flashback shows Rana losing patience with Aron at a ball game. He makes no attempt to stop her leaving. Her parting shot is: 'You're going to be so lonely, Aron.'

A sofa appears in the canyon, crowded with his parents and then friends. They look at him expectantly. He apologises to his sister for not being able to make her wedding. He talks to himself: 'It's me. I chose this . . . This rock has been waiting for me my entire life.' We see he's scratched an epitaph on the wall: 'Aron Ralston RIP 75 – 03'.

Thursday. Aron sees a young blond boy grinning at him from the sofa. He watches himself play with the boy. With tears in his eyes, he wrenches his arm till the bone snaps. He uses the blunt penknife to hack off his lower arm. His blood is gloopy. He is methodical. In the background are sharp, angular noises reminiscent of tweezers touching metal in the board game Operation.

Aron cuts his arm off. He stares in disbelief at his lower arm, stuck between the chockstone and the canyon wall. He makes another tourniquet for the stump, puts his rucksack on, takes a photo of the abandoned lower arm. He says 'Thank you' to no one in particular. Or, perhaps, to God.

He stumbles out of the canyon, abseils down a rock and dunks his face in a stagnant pond. He staggers around in the heat until a Dutch family appear. The father stays with Aron, the mother and son run off to get help. Aron is on the verge of losing consciousness when a helicopter arrives and transports him to hospital.

A triptych shows a generic crowd on the left, Aron swimming athletically underwater with a healed stump in the middle and, on the right, climbing a mountain. He emerges from the swimming *pool to see the sofa – no longer a hallucination – populated by his parents and friends.*

Text on the screen tells us that Aron's premonition came true: 'He met his wife Jessica three years later.' On the sofa now is the real Aron Ralston, his wife and baby. Further text updates the story: 'Their son, Leo, was born in February 2010. Aron continues to be a climber and canyoneer. He always leaves a note to say where he has gone.'

* * *

AMY RAPHAEL: *You talk at the end of the* Slumdog *chapter about how, after Oscar success, you did endless months of press and received crazy offers. And all you really wanted to do was get back to doing what you do best: making films that really mean something to you, for around $20 million, with your small team of mini-directors.*

DANNY BOYLE: François Invernel, who runs Pathé, is a serious climber, and he gave me Aron Ralston's book, *Between a Rock and a Hard Place*, some years before we started working on it. Superficially, it's impossible to imagine the book being turned into a feature film, but I had a very strong sense of being able to tackle it. It reminded me of Joe Simpson's *Touching the Void*, which I'd read a long time ago when it was doing the rounds. It was an extraordinary book, but I had no interest in climbing. Kevin Macdonald did an excellent job in the end.

Early on you had issues with the presence of Ralston's mother in the book.

In the book he tried to vary the tempo of the chapters by alternating his ordeal in the canyon with his 'home life'. But to make his story work as a film, I knew I'd have to take the biggest risk of all and not vary the tempo. His testimony about his experience in the canyon was completely riveting and brutally honest, and that's what the film had to capture. Aron wanted to include his family in the book because of the regret he felt for not being in regular enough contact with them, but to tell the story of his accident alongside his love for his family would have made it into a television movie.

I had a profound response to the alternate chapters, which were

327

all about his actual entrapment and his gradual realisation that nobody would be looking for him because he was such a loner.

It's beautifully written, sparse and evocative.

Like Simpson, his experience turned him into a writer. Every time he started talking about his mum, I wanted to be back in that canyon, while at the same time thinking I couldn't bear to be there. Which is why I realised so quickly that the film had to focus almost entirely on Aron's experience in the canyon. I gave a copy of the book to Christian [Colson], and he suggested I show it to Simon [Beaufoy].

Christian was sceptical at the start, and Simon just laughed: he didn't think he could create a script out of Ralston's story.

Yes. At which point Christian and I agreed that I should do a treatment. I literally sat in my kitchen and tried to carry the story through. It happened very quickly; it felt very natural. I gave it to Christian and then to Simon. Simon got it; he's a climber and he knew a way in that I didn't. He agreed to improve it. Simon is brilliant at structure, which is critical in a film like this because the story is so narrow.

Aron (James Franco), Kristi (Kate Mara) and Megan (Amber Tamblyn) shortly before Ralston traps his arm.

Did Beaufoy have a better understanding of how Ralston could have gone out that day without telling anyone where he was going?

He had a climber's insight, yes. As soon as he did a draft, it was amazing. That's what writers do – they go right inside the character. I rely on actors to do the same thing. I always imagine I think like the character, but I don't really. Coming from a theatre background, I expect the actors to provide the character and tell me when I'm wrong – or tell me when it could be better.

In other words, you're actor-led?

I am in terms of character. It was a real education for me when Simon presented the draft. I'd written this dynamic structure, which is how I'd seen it, and then he put a character in it. He went off to meet Aron, and it didn't take many drafts from that point.

Ralston didn't initially respond to your approach because he still envisioned an adaptation of his book along the lines of Touching the Void. *But he changed his mind after the Oscars.*

I went to meet him in late 2005 or early 2006 outside Amsterdam. At this point I hadn't written the treatment, but I did have the idea of how I wanted to make the film. He insisted his mum stayed in the script. He was very impressed by *Touching the Void* – and who wouldn't be? – but he also wanted Kevin Macdonald's structure; in other words, the ordeal intercut with retrospective testimony.

It's a problem for authors who sell their books for film rights. Do you take the money and wish the director good luck? Or do you try and keep some sort of control? Aron was trying to keep control at that point. It's very much part of his character and it's very much part of the drama of the book. He loves controlling things!

Was he suspicious of your intentions prior to your Oscar haul? Did he think you would retell his story and perhaps devalue it in some way?

It's a tricky situation. A Brit turns up whose life experience must feel a million miles away from his. Why would he trust me? And then *Slumdog* had huge commercial success. Aron is an astute businessman who's made a living out of his experience by giving motivational talks for big companies. The core values of his story are used to inspire people on a non-commercial basis as well. In other words, he's no fool. The Oscar success of *Slumdog* was obviously a turning point. It also showed him I can work outside the comfort zone of my own country: India's a long way from Britain, in the same way that Colorado and Utah are a long way away. Maybe he thought I could only do period dramas!

This was your one chance to make such a wildly daring film: by making it on the back of Slumdog's *success, the studios might not wonder what the hell you were up to.*

Of course, *Slumdog*'s success gave us a huge advantage in the mechanics of getting a film set up. After winning eight Oscars you have an open door. And that was one of the reasons we wanted to do it – because it was, in a way, a deeply uncommercial film. It's an impossible movie to sell, other than with a big hit right over your shoulder. You'd be very lucky to make it otherwise – or you'd have to make it for very little money.

You stuck with 127 Hours *despite being offered movies with budgets ten times the size. Wasn't your head turned even for a moment?*

No. I wanted to work with Christian and Simon again, if I could, because we'd had a great time. We'd stuck together and I'd learned so much. Christian's a very good producer and very sharp on script and edit and story. Sure, this was an opportunity to direct some sort of blockbuster, but I wanted to keep working with those guys. And anyway, nothing out there appealed. There's no point in trying to fake it with someone else's script because then it just becomes a commercial operation with no soul.

Are you saying, in effect, that the success of Slumdog *facilitated 127* Hours, *but you would have attempted to make it regardless?*

I'd have tried to. I think most probably we would have been knocked back. But the trouble with *127 Hours* – unlike *Touching the Void* – is that you have an amputation. So, as a prospect for the people backing your movie, it's like, 'Woah, we're going to spend six fucking days in a canyon alone with this guy, while he starves

and dehydrates to death – and then he's going to cut his arm off!'
It's the kind of film that's got an inbuilt need for a big success to
push it through, which is how we used *Slumdog*.

It was wonderful to have done *127 Hours* and to have made it
work. I loved directing James Franco. He really is a very underrated actor. Seriously underrated. I knew he was good, but you
need a very special actor to pull off a part like that.

What had you seen him in? Pineapple Express *and* Milk?

Yes. Also as James Dean and in *Spider-Man*. I always liked him as
an actor, but it was the audition that swung it.

What did you ask him to do?

He read a couple of pieces, including the video message that Aron
recorded for his mum when he thought he would probably die.
That directness, even in an audition room, was incredibly moving. The relationship that American actors have with the camera
is interesting. It was one of the fascinating aspects of shooting
the film. We'd started to use smaller digital cameras on *28 Days
Later* and *Slumdog*, and on *127 Hours* we combined them with an

'You need a very special actor to pull off a part like that.'

American actor's understanding of the camera. We are learning, as a nation, what it means to engage with the camera as our culture becomes increasingly about reality TV, but Americans have it in their blood. They're not suspicious of cameras.

Cameras aren't seen as intrusive.

No; they see them as a channel they can use. Which is how James treated them. He worked brilliantly with our two cinematographers, Anthony Dod Mantle and Enrique 'Quique' Chediak. There was a level of comfort between them and the cameras.

The first time you met Franco he pretended to be stoned. That must have made it tricky.

We had a terrible first meeting in New York. I was convinced he was stoned. He hadn't even finished reading the script. But he swears he never touches anything and, knowing him now, I think it's his way of sussing people out. He pretends to be out of it when in fact he's watching you microscopically to see what your reactions are. We asked to meet him again after he'd finished the full script. He agreed to read for us, which is great. A surprising number of actors refuse to read on the basis that they should just be offered the part. But James was happy to read, and he was excellent.

How many other actors did you see?

I can't actually remember. We auditioned a handful. But there weren't many because it's a massive part.

There was talk at the time of Ryan Gosling, Sam Rockwell and Cillian Murphy all being up for the part.

We talked to Ryan Gosling and Shia LaBeouf. LaBeouf was a serious contender, but he had had a terrible car accident and was still having his finger rebuilt. It was one of the things that interested him in the story, but in the end it was what counted against him. We had to have an actor who was fully fit, as it was going to be very demanding physically. We were delighted to offer the part to James. Casting always sounds so definitive: this actor was offered that role. But the reality is that casting in America is like a little dance. You have to dance around their other jobs, their deals with the studio, their home life. Often it's these issues which decide who does the job in the end.

I'm never that comfortable doing the dance because everyone in the States knows it's a dance but pretends it's not. And I'm not really like that. So you have to be careful.

Christian Colson said that Franco has real charm and that when he smiles, you smile. It's central to his success playing Ralston, because here's a guy who is so full of himself and so careless about his family and his girlfriend. It would be very easy not to empathise with him, even if he has trapped his arm.

It would be very easy to blame Ralston for his agony.

But, still, you like him. You are desperate for him to survive.

Yes, because James has got oodles of charm. But he still had to earn his place in the canyon. He's not a climber himself and doesn't have the physique of one; they're wiry as fuck and can scramble through small spaces. We shot the film in sequence, first on location and then in the old furniture factory in Salt Lake City. As one of the first takes of the indoor shoot, I asked James to try and get his arm free of the boulder. He has just realised that his arm is trapped. There is no way he can shift the boulder, but of course his brain won't accept this, so he keeps trying to move it. We set up all these cameras and said they could run for an hour without stopping. Until James collapsed.

After the pyrotechnics of the fall – some of which was being shot separately with stuntmen – we had to shoot the scene in that way. Aron trying to move the boulder is a big moment in the book, and for James it was important because it established his right to be there. He just went at it. He went on and on and on. He went insane. He didn't last an hour, but he went at it for a good twenty minutes. At the end the crew burst into spontaneous applause. He'd earned his right to be there: not just as an actor, but as a presence. He was saying, 'This is my film now.'

How did you trap his arm so effectively without damaging it?

The actual rock weighed about a ton, but we fixed the fake one to the wall for James. We made sure that even ten men couldn't move it. There was nothing James could do to move it. I didn't tell him it was fixed; I told him he might be able to move it. If he really tried. He believed he could move it, and the viewer does as well because its dimensions are not that enormous. It's the density of the thing.

And the angle. But didn't James actually move it very slightly with the pulley?

He did. He moved it fractionally, in agony.

As you said earlier, you filmed 127 Hours in chronological order, partly on location and partly on set. But you initially thought you could shoot entirely on location in the Blue John canyon.

Many factors made that impossible. There was accessibility. It took a huge operation to get near the actual canyon because it's so far away from anywhere. I was told that it would be almost impossible to service the crew, and initially I said it wouldn't be a problem as we'd just take a much smaller one. But then there were issues of safety. There was a high chance somebody would slip or fall because it's treacherous, and it'd be very hard to get anyone out of there in an emergency. And, technically, it would be virtually impossible to actually shoot. The space is narrow and deep and dark.

When we went to the canyon for a recce we saw just how inhospitable it is. We very quickly realised it would be virtually impossible to illustrate Aron's journey over six days. We were going to have to cheat anyway for scenes such as the one where he imagines his family gathered around the sofa. So we recreated the canyon in the old furniture factory and decided to spend just a week in the canyon to shoot the build-up to his accident.

How did you feel when you first visited the spot where Ralston was trapped for six days? It must have been emotional as you'd read the book, met Ralston and watched what he thought was his final video message to his mum.

It was emotional. And kind of surreal. The rescue services, who eventually removed the lower part of Aron's arm from behind the boulder, showed us some photos. I immediately knew we couldn't use them in the film. The arm was flattened. It made me think of the end of *Who Framed Roger Rabbit?*, when the evil guy gets flattened by the steamroller. His hand was like that. You couldn't show it; people would just laugh and think it's ridiculous. Anyway, they took the remains of the arm and cremated it. Aron then took the ashes and scattered them in the canyon.

I remember that first visit very clearly. Funnily enough, though, it was the approach to the canyon that startled me. It was just so dramatic.

Did you get dropped off by helicopter?

Yes; it was the only way. Other than by horse, which I didn't fancy. Cars can get within an hour of the canyon, but then you have another hour's trek, which is what we eventually did when we camped there. All the equipment was brought in by helicopter. The first time we went, it was really too hot to walk, so we took a helicopter. As soon as you step into the canyon, you realise how brilliantly Aron described the coolness and peacefulness of it.

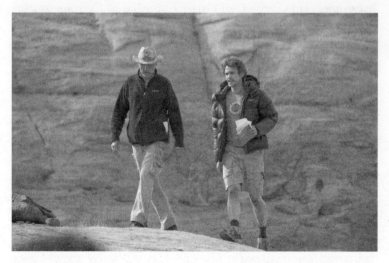

Danny Boyle and James Franco in Canyonlands. Boyle: 'I loved finally seeing where the story had unfolded.'

Did you have a sense of why guys like that would go on those kinds of adventures?

I did. I liked it when hikers came past, following the Aron Ralston path. It was interesting to watch them. They had a lovely spirit about them. The particular section where Aron got caught is innocuous really, but the canyon gets much more interesting as it goes all the way down. I loved being there and finally seeing where the story had unfolded. By then I was obsessed by the film and it no longer felt like an alien world. I knew what I wanted to do on screen, how I wanted to tell his story. I was never intending to make a film about how great it is to be in the countryside and – hey! – look at this fauna. I'd be lost even if I tried.

I went back with Quique and Anthony in the thick snow. It was amazing, but in the end the shoot was delayed because of the bloody snow.

Was it out-of-season snow? Part of global weirding?

It certainly wasn't supposed to snow!

To add insult to injury, you were also stuck in the furniture warehouse because Disney's John Carter *had taken all the soundstages.*

(*laughs*) We met them actually; they were scouting for locations at the same time. The size of that movie was overwhelming. That's a serious-scale movie. There was an AD from Scotland and I know the director, Andrew Stanton, who's a lovely man. Bumping into them at night was nice.

So you did your recce, found your furniture factory and Suttirat Larlarb built both a vertical and horizontal canyon. When I visited the set, I walked through the vertical one and immediately felt claustrophobic.

Suttirat did a brilliant job. She's one of those hidden geniuses who make a film both possible and richer. She's constantly filling up the creative space, building the image of the project in tandem with the narrative and character. Her brief here was to try and re-create the canyon both for the actor and the audience. James needed to feel that claustrophobia and panic so that the audience could feel

Danny Boyle peers into Suttirat
Larlarb's fake canyon.

it too. We spent about thirty days in the factory. Every day I used
to watch James come in, have a quick chat and resume his position
in the canyon. And, bless him, his habit of reading, of devouring
books, kept him sane.

What James didn't have was other actors. He was robbed of that
contact. Of course, there's something attractive about not having
any competition – 'It's going to be all about me!' – but the downside is the lack of camaraderie. I don't know if he realised how
solitary a job it would be. All he had was his books. But maybe it
suited him; I think he's solitary.

*Ralston is a loner too, although his thing is undertaking physical
tasks alone, whereas Franco is perhaps more cerebral.*

I didn't realise that at first, but it became clear later. James told
journalists that being in the indoor canyon drove him mad, but
I don't think it did. He had his books and he was able to work.
To act. When he did work, he was able to stretch himself. It was

a great challenge for an actor, a lovely way for him to express himself.

When we talked in Salt Lake City, you said you wanted the entire crew to work exceptionally hard. You wanted them to be in the zone of Ralston's story, to almost feel as ragged as he did. You certainly didn't want them floating in at 9 a.m. and sloping off at 5 p.m. They had to be as committed to the film as Ralston was to the boulder.

One of the dangers of working on the back of a film as successful as *Slumdog* is that we've been indulged by the awards and the general fuss. There is the opportunity to relax and take things for granted. No one is immune to that. But I don't think they could ever have had a half-hearted approach to this film because it was so extreme. I thought that it was crucial for everyone to feel they were being locked into the film right until the end, until they were released from it. So many of the crew were from Utah and were 'outdoors' people; it felt to them that this was their story, and they responded magnificently. Big thanks to John Kelly for that and to Bernie Bellew again.

We had two cameramen so that we could keep working. We had a similar ethos on *Slumdog* of never really stopping. I like that intensity, because when you're shooting I find the days off quite hard.

Because you're so consumed by the film?

I'm sure people go off and do something relaxing on a day off, but I wouldn't do that anyway. I'd just look at rushes or plan what we were going to do next. So I find a day off – or, God forbid, two days off – very, very difficult in terms of the health of the film. On *127 Hours* I wanted, as I was saying, to create this condition on set by shooting the necessary material in two months. I wanted to be able to feel the energy of such a short shoot. A three- or four-month shoot would have been wrong for the film; it would have been too languorous.

It was great to work with Anthony and Quique. They are both confident enough to work in tandem. It's weird to ask two cinematographers to shoot a film, because normally their relationship with the director is unique.

You had worked with Dod Mantle since the turn of the century, and then Quique stepped in as the new guy.

I met Quique on *28 Weeks Later*, which I executive-produced. I felt a great affinity towards him, a great warmth. And he knew the American system much better than Anthony did, because at that point Anthony hadn't worked on a larger-scale American film. I had a hunch they'd get on, given the kind of people they are. I know that Quique was able to advise Anthony on the way the system works in the States.

How does it differ?

The union rules dominate much more. You have to accept it and work your way round it; it's not something you can challenge.

You had this idea of having Dod Mantle and Chediak playing good cop/bad cop with Franco. But it didn't work in the end.

No. I ended up being both the good cop and the bad cop. I was standing outside the canyon shouting at them all, which forced them to bond against me. 'We're stuck here and that fucking twat wants us to do this. Again . . .'

My set visit happened to coincide with what I think is the best scene in the film: Franco as talk-show host, interviewing himself and thus acknowledging the stupidity of not telling anyone where he'd gone.

Amazing bit of writing by Simon. It was brilliant to actually watch that being shot. James was in the canyon, and Anthony had nipped in even though it was his day off. So it was Quique, Anthony and me shouting instructions very loudly at all of them.

You said earlier in the book that if you're critical of yourself, it's because you instruct the actors too much instead of just letting them get on with it.

I've got better at that, I think. It helps to work with more experienced actors like Franco and the three actors in *Trance* – James McAvoy, Vincent Cassel and Rosario Dawson – because you realise they know what they're doing. If they need help they will ask for it. In fact, they will demand it. So, yes, I'm better at it. But I do still like shouting from a distance. It does help if there's another lunatic on the set, enjoying it or experiencing it as much as the actor is. It's good for the actor not to feel as though they're on their own. Even with a full cast, there often isn't anyone to react to because you have to do the scenes in such tiny little bits.

Wasn't it quite hard in the canyon – both in the real one and in the ones Larlarb built – because there wasn't room for you to see what was actually going on, except on a monitor?

I was determined to make the fake canyons as realistic as possible. Everyone thought I was mad not to want floating walls, but I didn't want to cheat. I also thought that it would help James psychologically if the walls were solid. Anthony and Quique scrambled in the small entrance at the back to look over the rock at him. That was the access point. But otherwise the canyon was real. I was fine to watch it on the monitor, especially with this film, because it was so much about Ralston's relationship with the camera. We would leave James to it sometimes. We gave him a camera, and he shot material on his own.

Which Franco loved because he wants to direct.

He has that instinct in him anyway.

Did you find yourself adapting to Franco as you went along?

You discover things about actors as you go along. Actors are chameleons and they turn themselves into what they need to be for a particular role. They learn how to emphasise a certain aspect of their personality. And suddenly you think, 'We're so lucky to have James, he's serious and committed and can direct himself too!' Seriously, though, he's very bright and totally gets everything you say to him.

You may have got lucky with Franco, but nonetheless it took you time to find the film. In July 2009, you said to me: 'Deep down, I've absolutely no idea how to make this film.'

I like being in that situation. You have to forget how awful it was last time and go into it again. You sent me a *New Yorker* interview with James Cameron in late 2009, and I always remember his analogy about film-making being comparable to giving birth. Not that either of us would know, of course, but the basic concept is the same.

I'm involved with the London Film School and I occasionally give talks to the students; one of them asked about how much I prepare for a film. I told them how important it is on the one hand to be prepared, but on the other to not know what you're doing. It sounds perverse, but it's so dangerous to think you know what you're doing. I think it's where so many films go wrong. When you're open to possibility, to anything happening, films sort of make themselves. So little of it is about you as director anyway. Bertolucci said you have to leave a door open on your set for real life to walk through at any moment.

Have you increasingly come round to that way of thinking?

At the beginning, when you've got no track record, you have to give the impression that you know what you're doing.

You're almost bluffing.

But now you can be much more confident because you know it's worked in the past and you think, 'No, don't panic. That wasn't very good, but don't panic because it'll be interesting when you get it in the editing room.'

You get a thrill out of not quite knowing what you're doing, but you must have sudden points of clarity when you start to shoot?

You get flashes of clarity, but it comes and goes. I can't really speak for other directors, but judging by what some say they're constantly in a state of clarity. But I'm certainly not. It's about honesty as well. You have to admit you don't know what you're doing.

Anthony Dod Mantle said elsewhere in this book that the first words he heard from you about 127 Hours were: 'It's a little thing shot from the hip.' Coming from someone else, that could sound incredibly pretentious.

Well, that's Anthony speaking, and he has a tendency . . .

He was quoting you! But yes, I'm sure he would agree that he has pretentions: after all, he did give you Bill Viola DVDs for inspiration ahead of 127 Hours.

The problem I constantly have with Anthony is that he really wants to be a 'proper' cinematographer using big cameras. He is, without doubt, a genius. An absolute genius. But he doesn't really want to be shooting small indie films. He'll pretend he likes to shoot from the hip, but actually, unless you keep an eye on him, he orders all this expensive equipment. Which I don't want.

I got angry with him on *Trance* because he ended up using this big Alexa camera all the time. He deals with my anger by telling me that some guys from Sony are coming down to the set with a little camera. I realise I'm being dealt with, in a way. He loves all the big, expensive, complicated gadgets, but I much prefer him to – and I'm sure these are his words – shoot from the hip.

I suppose he is just a modern cinematographer. And all cinematographers are being dragged into the modern world by the inevitable – by the closure of labs. The fact that there's no film any more is forcing them to change. It was wonderful when Anthony was given an Oscar for *Slumdog* because it's a big statement about how the world is changing.

Ironically, however, the Alexa is exactly the same as a film camera, only it works electronically rather than chemically. All the cinematographers love it and want to use it constantly. I look at it and say, 'I'm not interested what format it records in or how highly interactive it is with its environment. It's just like a big 35mm camera.' I suppose it's good that you can run it for longer because you don't have to stop every ten minutes.

You have such a close relationship with your cinematographer that it's inevitable you won't agree about everything. I can't imagine you working with a DOP who doesn't have a certain amount of attitude, nor with one who's director-led. You need someone who is going to bring something to your vision, to give it added value.

You're right, of course. Anthony is a fantastic cameraman. His taste is a bit art-house, but he knows everything about storytelling. Cameramen are often great storytellers because they watch the actors telling the story through the camera. There's an umbilical cord between them. So they will then make suggestions that add to what's evolving. They're not really involved with pre-production – they will read the script, but not be around when the film is being set up – nor with editing, so their job is live. They gather the material and then see what the editor does with it.

There's something acute about the way they gather material. They know how to gather that material for you, especially a great camera operator like Anthony. I'd go as far as saying he's the world's greatest operator. And by operating I don't mean the wheels and the crane and all that stuff. That's not his world. I mean rather how he tells a story through the movement of the camera. He is always right about the simplest things, such as the point at which you move the camera from one place to another. Cinematographers have no oversight of the whole process, but their attention to detail is invaluable.

It must be a little odd for them, parachuting in and out of the process.

It's a case of needs must. And it's a process they become addicted to.

A cinematographer with fresh eyes must be hugely useful.

Yes, because he can give you another angle that you haven't seen before. Anthony is a team player – with the whole crew and not just with members of his own team. I would never want to work with someone who wasn't a team player.

We should talk about other members of the crew. Sound, for example, is really important, especially in 127 Hours.

It certainly is. Glenn Freemantle did a great job. Just the other day, in fact, he took me to Dolby to hear this new surround-sound system called Atmos. It was first used in *Brave* and then in *The Hobbit*. It's being slowly introduced into theatres in America and it will slowly be rolled out here in the UK. Dolby think it's going to be great for action sequences because there will be noise everywhere – if a car is going to fly over your head, the sound is going to start at the screen and then travel over your head and behind you.

We watched various examples of it, and I thought it didn't make much difference with action movies because they're so full of noise anyway. But then there was a rainy scene and I've never felt so wet. Which makes me think that it will actually be amazing for quieter scenes. I would have loved Atmos for *127 Hours*.

Could you go back and re-dub 127 Hours?

I guess you could, but it wouldn't be worth the cost unless it was a major film like *Titanic*. Glenn was very fired up about Atmos, though, and I could see why.

I'm not so sure I'd have appreciated hearing Ralston break his own arm in Dolby Atmos. Which leads us to the question of how you decided what to show and what to leave out in the film. Not just the breaking and cutting off of his arm, but also the drinking of his own urine and the up-close changing of his gritty contact lens.

Because the external world is so limited, you have to expand what you have to such a degree that everything has to become a character. Each of the possessions he has – the video camera, the blunt knife, the backpack – have to become a character. You have to make them as acute as possible, as vivid as a great piece of casting. They have to refresh the film. You see it in *Argo* when John Goodman walks in. It's like, 'Ah, yeah! Here he is!' – he freshens up the film. But no one else walks into the canyon, so you're left with the objects he's taken with him.

And the boulder.

All these friends that accompany him on his journey.

Ralston certainly relies heavily on the video camera, both to record a diary of sorts and to look back at the existing footage. At one point he gazes at Kristi and Megan in the pool and considers masturbating. You were desperate for him to masturbate.

Yes, but Aron absolutely said he didn't.

You were convinced he would.

But in the end you can't say, 'Ah, you're not telling the truth.'

Very true. So no masturbating, but a very realistic scene in which he finally decides he will die if he doesn't cut his arm off, so he may as well die trying to hack it off. There was then a fuss about people fainting in cinemas during that scene, which detracted from the fact that it's actually a very watchable film.

Obviously a story like this is going to struggle to get an audience. We did remarkably well, considering. Part of *127 Hours*' success was down to post-*Slumdog* curiosity and part was Franco. But unless a mega-mega-star had been cast, you would never have increased the audience. I think that even Leo [DiCaprio] would have ended up pulling in the same audience.

The film did okay. But you can't hide from the story. If you're doing it properly, then you have to ask all those questions about shitting and pissing and wanking. You have to ask every single question about every single thing to make sure it feels unflinching – and honest. Going back to Aron's book, I found the chapters on the canyon so honest. So when he said he didn't masturbate or get an erection, you have to accept that because he's so honest about everything else.

You had no interest in making a documentary, which means you were making a version of his story. You were borrowing it, enhancing it and making it cinematic. That must have been tricky: Ralston was keeping the story alive with his motivational talks, and he also made the odd set visit.

You have to keep the subject of the film on board. There is a constant pressure with this kind of film to keep the subject onside, because if he or she condemns you, then it's the death of the project. We tried to minimise Aron's involvement in the film, while keeping him happy and ensuring he was involved in many key decisions. We wanted to tell our version of his story, but we didn't want to get anything wrong.

You've got to feel confident that it's now your story, and you've got to tell it through your eyes, because otherwise you'll always feel at a slight distance. It's a weird balancing act between the two, and you can only hope that you get away with it in the end.

I'm sure there are details in the film that Aron didn't like. But, overall, I think he thought it was okay. I also think he'd got to the stage where he's told the story so many times that it was probably a relief for him to have somebody else tell it.

I imagine the film helped him. Although it's opened up the story again, it has allowed it a natural closure as well. Because, otherwise, when is he going to stop telling his story?

It must have been such a strange process for Ralston. He was on set when I visited and he talked about going into the prosthetics room full of fake arms and to wardrobe to see the twelve T-shirts of varying sizes – because Franco wore bigger T-shirts as the days went by to exaggerate his dramatic weight loss. He had an idea of what you were doing with his story, but the final result must still have been a shock.

The first time he saw it was when we smuggled him into a test screening in New Jersey. He put a cap on and I think he wore his prosthetic arm that day, which he doesn't like wearing very much. Christian and I had talked about it at length because we knew that the first time Aron saw it would be absolutely critical. It goes back to what we were just saying about trying to make his story our story. We knew it was going to be so difficult for him not to give

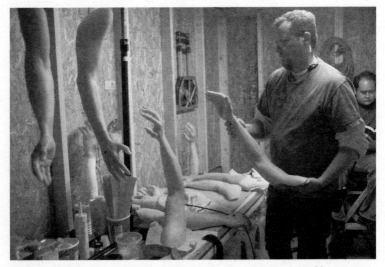

The prosthetics room on set in Salt Lake City, and some of the fifteen prosthetic arms.

us copious notes. We had to give him that right, but you know it's very dangerous as well because they might be the kind of notes that won't help a general audience.

He's a very meticulous man in the way he covers detail, so we decided the best way would be to show the film to him with an audience. It was an extraordinary experience because they went mad and were shouting when he cut his arm off. That threw him right into it in a way. It allowed him to temper his subsequent experience of the film with the knowledge that the film worked. He'd seen the audience response with his own eyes! Had he seen it on his own, in the cold empty atmosphere of the cutting room or with a few people who are not going to laugh, cry or react particularly, it would have been very intimidating. He might have thought his story hadn't translated onto the screen.

The New Jersey experience was memorable, if only to see his face afterwards. What a journey for him.

Poor guy! He must have played his own particular film in his head so many times, a very personal film that was ever evolving and no doubt getting further and further away from the real story – because that's how our memories mutate over time – and then suddenly the Danny Boyle version is out there for public consumption.

God, yes! *127 Hours* would have been different not only to Aron's own story, but also to what he might have expected of the film from the conversations we'd had.

He cried, didn't he?

Yes. I think it was a fairly overwhelming experience for him. James gave a pretty intense performance.

I presume that early screening included the longer ending, in which we see Ralston playing piano with his sister at her wedding and sitting on a roof with his girlfriend Rana, surrounded by fairy lights. I vastly preferred the much less saccharine ending you eventually went with.

We took all those scenes out. I guess we just felt we were trying too hard to make it conventional.

Because it was the kind of ending Hollywood likes?

You could say that. Or you could just say we were trying to make it more palatable. But actually, when people have been through that experience with Franco, the last thing they need is some kind of easy comfort.

I've watched 127 Hours half a dozen times in all and I still tear up every time the Dutch family appear. It's the relief of knowing he's going to be saved.

After all that time of thinking, 'Will he make it? Will he die?' Which you can't help doing, even though you know it's a real story and obviously he survives. A. R. Rahman does a great job with the music too!

Was it hard to cut the wedding and Rana scenes, or are you quite ruthless?

Oh, I've never had a problem with being ruthless.

You shoot knowing you're going to lose a certain amount of material anyway?

No, you kind of shoot everything as though it's the most important thing in the world. But the editing room is amazing. It's the most wonderful part of the process because you ask: 'What would happen if we dropped that?' And you debate with the editor for a while and then you do it. Obviously you can also change the experience of a film by moving the material around. The hard part is retaining sufficient distance so you can judge it when you put it in a different order.

Everybody knows you make the film in the edit. It's no secret.

After the slog of the shoot – and it is just that, regardless of how much of a buzz you get out of it – it must be a joy to sit in the editing room and work out how to assemble the jigsaw puzzle with your editor.

It really is. It's also why editors never come to the set. I've always been amazed by their lack of interest. You'd think they'd be curious, but they're just not. They know that the film won't really start being made till it reaches the edit. I've been very fortunate to have worked with some really good editors, but Jon Harris, whom I worked with for the first time on this, is very, very good. We just sit there and I watch. I love leaving him to it. I trust him. And it's fascinating to hear what an editor has to say about a film because they are outsiders and have a fresh perspective.

Let's return for a moment to Ralston's involvement in 127 Hours. At what point did he show you the video tapes he'd recorded in the canyon?

He showed them early on to Christian and me, and then to Simon and James. He doesn't show them to that many people. I don't think he likes letting them out of his sight. He keeps copies in a bank vault for safety. The tapes helped James enormously. Aron is surprisingly breezy in them. He is clearly trying to keep spirits up. It's evidently where James and Simon got the inspiration for the chat-show-host performance.

How much footage is there?

About forty-eight minutes. There's a weird kind of ghosting of other images on it occasionally. There's a fault in the tape, so you get him stuck in the canyon and skiing at the same time. It's very odd. We were going to try and repeat that effect. But in the end we kept it pure. He loops back on the girls rather than going back to a few days before when he'd been skiing. One of the processes of making the film is that you have to forget the original footage. We didn't use the tapes as a pinpoint reference.

Still, watching footage of a guy who thinks he's about to die must have been moving.

It was moving. Of course it was moving. This is going to sound funny and inappropriate, but after I'd watched the footage I kept thinking that we can do better than that! It's a terrible thing to think. But you think it because you've inhabited your fictionalised version of the story that you can present through an actor. I never wanted James to do an impersonation of Aron. If you're creating a version of someone, you emphasise and exaggerate certain characteristics.

I'm sure Aron wouldn't have allowed us to have the tapes as a continual reference point, and I remember thinking that we didn't want them anyway. I didn't want to be imprisoned in the truth of his story. The process by which we made all the day-to-day decisions with James about how he would harness this bit of climbing rope or sleep or spill his water would have been too influenced by the video tapes. We'd have been standing around saying, 'Aron didn't do it like that.' 'Truth', as Orwell says, 'is less important than emotional sincerity.'

And there's so much missing because Aron obviously didn't record all six days. Nothing changes: the environment certainly doesn't change, and he barely changes the position of the camera. Nothing changes, other than Aron slowly shrinking.

As a result of chronic dehydration.

It's awful to watch. On day four or five Aron turns the video on and . . . fuck. It's shocking. Because up until then you didn't really notice it. You see him growing more and more tired, and then suddenly he all but vanishes.

Franco lost twenty-five pounds and wore bigger and bigger T-shirts, but you couldn't ask him to do more.

Of course not! And anyway, when you do that with a movie you're kind of faking it. The actors look fake. 'Oh, he's really starved himself to get to that position!'

I'd argue that Michael Fassbender does a pretty convincing job of fading away in Hunger.

True. He's very, very convincing. But it's rare.

If it looks fake, then obviously it stops you from being lost in the story and going along with it.

That goes back to what I was saying earlier about being able to do it better. I wanted the film to be not an incredibly precise retelling of exactly what happened, but a story in its own right that felt compelling and involving. I wanted the audience to experience his highs and lows with him.

Why do you think you're so attracted to the trapped-person story? The three flatmates stuck in their flat in Shallow Grave, *drug users trapped in their addiction in* Trainspotting, *the kids trapped in poverty in* Slumdog . . . *and the Brian Keenan story that never happened.*

It's a good question. I was also involved briefly with this amazing script called *The Birthday Party*. Nothing to do with the Pinter play. This was a true story about a white guy in New York who was kidnapped for a weekend by a bunch of kids. They took him to where they lived, used his ATM card and kept a bag on his head. He only gets to glimpse what is going on. They threatened to kill him, but let him go in the end. Amazing story, but it's told from inside a bag! He only gets to glimpse what is going on (*laughs*).

That's worse than Buried, *for God's sake!*

You could say that it's to do with the idea of people escaping from their environments. For me, it's actually more about the technical challenge, funnily enough. I think that's riveting.

How do you tell a story . . . through a bag?

Well, that's the challenge! When you get those kinds of experiences in a cinema, it's just like, 'Woooah!'

When it works.

When it works, yeah. I think that's maybe one of the unconscious reasons I'm drawn to that kind of narrative arc; it might illustrate something profound to everyone else, but my focus is on the exhilarating challenge of how the hell you'd bring the story to the screen.

So it's not a conscious decision to make films about people who are trapped or stuck?

(*laughs*) I don't think it's about some deeper idea to do with escaping your background.

It's more to do with the way you approach film-making. Without wishing to sound rude, you approach films in a visceral, visual way, as opposed to a cerebral, profound way. You don't weigh your films down with intellect like, say, Michael Haneke.

It's very true. I was very fortunate that I worked at the Royal Court as a young guy. It taught me that just talking to yourself can alienate. There was a beautiful play which I saw being created called *Other Worlds* by Robert Holman. There was a rule that if the actors outnumbered the audience, the play was cancelled. Despite handing out free tickets to nurses up the road and whoever else, *Other Worlds* was cancelled some nights. It's a beautiful play, but for some reason it wasn't what people wanted to see.

My point is that you don't just make films or plays to please yourself. You have to think about what the audience wants, what they are prepared to experience. As I moved away from theatre into television and then on to film, I learned that it's a commercial world. People who are not making commercial films are supported, unwittingly, by ordinary people paying their taxes. They often behave in a way that suggests they feel they have no responsibility to anybody. I think they do have a responsibility. I think your job as a film-maker is to make the material as interesting as possible; there has to be access for more than just your mate.

Sounds to me as though you're not keen on auteurs.

My very personal take is this: every day, when you wake up as a director, it's important to remember to relax and enjoy your job. You're not Picasso, you're not Tarkovsky, you're not even Ken Loach. I have no interest in being an auteur; I see it as a kind of construct after the event. Very few directors aren't thinking, 'Am I going to be able to get this made? Am I going to be able to cast this?' Everybody's got to raise money to make films. Even Michael Haneke – and he's probably the guy who more than anyone can exist in the auteur world at the moment. It's a matter of perception: there are some auteurs out there who are seriously special, but they still rely on other people to make their films. Whereas Picasso just needed a crayon and off he went.

You're not interested in elite film-making. You want to put bums on seats.

I do. I'm not in this for posterity. I make the films I make because I live a life amongst people. You make films, some of which they'll like and others which they won't. Some will think my films are profound. Or trash. Most of the films I make are halfway between the two probably, which I'm happy with.

I do respond to film viscerally and visually. It's the only way I know. Otherwise, how can you equate how much you love an action movie with a seemingly more mature appreciation of a Kieślowski or Tarkovsky film? So your question is not rude. It's accurate. And I'm proud to be that way.

Thinking about it, I wasn't suggesting you were anti-intellectual. It's more about being anti-elitist.

I know. Film is a public medium, really. It might be made in a commercial way, but it's experienced in a very public way. Other art forms are more private. Although it is sidelined too often, poetry is, I think, the purest form of art.

I recently discovered the Martin Amis short story 'Career Move', in which poets swagger around Hollywood and are fed drugs, while scriptwriters desperately try to get published in snotty little magazines.

That's a great idea! As Poet Laureate, Carol Ann Duffy has a public role, but for most poets it's a very solitary, private life. A poet like Paul Farley, whose work I admire greatly, takes his new set of poems to his publisher and either they are published or they aren't. The publisher is hardly going to ask Farley to make the poems more accessible. I don't think much bargaining goes on. 'Hey, Paul, can you make this poem more groovy?'

A poem is a one-to-one experience. Because how you appreciate a poem is usually to do with solitude as well, isn't it? Certainly, that's how I experience poems.

It's also rare to read a poem just once. You read it over and over, working out the rhythm and the texture of the words. Whereas you might only re-read a novel once or twice – like, say, The Great Gatsby *– generally after a ten- or twenty-year gap.*

To read a great poem time and again is a special experience. Parts of *The Great Gatsby* are pure poetry. It's so condensed, with the perfect choice of words.

It's hard to find that language in cinema, but you can certainly create moments.

That's what you try to do. You try to smuggle in moments of that for people. But by its nature cinema is a public experience . . .

Created by so many people that it's hard to have a singular vision?

One thing I have learned is that despite everything I'm saying, directors do provide a singular vision. It's interesting to see what happens when you let people work without the director. It just doesn't work. You brief your second unit. Off they go. Back they come. With something that doesn't follow the brief. You think to yourself, 'Is it just me being dissatisfied?' Or, 'Has it not worked because there isn't a director there?' And it's the latter. Because for some reason – given how public it is and the fact that we don't work by committee – you still need strong leadership.

Which is why you can spot a Danny Boyle film, much the same as you can spot a Heston Blumenthal dinner.

Films clearly don't work without the director's vision, even though directors are pains in the neck. They're expensive in terms of con-stantly demanding more. The system would definitely get rid of them if it could. But for all their failings and for all the annoyance and irritability of having directors, they are irreplaceable.

I bet studios love you, though. For myriad reasons: you won a truckload of Oscars; you are less of a pain than most successful directors; you genre-jump; you are far from anonymous – your films can reasonably roll the credit 'A Danny Boyle Film'.

I give them something to sell. They like that. Equally, you don't do the things they want you to. And you make decisions that aren't based on the way they're making decisions – they want everything to be more commercial. Obviously, in the old days directors were on contracts and belonged to the studio. They had less freedom.

Returning again to the specific way you work, I'd like to talk about how your Catholicism – or lapsed Catholicism – has informed your film-making. We discussed it earlier on in the book, but I'm thinking specifically of Ralston looking skyward and saying 'Thank you' when he cuts off his arm. I'm amazed he didn't try to make a deal with God as so many of us – believers or not – would probably have done.

Aron himself was surprised he didn't turn to God.

I suppose my question is about the opaque Catholicism in your films . . .

(*laughs*) We talked earlier about the overall theme of my films being about escaping from or being trapped in circumstances. You could certainly argue that they are an escape from Catholicism, if only because they're morally quite expansive. They are not rigid films. They're about pleasure, if only the pleasure of watching the film. We even tried to make *127 Hours* a pleasure ride in a way, albeit in grim circumstances. It could so easily have been a cinematic ordeal in which the camera didn't move for forty-five minutes.

I can't pretend to have entirely escaped Catholicism. There are values that you hold and carry through your upbringing. But for me, they're more to do with family than with religion itself. Do I believe in God? No, but as Billy Connolly said, I believe in people who do. Those people seem like good people, even though you cannot understand why they believe.

Sometimes religion bleeds into fatalism. On the set of 127 Hours, *Ralston said he believed the rock was waiting for him.*

I don't really believe in all that, but fate is a mystery. You appreciate it more in India.

The notion that 'it is written'?

Yeah.

It's easier to take from a different culture.

Yes, it is. It really is. And especially in a strange culture that you

355

can't really make sense of. Nothing makes sense in India, so you may as well believe in fate, because that might explain some of what goes on in this sea of possibilities.

And India is, after all, the country that uses 'it is written' as a kind of convenient catch-all.

It is, yeah. But I still think you make your own decisions, and *127 Hours* makes that clear. Ralston makes his own decision not to tell anybody where he is going and not to keep looking for the Swiss army knife. Now you could say that was fate, but rather than it being preordained, there's always the possibility he could have phoned his mum. He could have said where he was going.

He chose not to or he didn't think about it? He compared that day's climbing to a walk in the park.

He didn't think about it. You make your own way in life. You make your own decisions. But I believe there's always the possibility to change.

127 Hours *is secular film-making infused with spirituality, or perhaps just good old humanity.*

Visionaries are often so fucked up and riveting because it's difficult to believe in something different. But you have to believe that things can change. If we sat here and tried to imagine Britain as a republic, it would be really hard. We'd both be thinking, 'It's never going to happen.' But it will. Absolutely it will. And the country will be different and better because of it. Ten or even five years ago it was hard to imagine America with a black president, but it happened. It's about believing in progression. And if enough people believe in progression, then you will make it happen. It's how you make change.

In the chapter on the Olympics opening ceremony you talk at length about how the volunteers taught you about belief and possibility, both of which enabled progression.

I learned that even with an institution such as the Olympic Games, which is so controlling and so limited in its horizons, you can do something good and make it progressive. People thought I was nuts for taking on the opening ceremony because of the possibility of failing after Beijing. But for some reason I didn't care about that. Obviously I'm thinking about it retrospectively, but I knew the volunteers were a symbol of possibility. And that's why I wasn't scared on the night. Everyone assumes a country's core is its institutions, but it's not. It's about the people who actually believe in something.

Your films are, in fact, as much about belief as being trapped: Renton believes he can get clean in Trainspotting; *Capa believes he can save the earth in* Sunshine; *Jamal believes he can win a million in* Slumdog; *Ralston has to believe he can beat the boulder. Did you talk to Simon Beaufoy about such concepts when you handed over your treatment?*

Not directly. What Simon gave us was something of a masterclass in scriptwriting. I remember reading his first draft. I was blown away. I had already made the film in my head, but Simon's script made me realise how incomplete my work was. He did what good writers do: he told the story through character and character choice. He's very good at tricks, like the scene at the start where, from a camera sitting at the back of the cupboard, we see Aron's hand fishing around in the cupboard for a penknife.

Well, I say tricks, but in a way they're not tricks. Dialogue is a trick, but it has to be believable. One of the real tricks of writing is to let characters say things that they don't look like they've been forced to say. They look natural and yet they illustrate a point about their character.

The humour is integral too. And I'm going to reference the 'Good morning, America' speech again.

This also goes back to what we were discussing about cinema being a public medium. Very few people can write without humour and get films made. Every writer that I've worked with knows that you need humour in there.

It buys you everything, doesn't it?

It does if you're going to ask people to sit there for ninety minutes. You'd better make them feel like they're having a good time, even if they're not, even if the film is ultimately deeply disturbing. You've got to make them feel that part of the bargain is you're supplying them with nourishment all the time. Humour's a great way of making you feel like time is passing. All the writers I've worked with do it automatically; it's part of their nature. I don't think any of them write a scene and then think, 'Fuck . . . there are no jokes in there. I'd better go back and put some in.'

Humour carries the story along.

And it's probably what carries the writers along too (*laughs*).

Did you let Beaufoy get on with the script or did you actually collaborate? You share a scriptwriting credit.

Simon came back with his first draft and then we just talked, much like we'd done on *Slumdog*. Slightly less than we'd done on *Slumdog*, because then I came on board after the script was written and I had various very specific notes about it. Whereas Simon's first draft of *127 Hours* was a more complete version of what I'd written. We just nurtured it along a bit really.

Beaufoy talked to me about how he saw 127 Hours *as Samuel Beckett's* Endgame. *Franco also referenced Beckett.*

I did my thesis at university on Samuel Beckett. I've been through my Beckett stage.

So you're not projecting Beckett onto every Waiting for Godot-*like situation?*

(*laughs*) Certainly not! And I didn't want *127 Hours* to feel like a Beckett play. Any good Beckett production will bring out his humour, but it's very deliberate humour and I didn't want James's performance to feel deliberate or in any way self-conscious. I wanted it to feel like that accident could happen to anybody. This is not a rigid schematic idea to illustrate humanity; it could literally happen to anybody.

It could happen to anybody anywhere. You were adamant that it wouldn't look like a National Geographic *film either. The story could have been set, at a stretch, in a lift. Anywhere he's isolated from humanity.*

Exactly. Everyone talks about how Aron was lost in the wilderness. But it struck me that he goes into that wilderness with a movie camera and a Walkman that's blasting out urban pop music.

Which means that, in the end, you managed to achieve the near impossible and make an urban film set in a canyon in the middle of nowhere.

(*laughs*) I think I probably did. I hope I did. Aron is a modern character, not some kind of transcendental-meditation person losing himself in the country. So yes, it's a completely urban story. He could have just as easily been trapped in a lift, in a sealed room. It doesn't matter really. The fact is that he got trapped in a canyon, believed he could survive and is around to tell his story.

Frankenstein (2011)

Europe, circa 1818. As the audience take their seats in the theatre there is the loud, resonant sound of a heartbeat. A large, womb-like pod sits centre stage. In it is the outline of a suspended human form. There is a flash of lightning – the densely packed light bulbs in the ceiling are switched on simultaneously to create blinding white light – and the naked Creature (Jonny Lee Miller/Benedict Cumberbatch) pushes through the membrane and flops onto the stage. He thrashes around, looks anguished, groans. He is pre-verbal. His body is fully formed, but he is like a small child.

As the Creature is in the process of evolving – literally finding both his feet and his voice – he meets his creator. Victor Frankenstein (Benedict Cumberbatch/Jonny Lee Miller) is both fascinated and repelled by him. The Creature clumsily approaches Frankenstein, who throws his cloak over him in a panic and runs away.

The Creature roams the streets of Ingolstadt, which is finding its feet as an industrial hub. He is still inchoate, a stranger in this brave new world. Yet he must learn about this world, and fast. A sparking steampunk locomotive briefly appears from nowhere, ridden by a gaggle of chained workers. Everyone he meets is scared of him; some throw stones.

The Creature wakes up in the countryside. A flock of birds shoots up into the air. He stares in wonder at nature. He bathes in the rain.

Two beggars sit round a fire. The Creature appears and grunts. They run, leaving him to work out how to eat the rabbit cooking in the pot. Later, they return to verbally and physically abuse him. This time it's the Creature that runs away. Alone, he howls. He is learning about pain.

We see a blind man, De Lacey (Karl Johnson), being given food by his son Felix (Daniel Millar) and daughter-in-law Agatha (Lizzie Winkler) before they head out to clear the field.

The Creature, dressed in ragged old clothes, approaches the house. The blind man assumes he's come to burgle them and offers food and books. The Creature crams food in his mouth. De Lacey, unable to see and unable to judge, is kind. He plays guitar for the Creature, whose first words are the expletives that have been aimed at him.

As Felix and Agatha clear the field, De Lacey teaches the Creature to talk and read. The Creature learns to recite Milton's 'Paradise Lost'. They discuss feelings, love and human behaviour. The Creature, now able to read the journal he discovered in Frankenstein's cloak, discovers his creator is from Geneva.

Eventually, De Lacey suggests the Creature meet his son and daughter-in-law rather than fleeing every day before they return. The Creature is reluctant and puts it off. One day, Felix and Agatha return from work before the Creature has had time to leave. Agatha, heavily pregnant, screams; Felix's instinct is to defend his wife and father by beating the Creature.

The Creature feels he has been betrayed by his teacher. He returns to burn the cottage and its three inhabitants. No one hears their screams for help.

On the edge of a lake, the Creature approaches a boy who turns out to be Frankenstein's younger brother. When the boy refuses to take him to his brother, the Creature kidnaps him. A search party, including Victor's fiancée Elizabeth (Naomie Harris), looks for the boy. Victor joins them. He is distracted, unkempt. There is talk of a monster living in the mountains.

The boy's limp body is found in a boat, alongside pages ripped from Victor's journal.

Victor searches for the Creature in the mountains. When he finds him, he is dumbstruck by the Creature's fluid movement and use of language. The Creature, in turn, wants to know why he was abandoned. Victor wants to avenge his brother's death, but is fascinated by the progress of his creation. The Creature has one request: he will disappear from society if Victor will create a female companion as hideous as him. Now that he can feel, he is lonely.

Victor is excited by the challenge of creating a female, a goddess.

He plans to postpone his wedding to Elizabeth and go to England and then Scotland. She is furious, but his mind is made up.

A dilapidated croft in the Orkneys. Victor arrives with a trunk, helped by two crofters. He asks for their help in securing fresh human remains. They are reluctant to rob graves – at least not until they are convinced that it's for important medical research. And the price is right.

Victor works for months on his new project. The Female Creature's body is suspended in a frame.

He dreams his brother is alive and quizzing him on his work, his early experiments with galvanism and his fascination with rotting bodies.

The Creature wakes him up. He demands to see his perfect companion. Victor isn't sure they should be together. How will she respond to him? To a life in exile? Is the Creature sure he can love? Does he have a soul? The Creature in turn swears to adore and cherish her.

Victor, who himself knows very little of love, says he will bring her to life, but instead hacks her body apart. The Creature is devastated.

Victor's father (George Harris) arrives, worried by his son's continued absence. Victor is taken away. He asks his father to burn his journal so that no one may create another Creature.

Back in Geneva, Victor and Elizabeth are married. Elizabeth is in her bedroom, preparing for her wedding night. Victor appears, edgy. He says the house is secure. He tells Elizabeth about the Creature. She simply laughs in disbelief and thinks he is suffering from nervous exhaustion. She suggests it might have been easier for them to create life by having a child.

Victor stalks off. The Creature suddenly appears from within the bed, where he's been hiding. He talks to Elizabeth. He tells her he has no name. He tells her all he wanted was a companion. Slowly trusting him, she sits next to him on the bed. He explains how, by studying human behaviour, he learned how to lie. Victor lied to him about his companion; now he will break his promise not to kill. He rapes and then murders Elizabeth.

The Arctic Circle. The Creature talks of his black heart. Victor stumbles towards him. The master has become the slave. The Creature is full of questions about being an outsider. Victor is *weary. He passes out. The Creature tells him that all he wanted was his love. Victor, drifting back into consciousness, says he doesn't know what love is. They both say they will only die when the other is dead. The Creature taunts his creator to kill him as they disappear into the distance.*

* * *

AMY RAPHAEL: *You had already signed up to direct* Frankenstein *at the National Theatre when you were approached to do the opening ceremony of the London Olympics, so you decided to use the play as a dry run.*

DANNY BOYLE: When I was approached about the opening ceremony, we were just finishing *127 Hours*. I said my only commitment was to direct *Frankenstein* at the National. By the time I started on *Frankenstein*, I was already working on the opening ceremony with production designer Mark Tildesley, costume designer Suttirat Larlarb and writer Frank Cottrell Boyce. Mark and Suttirat came with me to the National as they both had experience in theatre, and I used *Frankenstein* as a dry run for composers Rick Smith and Karl Hyde from Underworld, as they had never scored a play before. I wanted to see how they responded to the challenge before offering them the opening-ceremony job. Toby Sedgwick was also a great influence on both jobs.

We certainly used to joke about how it was a dry run for the Olympics. Mark, Suttirat and I hadn't done theatre for such a long time, so *Frankenstein* was very much a way for us all to reintroduce ourselves to the theatre. As a director I needed to find out about live entertainment again and whether or not I could still do it (*laughs*).

After a fifteen-year hiatus.

After a hiatus in which you work in a medium – film – in which you can literally change everything all the time. Endlessly. Until someone drags you away at the end, you can reshoot, add and take away scenes. Whereas live entertainment is live entertainment. You can rehearse and rehearse, but then you have to let go. And fifteen years is a long time to be away from the theatre. A very long time.

Other than assembling a team, what was your starting point for Frankenstein?

When I was doing research for both *Frankenstein* and the opening ceremony, I kept going back to the late eighteenth and early nineteenth century. It's when the age of science begins. Queen Victoria used chloroform for the delivery of her final child, which then legitimised it. The inner world of our bodies was just starting to be explored by surgery. Scientists were also beginning to look outside the body. They were on the verge of discovering how to harness electricity. In terms of what we understand now to be the modern world, it's the very start of it.

Mary Shelley obviously found a poetic, thrilling, outrageous way to manifest it. You see where the genesis of *Frankenstein* came from, because in the early days of surgery they were beginning to dig up the bodies. The resurrectionist men dug up fresh bodies, and the hospitals, which were only supposed to dissect convicted murderers, were beginning to explore and understand the inside of the body. Burke and Hare obviously went a step further and killed people before taking them straight to the hospital. That way you miss the inconvenient bit of having to dig the bodies up and getting caught.

Back then people thought you went to heaven in your body. The rich were worried about being dug up and experimented upon, so they had iron coffins made with security traps on. If you tried to break into the coffin, your hand would be cut off.

It's important to trace *Frankenstein* back historically and understand the context in which Shelley wrote it. Hollywood has created the idea of horror about it, but in fact it doesn't come out of horror at all – it comes out of a morbid fear of being born. It makes us question where we come from.

Science was as much of an influence on Mary Shelley as the arts.

Absolutely. She was watching everyone around her searching for answers about electricity. She lived in a house that was full of bright, enquiring minds – in other words, the people who hung around her husband, Percy Bysshe Shelley, and his friend Lord Byron. Science and the arts were much less rigid disciplines in the early nineteenth century and there was far more cross-over between the two.

'*Frankenstein* comes out of a morbid fear of being born. It makes us question where we come from.'

I had talked endlessly to Nick Dear, who wrote the stage play, about the science that hovers over *Frankenstein*. Electricity is obviously embedded in Mary Shelley's story, which was written in 1818. It is made fun of in the early Hollywood versions, but Shelley knew there was force in electricity. She knew from all those scientists that it was powerful and had huge potential. Could they harness it? Could they trap it? How could they then release it? These were the key questions of the time.

When I told Frank that I was directing *Frankenstein*, he gave me a copy of Humphrey Jennings's *Pandaemonium*, which documents the Industrial Revolution between 1660 and 1886. There's this amazing chapter called 'Effects of Lightning in Northamptonshire', in which a shepherd is killed on a hilltop alongside five of his sheep. The scientists arrive to try and figure out the force that has taken this man's life. It's explained, in intense detail, how they go through his pockets and find a stone that's been cleaved clean in two by the lightning: 'In one [pocket] we found a hard glazed stone, about ten inches long, six wide, and four thick, cracked in two.'

Pandaemonium is subtitled *The Coming of the Machine*, and we thought we'd literally manifest the new science and engineering of the period on the stage in the steampunk scene. The creation of

'We thought we'd manifest the new science of the period on the stage in the steampunk scene.'

power drove the revolution and changed societies. The railways appeared and, with them, the idea of travel, which changed everything. It's said that it was the biggest-ever change to warfare. You could move thousands of men to a different place by train.

And, of course, the heart of the Olympics opening ceremony told the story of the Industrial Revolution.

The original idea for the Olympics was to start with the Industrial Revolution. That was in play right from the beginning. You really have to deal with some element of the history of Britain in the opening ceremony, and I always knew it was going to be the Industrial Revolution. It felt as though the Industrial Revolution connected *Frankenstein* to the opening ceremony. We were tackling it in the Olivier theatre at the National, while simultaneously thinking about how we were going to tackle it in the Olympic Stadium.

Even now we are still children of the Industrial Revolution. And yet we're about to say goodbye to it. Well, not us personally, but in a few generations it will have faded from our memories. Its impact will have been totally subsumed into society. And yet it's such a massive thing: for God's sake, the Industrial Revolution started in our country!

The expectation at the opening ceremony was to cover kings and queens. When you look at our country you have to ask yourself what the root of it is. What made Britain the country it is today? It's not political to choose the Industrial Revolution, it's just common sense. Everything else just falls away. Kings and queens are just peripheral. This is gigantic, colossal, world-changing. The Industrial Revolution is a complex and wonderful thing. And, as we all know, an awful thing at the same time. We're still living through its consequences.

You explored the Industrial Revolution on a small stage before taking it to the world stage.

You say small, but the Olivier is a famously intimidating stage. Compared to anything else I'd done on the stage, it's enormous! I'd never worked in the main house at Stratford. I'd worked in the main place at the Royal Court – very intimate, four hundred seats, proscenium arch – but the Olivier is known as a killer space. It's very difficult to conquer. Even Nick Hytner, director of the National, warned us about it.

Normally, you go to the Olivier rigid with panic, terrified about how you're going to deal with the space. By rights we should have been intimidated. I hadn't done theatre for fifteen years, and Mark had only really done community theatre. But because the opening ceremony was looming over us, the Olivier actually felt quite intimate. It felt like a box where we were trying out some ideas. Which isn't to take away from performing *Frankenstein* at the National, because it was a brilliant experience.

You'd been talking to Nick Dear about staging Frankenstein *back when you were both at the RSC.*

Nick had done a dazzling adaptation of a Tirso de Molina play called *The Last Days of Don Juan*, which I directed. It was fantastic fun. A real belter of a time. It started at the Swan theatre in Stratford and then came down to the Barbican. We talked about working on something else together. Nick did a first adaptation of *Frankenstein* that just didn't work. It was a literal adaptation of the novel, which is, of course, letter-based. We left it, but over a ten-year period kept going back to it every now and again.

I felt that there had to be a unique approach to the play because there had been so many films: the first version was in 1910, and subsequent adaptations have starred Boris Karloff and Bela Lugosi. Since Nick and I had put the book on a back burner, Ken Branagh's *Frankenstein* had come out. There was, basically, way too much baggage associated with Shelley's novel.

And then, out of nowhere, we realised that no one had ever told the story from the Creature's point of view. Everything else had been done but, as far as we could tell, no one had thought to flip the perspective.

The minute you flipped it, Dear could get on with his adaptation.

Yes. The only problem we had was how to end the story. It took Nick quite a long time to come up with the final scene in the Arctic wasteland. But the rest of the story was released by that one idea. Nick immediately wrote the beginning of the play, in which the Creature comes to life and blinks furiously in the bright light of the world.

Is that when you thought of creating the ceiling of light bulbs above the stage?

Mark and I were inspired by Jeff Wall's photo *After 'Invisible Man' by Ralph Ellison, the Prologue,* which is inspired by Ellison's 1952 novel. It's about a man who lives in a secret basement on the edge of Harlem. Have you never seen the photo? It's amazing. *Invisible Man* is one of the first African American novels in America.

Anyway, we created a ceiling of light bulbs inspired by Jeff Wall, who was inspired by Ralph Ellison . . .

Let's talk about the first time you read Frankenstein, *which you often refer to as the first sci-fi novel.*

I read it when we were at Stratford doing the Tirso de Molina play. I thought it was hopelessly antiquated in terms of its structure, but obviously she's imprisoned in the letter format because it was fashionable at the time. But what a story! Enough, certainly, to make people pick it up and rave about it. It *is* the first work of science fiction. It is, literally, the beginning of science fiction.

I can never get over the fact that Mary Shelley was still a teenager when she wrote Frankenstein. *She is referred to as a 'literary heiress' – the daughter of Mary Wollstonecraft, the writer who died shortly after giving birth, and the writer and philosopher William Godwin – and eloped with Percy Bysshe Shelley at sixteen. I know she would have been stimulated by being around Shelley and Byron, but* Frankenstein *is very much her story. If anything – in my mind at least – she is the pioneering writer among that trio.*

I agree. I don't find her intimidated by those two at all, because I'm not a big fan of either's work. They're not Wordsworth and they're not Keats. I honestly think they're seriously overrated. Which means that I've never thought she was lucky to be around them; as though that in some way helped her write *Frankenstein*. She was this extraordinary presence in this world of scientists and literary types flying in and out of the house.

It's a stunning book, not in terms of the writing, but the ideas. Had she lived in a different age, she would have written it differently – she wouldn't have been imprisoned in the letter format. The fact remains that it really is a bizarre novel. And so incredibly radical.

In an era when women weren't really supposed to share their ideas with the world – her authorship was only finally acknowledged in 1831 with the third edition – Mary Shelley was exploring the idea of creating life without women. And she was pregnant as she wrote, growing her own creature.

The manuscript of *Frankenstein* was delivered a month before her baby was born. As Mary Wollstonecraft's daughter and an intelligent woman herself, I don't suppose Shelley wrote a story about men's desire to create life without being unaware of what she was writing. I think she knew exactly what she was doing. It's like she could foresee the science that was about to change the world. It's all documented in *Pandaemonium*, which is full of men chasing electricity. She was surrounded by men – whether she was lovers with both Percy Bysshe Shelley and Byron is irrelevant, they were both constantly around – and far from being a benign, bovine presence, she was busy absorbing everything that was going on around them and her.

She didn't write *Frankenstein* as some kind of feminist pamphlet, but she could see that these men around her were in a frenzy typical of a society on the edge of change. She could see that science had the power not only to create, but also to destroy. In *Frankenstein* the men pursue each other until they destroy one another.

The brilliance of Frankenstein *is that it's timeless. It seems modern now; it could just as well be about genetics.*

Because you can transpose ideas easily. We were aware of that, obviously, and discussed it at length. But really our focus was on telling the story from the Creature's point of view. It was just a wonderful release.

Your second radical idea was to double-cast so that the two lead actors would play the Creature one night and Frankenstein the next.

One of the first times I went to the theatre as a kid was with my secondary school, Thornleigh Grammar in Bolton. Mr Unsworth, the English teacher, took us to Stratford to watch *Richard II* because we were studying it at A-level. It was the famous production where they double-cast Richard and Bolingbroke. When we got back to school we talked about it at length. The idea never left me because it was so interesting. As soon as Nick started to write *Frankenstein*, I thought we had to double-cast because it's the creator and the created. By extrapolation it leads to universal questions: is there a God? Who created me? Am I created in His own image? So we set about looking for two actors capable of playing both roles. And I immediately wanted Jonny Lee Miller.

Why? You hadn't worked with him since Trainspotting *in 1996.*

Instinct. I had a hunch it could work with him.

Had you stayed in touch?

No; we weren't mates because that's not really what happens when you make a film together. I don't know why Jonny jumped to mind.

'Jonny had a young son, and he brought the experience of a pre-verbal child.'

But it worked. He had a young son, and that's one of the things he brought to the rehearsal room – the experience of a pre-verbal child. The Creature has to learn language right at the start of the play, and Jonny would imitate his child for us. There is a clownish – in the best sense of the word – element to the Creature, and Jonny helped us get a feel for that.

What did Benedict Cumberbatch bring to the role?

My only concern with Benedict was his physicality. I wanted the piece to be *so* physical, and I knew Jonny would be fine with that because of the work we'd done on *Trainspotting*. Certain actors are verbal, while others are physical. Jonny is a physical actor, but I thought Benedict, wonderful actor that he is, might be too cerebral; he's a seriously intelligent actor. At the time of his audition he was starring in Terence Rattigan's *After the Dance* at the Lyttleton and everyone at the National was raving about him because it was a huge hit. He gave a very physically restrained performance, which was obviously required for that particular role.

I knew he'd be able to do the speeches in *Frankenstein* because

371

'I was blown away by Benedict's physicality. He was electric.'

that's what he excels at, so I asked him to come and audition the very opening scene of the play so that I could see him emerge as the Creature and crawl over the floor. And I was blown away by his physicality. It was similar to James Franco's audition for *127 Hours* in that Benedict nailed it. He was electric. I wasn't sure he'd be able to physically release himself, but my God he did.

It wasn't a traditional theatre audition where everyone sits at one end of the room and watches. I'd been off doing films for fifteen years and auditioning actors by watching them close up – and that's what I did with Benedict. I was following him around the room as he was doing all this birth stuff, talking to him all the time. It was fantastic actually.

Were Miller and Cumberbatch both up for double-casting?

I guess they must have been (*laughs*). And it's a credit to them because it's a nightmare idea for an actor. If they had thought about it too much, they'd probably have turned it down. For different reasons I think they both thought it was the right time to do something like this.

I interviewed Miller ahead of the production, and he said that

*initially he kept on getting confused with the cues and forgetting
which character he was playing.*

Before they could even begin to be confused, we had to discover the
characters. I don't think Victor was a difficult character to discover
for either of them, but the Creature certainly was. You can make
anything of him. Who or what is he? They had a long journey to
go on, but equally it was a wonderful opportunity for an actor to
show you a character who at the start is pre-verbal and who slowly
has to find his place in the world. He has to deal with the inadequa-
cies of language and the human responses to him.

Telling the story from the Creature's point of view stops him
being a victim. The two iterations of him are that he is a malevo-
lent monster reflecting the worst side of us humans, or that he is a
victim of circumstances.

*But as soon as he develops feelings – which even Karloff's Creature
does, but in a clumsy, childish way – he is instantly humanised.*

He also learns feelings second-hand and so sees their power. He
learns love and cunning and deception. There's a great speech Nick
wrote in which the Creature discovers that the ultimate human trait
is the ability to lie. It's heartbreaking to watch really. Jonny and
Benedict played the Creature in their own style – which was the
whole point – so each brought a subtly different reading to the role.

Both actors were willing, I presume, to swap and share ideas?

Right from the beginning they were happy to steal ideas from each
other. Well, not steal, because it isn't stealing but rather blending
or borrowing. They were very generous with each other. One of the
tricky parts of being an actor is that you will always be judged. It's
doubly painful when you're not only judged, but also compared.
There was always the danger that a review would say X was a
little underwhelming as the Creature, but Y excelled. Inviting such
comparisons isn't easy for any actor.

Did you encourage Cumberbatch and Miller to spar?

In a very open way. It was like a wrestling tag team; they'd concentrate on one part for one day and then switch. But sometimes

Cumberbatch as the Creature and Miller as Dr Frankenstein: 'They borrowed ideas off each other.'

they'd say, 'Let me have a go at that.' They'd borrow ideas off each other, copy each other. They had the conundrum of balancing the two parts. They had to share discoveries and yet also protect their own. That's a bit of a challenge for a lead actor.

The only nightmare was, literally, how to keep the indivisibility of the evening. So I insisted on two press nights because I didn't want a situation where they had a press night as one character and not the other. That would have been ridiculous. Over the run they did exactly the same number of performances. Then the biggest remaining challenge, which we fought and thankfully won, was that they would film the play for NT Live twice. Meaning there are two versions of the play. And we've insisted that cinemas across the world show both versions.

They were both naked on stage. In every possible sense.

Yes, but both were strong enough to handle it. Physically and mentally. Benedict is led by intelligence – which is why people think he's cerebral – but he's a total actor who transforms that into physicality straight away. Jonny's more instinctive; he feeds in the intelligence afterwards. They were an almost perfect balance of two different approaches to acting. Although Nick wrote the script and I was hands-on as director, they created the Creature together.

They had a great time playing the Creature, even though it was extremely demanding in terms of physicality. They had to spend two or three hours in make-up and then drag themselves across a stage floor that gave them splinters and inevitably had nails sticking up. They were covered in gashes and cuts. When they played Victor, they got a night off from punishing their bodies.

Were they both happy to be naked on stage? There is no camera to hide behind, after all.

We talked about it at length. It wasn't gratuitous, so they were fine. There was no point in being half naked; they had to go for it. But I suggested they wear nappies – or wraps – when the play was filmed for NT Live. It's different, I think, when something can be watched over and again on a screen.

What else did you discuss? You've mentioned Miller imitating his young son. Did you send them off to do further research?

One or both of them visited stroke victims in recovery. They both went off to these special schools for kids who don't communicate very well through language. Because we wanted the Creature to be sympathetic and not a gorgon who doesn't evolve, we had manifested him initially as a child. He's not a monster because he learns to be one of us. In the novel he laments not having a name. Once he learns language and identity, these questions begin to plague him. A woman came in to talk to us about the brain and language. That was fascinating. We also went to an autopsy.

That sounds perfect. But isn't it tricky to see autopsies these days?

It's virtually impossible to do now because of the Human Tissue Act, which was passed in the wake of the Alder Hey organs scandal. Autopsies are very strictly controlled now because people were taking organs without consent and keeping them for experiments. You need a relative's consent, and because the autopsy happens so quickly, you're never going to get that consent. The families involved are too upset.

But we gave it a go. And Abbey Wright, who was the assistant director on the show, finally managed to get permission from St Thomas's. This young guy's body had been found in a toilet and they couldn't find any relatives. They knew it was a drug overdose, and so it was no problem. We went along to this autopsy and it was absolutely amazing. He was lying there on a slab. He was totally white because the blood was no longer being pumped around his body and so had settled. There was a line of blood at the lower sixth of his body, where gravity had done its job.

They cut the skull off and then took the brain out as casually as if removing something from a tin can. Out comes the brain! Once they'd done that, they peeled off the face, and it's as though the guy's identity just completely disappeared for a second. When they put the face back on, getting him ready for burial, his identity returned. They basically took everything out, using sections of it for analysis, to prove that he had indeed died of a drug overdose. Even though there were no known relatives, it ranked as a suspicious death, so they had to do the autopsy.

Were you squeamish?

Not at all. I was just full of wonder. It was an incredible thing to see. The most extraordinary part of it is that since this Act came in, everything has to be put back in the body. All the fluid, the detritus. When the pathologist opened up the bladder, the urine flooded everywhere. Some of it obviously drained off. But the letter of the law means that everything is meant to go back in that body. Everything, including the brain and the urine.

Once the brain comes out, it expands and won't go back in the skull. So it goes in the stomach cavity. You're buried with your brain in your tummy. They stuffed it all in there, in a heavy-duty yellow bag, along with the liver, kidneys and so on. The idea of the bag, I think, is that if they did come to dig up the body ten years later, those body parts will have been better preserved than the outside of the body.

Jonny didn't make it. I don't know if he was squeamish or not. Benedict was there, as was my daughter Grace. Abbey had to leave halfway through. But it was very civilised. We were standing behind a three-quarters Perspex screen which you can look through. If you don't want to smell it, you can choose not to. And it does smell because obviously the body is decaying.

It was a big moment for me. It made me realise what an amazing job I have.

Mike Leigh insists that his actors have all seen at least one dead body as part of a rite of passage. I think it's a smart idea.

I remember seeing my gran when she died. I was seven or eight. It was my first dead body. You need to touch a dead body too because it feels so different.

Did you embrace death on previous films?

(*laughs*) When we did *Shallow Grave*, we went to a morgue in Glasgow. The guy who was showing us around was trying to make us faint. He kept on whipping the corpses out, and some would have their skulls open. I remember him pointing out this overweight guy in his fifties with a huge lump on his head and saying he'd obviously died of a massive heart attack. When they suffer the attack they fall forwards, and the head's so heavy that it just goes 'thump'. He explained they'd need to do an autopsy on him because there was no obvious sign of death, but he knew what it was. He knew 100 per cent before they even opened the guy up. A massive, instant heart attack.

I don't think I ever told you about the morgue we went to in Bangkok when we did *The Beach*. That was unbelievable. We filmed a sequence there which was cut in the end. It wasn't air-conditioned; obviously the climate is tropical, so you can imagine how bad the stink was. We walked in and the smell hit us like a truck. The bodies were laid out, and they were doing autopsies on them. The heads were off like tin cans. Saw it off and open it up!

Out the back was a big room full of containers in which they kept the bodies. It wasn't like a refrigerator morgue with shelving. This was their idiosyncratic version of it. The bodies were laid out in shawls and they were all tagged. There were two or three containers and then there was a separate one for the Chinese. They were tossed in like animals. Appalling racism; the Thai people don't like the Chinese, even now.

That's awful. It must have been deeply distressing to witness, but fascinating nonetheless. Did you do any more traditional research? In other words, did you discuss the genesis of Frankenstein, *of how Mary Shelley wrote it at Villa Diodati, close to Lake Geneva; of her life with Percy Bysshe Shelley and Byron; of the furore when she started her relationship with Shelley while he was still married?*

We did talk, briefly. Hers was a life of scandal and judgement. There was a rumour that Mary and Percy consummated their relationship in a cemetery in King's Cross. Maybe that's just ghoulish, given what she went on to write. I was more interested in what was going on around her, with the dawning of a new science and the Industrial Revolution. All of which, of course, feeds back to the opening ceremony.

She was living through great changes in history, just as we are now.

We're going through a very similar period as we finally move out of the industrial age. If it keeps going, with machines being able to intuit and read our minds, the age will definitely shift. We're right at the end of a period that has seen the mechanisation of war and the invention of the atom bomb – both of which can be traced back to the birth of science.

Are you excited by what's coming our way?

No. Yes. I'll stick with yes (*laughs*). Every year the power of what you have in your pocket is increasing. Historians might well look back on the last twenty years as nothing. But for us the progression has been massive. Life-changing.

Has your reading of Frankenstein *changed over time? Did you find new layers when you returned to it after a decade, in terms of how it speaks to us of our fear of the unknown, genetics, cloning, the diminishing role of God . . .?*

We decided to tell the story through the Creature's eyes, and thus the doctor character is underwritten and undeveloped. We could have made the story more applicable, more modern by telling the story through Frankenstein's mind. We chose to emphasise the loneliness of the Creature as opposed to the visionary nature of the doctor. So, instead of exploring the questions about the existence of God which are in the novel, Nick's focus was the Creature's need for a father, for a sense of belonging.

The Creature ends up in the Arctic wastes, which is a metaphor in a way for the loneliness and isolation of man. Our production didn't attempt to include a big scene about God and who made us and whether or not we have souls. The Arctic waste is more like this wilderness that science is wandering off into. What's it going to find? It's not interested in worshipping any more. It's just interested in discovering. Certainly, in the early nineteenth century the Arctic wastes were the great undiscovered areas on the map.

Mary Shelley didn't believe in God, but she appears to have been almost possessed that night when the hallucinatory dream came to her and inspired her to write Frankenstein.

She probably was. When you have a really good idea, you have no idea where it comes from. It's just a good idea that makes a lot of sense. Then it almost writes itself and cascades forward. When you don't have a really good idea, it doesn't cascade forward. It's does anything but. Then it's like wading through treacle. But a good

Jonny Lee Miller as the Creature and Benedict Cumberbatch as Dr Frankenstein at the end of the play.

idea just seems to make itself. It makes perfect sense and everything seems to fit in.

Her mind must have been on fire with everything that was going on around her. She was watching and listening and growing a baby inside her, while these men were presumably asking the question, 'Can we create life?' And Frankenstein is, of course, really a perfect symbol of the rejection of God: we don't need a creator any more, we can do all this through science. At the time, the idea of creating a life without women and without God was an absolute profanity.

You were taken to church as a child, but are fascinated by science. Do you feel a pull between science and God?

I've only recently found science. It's been one of the great things about doing projects like *Sunshine*, *Frankenstein* and the opening ceremony: I do my dilettante research, and that opens up areas. It certainly opened up science for me. I wasn't good at science at school and I bought into the modern idea that art and science are separate disciplines. You choose one or the other. It's a great shame, because we should all have the chance to do both.

Let's talk about the specifics of putting Frankenstein *on at the National. You said earlier that you had to familiarise yourself with live productions again. What was your major concern? And how had theatre changed in your absence?*

I was worried about all the rehearsal time. I didn't know what I was going to do with the six weeks you get at the National. When I first started making films, I used to wonder how I was going to do it without the four weeks of rehearsal that I used to get at the Royal Court. With a film you get a couple of days, and you get used to it.

As soon as I started *Frankenstein*, of course, it just became self-evident that I would need the rehearsal time. Apart from that, the National is amazingly well resourced. It's all so diligent. The standard of work provided by the permanent staff, led by Sacha Milroy and David Marsland, is extremely high, whether they're building you a set or making your costumes. There is a danger that theatre has been starved, but I think that's a largely regional issue. I found it to be quite the opposite at the National. It felt like a step up from my time at the Royal Court. But that's the privilege of working in a main house. Nick Hytner and Nick Starr, the executive director, resourced our play really well. They knew it might just be a hit. It was a set text, and Benedict had been a big hit in *Sherlock*. The standard between him and Jonny would be very, very high.

Hytner and Starr guessed right: over 73,000 people saw it at the Olivier over sixty-four performances. That's a capacity of 98 per cent. It also proved a huge success in cinemas worldwide.

Is that right? Crikey. Well, we had a very generous budget in terms of how to execute it. They were hugely supportive of Mark and me. They knew I hadn't directed in the theatre for fifteen years and that this would be on a different scale for me. Technically, they knew that Mark hadn't designed at that level before.

The great thing about the National is that they're not rigid. It didn't start out with them telling us how *Frankenstein* should be done. There was that attitude in the Olympics, with people thinking they knew how to do it better than us, and we had to deal with that very quickly. At the National, everyone acted as great enablers. No wonder the place is such a huge success and everyone wants to take their work there.

The downside is that the backstage crew are doing so many shows. It's a constant turnover. We felt like outsiders coming in, but I think we brought a different rhythm. We brought a bell in that the audience could ring and we did some daft things like projecting the original *Frankenstein* film onto the tower outside. It all creates problems. The bell was so heavy. The bulbs on the ceiling would create power surges . . . They didn't complain; in fact, they seemed to love solving these problems. We used the rising drum in the centre of the stage. It isn't used very often because it has a very chequered history. But Mark and I loved it.

Other than the rehearsal periods being longer for theatre, were there other notable differences for you personally between screen and stage?

There always used to be this prejudice, which we've defied as a country, that you could never make the transition from being a theatre director to being a director working in film or television. I always felt that theatre was my wide shot. I'm a visual director who likes to create images, and that's why film suits me so perfectly. You have the luxury of the close-up and what that conveys. In theatre you don't have that. You have all those extra rehearsals because you have to find a way of generating that emotion through the rhythm and sound of the language and the physicality of the actor. You're trying to get that contact which cinema gives you automatically. The dynamism of cinema and the dynamism of theatre are just different ways of doing it.

In fact, the live filming of *Frankenstein* was hard. Filming a live show is a massive problem for actors because they act differently on stage and screen. It won't work as well if they interiorise for the camera in a big space. Because what they are doing in a big space is showing you the interior of their minds through language and physicality. In film they don't have to do that. The camera does that through their mental openness and discipline. So when you film a play, it's a hybrid of the two.

But the demand for seeing filmed versions of plays at the cinema has become huge. *Frankenstein* has been a great success and it's constantly being shown in different territories. I think that's just to do with access. The world has become so much more demanding in terms of shared information. You open up your computer in Winnipeg, Canada, you read about Jonny and Benedict in a production of *Frankenstein* in London, and you think, 'I want to see that!' That demand has to be served.

Actually, I was surprised at all the problems inherent in translating a play into film. The actors' expressions during the close-ups were so hard to get right. I couldn't instruct the actors so well when they asked if they should perform to the camera or for the people in the audience. It was a case of suck it and see. The theatre is full, and you've got to play to the people right at the back or it's not fair.

I guess you can't perform to an empty house when filming?

No, because it will feel like that in the cinema. I'm making a big deal out of it: the actors are the storytellers in theatre and they just deal with it. Some of it will be big, too big for camera. Some of it will be small, too small for the back of the house, but good for the camera. Actors know how to measure it.

Did you find yourself constantly tinkering with Frankenstein *before it opened at the National, or did you have to force yourself to let go?*

I used to tinker all the time in theatre. But the actors do push you away if you try to cling on. At a certain point, the play becomes theirs and you're useful only occasionally when things go awry. Some directors don't go back at all. You've got to let the actors get on with it.

Did you attend most nights?

No, I was hardly there at all once it opened. I was exhausted with it anyway. Actors have a different relationship in terms of their familiarity with the play. Your familiarity with it is exhausting by then. Theirs is the opposite; it energises them, I suppose because it allows them to riff on it. I went back for the understudy run-through – the pressure on Jonny's and Benedict's throats was incredible. Occasionally, the understudies went on and did very well.

Did you realise you'd missed the theatre?

I did enjoy the whole process very much. That's very much a tribute to Nick Hytner.

Would you consider directing a play in a regional city? I imagine you'd raise impressive funds with the right one.

I'd like to do another play and I'd be happy to work anywhere really. In the right space. I enjoy going to the theatre more since *Frankenstein* – after not going for a while because I lost the appreciation of it. When it's good, it's electric. There's nothing like it.

I'm encouraging you to talk about theatre and cinema as two very separate disciplines, but on the two occasions I saw Frankenstein *it struck me that the opening scene wouldn't have been out of place in one of your films: the pulsating heartbeat resounding around the theatre, the membrane out of which the Creature bursts, the extreme energy of the opening scene, the attention to visual detail.*

Toby Sedgwick, the movement director, and I wanted to make the opening of the play a complete sensation. It was part of the idea that we wanted to make the play a complete experience without a break. We were adamant about not having an interval. When we first started, it was approaching two hours, which would have demanded an interval. To do it in one go you need it to be between ninety and a hundred minutes. The theatre was great about it. If there is an interval, they make a lot more money, so it's an economic question as well. But we were determined to make it one experience.

That experience started as soon as you walked into the auditorium, and it would continue growing and nurturing. Really it was a way of experiencing the story from the Creature's point of view; although he was on stage as people were finding their seats, it was a full twenty minutes before you met the doctor. We wanted to involve the audience right from the beginning, to try and make it an immersive experience. So there was all this stuff going on. The heartbeat soundtrack. The bell. The bulbs on the ceiling. We were making use of the whole space. It was interesting to watch the audiences and see how they responded to the bell. Some never touched it; other times an extrovert would pull it and then everybody felt they could ring it. We neither encouraged nor discouraged it. It was up to the audience.

It was a challenge for the actors too, because whoever was the Creature that night had to be in the membrane for fifteen minutes before the action began. It wasn't the ideal prep for such a physical start to the play. They might have preferred to prep backstage and then slip into the membrane during a blackout. But they were brilliant about being strapped in there for all that time.

Both Benedict and Jonny talked about listening to the audience discuss who was playing whom that night, whether they'd already seen it 'the other way round' and how much they were looking forward to the naked scenes!

The membrane had a delicate, almost ghostly quality to it which hinted at the Creature's sensitivity.

We were going to be more brutal with it at one stage. Initially, we had this idea that it would burst and release all this red liquid. We tried it out and it was incredible; the Creature was skidding around the stage covered in fake blood. But it was a nightmare for the rest of the evening because all the actors kept sliding and falling.

The practicalities of theatre are about the longevity of the actor. On a film, you'll do anything to get one moment. You can push the actor. They'll recover. In theatre, it's about knowing they can get through the two hours. And then a number of weeks. In the end, we had to protect the actors by cutting the liquid idea, which was a real shame. We couldn't work out a way to get rid of the slime. We tried with cloths, but it was still an ice-skating rink for the actors, and that had the potential for disaster.

So you weren't stymied by health and safety but by your own common sense.

Yes! And the National are willing to push things as far as is reasonable. The way their staff developed the steampunk train was amazing in terms of the pyrotechnics and its proximity to the audience. In my fifteen-year absence the theatre seemed to have become good at dealing with incredibly restrictive laws in order to take many more risks.

You mentioned the drum in the centre of the stage being an issue. Was that a safety issue or was it the worry that it would just get stuck?

We used the drum to recreate a crevasse when the Creature and Frankenstein went up into the mountains. It was very, very dangerous because there was no safety rope around them. If either Jonny or Benedict had lost sight of what they were doing as an actor, they could easily have fallen down the hole. It's a serious fall. A death fall. But because they were both on stage together, they promised to look after each other. If one of them got possessed one night and started backing towards it, then the other would find a way to pull him back.

Apart from the red fluid, we did pretty much everything else we had come up with. Then it was just a case of using the mechanics of the stage and the space and being aware of the audience being in the same space as the actors. If you sit at the front of the Olivier, it's like a living room; if you're up in the gods, then it feels like this huge space. So you have to work out how to use it and how to fill it. It was a wonderful open space for Benedict and Jonny to perform in: they are both powerful actors who can easily fill it. I think they really loved that.

We've talked before about the problems you've had with third acts in your films. You did say that Dear had an issue with the ending, so did you worry about throwing everything at the start of Frankenstein *and leaving the end to stutter to a close?*

Nick had got as far as the amazing scene in which the Creature kills the doctor's wife Elizabeth. And then he got stuck. On a film you could just go to the Arctic and let the visuals speak. As a playwright he had to work out what the scene was about and how we were summing up these two men. So he wrote this very beautiful scene, and I rang him and said, 'Wow! That's it. Let's submit it now.' It felt like the right ending.

After a very ambitious opening like that, you had to let the pace settle down. The core of the novel is this debate between them in the Alps. The play had a different tempo. The Creature had to learn language and learn to debate. We couldn't rush through that.

I do concede, though, that the opening twenty minutes in which he learned about sensory perception was exciting. He just twitched and moved. And then he started to learn. You can compress twenty years of learning the skills of life into a few scenes, which is what they did brilliantly as actors. It was very entertaining. I think Nick did a fantastic job with those scenes. Normally, the Creature is an underwritten symbol of fear, but he really did redress the balance and flip the story around. It was wonderful to make him one of us.

Some of the reviews of the script were less kind: one described it as 'plodding'. Does that mean the script was not as successful as the staging?

I always feel script and staging are indivisible. People might ask if I preferred Benedict or Jonny. It's not that I won't answer as a matter of policy. If you're involved in that kind of operation, then it's important to realise that you're on a kind of voyage together. You don't think, 'Let's chuck him overboard because he's not pulling his weight.' You don't think, 'The design is not as good as the costume.'

Anyone can say what they like about your film or play, but it's no value to you when you're working on it. You select the people you want to work with. You find your cast, assemble your crew and set off on your voyage. As director, you take the blame. Or the praise. But the deal is that we all take responsibility for the production all the way through.

There are people who work in that divisible way. They take ownership of their own parts and couldn't care less about what everyone else is up to. To me, that's not being creative. Those are not good conditions for working in.

To answer your question more specifically, I didn't have any qualms about the script. I think Nick did an extraordinary job. As well as creating a very entertaining evening, he shifted the whole perception of this classic novel in one sweep. Perhaps people didn't have enough respect for what he'd done because they were too distracted by the double-casting. I suppose, if anything, the production didn't help people appreciate what an important shift it was in terms of an adaptation of a classic novel. I think time will show it to have been a landmark adaptation by Nick.

Quibbles about the script aside, Frankenstein *was ecstatically reviewed. It enabled you to make a triumphant return to the theatre and, as you said at the start, treat it as a warm-up for the opening ceremony.*

The fact that it was so well received by both the press and the public gave us confidence going into the Olympics. You would imagine that the scale of the job would increase the scale of anxiety. But it didn't work like that at all. The experience with *Frankenstein* meant that I didn't feel at all nervous about the opening ceremony. If anything, it made me relish the prospect.

The Opening Ceremony of the 2012 London Olympics

AMY RAPHAEL: *Let's go back to August 2010, when we were standing at the bar after an early screening of 127* Hours. *I started to tease you about the rumours that were swirling around: you were going to be involved in the opening ceremony of London 2012; you were going to be advising fellow director Stephen Daldry; you were actually going to direct the ceremony. You gave me an unusually stern glance, but said nothing. I realised in an instant that you'd accepted the job. I was baffled, before realising that it would have been more instructive to ask why you wouldn't do it. If you'd turned it down, you would never know what you'd missed out on. It turned out that I was wrong to mock and to doubt. Very wrong.*

DANNY BOYLE: (*laughs*) Well, I never had any doubt about accepting the job. When London was awarded the Olympic Games, I remember the very early discussions about who might direct the opening ceremony. I remember reading a list of names and thinking, 'They should give that job to me! I live in east London!' It was a casual response. I would never have sought the job and it never occurred to me that it would be offered to me. But I can't deny that I was excited by the thought of the Olympic Park being built so close to my house.

When did you have the first meetings?

I had a meeting with Martin Green, head of ceremonies for the London 2012 Olympics, when Christian Colson and I were in Los Angeles testing *127 Hours*. He sounded me out, and once I was back in London I met Seb Coe, chairman of the London Organising Committee of the Olympic and Paralympic Games (LOCOG). I was 100 per cent up for it, and Christian was hugely supportive about me taking time out from our film-making. It's all very well saying 'Let's do *Frankenstein*! Let's do the opening ceremony!', but your career in the film business is kept on track by the patience of people like Christian and Gaia Elkington at Cloud Eight Films.

Anyway, I was thrilled because I have a profound love of sport. You've got to be modest and remember that you're only a warm-up act for the athletes. Whatever you find out about the International Olympic Committee and the Olympics behind the scenes – and it's very disillusioning in many ways – what keeps you going is a life-long love of sport and of the Games.

I always watched the Olympics, first with my dad and then with my kids. By coincidence, my dad's birthday was 27 July, the same day as the opening ceremony. He died in 2011, and I knew he would have loved me to be involved in the Olympics. I remember missing the Commonwealth Games in Manchester in 2002 because I was filming. It was a big deal for my family, and I was gutted to miss it. I loved the idea of there being a Commonwealth Stadium in Manchester and I used to go and look at Thomas Heatherwick's *B of the Bang* sculpture before Manchester City moved in and before the sculpture was dismantled due to structural problems.

I had a practical idea about how to approach the opening ceremony. One of my first responses – which was heartfelt and instinctive rather than sentimental and PC – was to try and represent as many people as possible. And to invite the iconic people who are part of the fabric of our lives and as such belong to everyone, from Mr Bean to J. K. Rowling.

Did you have strong opinions about previous opening ceremonies?

God, yes. And you are unavoidably following in footsteps. Especially after Beijing. People thought it was crazy to follow that, but I thought the timing was perfect: you simply couldn't follow Beijing. I could see that previous ceremonies had escalated in a competitive way for too long, especially since LA in 1984. With Beijing they had got to the point where they couldn't go any further. Our trick was to inject some emotion and humanity back into the opening ceremony. It had become this massive, technically incredible event.

Beijing was eye-popping yet cold, cynical and calculated – a superficially brilliant piece of post-communist PR for China.

Absolutely. And even worse, people who had actually attended said that it was not a good live experience. So one of my first thoughts was to make this work for the people who paid money to see it in the stadium. If they are having a good time, that emotion will somehow transfer to the television audience. As a theatre director I've seen that happen.

Returning to your opening statement for a moment, I couldn't understand all those people – people like you – wondering why the hell I'd say yes (*laughs*).

I thought you might have political objections and not like the idea of the International Olympic Committee (IOC). They hardly have a blemish-free reputation.

There were issues, both specific and general. My lowest point was the Rapier missiles, which were positioned on buildings near where I live. The Olympics is a festival of peace, for God's sake. I was very close to walking away. I thought it was morally wrong. I wanted to go out and say, 'I would prefer to risk being blown up and all 80,000 of us die than have ground-to-air missiles on top of people's homes.'

Something as valuable as the Olympic ideal should open itself up and say, 'This is too important to destroy. And if you must try and destroy it, then you can try, but you'll only reinforce it for future generations. You'll only make these Games more important.'

It was just one of the inherent contradictions in the Olympic movement to do with scale and ethos which are just impossible to reconcile. For Frank Cottrell Boyce, who was a key collaborator on the opening ceremony, it was Dow Chemical and their sponsorship of the £7-million fabric wrap around the stadium.

Originally we designed the wrap for the stadium. It was to be covered in ivy and called the Hanging Garden. It got taken away from us. Damien Hirst was going to design it, and then he pulled out because he didn't want to be associated with Dow. I noticed that no story was made of it. Perhaps he didn't want it to come out. Good for him for making a private point.

I can understand why Cottrell Boyce took issue with Dow, which struck a $100-million, ten-year deal with the IOC in 2010: in December 1984, toxic gas from the American-owned Union Carbide pesticide plant leaked over the city of Bhopal, India. It is thought over 500,000 have since been negatively affected. When Dow bought Union Carbide, they paid out $470 million in compensation, but it is widely regarded as being far too little. I spoke to Cottrell Boyce, and he said that given India was competing in the Games, 'It seemed not only wrong, but also tacky and ill-mannered to take sponsorship from Dow.' What stopped either of you from walking?

Frank was going to pull out. He had terrible run-ins with Seb about its involvement. In the end we persuaded Seb to meet Amnesty, which LOCOG had refused to do. I can see why; they are besieged with people complaining about one thing or another. Frank felt a considerable amount of pressure from within his political community, but we both decided not to pull out. Him over Dow, and me over the Rapier missiles. It does help having one of the world's greatest-ever athletes in charge, because you have to accept sometimes that there's a different agenda to support – the worldwide need for a festival of sport that connects all the nations.

By that point I'd seen how the ceremony was beginning to take shape through the volunteers' eyes. I kept threatening to pull out – you have to in order to get what you want and to get through the various hurdles – but I didn't want to let the volunteers down.

It must have been like playing an extended game of poker.

Yes. But I'd seen the light in the volunteers' eyes, and they believed in a very romantic, idealistic version of the Olympics. Their belief in it was more important than what was actually true, and that belief made the event stronger. And passed on to the athletes too.

Did the volunteers – all 10,000 of them – anchor the show?

Oh God, yes. Completely. I made that clear to all the celebrities as well. I told them they were at the opening ceremony as part of the volunteers' show.

How did the celebrities respond?

They all understood. As far as I was concerned, the volunteers came first. They would finish work and jump on the Tube or get a coach down from Glasgow and line up in the freezing rain. People turned up from all over the country once or twice a week.

You had to make a decision very early on to trust the volunteers and hope that they'd keep a rather large secret for a very long time.

I met with resistance from the Olympics organisers when I said that I wanted to show the volunteers exactly what they'd be doing from day one. The organisers were convinced that the volunteers would leak anything and everything to the press. I realised at this point that volunteers always look confused and baffled at big events such as this because they clearly don't know what they're doing. They know they've got to raise their left arm at a certain point, but they don't know why.

At initial meetings I had to risk being disrespectful to LOCOG by talking to the volunteers so openly. LOCOG would be standing at the back of the room while I showed the volunteers the model of the opening ceremony. I'd explain that I was trusting them not to tell anybody about the ceremony either via social media or just while chatting to their mates. I told them it was their story too. I wanted them to inhabit it and when they walked into the stadium on 27 July 2012 to feel proud. I could see they were inspired immediately.

Of course, LOCOG and the IOC had very good advice to give because they have experience of major events. But, equally, we needed space to do things our way.

I can only imagine how challenging – not to say downright irritating – it must have been to deal with committees of inflexible people who insisted on doing things by the book.

Occasional threats to resign were useful. There's a terror of bad headlines in the press, which you have to turn to your advantage.

Whenever the interference weighed too heavily did you always think of the volunteers?

Yes. Always.

When did you first think of using such a big group of volunteers and of placing them at the heart of the opening ceremony?

Pretty much as soon as you take on the job you realise you're going to have to cast around 10,000 people to be in your sequences. The auditions started just as we were finishing *Trance* in late 2011. Originally 15,000 people were brought in, and we had to whittle it down. There were *X Factor* people in there who were doing it for the wrong reason.

Is that where you found Jasmine, the girl who led the digital-age sequence?

Yes. Talent sticks out a mile. She had a big beacon on her head saying, 'Look at me!' But in a good way.

Another stage of the relationship with the volunteers was the decision to cast them as the stars of the digital sequence rather than actors. The LOCOG imperative was to get actors because they are paid and so can be controlled and will turn up on time. But I insisted everyone in the digital section was from the volunteer corps. We used a sprinkling of professional dancers in each of the sequences because the choreographers wanted them, but they didn't need them; their work was astounding. The professionals came in quite late, by which time it was clear the standard of the volunteers' dancing was excellent.

You didn't need the professionals to glue it together.

Not really. The volunteers totally got it. Having said that, the choreographers – Kenrick 'H2O' Sandy, Temujin Gill and Sunanda Biswas – and Toby Sedgwick, the movement director who also worked on *28 Days Later* and *Frankenstein*, were brilliant. There was this amazing day when we moved from the rehearsal space in Dagenham into the Olympic Stadium and they all saw each other's sequences for the first time. The NHS workers dressed as nurses – all 800 of them – were waiting as we played out the Industrial

Revolution, and as the sequence came to an end they all applauded spontaneously. It was full of highly emotional moments like that. It was slick, but at the same time not slick at all.

I loved that element of it: it wasn't polished and there was a real feeling that while everything was under control, pretty much anything could have happened. It was thrilling.

Thrilling? Bloody nerve-wracking!

It had just the right number of rough edges.

I loved that about it. It was amazing. That was the other thing for me personally: I learned so much about entertainment, about culture and art. The most important thing – and it's incredible to have a refresher like this so late in your life – is to believe in something. It doesn't matter what anybody says, believe in something.

And that belief will see you through.

And it will reveal new worlds to you. It's a lesson I thought I had already learned. But I didn't really know how important belief is. You realise that if you're going to get involved with something like the opening ceremony, then you've got to believe in it. I know it sounds simple – obvious, even – but I just didn't realise how important belief is. So many people don't believe in anything. It's sad.

Not only have you got to believe, but you also have to convey that belief. That's all that matters in the end. We were lucky everything went well on the night, but so long as everyone believed, it would have been okay. I'd have been proud of the show whatever happened because we all believed, and we'd have conveyed that belief to everyone watching.

The volunteers weren't going to believe exactly what I believe. If you get 10,000 people together, then they're going to vote many different ways or not vote or not give a fuck about politics. But belief draws everyone together. I can't tell you how much I noticed the people – either behind the scenes or in charge – who didn't believe in anything. All they cared about was how the opening ceremony would be received by other people. I thought that was bullshit. Ignore the reviews! Believe in something and transmit that belief to the world. The volunteers believed in themselves and in each other, and in so doing created something really special.

We knew there were moles – journalists from the *Evening Standard* and the *Daily Mail* – in among the volunteers. We simply didn't regard them as a threat. We didn't want to be wary because of them. Instead, we said to them, 'We believe in you doing this.' They didn't write a word. It was quite bizarre.

Did it make you stop and reconsider everything?

Yes. I learned so much. You know you're going to learn something about scale, but you also learn about values and how you approach work. That's the great thing about doing something on that scale. There's always some ego involved in film-making, but something like this is actually beyond ego.

It could so easily have been all about you and how you created the greatest show on earth. But you took yourself out of the centre.

It was about trying to protect something, about trying to use the Oscars we won for *Slumdog* to try and protect the ceremony we wanted to create. And, of course, I didn't create the show alone.

On films you tend to work with a hard core of crew whom you refer to as 'mini-directors', and you did the same with the opening ceremony. Frank Cottrell Boyce scripted Millions *and wrote the 'script' for the ceremony. Suttirat Larlarb has worked with you as a designer since* The Beach; *she designed the show's costumes and the 'dove bikes' that glided around the stadium. Mark Tildesley has worked as production designer on your films since* 28 Days Later *and oversaw the overall design of the show. Visual-effects supervisor Adam Gascoyne has worked with you since* Millions. *You've worked with Underworld since their song 'Born Slippy' helped characterise* Trainspotting, *and the band's Rick Smith was musical director. Cottrell Boyce has talked of the room you created where 'no one was afraid to speak'.*

LOCOG were based in bland corporate offices in that huge Barclays tower block in Canary Wharf. I didn't really want to work there, so we took this office in Wardour Street in Soho. It was above

Adam's office and it was empty ahead of a big rental moving in, so the rent was cheap. There was space to create a model of the opening ceremony that evolved as our ideas became more concrete. But mainly there were huge boards on the walls upon which we collated imagery and ideas. We'd call different people in: for example, Brendan Houghton, who storyboards my films, would come in to discuss the storyboards for the opening ceremony.

It was a wonderful way to work. I'd say, 'Right, everybody, tomorrow you've got to bring in a list of your twenty favourite British songs and tell us why you like each one.' The following day it would be ten favourite paintings. Or photographs. Or poems. We'd have to think specifically about poetry that focused on London.

I wanted to include 'The Queen', a brilliant poem by Paul Farley, in the official programme. For some reason the powers that be weren't keen, so here it is:

> We have a Queen. We're living in a Queendom.
> This country has its best times under Queens.
> She brings out all the bunting and the courtiers,
> the peaceful demo and the strange headgear.
>
> She is a fifties Queen in black-and-white
> moving through the Commonwealth in newsreel;
> a sixties Queen with a sister in the Bahamas;
> a seventies Queen with a safety pin through her nose;
>
> an eighties Queen eclipsed by a princess;
> a nineties Queen advised not to lose touch.
> (And I have never known anything different.)
> She runs the House of Windsor as 'the Firm'.
>
> If we work at it, the word 'queen' will abrade
> to something strong and round and made of stone.
> She does regal waves from helicopters.
> Her wrist orbit's a well-worn ball and socket.
>
> On aerial views she is a great authority.
> The landfill and the scars, the motorways,
> the shrunken hunting grounds, the sea drawn back
> to reveal the tidal extent of her realm.

I couldn't do it. Imagine waking up
in the blue silence of seven hundred rooms
in a palace in the middle of a city
and realising, *Jesus, I'm the fucking Queen!*

What a fantastic pay-off line! You asked your team for quotes that meant something to them as well. In his foreword to Humphrey Jennings's Pandaemonium, *Frank Cottrell Boyce quotes G. K. Chesterton – 'The World is not perishing from lack of wonders, it is perishing from lack of wonder' – and says it's been his own motto for years.*

The quotes were really useful too. We ended up with walls plastered with the words of Jesse Owens, William Blake, Shakespeare ... You learn so much from other people's recommendations. And Suttirat, who grew up in California, had a slight outsider's perspective, which was useful. When I asked everyone for their key song about Britain, Suttirat said it was 'Cities in the Dust' by Siouxsie and the Banshees. I love the Banshees, but it seemed to me an obscure song to pick. She explained it was the song that made England seem cool. It made her want to come to London.

It sounds as though you were discussing what it meant to be British in an almost esoteric way.

Yeah, absolutely. I wanted to get to the heart of what it is about us that's unique. You have to ask yourself what people abroad know about us. Bond? Yes. The Queen? Yes. Dr Who? Possibly not. Or at least not enough people. Mr Bean? Yes. David Beckham? Yes. It's about what's British, but also what's universal, because obviously you have to be cognizant of the fact that you're doing it for a global audience. You can't make gestures: if you try and look after America, you'll end up in the middle of the Atlantic. You have to look after the home crowd first, but then think hard about what resonates around the world too.

We had to be brutal. Frank was desperate to include the Clangers. But, like so many other ideas, it fell by the wayside as it just wasn't quite right. Things die when you stand them up in a room. You might sit at home thinking you have a great idea, but as soon as you present it to a small, intimate team of people, you know if it has legs. Or something might sound great one day and then fall to pieces two days later. So the ideas that made it to the opening ceremony really had to stand the test of time.

Cottrell Boyce has said that you'd 'atomised and become the cloud where we store our knowledge'.

Ha! It didn't really feel like that. Although I was the leader of the group in the sense that I was the artistic director of the opening ceremony, I was still only first among equals. Which meant that I didn't ultimately have to take on all the responsibility! It was quite liberating not to be under all that pressure. I could be flippant, something of a dilettante. Whereas if you make yourself absolute leader, then you have this huge burden, and it inhibits you in the end. But I wouldn't say I atomised.

But you still had to make the final call?

Of course. But that's very easy to do when you're working with good people. Get good people on board and you've got a chance to make a global event like this work. We were going to make T-shirts that said: 'If we get good-enough people involved, it might not be shite.' But LOCOG said no.

One of Cottrell Boyce's major contributions was to give you a copy of Pandaemonium *when you directed* Frankenstein. *It's an astonishing collection of writing about Britain between 1660 and 1886, compiled by the co-founder of the Mass Observation movement.*

Pandaemonium really suited our method of working. Jennings collated all that material, so it's like a pick'n'mix book. It's a history of Britain that is not classic. Jennings had an idiosyncratic eye; no detail is unimportant. History isn't just about the key facts. Apparently there's a version of *Pandaemonium* that is three times longer; his daughter is trying to raise the funds to get it published.

Two years is a long time to spend preparing for an event that is both inward- and outward-looking. I presume your team gave it everything, just as you did.

Well, we nearly killed Suttirat. After 27 July, I didn't talk to her again till mid-October. She burned her mobile phone and disappeared back to the west coast of America. She's been hanging out in Seattle and recharging. The attention to detail she brought to 8,000 costumes was not sensible. It helped the volunteers, though, because they could see the attention she was giving to their individual costumes. And they got to take them home after the show.

After a fight, that is. It's traditional in these shows for the volunteers to take their costumes home as the only tangible thing they walk away with. As a kind of trophy or memento. Of course, LOCOG decided to ditch the tradition in favour of selling the costumes – to the volunteers. I said they had to be joking. We won in the end, and they took them home without having to pay.

Before Suttirat disappeared, she sent this blog feed from the *New York Times* of pictures people took on the Tube of the NHS workers going home in their nurses' uniforms. They all wore their outfits going home so they didn't have to go back and change – it was a forty-minute walk to the changing area and back – and they wanted to go and party in the gear. None of the volunteers could hang around in the stadium because there were just too many of them.

The point is that Suttirat's dedication meant the volunteers were really affected by how much care was taken with their costumes and how good they looked. They weren't actors and yet they were given proper costumes. It boosted their confidence.

Of course, some of the volunteers wanted to be actors. Others were opening-ceremony addicts. Some of them had been in four previous ceremonies.

You spent all that time in a room in Soho with your mini-directors; how closely did you work with Stephen Daldry, executive producer for the opening and closing ceremonies?

Stephen wasn't involved much until the start of 2012. He was a good interface with that LOCOG world and a great moral support to me. 'Keep it, keep it. Fuck 'em,' he kept saying. He also went off to film the sequence in which David Beckham and Team GB footballer Jade Bailey whizz along the Thames in a speedboat, before Beckham hands the torch over to Steve Redgrave at the Olympic Stadium.

So that wasn't filmed live on the night?

Ha! It was shot the night before at Tower Bridge. And the handover of the torch was shot forty minutes before it was shown. It was invaluable to be able to entrust that to Stephen. The 'Queen' jumping out of the helicopter had to be live, though, as it was buzzing above the stadium prior to her entrance.

Was that the biggest challenge on the actual night?

Technically it was, yes. Anyone with any experience would have advised us against it because the likelihood was it would go wrong. We practised with the guys jumping out without costumes on, and it didn't quite go right a couple of times, which was a bit nerve-wracking. They were going to land in the stadium, which would have been lovely, but it was too dangerous. I went up in the helicopter to take an aerial look at the stadium. It's one of the calls you have to make as a director. You do it on films; you watch your stuntmen practising. They will risk an awful lot, and you have to make a call – you have to stop them from taking unacceptable risks sometimes.

It was hairy being up in the helicopter. As we buzzed the stadium, the pilot was signalling that it was okay one second, but not the next. I knew it was just too risky for anyone to risk jumping into the stadium itself. Gary Connery, the stuntman who dressed up as the Queen, is just incredible. He's the one who made history in May 2012 by skydiving 2,400ft in a wingsuit – but without a parachute – onto a runway of 18,000 cardboard boxes.

Anyway, enough of the fake Queen. How on earth did you talk the real Queen into letting you film in Buckingham Palace, bringing James Bond with you, and then board a helicopter as though it was the most natural thing in the world?

When you accept this job, you realise that a huge chunk of time is passed over to the parade of athletes from all over the world. There's nothing much you can do with that element of the show. There are certain items of protocol, which include a series of official speeches and the arrival of the head of state. You can, of course, just let the head of state walk in and play the national anthem. But we decided to play around with ideas.

We initially thought the Queen could arrive by Tube, given that she was the first monarch to travel on the London Underground. And then Mark came up with the idea of shooting her at the palace and then in a helicopter. Frank wrote it up. We assumed that in the best-case scenario we'd have to use a double. In the submission to the Queen, I'd made it very clear that we'd find the best one possible. The worse-case scenario would have been a resounding no, in which case we'd have tried the Tube idea. And, if all else failed, we'd just walk the Queen in the door.

Word came back that the Queen was happy to shoot the film with Daniel Craig. We thought it was April Fool's Day. It was weird, but amazing. So we went to meet her. Edward Young, who is Deputy Private Secretary to the Queen, was hugely helpful; it was his responsibility to make sure the film wasn't naff. It was easy for us because the Queen has the instincts of a performer – she is, after all, 'on stage' all the time – and therefore knows that she has to change with the times.

The Queen knew that the Diamond Jubilee celebrations earlier that year would be quite formal, so here was a chance to be the opposite. It was a great instinct. She showed great instincts again when she decided that no one in her family should know about the film so that it was as much a surprise and delight for them as for the nation.

Who shot the film?

A Scottish guy called Michael McDonough, who was cinematographer on *Winter's Bone*. A fantastic cameraman. Another guy, Dan Carlin, shot the Rowan Atkinson and *Chariots of Fire* sequences. I loved meeting all these amazing new people – Thomas Heatherwick, Akram Khan . . . Akram had ripped an Achilles tendon and was out for seven months. He was just about fit in time to dance at the dress rehearsals. I went back to see his show *DESH* at Sadler's Wells a few months after the opening ceremony, and it was amazing. Thomas was there too. Lovely guys, but tough motherfuckers about quality control.

I bet James Bond producer Barbara Broccoli was no pushover either.

The Bond team were as concerned as the Queen's team about looking naff. Again, it goes back to belief: you hear their alarm bells but you push through, and your own unwavering belief should make them believe. Barbara was great, though. She believed in the idea and, of course, knew that you can't buy the kind of publicity we were about to give Bond. She saw it through.

It must have been incredibly complicated to get the Queen and Daniel Craig together once you had the green light.

It was insanely tricky finding a time when they were both free. Sam Mendes was right in the middle of shooting *Skyfall*, so Daniel hardly had any spare time. Technically, it would have been easy enough to splice them together, but I refused to shoot them separately.

It was a lovely afternoon. The Queen was very sweet. We filmed it in her private sitting room, where she usually meets with the Prime Minister. We set up in there and then went into another room, which was a much more human space. It was messy; there were papers and tea trays everywhere. She said she'd been to the dentist that morning and so wasn't in a very good mood.

She wanted to know what I wanted, so I told her certain specific things about pausing that were important. I didn't have to tell her a second time. You often have to remind actors, but she was as sharp as anything. I think she had a lovely time. It became clear that one of the reasons she agreed to take part was so that her immediate staff, who have been part of her life for so long, could also be in the film. It was a buzz for them. It was nothing to do with cameras, which they face virtually every day, but the presence of Daniel. Of Bond. A proper movie star.

There's a wonderful moment in the film where the Queen walks past Daniel, and you can see him thinking, 'I'm a fictional character, she's the real Queen. How is this even possible?'

Was the Queen aware of your work?

I have no idea. Absolutely no idea.

She didn't chat to you about Slumdog? *Or* Trainspotting?

No!

Did she have final approval of the film? I imagine you had to screen it for her before billions around the world gasped as she jumped out of the helicopter?

We showed the film to both her and Daniel as a courtesy – separately, obviously. You've got to be really careful. It's very interesting: this whole notion we bandy around in the film world about who has final cut is all about money; in the BBC world it's about ethics. I have final cut on my films, and that means I get to battle with the studio about controlling the culture of the film versus the money. But with the Queen film it was about fundamental ethics.

In the end, all I could do was hope that nobody objected to anything – because if the monarch objects to something, then the BBC has to listen. Or does it? Anyway, it was all fine. It was always meant to be fun and humanising.

One of the great things about the opening ceremony was its sense of fun and humanity. It was self-mocking instead of self-regarding. There was very little post-colonial pomposity.

It's very hard to inject humour. Sydney managed it. I always knew I'd be pleased if our opening ceremony was compared favourably to Sydney. They were 'the people's Games'. It's easy to repeat those kinds of phrases as they're constantly bandied about as PR, but I thought that the best way to make the London Games work would be as the people's Games.

And you wanted the opening ceremony to kick-start the people's Games?

Yes, to give everyone a way into the Games. Yet you mustn't overvalue the opening ceremony because even had it been terrible, we would still have had a great Games. People wanted those Games.

They needed them as a distraction from austerity and the Coalition.

Well, I think it was time. They wanted to believe in something.

As well as discussing what you felt was culturally important, did you and your team of mini-directors discuss what you believed in?

We bandied big ideas about. Tolerance. Dissent. Inclusivity. Big heart. Idiosyncratic. Modesty. Humour. We wanted to feel as though we were developing something as organically as possible. So we tried to create the circumstances where everyone felt safe and could bounce around ideas and feel okay about having bad days as well as good ones. That so long as they believed in each other, everything would be okay.

Was there a key moment when you realised you might potentially be creating something exciting?

Frank and I had a huge day that had nothing to do with the Olympics, but which fed back into the opening ceremony. We do this annual WaterAid auction, where people offer a few hundred or maybe, at a push, a few thousand quid to have dinner with us both. The dinner that had been auctioned in 2010 was delayed endlessly. Eventually, we agreed to have lunch in the House of Commons in early 2012 with the family who had made the highest bid. We all met on the day and walked over there. But there was a security check and they were sweeping the Commons and the House of Lords, so we couldn't go in either of them.

Our guide – Paul Oginsky, who is Youth Policy Advisor to David Cameron – suggested we visit the Chapel of St Mary Undercroft, beneath the House of Commons, which the public are not normally allowed into. Sitting MPs have the right to be married and their children can be baptised there. He said the best part of the chapel is the broom cupboard. Only one person at a time can go in – there's literally room for just you and a mop – so we took it in turns to go in. It's only when you close the door that you see this plaque.

It's a brilliant piece of PR by the suffragette Emily Wilding Davison, who had this fantastic idea of sleeping in the broom cupboard on the night of the 1911 census. The next morning she could say that she lived in the House of Commons and thus had to be allocated a vote. Her entry in the census recorded her address as the House of Commons, a declaration that meant she had the right to sit as well as sleep in Parliament. I stood in the darkness of the cupboard, thinking, 'Emily Wilding Davison slept here and then, two years later, died trying to put a suffragette sash round the King's horse on Derby day.' It was only a hundred years ago, which is just one person's very long lifetime. I stood there and filled up.

The fact that she got her name on the census is so important in our culture and our history. Tony Benn had put the plaque there in 1999 to commemorate her actions. He's been vilified in my lifetime, but an obviously brilliant man has realised how important it is to nail that plaque on that wall. The cute thing would have been to put the plaque on the outside, but it's far more interesting at the back of the cupboard. Who knows how many people will see it and whether it will have any value to them, but for me it is hugely valuable. It's up to people to find it.

For Frank and me that day was key in formulating the opening ceremony. We started to think about more hidden stories, the people who make those stories and how those stories are retold. People tend to think that Emily Wilding Davison leapt in front of the King's horse in an act of hara-kiri, but in fact she was trying to put a sash around the horse's neck. I don't know how she expected to survive such an audacious act, but it was a stunt rather than suicide. I was also touched by the fact that Tony Benn cared enough to get a plaque made – and to then place it inside the cupboard rather than making a song and dance about it.

Is that when you got in touch with the extended families of various suffragettes?

Helen and Laura Pankhurst, who are great-granddaughter and great-great-granddaughter of Emmeline, both appeared in the opening ceremony. Sadly, Emily Wilding Davison's sash was too delicate and is encased in a huge box, so it did make it to the stadium, but not into the show itself.

We also had Isambard Kingdom Brunel's relatives in. Brunel's great-great-great-grandson Inigo Thomas brought along his Uncle Miles, Lord Gladwyn, who is the oldest living descendant. Inigo sent us a lovely email afterwards: 'You know that it's fairly spot on that Brunel should quote Shakespeare: in his house on Duke Street, off Piccadilly, he had a Shakespeare room and he commissioned various Victorian painters to depict Shakespearean themes. Also, he, like Berners-Lee, thought technology should be public; he took out no patents on any inventions.' Inigo assumed we'd deliberately chosen famous figures who insisted on their work being publicly owned, but not at all. It was pure chance.

It was terribly sad that Mark Rylance wasn't able to play Brunel after the sudden death of his step-daughter.

Awful. But good old Kenneth Branagh stepped in, God bless him, to play Brunel and read from *The Tempest*. I wanted someone who was closely associated with Shakespeare. We wanted to begin and end the ceremony with an engineer because we are really good at engineering. It runs in our blood. And yet we've never made the best of it, never really showed off about it. All the Formula 1 cars, apart from Ferrari, are made in Britain. We have top-end engineering and yet no car industry of our own. How have we allowed that to happen?

Thomas Heatherwick is an engineer really. The cauldron he designed and built is an amazing piece of engineering. Everybody said it wouldn't work. They said it would go wrong on the night. At the 2010 Winter Olympics in Vancouver, where the cauldron had four moving pieces, one of them didn't work. We had 204 moving pieces, and they all worked. That's Thomas.

Was it your idea to ask Heatherwick to design the Olympic cauldron?

Yes. It goes back to the time I spent sitting under his *B of the Bang* sculpture at the Commonwealth Stadium. I loved it so much; it's a tragedy they took it down in 2009 because of structural problems. It's like Rachel Whiteread's *House*; it should be a permanent fixture in Tower Hamlets. These public sculptures breathe life into you. You may not be able to understand why, but that's not important. They work on you over time.

The cauldron was so simple and yet so poetic, with a petal for each of the countries participating in the Olympic Games. When Heatherwick first showed you it opening out, I imagine you had goosebumps.

Oh God, yes! We rehearsed the opening of the cauldron in the middle of the night because we really had to avoid photos of it leaking out. It looked completely different depending on where you stood in the stadium. It was like a living thing.

'Thomas Heatherwick's cauldron is an amazing piece of engineering.'

But we had to fight to have it on the floor of the stadium. The organisers had already decided that the torch was going to be on the roof, which is where they always are. The roof had even been strengthened. Why would you do that? It had already been done in Beijing. I was really clear that wasn't going to happen. I hate that. Those traditional cauldrons have no humanity about them at all; they're just vast, bombastic pieces that weigh fifty tons. We wanted something that had some humanity and warmth about it rather than shock and awe. It's a key moment in the opening ceremony, and it's what all the other events are leading up to. It's really what you're there to do: to light the cauldron.

I can imagine certain people had doubts about the petals all opening on the night too.

Of course. And yet again, it's about exhibiting belief. You have to maintain it steadfastly – outwardly, at least – even if doubts start to creep in. It's not about having phenomenal abilities, but about being the kind of leader who can lead everyone into this maelstrom. And make something that could be great or . . . crap.

There was this Australian guy, Scott Buchanan, who delivered the cauldron for Thomas, and an engineer from Yorkshire called Jim Tinsley, who built it. *So* many people were saying that the cauldron would fail, that it wouldn't open properly. They said it should already be open. I was having none of it; we had to believe that it would work on the night. I looked at Scott and Jimmy and knew it would work. I'd tell the dissenters not to curse it with their negativity.

Did you sometimes despair?

I certainly went through some tough times.

Every time you wanted to do something differently – or in your own way – did you have huge fights?

Yes.

Was that more challenging than the actual conception of the opening ceremony?

Yes. The battles were exhausting. The problem you've got is that you're working with people who have worked on global events many times before. They therefore bring with them invaluable experience and knowledge of the pitfalls. Interlaced with that confidence is this horrific knee-jerk response they have if they sense any doubt. They assume their experience means they know best. You have to learn how to accept their experience, but make sure they don't make it their show. Which is when my own experience came to the fore, because it's something I do all the time on films.

You would have been surprised to see me in those meetings. I was horrible. Mark Tildesley, who's the sweetest man on earth, was also vile. We used to sit there and watch each other being so unbelievably unpleasant.

It's just as well your little group knew and trusted each other so much. A less intimate group might not have handled or absorbed the stress so well.

That's so true. It was a full-on, protracted commitment. All of them are in demand and could have gone off and accepted other jobs. We managed to keep them on board for different reasons. Suttirat had an emotional connection: she went to the 1984 Los Angeles Games as a child. They were the first Games in which each spectator was given a coloured card to hold up. It was a big part of her childhood and stayed with her for a long time. Mark is a big sports fan, and his family were desperate for him to do it . . . Everyone was locked in by a personal agenda, as well as the fact that we had all worked together before.

You seem to be effectively saying that you were pretty much able to put the corporate element of the Olympics to one side – apart from the times you and Mark were vile in those meetings – and focus on the nostalgic and romantic elements instead.

I understand why there is a corporate element to the Olympics. Someone has to pay for it, and governments won't – and can't – afford to hand over the huge sums of money required. My point – which no one listened to – was that handing over £100 million doesn't give you carte blanche to do what you want. It gives you commercial rights, but it also gives you responsibilities. You are inhabiting a myth that is so powerful and so transfixing for people that you have to behave properly. I heard that BMW behaved well. When the torch was lit in Greece, the government literally had no money, and BMW paid for the event without saying a word. Whereas another sponsor behaved in a disgusting manner. They would only give us some of their product – which we needed for practical reasons – in return for Danny Boyle presenting an advert for their home market.

It's funny to think that you started off your career working for Joint Stock, a radical theatre company founded in London in 1974 by William Gaskill, David Hare, Max Stafford-Clark and David Aukin, and here you are, nearly four decades later, getting irate about the corporate nature of the opening ceremony standing in the way of the performance. I noticed that Mark Lawson, appraising the ceremony in the Guardian, *decided that it was a triumph of agitprop theatre: 'It marked the apotheosis of a dramatic tradition that had previously been marginalised in this country.'*

I can see why he came to that conclusion, but I don't agree. If you get the job of looking at our country and you decide to separate it into three segments, one of them is going to be historical in some way. You have to include the Industrial Revolution. Every other piece of history pales. And it's not because I come from the north of England; it's just a no-brainer. The stadium was built on land which they sealed and recovered from the Industrial Revolution poison. It's the area Dickens wrote about.

Britain's Industrial Revolution was exported all over the world and is still happening in certain countries, as they go through the painful process of mechanisation. We invented that. Wow! All this talk of British kings and queens is irrelevant by comparison. We wanted this to be an international show.

And then there's the National Health Service. Whatever successive governments think about changing it or making it more efficient, we have clearly decided as a nation that we want universal

'You have to include the Industrial Revolution. It's a no-brainer.'

healthcare. You can fuck about with it, but when you get down to the absolute fundamentals, we're keeping it. If you get seriously ill, it doesn't matter how much private healthcare you've got, you go straight into the NHS.

That's not politics. That's beyond politics. It's something we've collectively decided: 'We're having that.'

I personally think that the BBC is also absolutely fundamental. We've decided, as a nation, that we'll have a national broadcaster paid for via a licence fee. Rupert Murdoch, with all his power, can try his best to replace it. Various governments can fuck about with it. But there will come a certain point when we say, 'We're keeping that.'

So I really don't believe the opening ceremony was agitprop. If it was, then it would have been rightly disowned by people who don't believe in it.

Right from the start we believed in what we were doing, in what we were going to present. We weren't going to be knocked aside by people saying something was too left-wing, or not left-wing enough. Or too right-wing, or not right-wing enough. We decided to ignore it all, regardless of who might be saying it. If you don't, then you quickly find yourself being committee-led.

People asked how the opening ceremony could please so many people, but the values it believed in are those that we hold true despite our politics: tolerance, dissent, inclusivity, engineering, culture, humour, ambition, modesty.

I understand your explanation and your reluctance to allow politics to marginalise the opening ceremony. At the same time, I know that many people were thrilled that the NHS acronym was projected onto the floor of the stadium and that nurses were celebrated. It felt like you were flicking a V-sign at the Coalition, who appear determined to introduce two-tier healthcare into this country.

But again, these governments come and go. I remember thinking that you can't base your show either for or against what these people are about. It's more about providing some kind of timeless marker. We showed the plans for the ceremony to Labour as well as to the Coalition. To Ken Livingstone as well as to Boris Johnson. Ken, especially, did so much to bring the Olympics to London. But you need the support of the current government to make it work. It's also about the regeneration of a particular area of London. Which is why it's beyond the agendas of politicians worried about their jobs.

And it's another reason why I didn't want to speak about the opening ceremony before it happened. I knew it would get dragged into agendas, no matter how eloquent I might have tried to be. I even avoided talking about it on the director's commentary on the BBC DVD of the ceremony. I didn't want to narrow it down like that.

You say the opening ceremony was 'beyond politics'. Others thought differently. It has been described as having a Marxist view of history.

I know. But it didn't. Not at all. Isambard Kingdom Brunel wasn't Marxist. Nor is Tim Berners-Lee. It was about the things that are important to you, the things you hold true as part of a stable, progressive, courageous country.

I have to keep pushing here: the very fact that you told the story of the Industrial Revolution instead of stories about kings and queens makes it, in my mind at least, a left-wing reading on some level. And a right-wing artistic director would hardly have projected 'NHS' onto the floor of the stadium.

I really do disagree. I was very conscious that the responsibility of this job effectively meant I was doing it on behalf of a huge number of people, some of whom would share my own political views, some of whom obviously wouldn't. I had to represent everyone equally. Of course, I was tempted, at the start at least, to please myself and indulge my own left-wing leanings. But it wasn't that kind of job. It was bigger than that.

The values espoused by the opening ceremony are not left-wing values. They're more to do with the fact that we can be a modern, progressive country, and as such we can be an inspiring beacon for people everywhere. Tim Berners-Lee was a hero of the show because he chose to do something that genuinely had at its heart the welfare of everyone. He *gave* us the World Wide Web.

We fought all those wars in the last century to ensure we could continue going forwards. It's about fighting for simple values: we're all in this together and we have to respect the people we are in it with. You may not have exactly the same values, but you can still be on the same side. If I had just gone off and created a Marxist opening ceremony, then I'd have been insulting and alienating so many people. You can take pride in your country without taking sides. Politicians tend to limit beliefs sometimes by being combative about their own particular brand of politics. It can diminish people and make them feel as though they're not part of something. It can shut them out and be elitist. We didn't want our opening ceremony to be any of those things. So I don't agree that it was a left-wing reading of our history.

I take your point. I think we can both agree that the opening ceremony was at least radical in the sense that it made the grudgingly patriotic amongst us proud to be British: proud of our literary, musical, film and television heritage, of the Industrial Revolution, of our engineering and technological feats, and of our trade unions. If the ceremony was non-partisan, then you certainly seem to be using your new status to promote certain good causes. In October 2012, you recorded a statement that was broadcast via a big screen in Hyde Park after the TUC's 'A Future That Works' march, in which you talked about marching as a 'wonderful thing', your dad being a huge trade unionist and the trade-union movement being 'very much part of the fabric of my life'. You have also been vocal about the withdrawal of funding to regional theatre and the much-discussed reduction of arts subjects in future secondary-school exams.

After the opening ceremony I now have the kind of profile that people want to use to further good causes. The TUC march was about employment. A massive part of any government's job is not to spend all their time trying to persuade us of their philosophical beliefs, but to provide employment. People need the dignity of a job. They need the funds to bring up their family in the way they choose. It's all part of this idea of being a progressive country.

Education that encompasses the arts as well as the traditional subjects seems like a given to me. After all, culture civilises us. We are not going to be creating a huge amount of jobs in mass manufacturing any longer, but we are very good at all things cultural – so long as the opportunity is there in schools and funding for the arts isn't slashed year after year.

Cuts to the arts are, in my opinion, bloody foolish. I know the current government has to make all-round cuts, but the relatively small amount of money they are taking away from the arts won't help pay off debt elsewhere. It will, however, cripple the arts. As an insider who has worked for film, television and theatre, I can see the damage those cuts are going to do. Again, it's not about having right-wing or left-wing ideologies: taking money away from the arts will damage this country in ways that no one can quite foresee. The return you get from sustained investment in the arts is incalculable.

Slashing arts funding certainly seems crazy to me. For the simplest example of the theatre bringing money into the country we need look no further than Skyfall: *it is the UK's most successful film of all time and its director, Sam Mendes, started out at the Royal Shakespeare Company and the Donmar Warehouse.*

Their argument would be that Bond will happen anyway. Which is true. What they don't know is how successful that Bond will be. Or good. Look at the huge success of *Billy Elliot*, which Stephen Daldry took from the screen to the theatre. It's now being staged all over the world. The people involved in the arts in this country have huge potential, but what will happen if they are effectively silenced by a lack of funding? They may find a way to punch through, to be heard – but they will also, at some point, lose their self-belief. If they are constantly told they aren't worth anything, how are they going to come up with the goods? On a very basic level, theatres sustain local communities, they offer a sense of belonging – all of which can, at some point, build up to big expression like the opening ceremony.

We aren't economic leaders any more. Our industrial importance has diminished. What we can do effectively is continue to nurture the creative spark. Look at how the local council has invested in Oldham Coliseum: it has refurbished the theatre and created a positive night-time economy. Newcastle's principal cultural venues estimate that for every pound invested in their buildings, £4 is returned into the local economy. If we had cultural secretaries who were remotely imaginative, then they'd be finding a way to make the arts add to an uncertain economy, instead of letting them fall into decline.

The biggest celebration of the arts in the opening ceremony came in the digital-revolution section, after the stories of the Agricultural and Industrial Revolutions had been told. It was a fantastic celebration of music, film and television, but also, to my eyes, the least coherent section; perhaps because we've had so much time to look back and assess the impact of the Industrial Revolution, whereas we're living through the virtual revolution without any clear idea of where it's taking us.

It's a good point. It was basically the young people's section. Most of the volunteers and dancers were young. They certainly didn't know, for example, that Tim Berners-Lee had invented the World Wide Web. They had no clue who he was! Some had barely heard of The Beatles. You realise very quickly how old you are when you see how baffled these kids look when you're talking. So it was great to give them their own section.

There are two ideas in it. One is that, whether you've seen a film like *Kes* or not, it's part of your culture. Your heritage. It's running in your veins. It's an invisible fingerprint that everybody carries, whether you ever sit down and watch it or not. I love that idea. *A Matter of Life and Death*, the Powell and Pressburger film, is in your subconscious somewhere. It might sound ridiculous, but it's true.

The second thing is that right at the end all the kids went up the hill in their spangly gear, and this weird old inventor bloke applauded them and they applauded him.

Without really knowing what they had to thank him for.

We'd explained the Berners-Lee story to them, but maybe they didn't quite get it as much as me. It was certainly a profound moment for me.

What an incredible invention. And, as we were discussing earlier, he insisted it stayed public. Hence his tweet, 'This is for everyone,' being broadcast across the stadium.

Only a genius visionary would look ahead in time and think that a decade into the twenty-first century everyone would be shopping on the internet and communicating minute by minute on it. It's why it was vital he didn't become a corporate entity, but put his invention in trust. Lovely man. He can't keep still. He's ahead of you the whole time. As soon as you start a sentence, he's finished it.

How did you choose the snippets of films, from Kes *to your very own* Trainspotting, *that were projected onto the Barratt-style house that was part of the digital-age segment? They flickered past so fast that it was hard to see them all.*

You can see them better in the DVD. There's an extra where you can see exactly what is projected onto the house. Those who were in the stadium saw different snippets depending on where they were sitting. I loved that. Great work by Leo Warner and his team.

But, in the end, you have to exclude so many films. And so much music. We got the knockback on a few things that we couldn't have or that the artists wanted too much money for. The deal was that they were paid a quid for letting us play part of their song or for performing. It's a rule created by the Olympics in order to avoid competitive bartering for rights. Everyone gets the same.

Knowing their record sales will go through the roof.

Absolutely. It would be foolish to ask for more than a quid. I can't name them, but a certain band wanted £20,000 and would not budge. And a solo artist point blank refused to let us use one of his songs. Nothing to do with money; he just will not be associated with the Olympics.

You used to dress up as a glam-rocker, and earlier in the book you told me that David Bowie is 'everything' to you. So of course you asked him to perform at the opening ceremony.

For some people the most important 'great' might be Paul McCartney or Mick Jagger or Elton John. But for me it's always been David Bowie. I've loved his music since I was a teenager, and time has only enhanced my respect for his body of work. He's a titan for me . . . Anyway, I wrote to him trying to explain myself.

You wrote saying you were a huge fan?

Yes! He agreed to meet, so I flew to New York. I played Bowie the showreel we played to everyone we asked to appear in the opening ceremony. It was basically a preview made up of a combination of moving storyboards and animated footage put together by Brendan and Adam, or Sascha Dhillon, our brilliant video editor. We wanted to try and illustrate what the final sequence of events might look like, rather than just trying to explain it all verbally.

How did Bowie respond?

He was very complimentary and lovely. We also created a sequence based on some of the concerts from the last tour he did in 2004. He loved the Industrial Revolution sequence; it did occur to me to put him into that sequence as a kind of strange avatar figure, but it wasn't practical and Brunel was already leading that section. I'm not being trite when I say it was an honour simply to have spent a couple of hours with him and to have the chance to present our ideas.

Were you nervous?

Goodness me, yes. Yes!

You're not often nervous.

I'm not, but I was incredibly nervous meeting Bowie. Far more nervous than meeting Her Majesty the Queen.

In case he disappointed?

In case *I* disappointed! And he's just lovely. And he's still a Londoner. Which just made me want him to agree to appear even more. The Games were in his home city, for God's sake. But, in the end, he didn't want to make any kind of live appearance. At the same time, he made it clear he wanted to support us and was more than happy to help us with video footage and the rights to songs. I loved it when 'Heroes' played as Team GB entered the stadium.

For a long time there was talk of him being in poor health. And then, out of the blue, he released 'Where Are We Now?' on his sixty-sixth birthday. Did he tell you about the single? Or even play it for you?

He did not! I wish! I knew we'd be hearing from him again because I guessed he had something up his sleeve. But I had no idea about the single. I was as surprised and delighted as anyone else.

Why do you think he declined to play live?

He didn't give one specific reason. Perhaps he wanted to concentrate on other things. Perhaps it was health-related and he didn't want to face the stress of live performance.

I suppose he couldn't just turn up and sing 'Bonkers' like Dizzee Rascal. The expectation of Bowie playing live for the first time since 2004 would have been huge.

That's very true. Maybe he's happy with the thirty or forty years he has been in the public eye. After I met him I read about how he writes lyrics very late on in the songwriting process. During the Berlin years he'd record everything, including the backing vocals, before he had written all the lyrics. It's a bizarre way to work. He wouldn't record his own vocals until the studio was virtually empty. His most memorable songs are great tunes, but it's the vocal performance you remember.

In your new role as concert booker you also flew to the Bahamas to meet Mike Oldfield and ask him to perform rearranged segments from Tubular Bells, *the debut album he recorded at just nineteen and released in 1973.*

I flew in and out of the Bahamas on the same day. Crazy, but you obviously have to personalise the relationship. You can kid yourself about Skype or email or any other non-personal type of contact, but it just doesn't work as well. Mike was wonderful; he was immediately receptive. I think he's in some sort of semi-retirement, but he was really pleased that *Tubular Bells* would be remembered as part of the opening ceremony.

The curious thing about *Tubular Bells* is that it's known around the world as the theme to *The Exorcist*. I talked to Mike about this, as we wanted his music to introduce the sequence on children's literature – which included, of course, great iconic figures who happen to be villains. It was a lovely connection to make because the music is quite chilling. We wanted to play around with the idea of frightening the kids – in the sense that it's good for them to learn about fear from literature – and then Mary Poppins rescues them, so everything is okay in the end.

Tubular Bells is one of those serious staging posts in modern music, and I wasn't sure he'd want to play around with it, but it turned out he was delighted to have the chance to rework the album – to do a kind of jazz version really, I suppose – and to perform it in the children's literature and NHS sections of the ceremony, as they were both so vibrant and celebratory. The NHS staff who dressed as nurses loved dancing to it. Temujin and Sunanda did a lovely job binding all those elements together. I was very pleased, but who could have predicted that?

Were you surprised that so many of the artists you approached weren't just willing to give permission for their songs to be used or to perform live for the nominal fee, but were also interested about the context in which those songs were going to be used? John Lydon, for example, wanted to know how you were going to use 'Pretty Vacant' and 'God Save the Queen'.

'The NHS section of the ceremony was so vibrant and celebratory.'

Lydon is a very smart guy. Sensitive. Before approaching him, I spoke to Julien Temple, who, of course, had worked with him on *The Great Rock 'n' Roll Swindle*. Julien said that women especially find him to be sensitive, but that he tends to do this macho, alpha-male thing with men. He was terrific with me. He was very concerned that those two songs by the Sex Pistols weren't somehow being hijacked for the wrong reasons. People kept telling me he'd be unpredictable and unreliable because that's part of his public persona. But I didn't find him to be either of those things. Instead, he was very clear that he wanted to see the context in which 'Pretty Vacant' and 'God Save the Queen' would be used. We showed him the same preview showreel we'd shown Bowie and everyone else. Again, people questioned the decision to trust Lydon not to blab about the ideas we shared with him about the opening ceremony, but he was very faithful to us.

It's odd how suspicious people were. And interesting that your decision to trust people ultimately paid off big time, because everyone seemed happy to keep quiet about the ideas you shared with them.

It's not really about the trust paying off. Not for me, anyway. You have to trust because otherwise you'd become suspicious. You'd be looking over your shoulder the entire time.

Seb Coe, who is a good judge, very cleverly suggested we use the word 'surprise' rather than 'secret'. The notion of a secret unsettles people and gives them too much responsibility. Whereas the notion of a surprise is much more positive. You have to be careful about the use of the word 'secret', especially when there are lots of kids involved. It can have very, very dangerous connotations, as has been recently revealed in this country with the unveiling of the behaviour of certain celebrities towards children. Whereas kids love surprises and there's nothing sinister about them – it's something that is going to be revealed and shared by everyone.

The idea of using songs by Bowie, the Sex Pistols, The Beatles, the Arctic Monkeys, et al., was to bring together a kind of loose history of British songwriting. The opening ceremony was clearly a celebration of our great musical history, but the songwriting element of your theme fell away in the end. Still, I assume it helped you with the agonising job of choosing the soundtrack for the evening?

It didn't really come across, but I wanted Paul McCartney there as a songwriter as much as a performer. We had this idea of celebrating songwriting, because that's one of the things we're good at, for such a small country. But 'Hey Jude' is also the most famous singalong song in the world. You don't have to be able to speak English to sing it.

It's The Beatles at their nursery-rhyme best.

At their absolute best. The purity of the tune . . .

Had you met McCartney before?

A few times, yes. He's lovely. Good sense of humour. He came into the stadium to do his soundcheck on the Thursday evening. There were only about fifty of us there. We were shouting out requests in the end, and he'd play them. It was pretty cool. A moment to remember.

To go back to your question, I've always spent time carefully choosing music for my films, whether it be Underworld's 'Born Slippy' for *Trainspotting*, Moby's 'Porcelain' for *The Beach* or M.I.A.'s 'Paper Planes' for *Slumdog*. I'm losing touch with new music a little now, so I'm more voyeuristic, I suppose. I rely on people tipping me off about new artists or albums, whereas once I might have discovered them myself. But I'm still incredibly proud of our musical heritage. It's clearly one of the most outstanding things we've given to the modern world. It shows how, as a nation, we have the possibility to be progressive, because pop music is about imagination and newness and pushing boundaries.

Historically, we changed our attitude to music in the aftermath of the Second World War. We were no longer the nation constantly looking back at our empire. I really believe that pop music has helped liberate us from that colonial awfulness. It's an incredible force for good. There will always be individual moments in history where the tabloid press reacts in a hysterical manner, as it did to the hedonists taking Ecstasy in the late 1980s and '90s. But why not focus instead on the absorption of the Caribbean population into

London from the 1950s onwards? It changed us musically in a way that is progressive. And impressive.

We should, as a nation, be proud of our musical heritage. Any economist could tell you that it's made us a ton of money. After America, we are the biggest exporter of music in the world.

Which is mighty impressive for a small island.

For a tiny island we're brilliant at music for some reason. You'd think there would be no basis for an argument against making music a more central part of the curriculum or for building more music schools. Young people are drawn here by music, possibly because it's constantly refreshing itself.

And, at its best, it's classless as well.

Absolutely. So you're right, the songwriting idea didn't really come across, but that's okay. We still did our best to represent the key songwriters.

I wonder how many people noticed the presence of Fuck Buttons with their song 'Olympians' – although I notice they are credited as 'F Buttons' on the Isles of Wonder CD. *I assume that was Rick Smith's idea rather than an attempt to push your luck?*

I knew their albums, *Street Horrrsing* and *Tarot Sport*. We did talk about the fact that we'd never be able to use their full name, for similar reasons to not being able to use Paul Farley's poem 'The Queen' in the programme. I had to get used to the fact that this wasn't *Trance* or another film; this was my family-viewing item. Anyway, the band were very gracious about amending their credit to 'F Buttons', otherwise it would have hit that wall of corporate checking about what was acceptable.

After using 'Born Slippy' in Trainspotting *and working with Underworld again in* The Beach, Sunshine *and* Frankenstein, *you asked Rick Smith to be musical director of the opening ceremony. He wrote the music that effectively pulled together all the disparate elements of the evening, but not before you'd given him a dry run on* Frankenstein.

I wasn't sure Rick and Karl [Hyde] from Underworld were going to do *Frankenstein* because they hadn't composed a soundtrack to a play before, and it's unusual to pull people from the pop world into the world of theatre. But, in the end, they had a great time and really enjoyed the discipline. And it *is* disciplined because you're no longer your own boss. Rick has his own studio, writes, performs and produces his own music with Karl as Underworld, and is basically his own boss. We'd done *Sunshine* together in tandem with John Murphy, so I had a glimpse of what Rick was capable of. But it wasn't until we worked on *Frankenstein* that I realised how gifted a musician he is. He can put his hand to anything.

We decided fairly early on which songs we hoped to play and which artists we'd like to perform live, but Rick oversaw all the music. He helped ensure we achieved the right balance. He scored 'And I Will Kiss' for Evelyn Glennie and the Pandemonium drummers, which played during the Industrial Revolution sequence. It was seventeen minutes and fifteen seconds long, so it's a proper piece of music score. He also composed 'Caliban's Dream' – a little shorter at just over seven minutes – to accompany the entry of the torch into the arena and the lighting of the cauldron.

I have to say that some of Rick's titles are absolutely baffling. I have no idea why he called the drumming track 'And I Will Kiss'. I've tried to ask him a couple of times, but have never quite got the answer. He also wrote numerous incidental bits and pieces as well.

Did you want Smith's music to glue the disparate elements together? The music might otherwise have been in danger of being fragmented and stop–start.

It would have been like that anyway because of the snatches of music played in the digital-revolution section towards the end and then the entry of the athletes. You can't score the athletes coming into the stadium because it could take over two hours. It's a real live event that's pretty much out of anyone's control, so we decided to use existing pop-music tracks.

By the way, have you read Rick's introduction to the *Isles of Wonder* CD? He wrote that 'music is the fluid architecture all around us'. He is absolutely spot on. I was blown away when he sent me that.

Smith also describes music as Britain's cultural heartbeat and asks, 'How do you soundtrack a city?' Among his answers was 'the bosh of a drum'. The thousand volunteer drummers on 'And I Will Kiss' were bold, insistent, euphoric, celebratory and just short of chaotic. I loved the punk nature of the drums too; I'm guessing they were plastic because the budget didn't quite extend to a thousand real drums?

To start from the beginning of this particular concept, we wanted to create a sound that reflected the Industrial Revolution. A kind of percussive landscape. I knew from the Beijing Olympics how powerful a large group of drummers can be. But that particular drumming was so regimented, and I wanted something a bit more organic. I started thinking about how many drummers we'd need. Perhaps 500? Why not 2,000? In the end, we decided a thousand would suffice.

Rick is brilliant at drum work. We started to discuss the details of the Industrial Revolution sequence and how the Olympic rings would be bashed out of molten metal before rising up towards the top of the stadium. I wanted the accompanying drumming to be primitive. No, not primitive – tribal. Rick and I shared drumming tracks and ideas. We then had a meeting with LOCOG where we were told we could have a thousand drummers, no problem. But only 200 drums. I was dumbstruck. They started listing the price of drums. I can't even remember what they said. It was bloody ridiculous. I wasn't asking for high-quality drums. Just the kind you see guys playing outside Liverpool Lime Street station or outside McDonald's.

And they're bashing away?

They're bashing away. Rick and I could visualise the drumming; we just knew how brilliant it would sound as the rings went up. But I think that was one of the moments when some of the people involved in the Olympics took a step back from us. Detached themselves from us. They thought we weren't going to represent Britain properly. I was arguing with them, saying it wasn't the bloody Royal Tournament!

There was also a minor fuss about not being able to afford a thousand professional drummers. And how would we find a thousand volunteers who could drum or whom we could teach to drum?

Did it feel as though unnecessary obstacles were undermining your enthusiasm and innate can-do attitude?

At times. But it didn't stop us. We decided to use plastic drums and wrote to drum clubs asking if anyone wanted to do a try-out. We picked the existing volunteers who were musically inclined, and Rick and his 'captains' – these amazing guys he got on board to help him – taught them at the rehearsals. Just as Temujin and Sunanda taught the NHS workers to dance to *Tubular Bells*, so Rick and his captains taught the volunteers how to drum.

How did Rick and his captains teach them in such a limited time?

Those rehearsals were amazing . . . It's done through speech. They had to drum to the very specific and repetitive rhythm of 'Bang the drum so your mum can see you on TV/Bang the drum so your mum can see you on TV' and 'I am in need of a drink/I am in need of a drink'. It's amazing how quickly they then learn.

That sounds brilliant.

It really was. When they started learning, they'd hear Rick saying: 'I am in need of a drink . . . three, four . . . I am in need of a drink.' You could learn to drum that way. So could I. Pretty much anyone could. Initially, you watch the really good drummers in awe. You're thinking, 'Fuck me, how does the right hand do *that* while the left hand is doing *that*?' But if you follow the rhythm of those lines then you basically forget to panic. The delight on people's faces when they got the rhythm was just fantastic.

Did you have a go at drumming?

No, but I attended as many rehearsals as I could. The volunteers seemed to like having me around, as though it was a surprise. I don't know what they expected. That I wouldn't bother to turn up? I couldn't understand that at all.

Maybe they thought you were a mysterious Oscar-winner who would direct them at a distance rather than getting his hands dirty.

That kind of attitude is why the volunteers in previous opening ceremonies haven't had a clue about what they're doing.

You take it for granted that everyone is as hands-on as you are. One of your key skills is relatively ego-free leadership, whether it be directing a film or a play or a cast of thousands for the opening ceremony.

Well, you can say that . . . Of course you get involved. Of course you're visible, accessible. It would feel very awkward for me to do it any other way. We got rid of any sense of . . . not elitism, but separation. And as an extension of all being in it together, we were happy to ditch proper drums and go with the makeshift plastic ones. I didn't want the pressure of having to look after proper drums anyway. I knew there'd be complaints about people ruining them, whereas you can't ruin a plastic drum, no matter how hard you try.

The idea for plastic drums initially came from that scene in *28 Days Later*, where all those multicoloured buckets are placed on top of the roof to catch rainwater. I remember telling Mark, who was production designer on *28 Days Later*, that we needed another thousand buckets for the opening ceremony, but this time they had to be black!

I also felt there was a link – however tenuous – between the Industrial Revolution and the plastic drums. So many wonderful things came out of the Industrial Revolution: education, newspapers, the organisation of trade unions, protest, dissent. Plastic ultimately came out of the Industrial Revolution, and until we come up with a way of making it completely decompose, we are stuck with vast amounts of it.

At least Evelyn Glennie was allowed to play real drums. And the fact that she's been profoundly deaf since the age of twelve means she plays in an almost primal way, often barefoot to feel the music better, which again makes the connection with the land.

I was vaguely aware of Evelyn when Rick mentioned her. He showed me some online footage of her playing drums. I don't know how you'd describe her style. She's possessed. Rick explained this was because of her profound deafness. As soon as I saw her, I knew she had to lead the drumming. Rick obviously wrote parts for her in 'And I Will Kiss' and 'Caliban's Dream' that were more complex than for the volunteer drummers. When we told the volunteers that they were going to be led by Dame Evelyn, they were thrilled.

I know you rehearsed the musical sequences as much as time allowed, but I assume everything was pre-recorded in case of technical failure?

I'll try my best to explain this properly because it was really complicated. You have to pre-record everything. Everything. It was a live show that could not stop, so it was vital to have a back-up in case anything went wrong with the microphones. That's the first thing. Then there's the fact that the sheer size of the stadium meant it was very hard to get everything in sync: the time it takes for the sound to travel across the space is different to the time it takes light – the image – to travel. Anyone who was watching the drummers through binoculars from the opposite side of the stadium would have heard them playing out of time. You just cannot get it in sync. It's very frustrating, but you have to go with it.

Everybody who was performing live had a click track to follow. The television coverage followed the click track. The emergency pre-recorded material was also in time with the click track. But then the bloke watching the drummers through his binoculars would hear the music out of sync!

At first I thought it was all bullshit. I kept on saying we should just get on with it. What was all the fuss about? But the sound people were right. You can't take any risks with sound as it's so complicated.

Did Paul McCartney suffer a technical issue when he was performing 'Hey Jude'? His voice seemed wobbly and out of tune.

Yes. He started singing 'The End' and 'Hey Jude' live, and the pre-recorded versions kicked in at the same time. Like I say, it was a risk. He dealt with it, though. He's seen just about everything in his career.

With such a long and complicated event there is endless potential for things to go wrong. Were you anxious in the week ahead of the opening ceremony?

It wasn't like, say, rehearsing the final week of a play, where the actors are available to you every day. We could only call the volunteers in a few times a week. And then they wouldn't all turn up because they are human beings with complicated lives. I'm sure there were volunteers missing on the night itself because of unexpected personal crises. There's nothing you can do about it. One woman had a seizure during one of the dress rehearsals, and it was very upsetting, but with so many people involved it's going to happen.

On the night itself, I went outside the stadium at one point during the athletes' parade, and there was an ambulance looking after someone who had had a heart attack. With an audience of 80,000, statistically around six people are going to be taken ill. It's really distressing when you think of it in an individual way.

Anyway, the point I'm making is that the final run-up to the actual night was more than a week. By the time we got to the last week, we were pretty much trying to run the whole night, or at least run sequences of it, because you couldn't call the volunteers in every day.

Did you have a sense at that point that you might have actually pulled it off?

I always believed it would work. I had to. But a big revelation for me was the response from some of the specialists who were coming in and out of the stadium. They might be the Queen's security team checking out everything in advance, or the workers sorting out the rigs. None of them had seen the rehearsals, but on quite a few occasions I'd be stopped on my way to the control box by one of these specialists saying, 'That was all right!' You could see this mixture of relief and surprise on their faces. It was very entertaining. And reassuring. They've just watched fifty minutes of the opening-ceremony rehearsals, and they're not baffled or embarrassed. They haven't declared it stupid or . . . shite. I remember thinking, 'We're going to be all right.'

So you never woke up in a cold sweat or blind panic?

No, never. That does happen to me with film and theatre. But I didn't feel anxious about this. I think it was because I felt very clear about why we were all doing it and who we were doing it for, and that felt really good. I just had to solve as many problems as I could as I went along. And that was a mixture of knowing when to listen to experience and when to ignore it. It was wonderful to have people around me who had extensive experience of putting on huge, global shows.

Although it's invidious to pick out individuals from outside our inner circle, Catherine Ugwu, an executive producer of the Olympic Games, Piers Shepperd, technical director, and Patrick Woodroffe, lighting designer, were brilliant at holding our collective hands. It's impossible to cover everyone or thank them enough: the famous faces who spoke to so many people around the world on our behalf; those behind the scenes who, against all odds, made it possible; Tracey Seaward produced the unproduceable – she kept pulling rabbits out of hats when even I was thinking of giving up. It really is a case of 'without whom' . . . Paulette Randall, the associate director; Adam Gascoyne, who 'made' the opening film and all our pre-viz material; Toby Sedgwick; the choreographers, Kenrick, Temujin and Sunanda; Steve Boyd, Gina Martinez and Rocky Smith from Mass Movement; audio designer Bobby Aitken; and Claire Terri and Jenny Hutt.

I couldn't have done the opening ceremony on my own. I didn't do it on my own. It would make a much better story if I was shitting myself or throwing up in the weeks ahead of the opening ceremony. But it never felt like that really.

By 'pre-viz' do you mean 'pre-visualisation'?

Yes. We had to have a manifestation of the opening ceremony, and the only way to do it was by using CGI from Adam and Tim Caplan's team to create animated characters and mix it up with Brendan's storyboards.

Back to the night itself: how did you feel as the evening drew ever closer?

I tried to get in amongst the volunteers. They were fantastic. Really great. I was surprised how ballsy they were. I was expecting them to be full of nerves – 'Oh, Danny, I can't do this!' The kind of thing you get with actors sometimes. But there was none of that at all. Instead, they were like, 'Come on! Let's get on with it!'

In a way, the volunteers carried you along both in the rehearsals and on the night?

Very much so. I remember going to see them on the night because they had to be dressed in an area that was twenty minutes away from the stadium. There wasn't enough transport for them, so they had to make the journey by foot. But nothing was a problem. They were having such a good time. And I thought, 'That will come across during the show. Their sheer enthusiasm will carry the evening along.' You can't legislate for that. You can't force people to be enthusiastic. It's something you've got to invest in, put effort into. We treated them right and we got them excited. However, saying all that, they were full of such goodwill anyway that you'd have to have been extremely unpleasant to negate it. All we really did was encourage it. Their spirit conveyed itself on the night the minute they stormed into the stadium.

I'm still thinking about your question regarding the lack of nerves. It was also to do with having to rehearse so often with the volunteers in the pouring rain. Both at the rehearsal site in Dagenham and in the stadium itself people were slipping, they were spraining ankles. The huge beds from the children's literature and NHS sequences couldn't be pushed and pulled around. And the

Children jumping gleefully on beds in the NHS section.

grass, which was a mix of real and artificial, was too heavy to move when it was soaked. But they kept going.

When the weather began to cheer up, we felt invincible. We knew we could do it in the pouring rain; we'd done complete run-throughs in the rain. They would have done it without complaining.

I'm sure they would, but it might have been less magical. If very British.

I don't agree; I think it would have been amazing if it had rained. No one would have believed they'd have been able to pull it off, but I'm 100 per cent sure they would have. Certain things couldn't have gone up in the rain – the gigantic puppet of Voldemort might have been cut – but we'd have made it work.

I guess the rings would still have worked in the rain.

I think so. We'd have found a way to make them work. They were so central to the show. They were a direct reaction against Beijing's diamante Olympic rings. I remember watching their opening ceremony live and thinking they were like Dolce & Gabbana rings. The Chinese made the world a millennium before we made the world, and the best they could come up with were these 'pretty' rings.

Bling rings.

Ha! It made me realise that the rings have to be part of the land. You have to show them within the first fifteen minutes, so that the image can be sent around the world. We wanted to build them out of the Industrial Revolution, so we had to forge them.

Were they as heavy as they looked?

They were not, of course, made of real iron. But yes, they were pretty heavy. We had a great guy, James Lee, doing the wires, which usually go wrong. I liked him a lot. He was absolutely resolute about what I could and couldn't do. He wouldn't budge, no matter how much I begged. I love it when that happens; he knew that he was right and that if he budged, the show would have been damaged. He delivered 100 per cent on the night. He was the one who

'People thought I was mad when I explained how I wanted the rings to work.'

got Suttirat's flying bikes up in the air. They were a bigger sequence at one point, and I was very keen on making a point about the future of bicycles in cities, but we had to cut it back due to running-time pressures.

People thought I was mad when I explained how I wanted the rings to work. They initially said no. But I insisted. Why not try? It was yet another thing that could have gone wrong on the night, but it didn't.

You took creative risks and believed in yourself and your co-workers to such an extent that it's almost as though you willed things to go right.

I think that's true. I knew if I had everyone on side, then everything would work. Everything was going to be just fine.

The point at which I knew you'd pulled it off and I stopped worrying about you was when the rings went up. I almost punched the air at that point. Instead, I cried. Given that you have talked about being moved to tears by certain songs in the past, did you find yourself crying unexpectedly at any point during the opening cer-

emony? I know the idea of crying at your own work is a little odd, but you've made it very clear that the show wasn't about you, but rather about the volunteers.

I was terribly moved by the remembrance of the fallen. I talked to Rick about the music because we needed to change tempo after the seventeen minutes of drumming. We wanted to acknowledge First World War soldiers in the ceremony because the mechanisation of war is clearly one of the many complex things that came out of the Industrial Revolution. We talked about whistling as the volunteers who were dressed up as soldiers appeared in the stadium. We discussed 'Snoopy vs the Red Baron' by the Royal Guardsmen and the 'Colonel Bogey March' from the *Bridge on the River Kwai*. We thought about getting everyone in the stadium to whistle. In the end we kept the drums, but they faded into the background and we used some whistling over the top.

Images of remembrance are always very moving. But you don't tend to cry at your own work.

Not even when a photo of your father – to whom you were very close and who died in 2011 – was shown among the collage of images of others who had also passed away recently?

It was incredibly moving seeing those photos. We asked everyone who had tickets to the opening ceremony to send us photos of loved ones who had recently departed. They were amazed when we used them in the actual show. I was also well chuffed to see my dad up there. He would have loved to have been there. He'd have loved the sport – especially Mo Farah, because he loved middle- and long-distance running.

You did well to stop the ceremony from being sentimental, despite its many emotional, passionate and heart-warming moments.

We even managed to avoid it when Akram Khan danced to Emeli Sandé's performance of 'Abide with Me'. John Murphy arranged a version of the song for *28 Days Later*, and a performer from Liverpool called Perri Alleyne sang it. It was perfect for the film: the heart of the nation had been ripped out and everything was gone. It was much harder to use in an original and striking way in the opening ceremony because of its long relationship with sport and its religious connotations. Emeli and Akram did so brilliantly. Regardless of anyone's faith, it's a really important song. It felt like a lovely way of extending the section on remembrance.

You asked Akram Khan to 'go away and think about mortality' when you first discussed his dance. Apparently he was baffled initially by your instruction, as he assumed his dance would be a celebration of the Olympics.

And it was a celebration – just a different type of celebration. We knew that thousands of the fittest people in the world were about to walk into the stadium to tumultuous applause and a standing ovation. There's nobody on the planet fitter than those athletes. They are at the peak of physical health. This is effectively the master race striding into the stadium. It's your ultimate Leni Riefenstahl moment!

But one day they will all die. Just like the rest of us. I thought 'Abide with Me' would be a wonderful way of reminding us of two things that we all share, but that nobody wants to talk about: birth and death. Everybody lives a different life between those two events, but there is no escaping our mortality. It was apposite to remind people of this, because as soon as the athletes walked into the stadium everyone would be cheering. As soon as the Olympics kicked off, everyone would be celebrating the very opposite of death.

It's a contrarian idea, I know, but then we are a contrarian nation. There is a wonderful balance between our contrariness and our tolerance. It's quite amazing if you think about it. I wanted that contrariness to inform a moment in the opening ceremony, rather than just steaming forward in a gung-ho fashion. Everyone is desperate to be optimistic and positive and kind because the Olympics are a big celebration, but I think you have to acknowledge reality too.

Emeli Sandé was a towering, incredibly poised presence on the night. I've no idea how she kept her nerve in front of the 80,000 in the stadium.

I discovered Emeli via Kenrick Sandy, the choreographer of the

434

'Thanks, Tim Berners-Lee' storyline. When we started rehearsing – and this is going back a long time – he was playing 'Heaven'. I asked who the artist was, and then when I got a copy of her album I was like, 'Whoa!' Kenrick has got fantastic musical taste. He's got this place in Stratford where he runs a workshop for kids off the street. I was blown away when I went there. He also introduced me to Wretch 32. We used a cleaned-up version of his song 'Traktor' for the entry of the athletes.

But back to Emeli: she would have been right to be nervous because at one of the dress rehearsals the click track had gone wrong. She was also thrown into the deep end in the show because she had to perform unaccompanied, which is pretty tough. She certainly does have poise.

And she's from Scotland. We talked earlier about the time I've spent in Wales, Scotland and Northern Ireland. I was pleased that Emeli is Scottish, as is Evelyn Glennie. Rick is from Wales. Dizzee Rascal is from London. Well, not just London – he was virtually born on the spot where the stadium was built. That's a pretty good thing.

You wanted to represent Britain as fairly as possible – although, as you have often said, the Olympics is awarded to a city – and you wanted to be as progressive as possible. So while the trip to the Bahamas to meet Mike Oldfield might sound dead glamorous, you were so blown away by the Kaos Singing Choir for Deaf and Hearing Children that you asked them to sing and sign the national anthem.

I love signing because my three kids' modern schooling included learning to sign. There was a scene in *The Beach* which involved a couple of people signing, but it was cut in the end. The national anthem is a bit like 'Abide with Me': it's been heard so often that you barely notice it any more. I wanted people to experience each moment afresh. I thought having the national anthem sung and signed would refresh it. And make it moving. Pull everyone together. I didn't have as much control TV-wise over that section as I'd have liked, but it worked in the end.

I like the way you used so many kids in the opening ceremony – and

The Kaos Singing Choir for Deaf and Hearing Children.

kids from ordinary backgrounds. It tied in perfectly with putting the volunteers at the heart of the evening.

That was a brilliant part of the job for me. The Dockhead Choir – which is made up of forty children and teenagers from the church choirs of the Most Holy Trinity Parish, Dockhead, and the St William of York Parish, Forest Hill – sang 'Jerusalem' at the start of the show and 'Caliban's Dream' at the end. Maggs Shepherd, the choir's director, is an amazing woman who guided them through the experience beautifully.

I have used 'visceral' to describe the opening ceremony, but a better word would be 'possibility'.

And, perhaps, 'positivity'? You have talked about the importance of belief. An extension of this is the way you excel at instilling positivity in people. You built the infrastructure of the opening ceremony around the notion that it was a community-based project for the people. I think you could really feel the belief you gave them, even when watching on the TV at home.

I hope so. Hamish Hamilton did an excellent job of the television coverage, but live TV is a brutal medium. I was obviously concerned that the television coverage would be great, and I did everything that I could to help Hamish to make sure it was as great as possible. LOCOG and especially Martin Green pushed hard for Hamish to have as much time as possible to perfect what is an impossible job – three to four hours of unstoppable live-event TV. He was amazing! At the same time, I wanted those in the stadium to get maximum enjoyment from the event. I heard that people who watched the opening ceremony in the stadium in Beijing were shocked at how different it looked when they saw it on TV: it was made with both eyes on TV.

Whereas your opening ceremony was emotional and real for those in the stadium too. You'd have to be hugely cynical not to be moved by certain elements of it, such as the people you chose to carry the flag towards its climax.

We chose those people – including Doreen Lawrence, Shami Chakrabarti and Ban Ki-moon – quite late in the day. I wanted to involve the peace process in Northern Ireland somehow, not only because I worked at the BBC in Belfast, but also because it's one of the most astonishing shifts towards peace in my lifetime. I remember leaving Belfast and feeling despondent because I really thought they'd never find a solution, a way forward. And they have. It's not perfect, but it's a major change from the way things were.

We decided against it in the end because we would have had to include politicians from all sides of the community, and the flag wasn't big enough! It would have unbalanced the event. It's also a delicate situation there still; the process is ongoing, and our interference might have hindered in some way rather than helped.

We decided instead to make it more a mixture of individuals. I was keen that the selection was biased towards women because they are still not represented fairly in society. At one point we were going to have only women, but then we thought people would complain about it, and that would detract from the idea of celebrating women. We were particularly proud that Doreen Lawrence led the flag-bearers. Her journey from tragedy to justice is truly inspiring.

It was terribly upsetting seeing Muhammad Ali appear in the stadium around the same time. He looked confused and frail. Equally, he's the most famous sportsman alive. And possibly the most respected.

It was a tough decision to ask him. He is heavily medicated, of course, to control the Parkinson's. It was a real shame to see him like that. He clearly wanted to be there as he knows what he represents to people. He's one of the great symbols of the Olympics. Ultimately, we felt that it might be the last Olympic Games he would be able to attend. I thought it would be wonderful to have him there. He's such a powerful and important symbol, a symbol of somebody who stood up for what he believed in. It's easy to admire him now, but to be a conscientious objector in the mid-1960s was a big deal. He had huge courage. My dad loved and admired Ali. He tended not to like loudmouths, even though he was a bit of one himself. But he liked Ali.

Apart from David Bowie, whom at least you got to meet, your wish list of cultural and sporting icons appears to have been fulfilled. You're a huge fan of cycling, and Bradley Wiggins, wearing his Tour de France winner's yellow jersey, opened the event by ringing the largest harmonically tuned bell in the world. Mr Bean did a perfectly judged turn in Simon Rattle's orchestra, before cheating on the beach by elbowing past other runners and being driven part of the way in a re-run of Chariots of Fire. *J. K. Rowling read from* Peter Pan – *although, according to Kenneth Branagh, you had to 'talk her off a ledge' because it was her first public performance.*

When, early on in the Tour de France, Bradley won the time trial by such a margin, it was clear he was going to win the race. At that point I said to Tracey Seaward that we had to get him to open the show, but we couldn't approach him because we didn't want to curse his race. It's so easy for a rider to have a bad fall, so we didn't get in touch with him until he'd actually won the Tour. The bell was commissioned from the oldest manufacturing business in Europe – the Whitechapel Bell Foundry – and was rung by our first-ever Tour de France winner. What more could you ask for?

It was brilliant to work with Rowan Atkinson and Richard Curtis. Not only was what they produced such good fun, but not to have included them in any kind of celebration of our country would've been unthinkable. It wasn't actually Mr Bean. Strictly speaking, the name of his character was Derek. Everyone assumed it was Mr Bean, but that's the penalty of being so famous around the world for a creation.

In the end, J. K. Rowling came up with her own personal motivation for getting over her nerves. I'm not really at liberty to say what it was; she's terribly private, and I respect that. She was, of course, also motivated by the importance of reading and how books stimulate the imagination. It's a big ask to walk out there 'live' for one night only, but Jo read beautifully, and I can't tell you how thrilled the NHS volunteers were that she was in their sequence.

It is almost universally accepted that your opening ceremony was a blazing success. You were even offered a knighthood, which you immediately turned down. Why?

People fought many battles to make everybody free, equal citizens. Ever since I became aware of the concept, that is how I've always thought of myself. I am very proud to be an equal citizen. I have no reason to believe that being a preferred subject would improve the pride I feel in being an equal citizen. I'm lucky because I've made money and people like the work I've done, but it doesn't make me feel I'm better than anyone.

You want the encouragement to keep going, but at the same time to be aware of the same pressures – that you've got to keep up your standards, rather than feel like you've passed into another sphere. You've got to be careful because it sounds like you're criticising other people who have accepted knighthoods, which I'm not doing at all. It's a very personal choice. I already feel uncomfortable when people call me 'Mr Boyle'.

So, Danny, how would you like the opening ceremony to be remembered?

Pretty much as it is, really! I'm sure it will change over time, but right now I'll take it as a snapshot of something that people look upon with great fondness.

Did you feel prouder to be British afterwards?

This, I think, is what is great about Britain now: the mixture of tolerance and dissent. It's just incredible. It's not leaders, it's all of us. It's a wonderful privilege to be put in a position where you can try and look at it from an unbiased perspective. Because your own perspective is, naturally, biased.

I felt very strongly when we were creating the opening ceremony – in a philosophical, theoretical and also practical way – that we are a decent country. One of our attributes is our self-criticism, which can sometimes stop us from really appreciating our basic decency. All sorts of people hijack the notion of being patriotic for all sorts of reasons, but that shouldn't stop us from acknowledging that whether you were born here or emigrated here, there are certain values that we all want to try and share. They're pretty sound values as well, to do with self-expression. It's a free country, and you can self-express. It can be ugly, it can be pretty; it can be joyful, it can be dissenting. It's a mixture of self-expression and well-being.

Well-being comes out of us all being in it together. You cannot abandon people. That goes straight back to our National Health Service. It goes back to the healthcare Obama is trying to introduce in America. That's the philosophical idea: you cannot just leave people behind in society. The American military have it as their philosophy: they won't leave anyone behind. It might be painful at times or not necessarily rational at others, but you can't leave people behind. I can't say it enough times. It has to be at the heart of the way we live.

Trance (2013)

Simon (James McAvoy) works in a high-profile auction house in London. He plots with nightclub owner Franck (Vincent Cassel) to steal a masterpiece by Goya during a major public auction. Simon double-crosses Franck and his gang and is violently knocked unconscious. He wakes up in hospital suffering from amnesia: he cannot remember where he hid the Goya. His ability to recall the location is not improved by the removal of several of his fingernails by Franck and his sidekicks. In desperation, Franck finds Simon a hypnotherapist, Elizabeth (Rosario Dawson). She sends Simon into deeper and deeper trances, until he can no longer distinguish reality from illusion. As the film unfolds, we discover that nothing is as it seems.

* * *

AMY RAPHAEL: *More than with any of your previous films, you have tried to keep the plot of* Trance *under wraps. You even sent a personal letter out to journalists writing about the film, saying that you hoped they would 'help us protect the film's most intimate secret for the future audiences who have yet to see it'.*

DANNY BOYLE: Spoilers are a huge problem for journalists. Do you talk about and explain the film as much as you like, or do you try and protect the film and its narrative arc? How much does that then affect people's enjoyment of the film? So all you can do is appeal to people and ask them to be on red-hot spoiler alert.

We have talked elsewhere in the book about how you always put

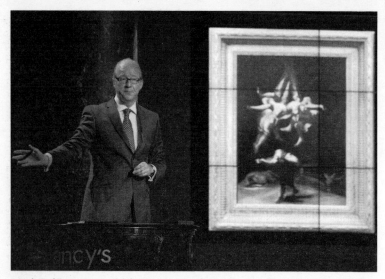

Mark Poltimore, a real-life auctioneer who advised on *Trance* and ended up acting in the film too.

men at the centre of your films. Is Trance *an attempt to redress the balance?*

I hope so. My films haven't only been populated by men, but this is the first time I've put a woman in the engine room. We want people to see *Trance* without knowing the narrative arc, which makes it tricky to discuss the specifics of Rosario Dawson's role. I will say this: I wasn't trying to be a feminist, be sensitive in any way or have a different aesthetic about it. I simply wanted to have a female character driving the film.

Redressing the balance was one instinct. The other was that I love femme-fatale movies. The question was whether you could make that genre relevant and update it – or rather, rethink it in a modern context. Give it a value other than the value it had, which is as a delicious device. I wanted to see if we could give it some meaning in a modern context, in a modern society. Those were always the reasons for wanting to make *Trance*. I'd always seen that potential in it.

The script for Trance *was around for some time, I believe. Didn't*

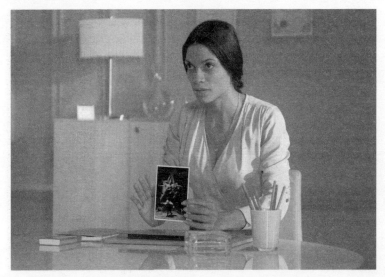

'I wanted to have a female character [Elizabeth] driving the film.'

it date back to the first time you worked with John Hodge, on
Shallow Grave*?*

Just after *Shallow Grave* I was sent a script that also centred around
three characters. I thought it was great; I was up for directing it.
Then I met the writer, Joe Ahearne, and he said he wanted to direct
it himself. I was baffled; why send it to me? Anyway, he went off
and made his own version of it.

But I kept thinking about the story. The idea of amnesia is
delightful in cinema because you can create these worlds where
you're not sure whether what you're seeing is real or not. The dis-
tinction between reality and illusion is blurred. It's very much in
the classic tradition of fantastic films like *Eternal Sunshine of the
Spotless Mind* and *Memento*. And, of course, those films all borrow openly from Nic Roeg. Most directors work in a rigid way
where the audience always know where they are and what time
it is. Roeg makes the past, present and future available at every
moment. He's an absolute master at it.

Did you think about cinema as a form of hypnosis in itself?

As soon as you start doing your research, you find out that the origin of the word 'mesmerising' comes from a German guy called Dr Franz Anton Mesmer. He was the architect of hypnosis. I realised it's a word I use all the time when I'm discussing my films with journalists. I must have been asked a thousand times what I want people to get from my films, and I always say that I want people to be mesmerised, to be caught like rabbits in the headlights for ninety minutes.

It's particularly relevant to *Trance*. What you're watching is twenty-four frames of still life flickering in front of you, except your brain fills in the flicker, because there isn't one. A good story and good performances accentuate that. You're left in what you hope is a trance; it's the effect Roeg's films, in particular, have on me. You forget, ideally, about the outside world. The characters seal themselves inside a bubble, which is a puzzle of their own making. There is no way out of it. As a film-maker you can puncture it by throwing something into the mix that isn't appropriate, but the bubble remains, and the characters circle each other within that puzzle.

Hypnotism is a particularly appropriate subject for a film. It's

Cinematographer Anthony Dod Mantle and Danny Boyle.

surprising there haven't been more films exploring it as a theme. Certainly, when you watch Derren Brown's live TV shows you can't help but think how cinematic they are. More films should be made about hypnosis.

Anyway, I worked on the story with John for some time, doing different things with it. I thought for a while that the painting should be stolen from a church, but that didn't work. John went away and wrote a solid first draft, which we showed to Christian [Colson]. John had a very good approach to the original idea. It's very much his script, although I wrote some scenes, such as the one with James McAvoy in the French countryside. It was great to be back with John because I hadn't worked with him since *The Beach*.

How did you fit Trance *in when you were working flat out on the opening ceremony for two years? I know you shot it before the Olympics and edited it afterwards, but you must have been very disciplined not to let them overlap.*

I started talking about the opening ceremony when we'd finished *127 Hours*, and it was evident that it would take two years to plan. I made it clear that I had a prior engagement: I was already committed to *Frankenstein*. They were fine with this, but there were heavy hints that I needed to focus entirely on the Olympics once I'd stopped working on *Frankenstein*. But I knew that if I was only working on the opening ceremony, it would drive me mad. So much of it is procedural, which means waiting around for things to happen. People warned me that there'd be times when I'd be twiddling my thumbs.

So I thought we should make a film. *Trance* was perfect because it's set in London. We were originally going to set it in Manhattan and cast an English actress; we had the idea that she would be an outsider, that she didn't actually belong to the country. I suppose the implication was that she had no one to turn to. I like the idea of creating a bubble in which nobody has anybody to talk to. There are no police. As soon as you puncture it with real life, you pop the bubble. There is no family to relate to; no mother or sister to ring. They can't text a mate. These are three characters living in a pleasure bubble.

Anyway, it made more sense to move the action to London because of the Olympics. The actress didn't have to be American;

Arwel Evans from the art department, cinematographer
Anthony Dod Mantle and Danny Boyle.

she could just have easily been French. It just so happened that
Rosario is American, and we felt that accent suited the language of
therapy perfectly.

It's a largely interior film, and not just in the sense of the 'mind',
so their respective flats had to be very distinctive, a kind of extension of the pleasure bubble. We found Franck's house in King's
Cross. We called it 'the lost house'. It's a slick black space with all
these glass surfaces and a long, narrow swimming pool. Amazing.
Simon's place was, ironically enough, right up James McAvoy's
street. Fifties, art deco-ish. James was delighted when he walked
in. He bought half of it! Mark Tildesley, the set designer, created an
idiosyncratic space to set Elizabeth in, this neon orange world with
a wall of mirrors to suggest a surface reality.

You've got three very distinct rooms. I learned that from *Shallow
Grave*. When you have a threesome, you have to be able to separate
them, because you're chopping and changing different points of
view. There's never going to be a single point of view taking you
through everything. You've got to know where you are.

You were saying on set that this is a film about language.

446

I think so. That's why I wanted Elizabeth's accent to be an outsider's. I always wanted that sense of slight distance; an accent we recognise and has an allure about it. Certainly, the Americans find the English accent very alluring. They attach an intelligence to it. Rosario's accent has a kind of movie allure, an ease. When Americans talk nicely, they talk with a real ease because they have that confidence which comes from being part of an ascendant nation. Also, therapy feels like it belongs in that very modern, Californian world; the idea that you can always find an answer – just keep talking!

So, yes, words are very important in *Trance*.

You talk about Dawson's American accent, but McAvoy is Scottish and Vincent Cassel is French. Did you want their very different accents to highlight the distance between them?

It wasn't intentional. It's weird actually because *Trance* is set in London, but there aren't really any English accents in it. We had the chance to get Vincent Cassel, a truly great actor. There are 200,000 French-speakers in London now, and they even have their own MP in the French parliament. James McAvoy was asking

'Vincent Cassel is a truly great actor.'

whether I wanted him to do English or Scottish, and, of course, I love a Scottish accent. He's worked in America often enough to know that they don't always want the Scottish accent, despite the fact that Sean Connery has probably been our greatest star. Quite often James will do straight English for safety.

You were determined to make a film to ensure there was no thumb-twiddling in the lead-up to the opening ceremony. Did you also want to make a violent, sexy film noir as a kind of punk response to the Olympics?

You have a responsibility with the Olympics, a public responsibility. It has to be for everyone. *Frankenstein* and *Trance* allowed us to have a much darker and carefree side while the Olympics was going on. Having said that, my focus was on the idea of making another three-hander. I loved the idea of telling a complex story with three actors. The last time I did so was, of course, with *Shallow Grave*.

As in the other films, the 'central character' has impossible odds stacked against . . . her. Elizabeth is clearly trapped in a nightmare. What can she do? Because no one will help her. The police certainly won't, because their record of helping people is just so bad. And yet somehow she finds a way out: she uses hypnosis to play the situation to her advantage.

Elizabeth does what people do in movies – she comes up with a solution. She does it herself. Nothing stops her. Not violence, not the danger of a gang. She just carries on. So, it's the same film – impossible odds that are somehow overcome. You just don't know who it will turn out to be.

Are there any other kinds of films? There must be. I've just got to make one of them.

You have to give your central character something to overcome, whether they're addicted to drugs, escaping zombies or trapped. It would be a little boring otherwise. And you make the viewer work with this film: we never quite know if the character is operating in real time or suspended in a trance.

Don't say any more! Ideally, we want people to see *Trance* knowing very little about it. That way they have to work it out themselves.

Dominic (Matt Cross) looks to get the heist under way.

We were so desperate not to give away clues of any kind that we ended up not putting enough in.

As soon as we started showing the film, both to individuals and at test screenings, we began a process of putting clues back in. It's supposedly what always happens with these kinds of films. You fear that the slightest look will give it all away.

Did you enjoy the challenge of playing with the audience, of bluff and double bluff?

One of the weird disciplines of messing with the traditional linear narrative is that the story has to make sense if someone watches it for a second time. There have to be clues which you think are huge elephant feet stamping down with great obviousness, shouting 'Look at me!', but which people watching barely notice. When they go back a second time, however, they think, 'Ah, I should have spotted that.'

I enjoyed planting the clues, but it's the story I'm drawn to. Here's a modern, professional woman who has to deal with appalling circumstances which you don't fully understand until right at the end. Its structure also shows the fact that men dominate everything. They dominate the film industry. They dominate how films are made. They dominate stories. They dominate the structure of stories.

'Simon [James McAvoy] *appears* to be the central figure, the hero.'

And James McAvoy dominates *Trance*. Or rather, his character Simon does. So much so that people find it very difficult to let go of him. It's classic. He appears to generate the film. He *appears* to be the central figure, the hero, if you like. That's what interests me about it, rather than just the laying down of clues. We were really doing the opposite when we were making it. We were going to give the audience very little help. Since we've made it, we've gone back and, either through editing or through pick-ups, laid down clues to help people.

I don't think those clues slow down the action. I certainly needed them; but then I tend to watch elliptical films in a passive way rather than frantically trying to work out what the reveal might be.

And it's important to consider the pleasure principle. On one level, *Trance* is about a modern woman making a series of decisions, but ultimately it's about what the audience thinks and what pleasure they will take from watching it. Do they like riding with it? Do they think they can follow it or not? It's about the pleasure of that ride.

For me, it's a very different responsibility from something like *Slumdog*, *127 Hours* or the Olympics. It's quite nice to do a pleasure-bubble film where you just live inside this bubble. Of course, there's a central idea in there: there's something magnificent about what Elizabeth does on her own terms. But, really, it's a pleasure bubble with a great French actor, a beautiful girl and James pulling out

'James pulled out all the stops to circumnavigate a nightmare part.'

all the stops to circumnavigate a nightmare part. Like the parts in *Memento* or *Eternal Sunshine*, where you can almost see the actor thinking, 'Where is my brain now?' James pulls it off magnificently, so much so that despite what is eventually revealed, you still feel a degree of sympathy for him.

It's interesting what you say about watching it passively. I was intrigued by the historical response to films that overlap reality and illusion. In America they say that men especially don't like to think they haven't worked it out: 'That's rubbish. I guessed that, I knew it all along.' Whereas women are more inclined to go along with the ride. They're able to enjoy the uncertainty.

Does it matter whether you work the reality out?

You'll just get something different out of the experience. People will leave the cinema to go to the toilet and they'll miss the fundamental moment. But you hope they get something out of it in the end.

Did you have the same issues and debates about the sex in the film as you did about the clues?

(*laughs*) We cut one sex scene between Elizabeth and Franck which was shot in detail. It was a very good scene, very funny too. The real reason we took it out was because we didn't want to see her properly naked until she walks across the floor towards Simon to put him in a final trance. She uses their most intimate secret to put him in the deepest trance.

Did you want that scene to be shocking?

Yes . . . well, powerful. Which is why we saved the nudity. As a viewer you only understand that scene in retrospect. I don't want to discuss the finer points of it here as I don't want to give it all away. The point is that Elizabeth shares their most intimate secret at a crucial moment, because it makes him feel secure that they share intimate knowledge. All these hypnotism sessions are about making you feel safe and secure.

You wanted Elizabeth's full-frontal nudity to be powerful in terms of the narrative arc, but people might find the specifics shocking.

You used to see this kind of nudity all the time, certainly in European movies. The film world has supposedly become a lot more prurient about explicit nudity because porn is everywhere and movies want to separate themselves from porn. That's the official line of the movie industry. So films have basically stopped using sex as an engine for stories. If you stop and think about it, you realise that sex is rarely present in mainstream films any more. Scenes like the one in *Don't Look Now* would never happen now. I'm not talking about specialist art-house movies that cater for a very small audience. Outside of that, sex has become a big taboo again. Before it was for moralistic reasons; now it's to put clear water between it and the porn industry.

You hope it's possible to shock people, but for the right narrative reason. Obviously it contains within it an idea of that violent control that Simon has as an instinct. He wants to shape her in his image. What's interesting for me is how she uses the power of his fantasy.

Was Dawson happy to film the explicit sex scene and appear naked?

Yes; she understood it was part of the story. Rosario reminds me of Cameron Diaz. Given how pretty they are, they're the least vain people. You're with them for three months filming and you watch them. Actors are understandably neurotic. They are on display in a way. I never saw Cameron Diaz look in the mirror once when we worked together on *A Life Less Ordinary*. The only thing that bothers Rosario is the idea she's got something in her teeth before a take. If you are really pretty and people tell you that all the time, I suppose you relax at some point and say, 'I guess they're right.'

Dawson told me that her only concern was her walk: how she would emerge from the bathroom and walk naked across the room.

There's a terrible Helmut Newton model walk, and she was terrified of it looking like that. So yes, that was her obsession.

How did Trance *test in terms of the varying reactions from men and women?*

What's been surprising is that women like the film more than men. Much more. On the cards they mark to say if they think there's too much nudity, the results were equal between men and women. Are those guys being honest? Or are they marking the card that way because of who is sitting beside them? Anyway, women seem to like the film more, and it'll be interesting to see if that follows through. I would have thought the opposite because of Rosario's nudity, because of the violence.

But maybe that goes back to what we were saying about women not needing to be in control of things so much.

It's interesting that the only way Elizabeth can control Simon is to hypnotise him. Did the actors experience hypnosis first hand?

We had a hypnotist in who tried to hypnotise James and Vincent. They didn't really go under. They were relaxed but not really fully under. They were possibly too aware of being watched. We also went to see a Derren Brown show. There's this tension within the hypnotism profession about recovered memories being implanted in people, and it was discredited legally. You could no longer use it in a court of law. Since then they've slowly been trying to rebuild its reputation as a serious medical procedure, like acupuncture.

Danny Boyle (middle) discussing an action scene towards the end of *Trance*.

Hypnotherapy can help people enormously, but it has a darker side to it as well. It has to be controlled in some way. They claim that they can't force people to do what they don't want to do, but there are also a small number of people who are extremely suggestible. If you pick the right person, you can get them to do things that are humiliating. So you can see where the tension arises.

I heard this funny story which actually happened at some point in the past few years, while we were preparing *Trance*. This stage hypnotist in East Yorkshire got four people on stage and put them in a trance. He was walking around the stage and walked straight into a scaffolding pipe. He was knocked unconscious. No one could get the people out of the trance. Not until he came round fifteen minutes later, at which point he brought them out.

As Elizabeth says in the story, only the person who puts you into a trance can take you out of it. You see that with Derren Brown on stage. They're clearly not stooges. These are people that he really has power over. Or, as is the truth, they want him to have power over them. They are susceptible. That's what he's doing in his show, finding these people . . . The talent is picking these people out. When he asks questions and asks people to stand up, they

454

spot the person who is first to stand up. That's the person who wants to get up on stage and humiliate themselves. A hypnotist can get the right person to do just about anything. And when the hypnotist is a beautiful woman with a past, you've got the start of a good story.

127 Hours Diary

It's our very first book session and Danny Boyle is raving about the importance of being 'hideously optimistic' when setting out to make a film. He talks about potential successors to *Slumdog Millionaire*: a musical, a thriller or perhaps a film about a man who cut his arm off in a canyon in Utah.

Boyle says he doesn't write, but he has adapted the story of the man in the canyon. Aron Ralston's best-selling book, *Between a Rock and a Hard Place*, has just one quote on the British cover: 'Riveting: think *Touching the Void* directed by Tarantino.' It's both an obvious and impossible subject for a feature film. Here is the true story of an experienced mountaineer who goes on a one-day hike through a remote Utah canyon when a falling boulder traps his right arm against the canyon wall. He has told no one where he is and, as the hours pass, it becomes clear that he must either cut his arm off with a blunt penknife or die.

Boyle and Ralston have been in touch for years, thrashing out how a film might work. Now, post-*Slumdog*, Boyle is as close as he's ever been to bringing Ralston's story to the screen. His treatment is influenced neither by *Touching the Void*, Kevin Macdonald's spectacular drama-documentary about two young British climbers stuck up a mountain in the Peruvian Andes, nor by the violent extravagance of Tarantino. Boyle talks about the film in the simplest of terms: 'I've written it as an action movie – Ralston is one of those American extreme-sports guys who is scared of nothing, and bam!' – he claps his hands together – 'that's it, he's stuck.'

Stuck – and then sawing away at his arm. My initial response is scepticism; it's an enthralling story, but equally it could end up as a desperately claustrophobic horror film with the boulder cast as the villain. Boyle doesn't disagree. 'I don't know whether anyone could actually watch it . . . but if you could pull the audience in, it would be incredible. What happens to Ralston's mind during the 127 hours he's trapped?'

Boyle knows one thing for certain: never again will he have the freedom to direct such an idiosyncratic film. Without *Slumdog*, there would be no potential film about a man and a boulder. Perhaps it will be his *Walkabout* – a survival story set in a huge visual landscape, albeit in the confines of a canyon as opposed to the Australian Outback of Nic Roeg's film. For now, Ralston's story is simply a six-page treatment with no funding and no cast. Yet Boyle and *Slumdog* producer Christian Colson have already agreed that a big injection of cash would do the film no good. 'We'd definitely shoot it on a microbudget,' says Boyle. 'We absolutely wouldn't want it to become an inflated film just because of the success of *Slumdog*.'

3 July 2009

For a while Boyle mentions only the musical: he has *always* wanted to make a musical. Then both the musical and the thriller fall by the wayside. Instead, all talk is of Utah. The trip he is planning later on in the month with Colson and Ralston – to revisit the exact place in Blue John Canyon where the adventurer's arm was trapped – is a logistical challenge. 'You can only drive within four miles of it. The desert heat would be too brutal to walk the rest of the way. So we'll be dropped off and – hopefully – picked up by helicopter.'

After a day in the desert, Ralston will show Boyle and Colson the video messages he shot in the canyon while contemplating his imminent death. 'I don't know what it's going to be like watching such incredibly personal messages. Aron has one copy of the video, the other is in a bank vault.'

Boyle is concerned about conveying Ralston's extreme fear and heroic resolve without resorting to voice-over. 'It would be really cheap to use voice-over, but we have to find another way of doing it. We need to find an actor who can talk to himself without looking

457

. . . naff. In reality that's what Ralston did in the canyon. He asked himself questions like, "How the fuck did you get yourself in this mess?" It's a dream part for an actor because he doesn't have to act or share close-ups with anyone else. He's not going to be cut out of the film.'

7 July 2009

Boyle is wondering if being hideously optimistic is such a good idea. 'I'm making a film that has no dialogue! I've been working on the script and it's driving me mad. How do I keep it going when I can't cut to another scene, another plot line, another character? There isn't any variation on the how-is-he-going-to-get-out-of-here plot line.' He pauses and pushes his hair up. 'But I'm excited! I don't really know how to make it work, and I love that feeling. Deep down, I've absolutely no idea how to make this film.'

10 July 2009

The film now has an official title: *127 Hours*. The treatment – which refers to Ralston's adventure as 'the triumph of the human spirit, of survival against Sisyphean odds, of rebirth'; which aims to tell the story 'compulsively', to remain steadfastly 'macro in scale' yet 'epic in intensity' – has evolved into a fifty-page script with triptychs, beautiful girls, parties and heartbreaking video messages. My scepticism has evaporated: this is gripping stuff; it jumps off the page like a Technicolor dream.

  Still, it's relatively early days. Boyle wonders if Ralston will be happy with the script, which is essentially faithful to his experience but inevitably embellished. It is now three years since Boyle first wrote to Ralston with the idea of turning his story into a film. Since the accident happened in April 2003, when Ralston was twenty-seven, he has become a celebrity in America. In 2006 he starred in an NBC documentary – *Survivor: The Aron Ralston Story with Tom Brokaw* – in which both Ralston and his mother talked about their respective ordeals. He has given motivational talks to major companies across America and the world. He is a celebrity with money in the bank; his ego may swell at the thought of Boyle filming his story, but he could just as easily turn the project down.

  Boyle is at the edge of weariness. 'We shouldn't talk about this too much right now. We have to get legal permission to film his story. We'll have to see how our trip to Utah goes.'

25 August 2009

The trip to Utah was a success – but also difficult. Boyle was shocked by Ralston's video footage, by his self-control, by 'how much he shrunk day by day due to water loss'. Meanwhile, Ralston has yet to agree to the film. Boyle and Colson will fly to New York in a few weeks to see him again. I ask if Boyle loses interest in projects when they become . . . Sisyphean. He laughs. 'You get on a roll with a project and that's where the best ideas come from. It would be a shame if Aron doesn't agree, but I'm hoping he will. It's now eighteen months since I finished *Slumdog*. I want – need – to start filming again soon.'

In the meantime, he's been talking to the playwright Patrick Marber about a long-term project. 'Christian and I would like him to adapt Andrew Miller's debut novel *Ingenious Pain*. It's about a guy born in the eighteenth century who can't feel any pain and becomes an excellent surgeon. It's a fantastic story.'

1 December 2009

Simon Beaufoy, who won an Oscar for the *Slumdog* screenplay, has been working with Boyle on the *127 Hours* script. 'I'm trying to turn it from an action film into Samuel Beckett's *Endgame*; there's something very Beckettian about this guy who can't physically move for the entire film, standing there shaking hands with a boulder,' Beaufoy says, laughing. 'Seriously, I'm trying to move it beyond a film about a superhero into one about a flawed individual who does something extraordinary. I'm interested in emotion and the psychology of a person; I'm trying to help the audience understand Ralston more. I met him last week for the first time. He's very complex, very aware of his failings. I climb too, so we talked about climbing for hours. He was incredibly open and likeable.'

He points out that Boyle has gone straight from one impossible film to another. Yet *127 Hours* is very different to *Slumdog*. 'Directors say they make the same film over and over again, but that's just not the case with Danny. However, I just sent him an email asking if he realised this is another memory film! Both of us hate flashbacks –

done badly, it's such lazy film-making. But *Slumdog* is one massive flashback, and elements of *127 Hours* also rely on flashback.'

Boyle is, of course, as incapable of lazy film-making as Beaufoy is of writing an anaemic script. The director embraces the impossible. His work is always risk-taking and often brilliant. 'It's going to be an extraordinary piece of cinema,' says Beaufoy.

8 December 2009

It's Tuesday and Boyle is back from an eight-day trip to Los Angeles, Utah and New York. He's been in endless finance meetings with Fox Searchlight – who will back *127 Hours* – followed by another recce in the desert and a visit to his daughter, Caitlin, who is studying at Parsons The New School for Design. He will have an early-morning meeting on Wednesday with Patrick Marber in his Sussex home which will play havoc with his jet lag. On Thursday he will take his son Gabriel to the premier of *Avatar* and, unable to find a black taxi, will walk all the way home to the East End after the party. On Friday he will have lunch with Nicholas Hytner at the National Theatre, where – in around a year's time – he will direct Nick Dear's adaptation of Mary Shelley's *Frankenstein*, his first play in fifteen years. On Saturday he will fly to Germany for the European Film Awards.

And yet his focus on *127 Hours* never wavers. We briefly talk on the phone late into the night on Tuesday. He reflects on co-writing a script for the first time. 'It's interesting watching Simon rewrite my draft. My impulse was to sweep through it, whereas Simon has built these little houses in the story that help make sense of it. He understands the architecture of script-writing so well; he sets Aron up as being a certain type of character at the start of the film and, by the end, he's clearly changed for the better. Simon is brilliant at manipulating little sequences to illustrate Aron's character.'

He is still trying to work out how to make the film. 'We're going to need so much material to sustain it, to keep the audience visually stimulated. It's through visual stimulation that the audience will become emotionally involved. There's no conventional dialogue, no looks shared between characters . . .'

On the internet, excitement is building around *127 Hours*. As is speculation. 'Danny Boyle's *127 Hours* to Have Over an Hour of No Dialogue' screams more than one headline. Cillian Murphy,

Sam Rockwell and Ryan Gosling are all reported to be up for the role of Ralston. One writer even suggests Ewan McGregor: he is friendly with Boyle again and, after all, *A Life Less Ordinary* was set in Utah. Boyle and Colson, meanwhile, are auditioning an outstandingly bright American actor who seems born to play Ralston.

16 December 2009

I meet Christian Colson in his Covent Garden office. He is buzzing with excitement; this is a critical time for raising money for *127 Hours*. 'There will be more gambling to do over the next week or so. I love it. It's something I feel I'm good at. A proper contribution to our process. In this case it's not about arguing against anyone or screwing anyone. It's more a case of putting it together so that everyone ends up happy.'

Colson says that a huge amount of goodwill will be carried over from *Slumdog* to *127 Hours*. 'And with that comes a huge responsibility not to become complacent or lazy. Anyone would give Danny $150 million like that' – he snaps his fingers – 'but I think he'd prefer to make ten films for $15 million. We want *just* enough money to make *127 Hours*. I'm thinking around $20 million – we certainly wouldn't want as much as $30 million. Perhaps $22.8 million. The schedule and budget will burst at the seams. Danny and I both want to keep working; if you fuck up a $100-million film, you might not work again.'

He explains the schedule: a staggeringly short period of time for pre-production, the shoot, the edit, everything. The shoot itself will last a brisk eight weeks and will use two full units. 'It's nuts. We shoot in nine weeks' time and we're not even financed. We've flown to LA four times in a month. The project has already got a high-energy feel to it. We want to have it ready for the Toronto Film Festival, as we did with *Slumdog*. Except that we'll finish shooting three months later than *Slumdog*. We'll come home at the start of May and cut it like it's our first movie, in eight weeks. If we need more time we'll take it, but because this is a film about a bloke who's stuck, we need the energy and rhythm of a fast turnaround.'

A little later, Boyle turns up to meet Brendan Houghton, the storyboard artist who has worked on *28 Days Later*, *Sunshine* and *Slumdog* (not to mention Tim Burton's *Corpse Bride* and Susanna

White's *Nanny McPhee and the Big Bang*). Houghton spreads two dozen striking drawings on Colson's desk. There's Ralston cycling like fury through the orange-red desert; dropping into the canyon; watching wide-eyed as the boulder approaches; looking horrified and confused as his right arm is trapped. Boyle moves the drawings around the table, then asks Houghton to make the odd change to a specific detail. It's a slow process involving much silent staring and frowning.

Before I leave, Colson talks about James Franco, the actor-director-writer who has a book deal with American publishing house Scribner and who is planning to start a joint PhD in English and Film Studies at Yale in autumn 2010. Sean Penn's lover in *Milk*, a stoner in *Pineapple Express* and 'Student with the Best Smile' at high school, he is to play Ralston. 'His audition tape was fucking brilliant. When he cries, you cry. When he smiles, you smile. He's very loose. He's got real charm.' Glancing up from the storyboards, Boyle nods vigorously in agreement. But there's a distant look in his eyes: his mind is already in Utah.

James Franco in the canyon moments before his arm is trapped by a chockstone.

I phone Boyle at his dad's house in Radcliffe, Greater Manchester. It's late afternoon on New Year's Eve and he's about to cook dinner for his dad and his kids. We work through a list of queries related to the book and then I ask how *127 Hours* is progressing. He seems to jump from utter terror to supreme confidence. 'Simon has made it slightly less a one-man film, but it's still like, "You've got to be joking! A one-man film!" I always have a phrase in mind: "It's an action film where the hero can't move." As a form, it contradicts what is expected. Much like making a drugs movie that's full of energy, appetite and relish. I want the trailer for *127 Hours* to look like an action movie, and the audience has to work out that Aron can't in fact move.'

His dad says something in the background; Boyle, his accent more northern than usual, pauses to gently reassure him he won't be long. 'The buzz of it for me even at this stage is: "How the hell am I going to do this?"' He laughs, wishes me Happy New Year and is gone.

8 January 2010

Boyle and Colson have just flown out to Salt Lake City, but Anthony Dod Mantle, the British cinematographer who won an Oscar for his work on *Slumdog*, is at home in Copenhagen for another few days. He talks about the 'extraordinarily restrictive nature' of *127 Hours* and then launches into his thesis on the film. 'It's not even camouflaged any more: it's an absolute glorification of an art movie. Coming after *Slumdog* I think this film, with its triptychs, is quite extraordinary. I gave Danny a Bill Viola DVD just because it stretches your brain. Because, in a way, that's what we have to do with this film . . .'

I'm not sure Boyle, who eschewed arty work after directing *Mr Wroe's Virgins* back in 1993, would agree with the suggestion that he's making an art movie. Dod Mantle laughs. 'I'm sure you're right! That's because he wants films to sell tickets. Bums on seats is very important to him.'

February 2010

Boyle tells *Empire* magazine that he will be using two cinematographers on *127 Hours*: Anthony Dod Mantle will be joined by

Enrique Chediak, who shot *28 Weeks Later*. 'One is from northern Europe and the other is South American. They'll bring different things to it. Like in a conventional film you'd have a comic character and a villain.' He doesn't say if Dod Mantle, with whom he's worked regularly since 2001, will be cast as the comic character or the villain.

March 2010

Shortly before I fly nearly 5,000 miles from London to Salt Lake City, the *Los Angeles Times* runs a feature entitled 'Oscar Bait 2011'. The shoot has barely begun and yet *127 Hours* is on the list. The accompanying piece talks of a 'riveting story of survival' and adds: 'Hopefully Ralston's happy ending will do more for Academy voters than Sean Penn's 2007 downer, *Into the Wild*.'

27 March 2010

It's a gloriously sunny day in Salt Lake City. *127 Hours* is being shot in an old furniture warehouse in the suburbs of the city: the soundstages are all booked up – notably by Disney's tent-pole movie *John Carter of Mars* – following the introduction of a 20 per cent tax credit to productions spending money in Utah.

The bright light outside gives way to a dark, dusty hangar littered with piles of orange-red soil, boulders and carpentry tables. At the far end, black cloth curtains hang loosely around a relatively small rectangular space. A machine pumps dust out relentlessly. A gap in the curtains allows a glimpse of red rock. A disembodied Mancunian voice booms out: 'Right, James, let's go. Action!' A row of directors' chairs face a monitor. The set is utterly silent. Franco is on the screen, his arm stuck, a shaft of light at his feet. His face – usually handsome and relaxed – is contorted with pain.

As only two weeks of the shoot will actually take place in the Blue John Canyon, Suttirat Larlarb – costume designer on *Sunshine* and *Slumdog*; costume and production designer on *127 Hours* – has created both a vertical and horizontal canyon in the furniture factory. They are astonishing: as Franco is doing his thing in the horizontal canyon, she walks me through the vertical one, telling me it's 98 per cent accurate, that filming in the real canyon is dangerous, that the transition from set to location will appear seamless on film.

The canyon is tall, narrow and terrifyingly claustrophobic. I knock on the walls and am almost surprised they sound hollow. I have to contort my body to get under a human-sized chockstone trapped in mid-air and begin to understand, in the vaguest way, how Aron Ralston might have felt. I scramble out of the canyon and feel instant relief. Larlarb laughs. 'Danny keeps cheating to a minimum.'

She leads the way to an adjacent building where the costume department is piled high with a dozen pairs of identical walking shoes, seventy-odd Phish T-shirts and various items of climbing gear. 'Aron lost a huge amount of weight through dehydration; James obviously can't do that, so we just have to dress him in bigger T-shirts.' As Larlarb is chatting, Ralston turns up for his first set visit. His right arm, which he successfully hacked off just beneath the elbow, is tucked into the pocket of his fleece.

He takes photos of the shoes and the T-shirts (Phish were a favourite band at the time of the accident). He then sits down to talk. He's bright, articulate, self-deprecating but also self-assured, just a little cocksure. He says that the canyon experience was a blessing. He didn't tell anyone where he was going that fateful day because, to him, it was 'a walk in the park, a trip to the beach'. He was anxious about hypothermia, dehydration, sleep deprivation and depression but, for the most part, not death. Love kept him alive – for his family, his friends and the son he might one day have (he met his wife in a bar in Aspen after the accident; Leo was born in February 2010). He was smiling as he cut his arm off because he was about to be free again. By the time he was airlifted to hospital, he had lost 40lbs and had just fifteen minutes left to live.

Ralston admits it was hard to let go of his story. 'There was the usual anxiety about a film of such a personal experience: will it be portrayed accurately? Will it be sensationalised or overdramatised? I have faith now that the film will echo my sentiments: this is not a man versus nature story, but man versus self; the boulders in our lives can be our blessings. After the Oscars, Danny was being courted by everyone in the universe, but he still had a dog-eared copy of my book. His personal interest kept me interested in the project. I'm really excited about the film now; the set is awesome.'

Apart from his family, Ralston showed very few people the video footage he shot in the canyon; now it has become integral to the making of *127 Hours*. James Franco, who almost nods off as we talk – he's embracing his own fatigue and there's some method going on too – talks in hushed tones about the footage. 'Aron, Danny, Christian, Simon and I were in a hotel room in LA watching this rough footage with a weird static line through it. Aron didn't say anything very profound, but I was like, "Wow, I'm watching a guy who thinks he's going to die and has accepted his own death." He wasn't weepy at all – in fact, he was very controlled. It was incredibly powerful watching someone confront his own death.'

Franco adds that Boyle is a 'very, very nice guy. Fun. Innovative. Fearless. Most of the time it feels like I'm just acting with Danny . . . and a rock.'

28 March 2010

Enrique 'Quique' Chediak is shooting today, but Anthony Dod Mantle drops in looking like an extra from *Miami Vice*. He says it's 'extremely unusual' to be working with another DP. 'Apart from time, which is the governing factor, this film is being made with two DPs because Danny has a feeling that it will be inspirational. Creatively it's interesting to have two sets of eyes working on the same story. I had never met Quique before; we had to learn to trust each other very quickly.'

Dod Mantle is used to tough filming conditions – he's a Lars von Trier regular, after all – but *127 Hours* is something else. 'Danny doesn't want it to be easy for me or Quique. There's no room for Danny in the canyon, it's just James and the DP, so he stands outside wearing headphones and shouting instructions. I shot two days lying down. Then I was sitting there like Quasimodo. I felt like I'd been in the ring with Tyson. Both elbows were cut, my knees were sore . . . but still he wants you to do the ultimate in operating and lighting.'

A little later, I sit on a director's chair and watch the monitor replay an earlier shot of Franco tentatively sipping his urine; in real time, I hear Franco waking up from a nightmare and the echo of his howl. Boyle yells: 'Fantastic shot!' During the break, Chediak asks if I'd like to see the horizontal canyon: it's even narrower and more claustrophobic than the vertical one. Awkwardly embracing a boulder is a Franco body double – the actor is doubtless off reading a novel, as he does in every free moment – and a padded blue mat for the DP to kneel on. Chediak points out the Si-2K camera, used to such great effect in *Slumdog*, and jokes that 'there are so many wires trailing in and out of the canyon that I feel like a meatball in a dish of spaghetti'.

Boyle appears, like Banquo's ghost, from behind the curtains. Two weeks into the shoot and he looks shattered: he is working every day from 7 a.m. to midnight. He has time – just about – to talk over lunch. We sit in Christian Colson's office, where the vast London desk has been replaced by a white plastic garden table. Filming, he says, is going well, despite it being tough, slow, a constant fight against time and 'like going to work in a poky corridor'.

127 Hours is a brilliant contrast to *Slumdog*; from a billion people in India to one man in a canyon in Utah. Boyle doesn't want it to be a wilderness film – there will be minimal shots of epic rural landscapes like those which define *Into the Wild*, Werner Herzog's *Grizzly Man* or Gus Van Sant's *Gerry* – and even suggests it's an urban film. 'When Aron sets up his video or his camera, they're like CCTV cameras. It becomes a story about how we record ourselves. When I first read Aron's book, I weirdly thought it was a story about a man who cuts his arm off. But it's not: it is, as I noted in the original treatment, a Sisyphean story.'

It's also about America. Since *A Life Less Ordinary*, Boyle has wanted to make another film here. America may celebrate the individual, but Ralston survived because he was part of a community; he fought for his life because he felt loved.

'People may think that *127 Hours* is about individual superheroism – I'm thinking of Lance Armstrong, Michael Phelps – but my take on Aron's story is that there's something wider and bigger that sustains us in the end. The film is not a polemic, but I hope it will very subtly suggest the idea that Aron wasn't almost destroyed by nature, he was saved by society.'

This is, as Boyle says, the subtle aspect of the film. The reality is that not everyone wants to watch a grisly, gory arm amputation, even if it is beautifully shot. 'I realise plenty of people might think, "Euuuughh!" But you have to be honest about the story and not approach it thinking you mustn't horrify people too much. The truth is that it took Aron forty-four minutes to cut his arm off. He didn't hack at it like a madman; he did it with precision. You've

467

got to show an element of that, but not in real time. I want the audience to be wondering if, put in a similar situation, they would try to cut their own arm off or give up and die.'

He is relying on Franco to beguile the viewer. 'He has a charm, an ease, a grace about him that's invaluable. He must be barking mad to have taken on the role, but he is totally immersed in it. He has a looseness that British actors just don't seem to have – Leo [DiCaprio] was the same. James is not only a very, very good actor, but he's also interested in the technology and the technique. He's at film school in New York and he's already directing shorts. Digital technology allows us to shoot hundreds of hours of footage and I've agreed for James to have access to some of this for his own cutting exercise, perhaps for his own amusement, perhaps to appear on the Blu-ray disc of *127 Hours*.'

With Franco's looseness and focus, Boyle has been shooting twenty-minute takes which will invariably be edited down to less than twenty seconds. 'We did one take of James trying to set up a pulley system, and he did it so well that I thought, "Fucking hell! He's going to actually move the rock!" It's obviously not a real 800lb rock, but it's been fixed with a steel rod and is almost impossible to move. I swear to God, he went mad trying to move it. It was a *fantastic* take.'

Despite feeling exhausted after just two weeks, Boyle is also exhilarated. His lunch break is over; our time is up. One last question: right now, two weeks in, does he think *127 Hours* will work? 'I watched the rushes at midnight last night and some of the stuff we shot on Friday was excellent. Fucking great, in fact. We've got a lot to do – oh my God, a *lot* – but it's coming together. I'm thinking about the music all the time and hopefully we'll be working with A. R. Rahman again. The film is going to be gruelling, slightly insane, but also funny.' He grins wildly. 'At this point I *always* think I'm making the best film in the world ever!'

A little later, Colson shows me a tiny side room full of upper limbs. Tim Huizing, who works for Tony Gardner in the prosthetics department, is bent over a forearm with a tiny paintbrush in his hand. He is dotting freckles on the arm in exactly the same pattern they appear on Ralston's skin. There are fifteen arms – all made from moulds of Ralston's left arm – on display: some are solid, others hollow; some are intact, others reveal smooth muscles and stringy white nerves. Huizing produces Ziploc bags of spare muscles that look horribly real, and a small box filled with bones set in synovial fluid. It's repellent yet strangely compelling, like a Victorian medical museum.

As we wander around the set and then sit in front of the blank monitor, Colson talks about the way *Slumdog* was positioned in the UK as 'the feel-good film of the decade', despite its subject matter. '*Slumdog* is pretty dark, like all the best fairy tales, until the very end. *127 Hours* will be the same; it will be dark before it's affirming. Hopefully it will put people through the wringer a bit.'

The monitor springs into life to show sunrise in the canyon and Franco/Ralston amusing himself by pretending to be an overenthusiastic chat-show host. 'Good morning, everyone! It's seven o'clock in Canyonland, USA. Today, on the boulder, we've got a special guest – the self-styled American Superhero Aron Ralston. Shout it out, Aron!' The scene unfolds with Ralston playing both the role of the chat-show host and himself. A faultless first take, it's funny, moving and full of pathos.

By 10 p.m., Colson is done for the day. He talks with some concern about the forthcoming two-week trip to the canyon: there will be no access at night, not even by helicopter, so a fully-trained doctor will be on site at all times. Satellite phones will be the only form of communication. 'We will have to drum into the crew that they are not on holiday. There can be no drinking, no wandering off. This is serious stuff.'

How does he feel about the camping? He is being playful but also serious. 'I fucking hate camping. I like the Four Seasons.' And what about Danny Boyle? Colson looks incredulous: have I not worked the director out yet? '*He* likes shooting.'

Danny Boyle on Photo Albums

There are three fundamental pieces of advice Danny Boyle would pass on to aspiring directors: don't be frightened to be enthusiastic, because it's completely disarming and 'the equivalent of a double first at Harvard'; get plenty of coverage; and, finally, stockpile images. According to Boyle, British films suffer from a lack of visual pleasure – something he could never be accused of in his own work. Ever since he started to direct television drama for the BBC back in the late 1980s, Boyle has been collating albums crammed with images of forests, drug users, football, council estates, urban landscapes, war, corpses and – for The Beach, *of course – paradise.*

I have always collected images. From photography books, magazines, record sleeves. I buy postcards from museums and keep cards I've been sent. The images can literally be from anywhere. If you see an image and respond to it, keep it. It doesn't matter if you don't use it. Don't discriminate. Don't just collect for a specific project. Collect them so that you create a kind of treasure trove you make your way through as you go from film to film. I've got a garage full of photography books. Once a film is up and running, I spend days looking through them.

When I'm preparing to make a film, looking at imagery is as important as reading any book. It's extraordinary the amount of imagery that's available. While we were making *Slumdog*, we talked about how India is a trap for photographers and cinematographers because, visually, it is simply jaw-dropping. All you want to do is stare at it. When you get over the initial allure, the images start to work in different ways. They trigger ideas about scenes, about the way you are going to see scenes, about the visual vocabulary of the film.

Some of the best and most urgent photography comes from awful circumstances, from war or famine. Photographers point and shoot because they can't hang around. It's extraordinary what those images, as opposed to composed photos, capture. I collected endless images of war for *28 Days Later*. Right at the start of the film, the small screens in the lab show incredibly violent acts of people being hacked to pieces. We shot those scenes in a gravel pit near the Blackwall tunnel and they were all inspired by these unsettling images I'd been collecting.

The albums inspire the cast and the crew. They help the costume department, the location manager and the design department. Mark Tildesley, who designed *28 Days Later*, *Millions* and *Sunshine*, also has oceans of imagery, so we could very easily share our vision for those films. Actors might play four characters a year and so they really value a visual prompt, which tells them more than the colour of their character's hair. As we prepare to shoot, I put the images up on the walls of the production office and we're surrounded by the film as we're discussing it each day.

One of the problems of film is that you can end up in a series of meetings, *talking* about something that is essentially a visual medium. Yet very little dialogue is remembered in films. What you remember are images. Every now and again a director comes along and changes the balance – Tarantino for one. He has a delicious love of dialogue.

Generally it is, as I say, a visual medium. And, God, you should prepare for it! Not by reading books and talking about them to your crew but by showing a photograph. It's an incredibly accurate way of making a film, simply because language is very inaccurate. You swear you had a conversation with someone about a certain thing, yet you each remember the conversation differently. You could ask for a Ford Zodiac and end up with a Ford Zephyr; if you showed a photo of a Zodiac, you're far more likely to get it. It's a far more precise way of working.

The touchstone for British film tends to be realism. It's something we all depend on. It's valuable and important, but sometimes you want to leave it behind; it can be crushing. Films don't always have to be plausible. Sometimes, as director, you want to lift off, to leave the realism behind. Photography can help you. Often it captures a moment of reality but, because it's a snapshot frozen in time, it transforms that moment into something surreal. Cartier-Bresson was a realist but his photos were magical.

Use images well and they can help you to leave reality behind and enjoy yourself. For instance, in *Millions* we wanted the saints to look like they were painted by El Greco. El Greco supposedly had astigmatism and therefore his characters were elongated, like a Giacometti sculpture. In the end, we just didn't have the money to create El Greco-style saints, so we created CGI halos instead. But the inspiration was there.

I started putting together albums when I was working in Northern Ireland for the BBC. I had a great book of Bertolucci's films and I used the imagery from that. A few years later, when I was casting for *Mr Wroe's Virgins*, the BBC drama series, I showed Jonathan Pryce the album I'd been working on. I could tell he was quite surprised – it was obvious this didn't happen that often. I thought we would never talk him into taking the role, but he agreed and I'm sure the album was part of what persuaded him.

It's very easy for British films to look visually impoverished, which we tend to blame on things like budget and landscape. Of course, we can rarely find the clean horizons so common in America, but I think that's a cop-out. We have grown up with a literary tradition and therefore rely too much on the writing. You don't have to abandon writing to make a great film; you just have to add a visual language to it. A visual pride.

Acknowledgements

With thanks to Ian Bahrami, Maria Boyle, Walter Donohue at Faber, Jude Edgington, Lizzie Francke, Corinna Gallup, Jonny Geller at Curtis Brown, Joanne Glasbey, Helen Johnson, Gareth Jones, Mike Leigh (for putting in a good word), Cheryl Roberts, Tracey Seaward, Karen Walter at *NME* and Jon Wilde.

Special thanks to Christian Colson and Gaia Elkington at Cloud Eight Films, and to Leah Clarke at DNA Films for services beyond the call of duty.

'The Queen' by Paul Farley, from his collection *The Dark Film*, is reproduced with the kind permission of Picador, London. © Paul Farley, 2012.

Photo Credits
Photos from *Shallow Grave* © 1994, *Trainspotting* © 1996 and *A Life Less Ordinary* © 1997 courtesy of DNA Films; photos from *Millions* © 2004 Pathé Entertainment; photos from *Slumdog Millionaire* © 2008 Ishika Mohan, courtesy of Celador Films and Pathé Entertainment (UK); photo of Danny Boyle as a teenager by Paul Hatzer.

28 Days Later © 2003, *Sunshine* © 2007, *Slumdog Millionaire* © 2008, *127 Hours* © 2010, *Trance* © 2013 courtesy of Fox Searchlight Pictures. All rights reserved. *A Life Less Ordinary* © 1998 and *The Beach* © 2000 courtesy of Twentieth Century Fox. All rights reserved.

Frankenstein photos © 2012 Catherine Ashmore. Courtesy of the National Theatre.

Filmography

Shallow Grave (1994)
Channel Four Films/The Glasgow Film Fund/Figment Films.
Screenplay by John Hodge, produced by Andrew Macdonald and
Allan Scott, photography by Brian Tufano, edited by Masahiro
Hirakubo, casting by Sarah Trevis, designed by Kave Quinn, cos-
tume by Kate Carin, original music by Simon Boswell. With Kerry
Fox (Juliet Miller), Christopher Eccleston (David Stephens), Ewan
McGregor (Alex Law), Ken Stott (Detective Inspector McCall),
Keith Allen (Hugo), Colin McCredie (Cameron), Peter Mullan
(Andy), John Hodge (Detective Inspector Mitchell). 92 mins.

Trainspotting (1996)
Channel Four Films/Figment Films. Novel by Irvine Welsh, screen-
play by John Hodge, produced by Andrew Macdonald, photog-
raphy by Brian Tufano, edited by Masahiro Hirakubo, casting by
Andy Pryor and Gail Stevens, designed by Kave Quinn, costume by
Rachael Fleming. With Ewan McGregor (Renton), Ewen Bremner
(Spud), Jonny Lee Miller (Sick Boy), Kevin McKidd (Tommy),
Robert Carlyle (Begbie), Kelly Macdonald (Diane), Peter Mullan
(Swanney), Susan Vidler (Allison), Pauline Lynch (Lizzie), Shirley
Henderson (Gail), Irvine Welsh (Mikey Forrester), Dale Winton
(Game Show Host), Keith Allen (Dealer), Kevin Allen (Andreas).
92 mins.

A Life Less Ordinary (1997)
Channel Four Films/Figment Films/Polygram Filmed Entertainment.
Screenplay by John Hodge, produced by Andrew Macdonald,

photography by Brian Tufano, edited by Masahiro Hirakubo, casting by Donna Isaacson, designed by Kave Quinn, costume by Rachael Fleming, original music by David Arnold. With Ewan McGregor (Robert Lewis), Cameron Diaz (Celine Naville), Holly Hunter (O'Reilly), Delroy Lindo (Jackson), Dan Hedaya (Gabriel), Ian McNeice (Mayhew), Frank Kanig (Ted), Stanley Tucci (Elliot Zweikel), Tony Shalhoub (Al), Ian Holm (Naville), Maury Chaykin (Tod Johnson). 103 mins.

The Beach (2000)

20th Century Fox/Figment Films. Novel by Alex Garland, screenplay by John Hodge, produced by Andrew Macdonald, photography by Darius Khondji, edited by Masahiro Hirakubo, casting by Gail Stevens, designed by Andrew McAlpine, costume by Rachael Fleming, original music by Angelo Baldamenti. With Leonardo DiCaprio (Richard), Virginie Ledoyen (Françoise), Guillaume Canet (Étienne), Robert Carlyle (Daffy), Weeratham 'Norman' Wichairaksakui (Detective), Abhijati 'Muek' Jusakul (Senior Farmer), Paterson Joseph (Keaty), Lars Arentz Hansen (Bugs), Tilda Swinton (Sal), Staffan Kihlbom (Christo), Jukka Hiltunen (Karl), Magnus Lindgren (Sten). 119 mins.

28 Days Later (2002)

20th Century Fox/DNA Films. Screenplay by Alex Garland, produced by Andrew Macdonald, photography by Anthony Dod Mantle, edited by Chris Gill, casting by Gail Stevens, designed by Mark Tildesley, costume by Rachael Fleming, original music by John Murphy. With Cillian Murphy (Jim), Naomie Harris (Selena), Brendan Gleeson (Frank), Megan Burns (Hannah), Toby Sedgwick (Infected Priest), Justin Hackney (Infected Kid), Christopher Eccleston (Major Henry West). 113 mins.

Millions (2004)

Pathé Pictures International/UK Film Council/BBC Films/Fox Searchlight Pictures. Screenplay by Frank Cottrell Boyce, produced by François Ivernel, David M. Thompson and Graham Broadbent, photography by Anthony Dod Mantle, edited by Chris Gill, casting by Beverley Keogh and Gail Stevens, designed by Mark Tildesley, costume by Susannah Buxton, original music by John Murphy.

With Alex Etel (Damian), Lewis McGibbon (Anthony), James Nesbitt (Ronnie), Daisy Donovan (Dorothy), Christopher Fulford (The Man), Pearce Quigley (Community Policeman), Jane Hogarth (Mum), Alun Armstrong (St Peter), Enzo Cilenti (St Francis), Nasser Memarzia (St Joseph), Kathryn Pogson (St Clare), Harry Kirkham (St Nicholas), Leslie Phillips (Leslie Phillips), Frank Cottrell Boyce (Nativity Teacher). 98 mins.

Sunshine (2007)
DNA Films/Ingenious Film Partners/Moving Picture Company/ UK Film Council/20th Century Fox. Screenplay by Alex Garland, produced by Andrew Macdonald and Bernie Bellew, photography by Alwin Kuchler, edited by Chris Gill, casting by Donna Isaacson and Gail Stevens, designed by Mark Tildesley, costume by Suttirat Larlarb, original music by John Murphy. With Cliff Curtis (Searle), Chipo Chung (Icarus), Cillian Murphy (Capa), Michelle Yeoh (Corazon), Hiroyuki Sanada (Kaneda), Rose Byrne (Cassie), Benedict Wong (Trey), Chris Evans (Mace), Troy Garity (Harvey), Mark Strong (Pinbacker), Paloma Baeza (Capa's Sister), Archie Macdonald (Child), Sylvie Macdonald (Child). 107 mins.

Slumdog Millionaire (2008)
Celador Films/Film4/Pathé Pictures International/Fox Searchlight Pictures. Novel *Q&A* by Vikas Swarup, screenplay by Simon Beaufoy, co-directed (India) by Loveleen Tandan, produced by Christian Colson, François Ivernel, Cameron McCracken, Tessa Ross and Paul Smith, photography by Anthony Dod Mantle, edited by Chris Dickens, casting by Gail Stevens and Loveleen Tandan, designed by Mark Digby, costume by Suttirat Larlarb, original music by A. R. Rahman. With Dev Patel (Jamal Malik), Saurabh Shukla (Sergeant Srinivas), Anil Kapoor (Prem Kapur), Freida Pinto (Latika), Iffran Khan (Police Inspector), Azharuddin Mohammed Ismail (Youngest Salim), Ayush Mahesh Khedekar (Youngest Jamal), Mahesh Manjrekar (Javed), Sanchita Choudhary (Jamal's Mother), Sharib Hashmi (Prakash), Rubina Ali (Youngest Latika), Ankur Vikal (Maman), Tiger (Punnoose), Chirag Parmar (Young Arvind), Tanay Hemant Chheda (Middle Jamal), Ashutosh Lobo Gajiwala (Middle Salim), Tanvi Ganesh Lonkar (Middle Latika). 120 mins.

127 Hours (2010)
Pathé Pictures International/Fox Searchlight Pictures/Film4 in association with Warner Bros Pictures. A Cloud Eight/Decibel Films/Darlow Smithson Production. Novel *Between a Rock and a Hard Place* by Aron Ralston, screenplay by Danny Boyle and Simon Beaufoy, produced by Christian Colson, Danny Boyle, John Smithson, François Ivernel, Bernard Bellew and Tessa Ross, photography by Anthony Dod Mantle and Enrique Chediak, edited by Jon Harris, casting by Donna Isaacson, design and costume by Suttirat Larlarb, original music by A. R. Rahman. With James Franco (Aron Ralston), Kate Mara (Kristi), Amber Tamblyn (Megan), Clemence Poesy (Rana), Kate Burton (Aron's mother), Lizzy Caplan (Sonja Ralston). 94 mins.

Frankenstein (2011)
Novel *Frankenstein* by Mary Shelley, play by Nick Dear, designed by Mark Tildesley, costume by Suttirat Larlarb, lighting design by Bruno Poet, music and soundscore by Underworld, sound design by Mike Walker, director of movement Toby Sedgwick, fight direction by Kate Waters. With Benedict Cumberbatch (Victor Frankenstein/ the Creature), Jonny Lee Miller (the Creature/Victor Frankenstein). Approx. 120 mins.

The Opening Ceremony of the London Olympics (2012)
Writer: Frank Cottrell Boyce; producer: Tracey Seaward; associate director: Paulette Randall; designers: Mark Tildesley and Suttirat Larlarb; costume: Suttirat Larlarb; visual-effects supervisor: Adam Gascoyne; music director: Rick Smith; movement director: Toby Sedgwick; tehnical director: Piers Shepperd; choreographers: Kenrick Sandy and Akram Khan; co-choreographers: Temujin Gill and Sunanda Biswas; cauldron designer: Thomas Heatherwick; video editor: Sascha Dillon; lighting designer: Patrick Woodroffe; executive producers: Catherine Ugwu, Stephen Daldry; executive producer (broadcast/TV): Hamish Hamilton. Approx. 240 mins.

Trance (2013)
Pathé Pictures International/Fox Searchlight Pictures/Film4. A Cloud Eight/Decibel Films production. Screenplay by Joe Ahearne and John Hodge, produced by Christian Colson, Danny Boyle,

Bernard Bellew, François Ivernel and Tessa Ross, photography by Anthony Dod Mantle, edited by Jon Harris, casting by Gail Stevens and Donna Isaacson, designed by Mark Tildesley, costume by Suttirat Larlarb, original music by Rick Smith. With James McAvoy (Simon), Vincent Cassel (Franck), Rosario Dawson (Elizabeth), Danny Sapani (Nate), Matt Cross (Dominic), Wahab Sheikh (Riz). 93 mins.

Index

Numbers in italics refer to photos

'Abide with Me', 433–4
Abrams, J. J., xiii
Acharya, Raj, 282–3, 284, 291, 297, 309, 317
acting, difference between theatre and cinema, 381–2
actors' exercises, 20
After the Dance (Rattigan), 371
Age of Innocence, The, 19
Agius, Lorenzo, 106
Agra, 287, 288–90
Ahearne, Joe, 443
Aitken, Bobby, 429
Albarn, Damon, 87
Alexa cameras, 342
Ali, Muhammad, 108, 437–8
Ali, Rubina, 259, 270, 278, 306, 316–17
Alien, 22, 236–7, 243
Alien: Resurrection, 113, 225
All Saints, 160
Allen, Keith: in *Shallow Grave*, 46, 61–3, 62; in *Trainspotting*, 81
Allen, Kevin, 61, 62–3, 274
Allen, Woody, 19
Alleyne, Perri, 433
Altman, Robert, 135
Amis, Martin, 353
'And I Will Kiss', 423, 424, 426–7
Anderson, Laurie, 193
Anderson, Lindsay, 26
Angel at My Table, An, xiv
animation, 42–3, 129
Annakin, Ken, 13
Apocalypse Now, 21–3, 42, 130, 151

Arentz-Hansen, Lars, 131
Argo, 344
Armstrong, Alun, 199, 215
Armstrong, Neil, 224
Ash, 126
Ashcroft, Richard, 160–1
Athens Olympics (2004), 409
Atkinson, Rowan, 401, 438–9
Atmos surround-sound system, 343–4
Aukin, David, 66–7, 71, 73, 83, 409
Austen, Jane, 6
Australia, 134–5
autopsies, 375–7
Avatar, xiii, 225, 228, 460

Bachchan, Amitabh, 258, 281, 314
Badalamenti, Angelo, 160
Badgered, 217
Baeza, Paloma, 254
Bailey, Jade, 399
Bailey, John, 5
Ban, Ki-moon, 437
Bangor University, 16–17
Barker, Howard, 23
Barmby, Nick, 67
Barve, Rahi Anil, 217
Battle of the Bulge, 13
BBC, xiii–xiv, xv–xvi, 5, 23–31, 168, 411
Beach, The: main discussion, 133–63; accidents on set, 142–3, 153; cast, 140–6; Danny Boyle (DB) on the novel, 133–4; DB's feelings about, xv, 39, 119–20; ecology issues, 153–5; ending, 160–1; filming and cinematography, xv, 137, 139–45, 155–9, 183; filmography entry, 342;

group dynamic in, 122; McGregor's expectation of being in, xix–xx, 137–8; marijuana field, 157–8, *158*; morality, 135–6, 157, 209; plot, 130–3; problems, x, xvii–xviii, 138–40, 149–51, 153; reception and revenues, 152, 160; research, 377; Richard's character, 37–8, 138–9, 150; setting and set, 134–5, 139, 147, 153–5; signing scene, 435; soundtrack, 159–60; themes, 135, 149, 152, 161; voice-over, 161

Beatles, The, 420; *see also* Lennon, John; McCartney, Paul

Beaufoy, Simon, 320; and acting, 54; attitude to press and publicity, 53; DB on, 330; and directing, 32; and *The Full Monty*, 265, 266, 319; and *127 Hours*, 328–9, 357–8, 459–60, 463, 466; and *Slumdog*, xii, xv, 37, 264–5, 266–7, 272, 288, 290–1, 298, 307, 313, 459

Beckett, Samuel, 358, 459

Beckham, David, 399

Beijing Olympics (2008), xxv, 389–90, 424, 431, 437

Bellew, Bernie, 245–6

Benn, Tony, 405

Bennett, Alan, xxxi

Berlin Bertie (Brenton), 61

Berners-Lee, Tim, 405, 412, 415–16

Bertolucci, Bernardo, 464

Best, George, 5

Between a Rock and a Hard Place (Ralston), 327–8, 456–7

Beyond Rangoon, 157

Bhopal gas disaster (1984), 391

Bigelow, Kathryn, 42, 181–2

Billy Elliot, 414

Birthday Party, The (script), 351

Bishop, Bob, 5

Biswas, Sunanda, 393, 419, 429

Bizet, Georges, 92–3

Black Friday, 292

Blondie, 92

Blood Simple, xv, 77

Blow-Up, 13–14

Blue States, 195

Blur, 58, 87

BMW, 409

Bollywood, 279–80, 282, 292, 303, 307, 313–14

Bolton Octagon, 15–16

Bond, Edward, 23

Boorman, John, 157

Bowie, David, 11–12, 91, 92, 416–18

Boyd, Steve, 429

Boyle, Mrs (DB's mother): background, 1, 4; death, 3, 10; employment, 4; and *Millions*, 10, 207; optimism, 34; politics, 3; relationship with and influence on DB, 3–4, 33–4; and religion, xxii, 8–9, 10, 206–7; upbringing of children, 14

Boyle, Bernadette (DB's sister), 1–3, 10

Boyle, Caitlin (DB's daughter), xiii, xxii, 43, 273, 460

Boyle, Danny (DB)

AS DIRECTOR: main discussion, 31–45; advice to aspiring directors, 470; on American actors, 331–2; on audiences, 43–4, 56; on big-budget films, 162–3; biggest ambition, xxii; on British films and film-makers, 245, 471, 472; on camera work, 24–5, 31, 68–9, 124–5, 183–4, 285–6; on characters in own films, 37–8; on coming down from filming, 39–40; core film themes, 351, 357; on differences between directing theatre and film, 20, 50; on differences between US and British directing styles, 18–19; directing style, x, 31–45, 301–2, 425–6; DVD extras, 216–17; on editing, 28, 40, 348–9; on ego in the film industry, 313; favourite art films, 55; favourite film and film-maker, 21–2, 35; favourite horror films, 193; favourite kind of cinema, 15, 42–3; favourite setting for own films, 120; on film as pop culture, 58–9; on filming as hard work, 38–9; on film-making process, 340–1, 352–4; group dynamic in own films, 122–3; ideal conditions for best work, 119–20; on importance of doubt, 45; on importance of humour in films, 357–8; on importance of sound in films, 251–2; on improvisation, 21, 36; lack of women at heart of own films, 41–2; on length of directors' golden periods, 44–5; lessons learned from theatre work, 19; love of action in movies, 126; morality in own films, 209; on music's role in films, 93; and press and publicity, 53–4; on qualities of own films, 35–8; relationship with cast and crew, xiv, xv–xxi, xxvi, xxix–xxx, 31–4, 54, 123, 162–3, 339–40; relationship with writers, 24, 25, 54–5, 290; romance in own films, 121; on sci-fi films, 223–4, 242–5; on scripts and stories, 36–8, 39; stealing from other directors, 119, 244–5; on technology, 124–5, 225; on theatre vs cinema work, 381–2; on theatre work, 363; variety of own films, x, xxii; violence in own films, 66–8; voice-overs, 82–3, 161; on own weaknesses, 41–2; working with child actors, 205–6, 211, 279, 297–8

GENERAL AND VIEWS: on arts funding, 413–15; attitude to criticism, xvii, 40–1; on Britishness, 398–9, 439–40; character, xxii; charity work, 404–5; on education, 209, 413–14; energy and love of pressure, xii, xv, 3–4, 145, 169; enthusiasm, 17–18; and football, 4–5, 9; and guilt, 2–3, 34; image collection, 470–2; on importance of belief, 394–5; on India, 267–8, 308–9; love of popular culture, xii–xiii, 10–13; on making money, 170; Mile End home, xii; on modern technological progress, 378; money earned, 97, 136–7; musical tastes, xiii, 11–13; on Northern Ireland peace process, 437; and opera, 290; on poetry, 353; politics, 3, 13, 209–10, 412–14, 440; on pop music, 58–9, 421–2; and reading, xxviii, 6; relationship with parents and their influence, 3–4, 33–4; and religion, xxii, 2, 6, 8–10, 12, 34, 58, 206–7, 225–6, 309, 354–5; on republicanism, 356; and science, 380; on success, 34–5; on women, 437, 442, 449; work ethic, xxii–xxiii, 136, 338; on writing, 329, 357–8, 379–80

LIFE: birth, childhood and school, 1–8, 370; as twin, 2, 3; involvement in school drama, 6, 7; gives up idea of being priest and stops going to church, 8–10, 12; growing interest in popular culture, 10–13; early trips to cinema,

13–14; first girlfriends, 14; summer jobs, 14; job as theatre usher, 15–16; at Bangor University, 16–17; directs first play, 16; joins Joint Stock, then Royal Court, 16–18, 19–21, 23; joins BBC, xiii–xiv, xv–xvi, 5, 23–31; reaction to mother's death, 10; partner and children, xiii; more BBC work, 168; refuses knighthood, 439

PHOTOS: in football team, aged ten, 5; aged seventeen, 11; on *Shallow Grave* set, 49, 69; on *Trainspotting* set, 82, 100, 104; on *A Life Less Ordinary* set, 112; on *The Beach* set, 133, 141; on *28 Days Later* set, 167, 183; on *Sunshine* set, 223, 233; on *Slumdog* set, 264, 284; at Oscars, 320; on *127 Hours* set, 335, 337; with Dod Mantle, 444; with Dod Mantle and Evans, 446; on *Trance* set, 451, 454

Boyle, Frank (DB's father): ambidextrousness, 5; background, 1; cinema trips with DB, 13; DB tries to share tastes with, 22–3; DB visits, 463; death, 389; employment, xxii–xxiii; favourite DB film, 74; and football, 4; and *Millions*, 207; musical tastes, 74; photo shown at London 2012 opening ceremony, 433; politics, 3; relationship with DB, 3, 433; and religion, 8; upbringing of children, 2, 3, 14; war service, 266

Boyle, Gabriel (DB's son), xiii, xxii, 3, 43, 129, 460

Boyle, Grace (DB's daughter), xiii, xxii, 43, 173, 302, 304, 376

Boyle, Maria (DB's sister): childhood, 1–3, 10, 13; as DB's twin, 2, 3; employment, 3; lends author tapes of DB's TV work, xiii; DB visits, 320

Bradshaw, Peter, 256

Branagh, Kenneth, 19, 61, 227, 406, 438

Brave, 343

Bremner, Ewen, 78, 85, 85, 89, 98, 104

Brenton, Howard, 16, 61

Brinks Mat robbery, 175

Britpop, ix

Broadbent, Graham, 201

Broadbent, Jim, 168

Broccoli, Barbara, 401–2

Brown, Derren, 444–5, 453, 454–5

Brown, Roy Chubby, 168
Brunel, Isambard Kingdom, 405–6
Bryce, Davey, 87
Buchanan, Scott, 408
Burchill, Julie, 10
Burke, Kathy, xiv, 30
Burns, Megan, 166
Burton, Kate, 325
Burton, Tim, 214, 462
Busby, Matt, 5
Buxton, Susannah, 212, 214
Byrne, Rose, 218, 234, 247
Byron, George Gordon, Lord, 364, 369–70

'Caliban's Dream', 423, 426–7
Calton Athletic, 87, 107
Cambodia, 181
Cameron, James, xiii, xxii, 225, 228, 237, 341
Campbell, Marvin, 167
Campion, Jane, xiv
Canet, Guillaume, 130, 142–3, 142, 146, 147, 155–6, 155
Cannes Film Festival, 75–6, 107
CanonCam, 285, 286, 294
Caplan, Lizzy, 323
Caplan, Tim, 429
Carlin, Dan, 401
Carlyle, Robert (Bobby): in The Beach, xviii, 130, 148–9, 149; in Trainspotting, 78, 82, 85–6, 85, 89, 96–7, 98, 99–100; turns down Shallow Grave, xx, 60; on working with DB, xx–xxi
Carpenter, John, 244–5
Carr, Martin, 168
Carrey, Jim, 35
Cartier-Bresson, Henri, 472
Cartwright, Jim, xvi, 168
Cassel, Vincent, 339, 441, 447, 447
Celador, 268
Celebrity, 19
CGI: and The Beach, 153, 159; and A Life Less Ordinary, 124–5; and Millions, 196, 214; and Slumdog, 214, 294; and Sunshine, 225, 228–30, 239, 240–1, 246, 249, 251; and 28 Days Later, 181
Chabrol, Claude, 13–14
Chakrabarti, Sami, 437
Channel 4, 50, 74, 83
Chaplin, Charlie, 144
Chapman, John, 30–1

Chaykin, Maury, 110, 123
Chediak, Enrique 'Quique': DB on, 339; and 127 Hours, 332, 336, 338–9, 340, 463–4, 466–7
Chekhov, Anton, 135
Chheda, Tanay Hemant, 260, 278–9, 289, 317
Children of Men, 192
Choudhary, Sanchita, 258
Christie in Love (Brenton), 16
Christine, 26–7
Chung, Chipo, 218, 247
Churchill, Caryl, 25
Cilenti, Enzo, 197
Cimino, Michael, 22
Cinders (Glowacki), 23
cinema, future of, 44
'Cities in the Dust' (Siouxsie and the Banshees), 397
City Slickers II, 40–1
Clark, Sarah, 139, 153
Clarke, Alan, 26–8, 38, 50
Clarke, Arthur C., 223
Clarke, John Cooper, 168
Clash, The, 12–13, 194–5, 215
Clear, 214
Clockwork Orange, 14–15
Cocker, Jarvis, 94
Coe, Seb, 389, 391, 420
Coen brothers, xv, 50, 77, 113–14, 116, 317
Cohen, Polly, 269
Cohen, Sacha Baron, 319
Coldplay, 238
Collins, Mick, 5
Colman, Sharon, 217
Colson, Christian, 320; attitude to press interviews, 53; background, 264; on Beaufoy and The Full Monty, 267; Covent Garden office, xi; DB on, 330; and DB doing London 2012, 389; on Franco, 333; and 127 Hours, 328, 349, 457, 459, 461–2, 463, 466, 468–9; and Slumdog, xxi, 39, 228, 264, 265, 267, 268–9, 291, 308, 313, 316, 317–18; and Trance, 445
Company, 292
Connery, Gary, 400
Connery, Sean, 448
Connolly, Billy, 355
Conway, Father, 9
Conway, Richard, 232, 239, 240, 249
Cooper, Alice, 12

Coppola, Francis Ford, 22
Coronation Street, 202
Cosmo, James, 80
Cottrell Boyce, Frank: as actor, 54; background, 202; charity work, 404–5; and *Frankenstein*, xxvii–xxviii, 365; and London 2012, xxvii–xxviii, 363, 390–1, 395, 397, 398, 401; and *Millions*, 199, 200, 203, 205, 206, 210, 212, 214–15, 217; motto, 397; on working with DB, xvii
Cox, Brian, 234–5
Craig, Daniel, 402, 403
Crazies, The, 171
Crosby, Bing, 11–12
Cross, Matt, 449
Cruise, Tom, xx
Cuarón, Alfonso, 192
Cumberbatch, Benedict: acting style, 371–2; and *Frankenstein*, 371–6, 372, 374, 379, 381, 383, 385
Curtis, Cliff, 218, 234, 249, 251
Curtis, Richard, 127–8, 438

Daldry, Stephen, 388, 399–400, 414
Dallas, Tony, 5
Dargis, Manohla, 201, 256
Dark Star, 244–5
Davison, Emily Wilding, 404–5
Dawson, Phil, 25
Dawson, Rosario, 339, 441, 443, 447, 452–3
Day, Angela, 176
Day, Michelle, 307
Day of the Triffids, The, 172
De Palma, Brian, 231
Dead Dad, 250
Dear, Nick, 365, 367–8, 373, 375, 379, 386–7
Decameron, 13–14
Dedhia, Mulchand, 285
Deer Hunter, The, 151
Departed, The*, 140
Desai, Mrinal, 287
DESH, 401
Devlin, Anne, xiv, 24
DGA awards, 317
Diana, Princess, 134
Diaz, Cameron: DB on, 453; in *A Life Less Ordinary*, xix, 109, 113, 116, 117, 117, 118, 121, 122, 123, 124, 125, 128; luminosity on camera, 140
DiCaprio, Leonardo: in *The Beach*,

xviii, 130, 137, 138, 140–5, 141, 142, 148, 149, 149, 151, 155–7, 155, 159, 161; DB on, 140–1, 468; effect on fans, 141, 144–5
Dickens, Chris, 302
Digby, Mark (Marco), 307–8
Dillon, Sascha, 417
Dirty Pretty Things, 186
Disneyland, Paris, 214
Dixon, Franklin W., 6
Dizzee Rascal, 433
Dockhead Choir, 436
Dod Mantle, Anthony, 444, 446; DB on, 341–3; and *Millions*, 215; and *127 Hours*, 332, 336, 338–9, 340, 341–3, 463–4, 466; and *Slumdog*, 215, 283, 284–6, 284, 308; TV work with DB, 168; and *28 Days Later*, 172–3, 182–4, 183, 188; on working with DB, xv–xvii, xxii, xxiii
Dolan, Terry, 5
Donovan, Daisy, 198, 203–4, 205
Don't Look Now, 50, 193, 452
Dow Chemical, 390–1
D:Ream, 234
Driver, Minnie, xiv
Duffy, Carol Ann, 353
Dumb & Dumber, 35, 37

Eagle of the Ninth, The, 245
Ebola virus, 180
Eccleston, Christopher: and football, 65; as mimic, 102; in *Shallow Grave*, xiv, 46, 57, 60, 61, 61, 62, 64, 65, 68, 70, 71, 72–3, 72; in *Strumpet*, xvi, 168; in *28 Days Later*, 166, 188
Ecstasy, 87
Edinburgh: Princes Street, 96, 97
Edward Scissorhands, 215
Einstein, Albert, x
electricity, 364, 365
Elephant, 26, 27–8, 50
Elfman, Danny, 215
Elizabeth II, Queen, 400–3
Elkington, Gaia, 318, 389
Ellison, Ralph, 368
Elson, Michael, 229
Emmerich, Roland, 246
Etel, Alex, in *Millions*, 90, 196, 203, 203, 204–5, 211, 213
Eternal Sunshine of the Spotless Mind, xiii
Eureka, ix, 44
Evans, Arwel, 307, 446

Evans, Chris, 218, 234, 240
Exorcist, The, 193

Fanshen (Hare), 17
Farley, Paul, 353, 396–7
Farrell, J. G., 225–6
Fassbender, Michael, 350
Federbush, Paul, 269
Fernandes, Longinus, 305
Film4, 267, 268
Final Curtain, The, 163
Fincher, David, 76, 317
Fitzgerald, F. Scott, 308, 353
Fleming, Ian, 6
Fleming, Rachael, xxi, 89, 99, 254
Fletcher, John (Pathé), 315
Fletcher, John (St Mary's primary
    school), 5
For the Greater Good, 29
Ford, John, 36
Forman, Milos, 76
Formby, 208
Forrester, Terry, 96–7
Forsythe, Bill, 101
Four Nations Choirs, xxv
Four Weddings and a Funeral, 59,
    106–7, 137
Fox, Kerry: DB on, 21, 30; in *Shallow
    Grave*, xiv–xv, 46, 57, 60, 61, 62,
    63–4, 72–3, 72; on working with
    DB, xiv–xv
Fox Searchlight: and *127 Hours*, 460;
    and *Slumdog*, 268–9, 319; *see also*
    20th-Century Fox
Framestone CFC studios, 159
Franco, James: DB on, 331, 332, 339,
    340; and directing, 340; and *127
    Hours*, 323, 328, 331–3, 331, 335,
    336–7, 340, 349, 350, 462, 462,
    464, 466–7, 468
Frankenstein: main discussion, 363–87;
    cast, 370–5; the drum, 385; as
    dry run for London 2012, 363,
    366–7; ending, 386; film versions,
    368; influences, xxviii, 365; lack
    of interval, 384; light-bulb ceiling,
    368; live filming, 382; nakedness in,
    374–5; the novel, 364–5, 368–70,
    379–80; opening scene, 365, 383–5;
    plot, 360–3; reception, 381, 386–7;
    research, 375–8; script, 367–8, 378–
    9, 386–7; soundscore, xxvi–xxvii,
    422–3; staging, 380–1; steampunk
    scene, 365–6, 366, 385

Frazier, Joe, 108
Frears, Stephen, 31, 186, 214
Freemantle, Glenn, 252, 319, 343
Fresnadillo, Juan Carlos, 192
Frost, Nick, 192
Fuck Buttons, 422
Fulford, Chris, 133, 198, 204
Full Monty, The, 265, 266, 319

Gajiwala, Ashutosh Lobo, 260, 278–9,
    289, 317
Gallagher, Noel and Liam, 4, 158
Gardner, Tony, 468
Garity, Troy, 218, 234
Garland, Alex: and acting, 54; *The
    Beach* novel, 38, 133–4, 151; DB on
    his central characters and writing,
    37–8; partner, 254; and religion,
    225; and *Sunshine*, 38, 179, 225–6,
    227, 242–3, 253; *The Tesseract*, 134;
    and *28 Days Later*, 170, 171, 179,
    181, 182, 191, 193
Gascoyne, Adam, 214, 294, 395–6,
    417, 429
Gaskill, William (Bill), 17, 19, 20–1,
    114, 409
Gerry, 467
Ghandi, Indira, 293
Gill, Chris, 174, 228, 229
Gill, Tamujin, 393, 419, 429
Gladstone, Alex, 187
Gladwyn, Lord, 405
Gleeson, Brendan, 166, 178, 179
Glennie, Evelyn, 423, 426–7, 435
Gluck, Christoph, 290
Godspeed You! Black Emperor, 160,
    173, 194
Godwin, William, 369
GoodFellas, 82–3
Goodman, John, 344
Gosling, Ryan, 332, 461
Grace of Mary Traverse, The
    (Wertenbaker), 23
Grande Bouffe, La, 13–14
Grant, Hugh, 128, 137, 237
Gray, Muriel, 93–4
Great Gatsby, The (Fitzgerald), 308,
    354
Greco, El, 472
Green, Martin, 388–9, 437
Greene, Graham, 6
Greenhalgh, Paul, 5
Grizzly Man, 467
Guinness, Alec, 137

Hamilton, Hamish, 436–7
Hamlet (Branagh version), 227
Haneke, Michael, 352
Hard Day's Night, A, 82
Hare, David, 17, 24, 409
Harnett, Ricci, 167
Harris, George, 362
Harris, Jon, 349
Harris, Naomie, 122, 165, 177–8, *178*, 182, 361
Hashmi, Sharib, 258
Heath, Duncan, 86
Heatherwick, Thomas, xxix, 389, 401, 406–8
Heaven's Gate, 22
Hedaya, Dan, 109, 116, 123
Hen House, The, 24, 55, 211
Henderson, Shirley, 79
heroin, 87
Herzog, Werner, 467
'Hey Jude' (The Beatles), 421
Hickey, Kieran, 26
Hicks, Jo, 198
Hirakubo, Masahiro, 31, 92–3, 174
Hirst, Damien, 390–1
Hitchcock, Alfred, 27, 41, 60
Hobbit, The, 343
Hodge, John: as actor, 54, 63; attitude to press and publicity, x, 9, 53; background as doctor, 55; and *The Beach*, xvii–xviii, 134, 137, 159; on DB, 54, 71–2; and directing, 54; and *A Life Less Ordinary*, 112, 113, 114, 121; relationship with DB, 31, 51, 53, 163; and religion, 58; and *Shallow Grave*, 48, 50–1, 52, 54–5, 57, 63, 66, 72, 73, 443; and *Trainspotting*, 83, 84, 88, 89, 90, 91, 92, 96, 97, 104, 107–8; and *Trance*, 445; work ethic, 136; writing style, 36, 38
Hodge, Lucy, 83
Hogarth, Jane, 200
Holm, Ian, 110, 114–15, *115*
Holman, Robert, 352
Holmes, Virginia, 307
Holt, Kevin, 5
Horn, Alan, 310
Horn, John, 310, 312
Hot Fuzz, 192
Houghton, Brendan, 230, 396, 417, 461–2
Howard, Ron, 317
Huizing, Tim, 468–9

Hunger, 94, 350
Hunter, Holly, 109, 114, *115*, 125
Huntley, Noah, 165
Hurt Locker, The, 42
Hutt, Jenny, 429
Hyams, Peter, 248
Hyde, Karl, xxvi, 363
hypnotism, 443–5, 453–5
Hytner, Nicholas, 460, 367, 380–1, 383

India: bureaucracy, 292–4; DB on, 267–8, 308–9; infrastructure and youth of population, 273; middle class, 314; police corruption, 295–6, 308–9; in Second World War, 266; use of the 'no', 282–3; *see also* Mumbai
India Take One, 269, 291, 303
Ingenious Pain (Miller), 459
Inglourious Basterds, xiii
Inspector Morse, xiv, 29–30, 213, 290
Intacto, 192
International Olympics Committee (IOC), 389, 390, 392
Into the Wild, 464, 467
Invernel, François, 327
Isaacson, Donna, 115–16, 234
Isles of Wonder CD, 422, 423–4
Ismail, Azharuddin Mohammed, 258, 270, 278, 289, 298, 316–17
Ivernel, François, 268

Jagger, Mick, 107
Jai Ho Trust, 315–17
Jenkins, Amy, 29–30
Jennings, Humphrey: *Pandaemonium*, xxvii–xxviii, 365, 397, 398
Jodorowsky, Alejandro, 13–14
John, Elton, 107
John Carter of Mars, 464
Johnson, Davey, 205
Johnson, Karl, 361
Joint Stock, 16–18, 19, 409
Jolie, Angelina, 41, 86, 98
Jones, Duncan, 245
Jones, Robert, 74
Joseph, Paterson, 131
Juno, 310, 312

Kaos Singing Choir for Deaf and Hearing Children, 435–6, *436*
Kapoor, Anil, 41, 257, 280–1, *280*, 306

Karloff, Boris, 373
Kashyap, Anurag, 281–2, 292
Kaufman, Charlie, xiii
Kaushal, Sham, 288, 297
Keats, John, 369
Keeffe, Barrie, 17
Kent, Nick, 10
Kes, 4
Khan, Aamir, 292
Khan, Akram, 401, 433–4
Khan, Feroze, 258
Khan, Irrfan, 257, 281, 282, 296
Khedekar, Ayush Mahesh, 270, 271,
    278, 289, 298, 299, 306, 317
Khondji, Darius, xv, 143, 156, 183–4
Kihlbom, Staffan, 132
Kirkham, Harry, 198
Kubrick, Stanley: *Clockwork Orange*,
    14–15; directing style, 169–70;
    Napoleon, 114–15; and *Sunshine*,
    179, 243–4; *2001: A Space Odyssey*,
    223, 224, 243–4, 252, 256; variety
    of films, xxii
Kuchler, Alwin, 182, 183–4, 238–9,
    241, 250
Kumar, Sanjay, 283, 291, 303
Kureishi, Hanif, 23

LaBeouf, Shia, 332
Larlarb, Suttirat: DB on, 336; and
    Frankenstein, xxvi, 363; and London
    2012, xxvii–xxix, 363, 395, 397,
    399, 409; and *127 Hours*, 336–7,
    464–5; and *Slumdog*, 306–7; and
    Sunshine, 231, 250, 251
Lawrence, Doreen, 437
Lawrence of Arabia, 208
Lean, David, 59, 71
Led Zeppelin, 12, 23
Ledoyen, Virginie, in *The Beach*, 130,
    142–3, 142, 146, 147, 155–6, 155,
    159, 159
Lee, James, 431–2
Lee, Malcolm, 5
Lee, Spike, 114
Leftfield, 107
Leigh, Mike, 21, 312, 377
Lem, Stanislaw, 244
Lennon, John, 58
Life Less Ordinary, A: main descrip-
    tion, 112–29; cast, xix, 114–17, 123;
    DB's feelings about, 126–9, 153;
    effects of failure on DB, 41; filming
    and cinematography, x, 119–20,

123–5; filmography entry, 341–2;
    plot, 109–12; reception, 129; sets
    and setting, 112–14, 124; sound-
    track, 126; subplot, x, xvii, 118;
    themes, 121
Lindgren, Magnus, 132
Lindo, Delroy, 109, 114, *115*
Livingstone, Ken, 411
Loach, Ken, xii, 18, 31, 86
LOCOG *see* London Organising
    Committee of the Olympic and
    Paralympic Games
London, 172–4; Bangabandhu primary
    school, Bethnal Green, 209; Houses
    of Parliament, Chapel of St Mary
    Undercroft, 404–5
London Film School, 341
London Olympics opening ceremony
    (2012): main discussion, 388–440; as
    agitprop, 410–13; athletes' entrance,
    423; author's impressions on watch-
    ing, xxv–xxvi, xxx–xxxi; budget,
    xxiv–xxv; cauldron, xxix, 406–8,
    407; *Chariots of Fire* sequence, 401,
    438; children's literature sequence,
    418–19, 438, 439; costumes, 399;
    DB's feelings of anticipation, 387,
    427–9; DB's relationship with Games
    organisers, 381, 392–3, 408–9,
    424–5; DB's role, 398, 425–6;
    digital-age sequence, 393, 415–16;
    dove bikes, xxviii–xxix, 431–2;
    drums, 424–7; *Frankenstein* as dry
    run for, 363, 366–7; Games spon-
    sorship and defence controversies,
    390–1; ideas generation, xxvi–xxviii,
    395–9, 403–4; ideas rejected,
    xxviii, 397–8; Industrial Revolution
    sequence, xxv–xxvi, xxviii, 366–7,
    405–6, 410, *410*, 417, 423, 424;
    influences, xxviii–xxviii; Mr Bean
    sequence, 401, 438–9; music, singers
    and bands, 416–27, 433–6; national
    anthem, 435–6; NHS sequence,
    xxv, 393–4, 410–11, 419, *419*, 430;
    Olympic flagbearers, 437; Olympic
    rings, 431–2, *432*; opening bell, 438;
    pre-recordings, 427; press preview,
    xxv; Queen's arrival, 400–3; recep-
    tion, xxx; remembrance sequence,
    433; secrecy beforehand, 392, 395,
    420; suffragette sequence, 404–5;
    team and other special helpers,
    xxvi–xxvii, 395, 409, 429; Thames

speedboat sequence, 399–400; treatment of protocol, xxviii, 400; TV coverage, 436–7; volunteers, 356–7, 391–5, 399, 425–6, 428, 429–31

London Organising Committee of the Olympic and Paralympic Games (LOCOG): DB recruited by, 389; involvement with opening ceremony, 392–3, 398, 399, 424, 437; offices, 395; sponsorship controversies, 391, 409

Lonkar, Tanvi Ganesh, 261, 271, 278, 317

Los Angeles Olympics (1984), 409

Lowe, Paul, 213

Lucas, George, 13

Lydon, John (Johnny Rotten), 419–20

Lynch, David, 93, 160

Lynch, Pauline, 79

M1 motorway, 187–8

McAnally, Ray, xiii, 25

McAulfield, Jenny, 211

McAvoy, James, 339, 441, 446, 447–8, 450–1, *450*, *451*

McCartney, Paul, 421, 427

McCracken, Cameron, 268

McCredie, Colin, 46

Macdonald, Andrew: attitude to interviews, ix; and *The Beach*, xvii–xviii, 134, 137, 139, 151; on DB, xxii; and directing, 54; and *A Life Less Ordinary*, 112, 113, 121; partner and children, 254; producing skills, 51–3; relationship with DB, 31, 51–3, 71–2, 163; and religion, 58; and *Shallow Grave*, xv, 50–4, 52, 71, 73, 74, 75; and *Sunshine*, 226, 227, 235; and *Trainspotting*, 83, 84, 88, 92, 97, 104, 107; and *28 Days Later*, 190, 191; work ethic, 136

Macdonald, Kelly, 79, 90–1, 204

Macdonald, Kevin, 245, 327, 329, 456

McDonough, Michael, 401

McDowell, Andie, 137

McGahern, John, 26

McGibbon, Lewis, 196, 203, 204–5, 213

McGregor, Eve, 121

McGregor, Ewan: and *The Beach*, xix–xx, 137–8; and football, 65; and *127 Hours*, 461; in *A Life Less Ordinary*, xix, 109, 113, 114, 117–18, *118*, 120, 121–3, *122*, 125–6, *128*;

relationship with DB, xviii–xx, 89, 137–8; in *Shallow Grave*, xviii–xix, 46, 57, 60–1, *61*, 62, 64, 65, 67, 68, 72–3, *72*; and swimming, 101–2; in *Trainspotting*, xiv, 70, 78, 83, 84, 85, 88–91, *88*, 96, 97, 98, 101–2, *101*, *103*, *104*, 105

McGuinness, Frank, xiii, 5, 24

McKee, Robert, 181

McKeown, Diarmuid, 318

McKidd, Kevin, 78, 86, 98, *104*, 106

McLeod, Robert, 248

McNeice, Ian, 109

McQueen, Steve, 94

Mad World, My Masters, A (Middleton and Keeffe), 17

Made in Britain, 26, 27

Madonna, 107

Mamet, David, 18

Man Who Fell to Earth, The, 23

Manchester: Aaben art cinema, Hulme, 13

Manchester United football team, 4–5

Manjha, 217

Manjrekar, Mahesh, 262

Mara, Kate, 324, *328*

Marber, Patrick, 459, 460

Martinez, Gina, 429

Mass Movement, 429

Maya (aka M.I.A.), 302–3

Mehta, Suketu, 283, 291–2, 294, 309

Memarzia, Nasser, 199

Mendes, Sam, 402, 414

Merchant, Riyaz Ali, 306

Mesmer, Franz Anton, 443

Mesrine, xiii

Michell, Roger, 128

Middleton, Thomas, 17

Mighty Heart, A, 281

Milk, 462

Millar, Daniel, 361

Miller, Andrew, 459

Miller, Jonny Lee: and *Frankenstein*, 370–1, *371*, 372–5, 374, 379, 381, 383, 385; and *Trainspotting*, 78, 86, 98, *98*, 99, 102, *103*, *104*, 106

Millions: main discussion, 201–17; as autobiography, 206, 207; cast, 90, 203–6; DB's feelings about, xvi, 43, 217; and DB's mother, 10, 207; and DB's use of images, 472; DVD extras, 216–17; filming, 162, 211–15, 298; filmography entry, 342–3; morality, 209; plot, 196–201;

politics in, 209–10; reception, 216; religion in, 206–7; scenes cut, 216; script, xvii, 201–3; soundtrack, 193, 215–16; special effects, 214, 232; themes, 206–7; warmth, x, 207–8

Miral, 276

Mirren, Helen, 248

Mission to Mars, 231

Mitchell, Julian, 29, 30

Mittal, Medhur, 262, 272, 274, 275, 278, 313

Moby, 160

Moon, 245

moon landings, 224

Mormons, 202

Morrissey, 13

Moving Picture Company (MPC), 229–30, 246

Mr Wroe's Virgins, xiv, 21, 30–1, 50, 214, 472

Mr Young's Preview Theatre, 189

MTV, 59

Mueck, Ron, 250

Mullan, Peter, 46, 63, 78

Mumbai, 291, 292–301, 304–6, 308; bridge linking two sections, 308; Dharavi slum, 294–5, 297; Dhobi Ghat, 297; Garai Beach, 300; Gates of India, 290; Juhu slum, 301; landfill sites, 264, 298–300; Queen's Necklace, 293; Slum Necklace, 293; VT station (Chhatrapabi Shivaji Terminus), 301, 304–6, *304*, *305*

Mumbai, 304

Murdoch, Rupert, xxx, 411

Murphy, Cillian: and *127 Hours*, 332, 461; in *Sunshine*, 218, 234–5, 237–40, *237*, *247*, *252*; in *28 Days Later*, 122, 162, 164, 172, 173, 176–7, *176*, *177*, *178*, 193, *195*

Murphy, John, 193–4, 215, 252, 433

Murray, Charles Shaar, 10

Muybridge, Eadweard, xxviii

Nada, 13–14

Naked, 21

Napoleon, 114–15

National Theatre, 380–1, 385; Olivier Theatre, 367, 385

Near Dark, 181–2

Neivelt, Thomas, 285

Nesbitt, James, 196, 203, 205, 212

New Musical Express, 10–11

New Order, 91

New York, 308

Newcastle, 414–15

Newman, Robert, 310, 311, 320

Nicholas, Eileen, 80

9/11, 174–6

Nischol, Natasha, 307

Nolan, Chris, 317

Noorani, Tabrez, 283, 291, 303

Norman, Barry, 93

Northern Ireland, 24, 202–3

Not Even God Is Wise Enough, 29

Notting Hill, 127–8

Noye, Kenneth, 175

nuclear submarines, 235

Oasis, 4, 58

Obama, Barack, 440

Oginsky, Paul, 404

Oldfield, Mike, 418–19

Oldham Coliseum, 414

Oldman, Gary, 21

O'Malley, Leonard, 47

127 Hours: main discussion, 327–59, 456–69; arm entrapment and amputation, 333–4, 335, 346, 354–5, 467–8, 468–9; cast, 331–3, 461, 462, 468; editing, 348–9; ending, 347–8; filming and cinematography, xxiii, 331–2, 338–43, 463–9; financing, 461; gritty reality, 344–5; origins and plans, 327–31, 456–61; plot, 323–7; Ralston's involvement, 329, 344, 345–7, 349–50, 456–60, 465–6; script, 357–8, 459–60; setting and set, 334–7, *337*, 340, 464–5, 466; soundtrack, 343–5; themes, 351, 355, 357, 467; as urban story, 358–9

Orchestral Manoeuvres in the Dark, 193–4

Orwell, George, 350

Oscars, x, 107–8, 318–21

Osmonds, The, 120

Owen, Clive, 192

Page, Jimmy, 12

Page, Louise, 23

Pandaemonium (Jennings), xxvii–xxviii, 365, 397, 398

Pankhurst, Helen, 405

Pankhurst, Laura, 405

Park, Nick, 43, 129

Parmar, Chirag, 260

Patel, Dev, 273; casting and working with on *Slumdog*, 272, 273–6,

277–8, 281, 296, 296, 304, 305–6, 305, 307; and Oscars, 319; and *Slumdog* publicity, 313, 315
Pathé, 208, 268, 269, 309
Patil, Siddesh, 261, 300
Pegg, Simon, 192
Penda's Fen (Rudkin), 26
Penn, Sean, 462, 464
Perkins, Tim, xxiv
Phillips, Leslie, 198, 204
Pine, Chris, xiii
Pink Floyd, 245
Pinto, Freida, 276; casting and working with on *Slumdog*, 276–7, 304, 305, 305, 306–7; and Oscars, 319; and *Slumdog* publicity, 313, 315
Pitt, Brad, 41
Pixar films, 42–3
Plato, x
Play for Today TV series, 26
Poésy, Clémence, 325
Poland, 23
Poltimore, Mark, 442
PolyGram, 59, 74–5, 76, 106–7
Pookutty, Resul, 284, 291
Pop, Iggy, 92, 95
pop music, 58–9, 421–2
Powell, Michael, 53
Precious, 310
Pressburger, Emeric, 53
Preston, Richard, 180
Prophet, A, xiii
Pryce, Jonathan, xiv, 19, 21, 30, 472
Pulp Fiction, 76
punk rock, 12–13

Q&A (Swarup), 267
'Queen, The' (Farley), 396–7
Quigley, Pearce, 197, 204
Quinn, Kave, 64–5, 98
Quinto, Zachary, xiii

Ragged Trousered Philanthropists, The (Tressell), 17
Rahman, A. R., 303, 320, 468
Ralston, Aron: book about experiences, 327–8, 456–7; canyon video tapes, 349–50, 457, 465–6; character, 337; DB on, 333; and fate, 355–6; later life, 465; and *127 Hours*, 329, 344, 345–7, 349–50, 456–60, 465–6; reasons for survival, 467
Randall, Paulette, 429
Rattigan, Terence, 371

rave culture, 30
Rea, Stephen, xiii–xiv
Redgrave, Steve, 399
Reed, Lou, 92
Rice, Peter, 190, 254, 281, 310, 312
Ritchie, Alison, 17, 18
Ritchie, Paul, 318
Roberts, Julia, 128
Rockingham Shoot, The, 26
Rockwell, Sam, 332, 461
Roeg, Nicolas: and big stars, 41; DB's admiration for, 13, 35, 444; *Don't Look Now*, 50, 193, 452; *Eureka*, ix, 44; golden period, 44; *Walkabout*, 13, 457
Rogers, Sue, 86
Romero, George A., 171, 179
Ross, Tessa, 267, 268
Rotten, Johnny *see* Lydon, John
Rowling, J. K., 438, 439
Royal Court Theatre: DB at, 16, 19–21, 23, 26, 61, 138; stage, 367; writers' importance, 25
Rudin, Scott, 51
Rudkin, David, 26
Rundle, John, 212
Ryder, Winona, 113
Rylance, Mark, 406

Sahni, Pravesh, 283, 291, 303
St John, Clare, 235
St Mary's primary school, Radcliffe, 4, 5
Salesian College, Bolton, 6–9
Salgado, Sebastião, 304
Salonika (Page), 23
Salt Lake City, 120
Sandé, Emeli, 433–4, 434–5
Sandy, Kenrick 'H2O', 393, 429, 434–5
Saneda, Hiroyuki, 218, 231, 232, 233, 233–4, 236
Satya, 281–2, 292
Saved (Bond), 23
Sayers, Tom, 319
Schlöndorff, Volker, 22
Schnabel, Julian, 276
Scorsese, Martin, 19, 77, 82–3, 93, 140, 206
Scott, Allan, 50
Scott, Ridley, 145, 236–7, 243
Scout, xiii–xiv, 5, 24, 25
Scum, 26
Seaward, Tracey, 214, 429, 438
Sedgwick, Toby, 184, 395, 429

Seoul Olympics (1988), xxviii
Se7en, 76
Sex Pistols, 419–20
Seymour, Richard, 235
Shakespeare, William, 6, 135, 370, 405–6
Shalhoub, Tony, 116
Shallow Grave: main discussion, 49–77; audience, 56; and Bowie, 92; cast, xx, 60–4; characters, 57–8; cynicism of, 41; DB's reaction to seeing it in cinema, 35; editing, 73; filming and cinematography, xv, 63, 64, 65–73; filmography entry, 341; group dynamic in, 122; humanity of characters, x, 56–8; humour, 135–6; McGregor on, xviii–xix; marketing, 59–60, 74–5; morality, 135, 209; plot, 46–9; as pop culture, 58–9; props, xv; research, 377; script, 38, 66; set, 31, 64–5; soundtrack, 73–4; themes, 49, 105; violence in, 66–8; voice-over, 161
Shanghai Film Festival, xii
Shaun of the Dead, 192–3
Shelley, Mary, 364–5, 368–70, 378, 379–80
Shelley, Percy Bysshe, 364, 369–70, 378
Shepherd, Maggs, 436
Shepperd, Piers, 429
Shukla, Saurabh, 257, 281–2, 286–7, 296
Sight and Sound, 56–7
Simpson, Joe, 327
Simpsons, The, 56, 130, 141
Siouxsie and the Banshees, 397
Skins, 273–4
Skyfall, 414
Sleeper, 92
Slumdog Millionaire: main discussion, 264–322; awards, x, xii, 76, 308, 313, 317–20, 321, 342; budget, 268–9; cast, 90, 269–82; child actors, xii, xvi, 205–6, 279, 297–8, 315–17; Colson's eagerness for DB to make, xxi; core theme, 357; costumes and make-up, 306–7; criticism, 154, 155, 314–15; DB's feelings about, xv, 39, 43, 84, 127; DVD extras, 217; editing, 73, 228, 302–3; effect on DB's career, 330; ending, 304–6, 304, 305; escapades, 287–9; filming and cinematography,

xvi, 139–40, 153, 214, 215, 241–2, 282–308; filmography entry, 343; marketing and press tour, 53, 185, 313, 315, 469; morality, 209; multiple timelines, 301; plot, 257–64; producers, 268; release problems, 309–11; revenue and reception, 311–15, 320; script, 37, 38, 264–7, 290; sentimental aspect, x, 41, 121; set and setting, 148, 282–3, 293–301, 307–8; soundtrack, 302–3; trust set up for child actors, 315–17
Smith, Andrew, 224, 233
Smith, Esme, xxx
Smith, Paul, 268
Smith, Rick: and *Frankenstein*, xxvi, 363; and London 2012, xxvi–xxvii, xxx, 395, 422–5, 426, 433; nationality, 433; *see also* Underworld
Smith, Rocky, 429
Smith, Will, 292
Solar Crisis, 243
Solaris, 243–4, 256
Spall, Timothy, xvi, xx, xxii, 168
Specialist, The, 75
Spencer, Julian, 235
Spielberg, Steven, xxii, 36
Stafford-Clark, Max, 19–20, 21, 25, 409
Stanton, Andrew, 336
Star Trek, xiii, 241
Star Wars films, 13, 22, 137, 223
Starr, Nick, 380–1
Steadicam, 27–8
Stevens, Frederick, 306
Stevens, Gail: and *A Life Less Ordinary*, 115; and *Millions*, 203; relationship with DB, xiii; and *Slumdog*, 273–4; and *Sunshine*, 234; and *Trainspotting*, 86; and *28 Days Later*, 171, 176, 184
Stiles, Richard, 169–70
Stone, Oliver, 38
Stott, Ken, 48, 52, 63
Strong, Mark, 219, 227, 252–3
Strummer, Joe, 12, 195
Strumpet, xvi, 168, 193
Sundance, 191
Sunset Boulevard, 71
Sunshine: main discussion, 223–56; Capa's character, 37–8; cast, 233–4, 237; CGI and special effects, 225, 228–30, 231, 238–42, 247–50; core theme, 357; costumes, 230–1, 250;

DB's feelings about, 217, 223–4, 228, 256; editing, 73, 228–9; ending, 237–9, 252–4; filming and cinematography, 226–8, 231–2, 236–7, 238–42, 246–55; filmography entry, 343; genesis, 225; influences, 179, 242–5; oxygen garden, 233, 247–9, 249; plot, 218–22; reception, 255–6; research, 234–6, 248; setting, 253–4; sound in, 251–2; soundtrack, 193, 238, 252; space ships, 230, 230, 239, 243, 249; spiritual dimension, 225–6, 237–40

Survivors, 179
Swarup, Vikas, 267
Swinton, Tilda, in *The Beach*, 131, 143, 145–6, 146, 151, 152, 156–7
Sydney Olympics (2000), 403
Synecdoche, New York, xiii

Taare Zameen Par, 292
Taj Mahal, 287, 288–90
Tamblyn, Amber, 324, 328
Tandan, Loveleen, 284; casting work on *Slumdog*, 269–71, 280, 282, 300; co-director credit on *Slumdog*, 283–4; coaching work on *Slumdog*, 278, 279, 300; role in *Slumdog*, 291
Tarantino, Quentin, 76, 198, 456, 471
Tarkovsky, Andrei, 55, 243–4, 256
Tarrant, Chris, 281
Telluride film festival, 310, 312
Temple, Julien, 420
10,000 BC, 246
Terri, Claire, 429
Thailand, 134–5, 139, 147, 153–5
Thatcher, Margaret, 105
Thaw, John, 29, 30, 290
Thewlis, David, 21, 168
This Life, 30
Thomas, Inigo, 405–6
Threads, 179
3 Mills Studios, 176, 226
Tiger, 260
Tildesley, Mark: and *Frankenstein*, xxvi, 363, 381; images collected by, 471; and London 2012, xxvii–xxviii, 363, 395, 401, 408–9, 426; and *Millions*, 208, 214; and *Sunshine*, 230, 238–9, 241, 247–8, 250; theatre experience, 367; and *Trance*, 446; and *28 Days Later*, 31–2, 184, 185, 186–7, 188
Till, Stewart, 74, 75, 106, 107

Tin Drum, The, 22
Tinsley, Jim, 408
Tirso de Molina, 367
Titanic, xxii, 141
Tong, Pete, 160
Topo, El, 13–14
Toronto Film Festival, 310, 312–13, 317
Touching the Void, 327, 329, 456
Toy Story, 43
Toye, Leonard, 5
Trainspotting: main discussion, 82–108; author on seeing, xxi; awards, 107–8; Carlyle on, xx–xxi; cast, 62–3, 84–6, 88–91, 204; cultural context, ix–x; cynicism of, 41; DB and the novel, ix, xi, 83, 84; DB's feelings about, 19, 126; drugs in, 55, 86–7, 93–4, 102; effect on subsequent DB films, 118; emotional and life-affirming aspects, 207, 208, 357; encouragement of tourism, 155; filming and cinematography, xiv–xv, 69, 70, 90–1, 95–105; filmography entry, 341; group dynamic in, 122; influences, 14, 82–3; McGregor on, xix; marketing, 106; narrative thread, 38; plot, 78–82; as pop song, 58; reception and revenues, 93–4, 107–8, 134, 152, 280, 282; Renton's character, 88–9; script, 84, 107–8; set and costumes, 98–9; soundtrack, ix, 91–3; special effects, 99–102; themes, 94–5, 105; US version, 105–6; voice-overs, 82–3, 161; Welsh in, 54, 78, 100
Trance: main discussion, 441–55; cast, 442, 447–8; clues in, 448–51; filming and cinematography, 342; hypnotism theme, 443–5, 453–5; language theme, 446–8; origins, 442–3; plot (no spoilers), 441; research, 453–5; script, 442–3, 445; setting and set, 445–6; sex scenes, 451–3; woman-centredness, 442, 449
Tressell, Robert, 17
Trier, Lars von, xvi
Truffaut, François, 27
Tucci, Stanley, 109, 116, 124
Tufano, Brian, 69, 82; DB on, 31; and *A Life Less Ordinary*, 124; and *Millions*, 215; and *Shallow Grave*, 64, 68–9, 70; split from DB, 156; and *Trainspotting*, 97, 101

Turner, Frank, xxv
20th-Century Fox: and *The Beach*, 136, 140, 154, 157; and *Sunshine*, 253–4; and *28 Days Later*, 190, 191
24 Hour Party People, 201
28 Days Later: main discussion, 170–95; cast, 176–8, 184; DB's feelings about, 43, 127, 162; editing, 174; emotional aspects, 207; ending, 181–2, 187; filming and cinematography, 31–2, 97, 172–4, 182–9, 232; filmography entry, 342; group dynamic in, 122; images collected by DB for, 471; Jim's character, 180; marketing, 190, 191; 9/11's influence, 174–6; plot, 164–7; reception and revenues, 152, 189–91; sequel, 191–2; setting, 172–4, 172, 184–8; soundtrack, 160, 193–5, 433; themes, 175, 185
28 Months Later, 192
28 Weeks Later, 191–2, 464
Twilight Samurai, The, 234
2001: A Space Odyssey, 223, 224, 232, 243–4, 252, 256
2010, 248

Ugwu, Catherine, 429
Underworld, xxvi, 92, 160, 252, 363, 395; *see also* Smith, Rick; Hyde, Karl
Union Carbide, 391
Unsworth, Mr (teacher), 6
Uzbekistan, 108

Vacuuming Completely Nude in Paradise, xvi, xx, 168, 193
Van Sant, Gus, 317, 467
Vanilla Sky, xx
Varma, Ram Gopal, 292
Venus de Milo Instead, The, xiii–xiv, 24, 42
Victory (Barker), 23
Vidler, Susan, 78, 85, 99
Vikal, Ankur, 259
Vinterberg, Thomas, xvi
Viola, Bill, 342, 463

Wai, Wong Kar, 233–4
Walkabout, 13, 457
Wall, Jeff, 368

Wallace and Gromit films, 43
Walton, Toby, 199
Wang Nang, xxx
Warner, Leo, 416
Warners, 268–9, 309–10
WaterAid, 404–5
Weaver, Sigourney, 113
Weinstein Company, 105
Welles, Orson, 24
Welsh, Irvine, *100*; cameo in *Trainspotting*, 54, 78, 100; on heroin, 87; *Porno*, 95; sayings, 118; *Trainspotting* novel, ix, xi, 83, 84, 94
Wener, Louise, 92
Wertenbaker, Timberlake, 23
Whedon, Joss, 113
Wheeler, Tim, 126
Whistle Down the Wind, 202
White, Susanna, 462
Whitechapel Bell Foundry, 438
Whiteread, Rachel, 406
Who Wants to Be a Millionaire?, 268, 280–1
Wiggins, Bradley, 438
Williams, Andy, 74
Williams, Robbie, 65
Williams, Treat, 324
Wilson, Richard, 20, 100
Winkler, Lizzie, 361
Winton, Dale, 100
Wollstonecraft, Mary, 369
Wong, Benedict, 218, 233
Woo, John, 206
Wood, Tim, 229, 250
Woodroffe, Patrick, 429
Wordsworth, William, 173, 369
Worthington, Steven, 5
Wretch 32, 435
Wright, Abbey, 376
Wright, Edgar, 192
Wyndham, John, 172

Yeoh, Michelle, 218, 233, 233, 249, 250
Young, Edward, 401
Young, Toby, 267

Zweger, Lisbeth, 214